MW01405329

THE HOUSE
OF A LIFETIME

THE HOUSE OF A LIFETIME

A COLLECTOR'S JOURNEY IN TANGIER

UMBERTO PASTI &
NGOC MINH NGO

FOREWORD BY
MADISON COX

Rizzoli
NEW YORK

New York · Paris · London · Milan

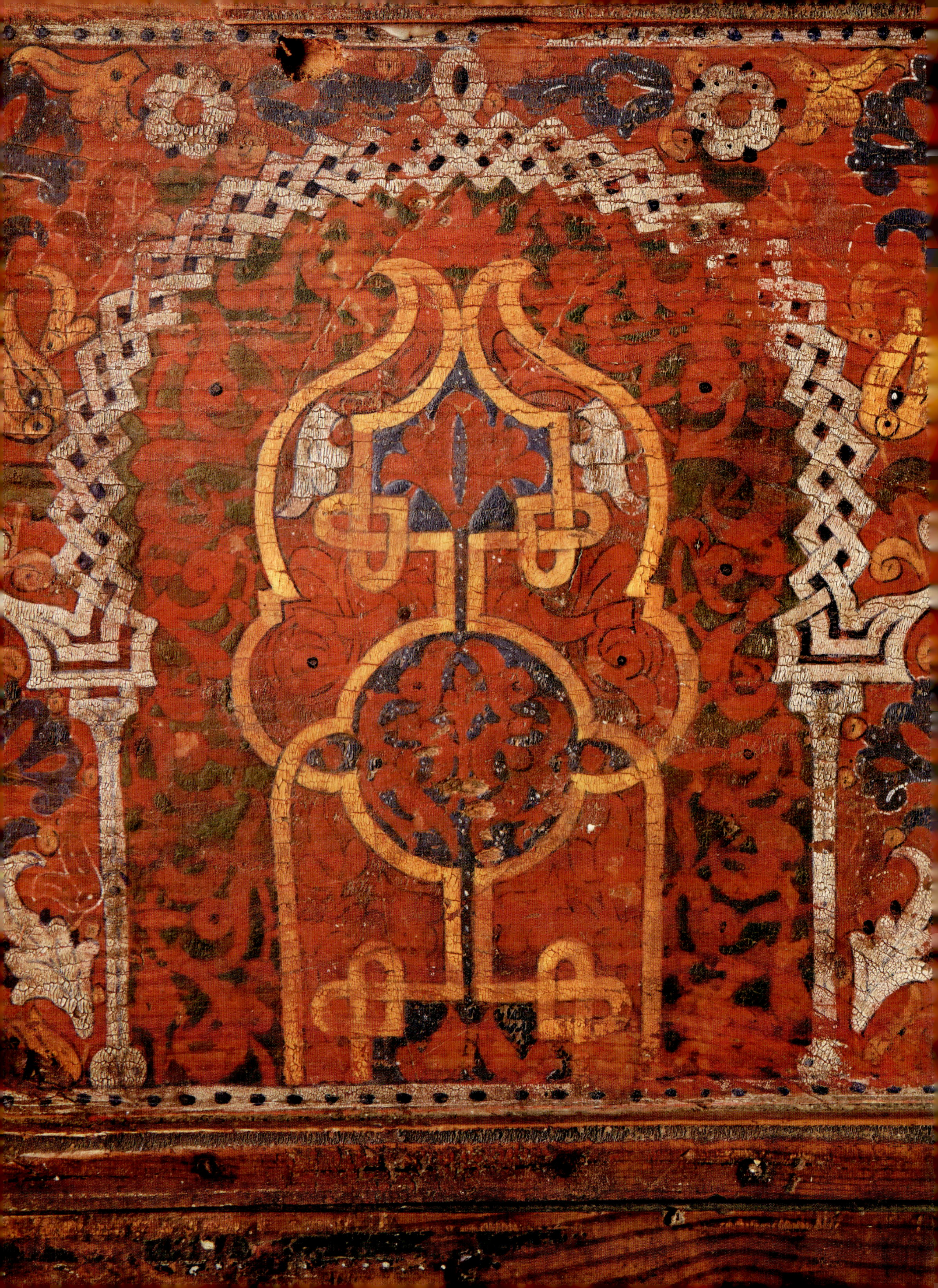

TO THE PEOPLE OF TANGIER

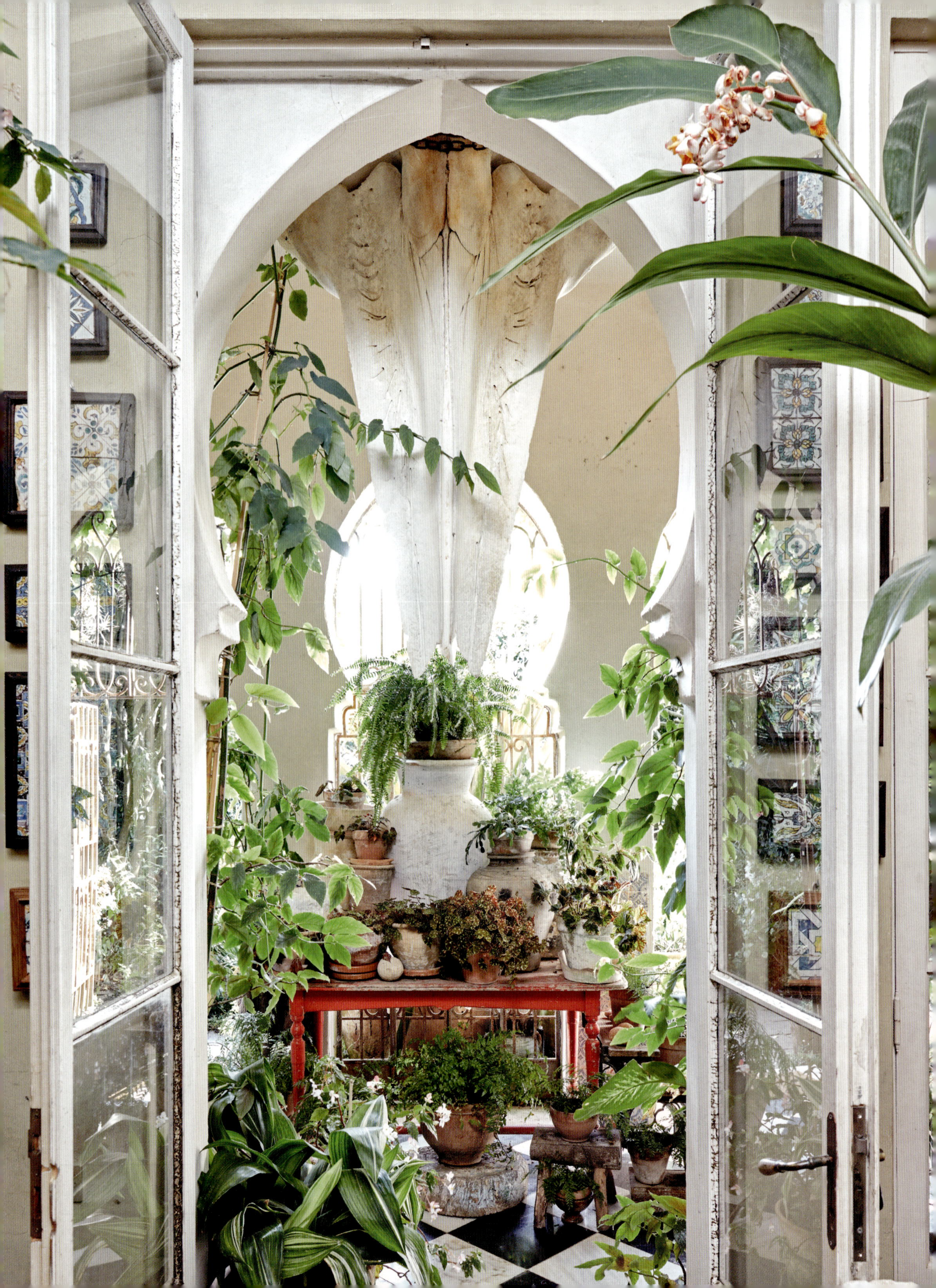

CONTENTS

    9   FOREWORD

  15   TIME REGAINED IN TANGIER

  25   THE UPPER PAVILION

        30   *The Painted Furniture of the Jbala*

        44   *A Bit of History*

        47   *Attributionism*

        48   *Painted Flowers*

  83   THE CENTRAL PAVILION

        87   *Tiles*

        87   *Tunisian Beauties*

        88   *Epigraphic Tiles and Tiles from Fez*

129   THE LOWER PAVILION

      134   *Textiles and Carpets*

      137   *Embroidery*

      139   *Carpets*

      141   *Fragments*

189   THE GARDEN

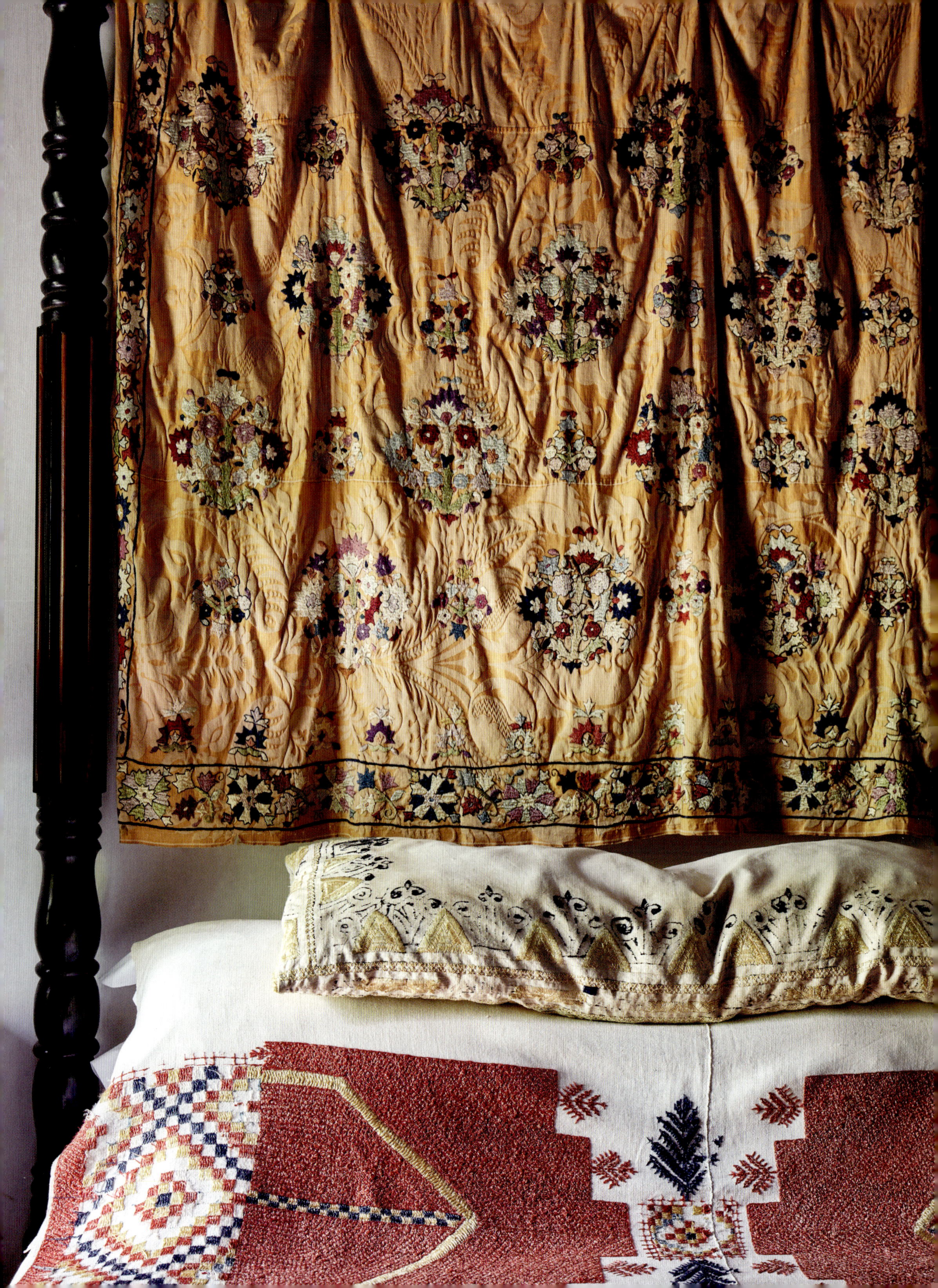

FOREWORD

MADISON COX

Oh, dear reader, what excitement awaits you! Within your hands is the means to embark on an odyssey that will take you across multiple continents, civilizations, and centuries to arrive at a most magical place called "Tebarek Allah." Just as in Homer's epic tale, the series of extraordinary experiences portrayed in this remarkable, one-of-a-kind book offers deep insights into its author, Umberto Pasti, and his life partner, Stephan Janson, and the world they have created on a south-facing hillside in Tangier, Morocco. This captivating, lavishly illustrated tale is rich in detail and encompasses all that a true epic must contain: passion, valor, adventure, and love.

In today's world, one of widespread global conformity combined with grand-scale stylistic copying, rare are the residences or personal retreats that strike a true note of originality and strong character. Sir John Soane's house on Lincoln's Inn Fields in London immediately comes to mind. Or closer to our age, the Roman apartment of the late Italian-born art and literature critic Mario Praz. Whether Harry Blackmer's highly stylized town house in Athens or the various interiors Christopher Gibbs conceived, each of these places subscribed to a deep-seated passion that in turn created a universe unto itself.

Between these pages, Pasti treats the reader to the historical evolution of his Tangier house as it was passed down from one eccentric expat owner to another, and finally to the couple's purchase and eventual expansion of the property, which enabled their garden to double in size. After *Eden Revisted: A Garden in Northern Morocco*, with the brilliant photographer Ngoc Minh Ngo—a window onto Pasti's idyllic country retreat near the coastal village of Rohuna, just south of Tangier—the duo has reunited to produce this most intimate volume that chronicles the beauty and genius loci of this Tangier home. It is Pasti's melding of both tangible and intangible components from the natural plant world with found objects and constructed elements, brought together within this urban context, which creates Tebarek Allah's unique spirit.

In conclusion, dear reader, I must in good faith provide you with full disclosure: I have been Umberto and Stephan's friend for over forty years, and it is to them that I owe my discovery of our beloved Tangier. It gives me great joy to see their very special home so beautifully documented in book form, and to know that in the future, Tebarek Allah will become a museum and remain a place where visitors can study and explore both the rich flora that graces the garden as well as the myriad examples of refined Moroccan craftsmanship that have been lovingly safeguarded by Pasti over the decades. Sharing one's world is a most beautiful gift, one that both Umberto and Stephan gave me so many years ago when they first introduced me to Tangier. For that thoughtful gesture alone, I shall be eternally grateful. *Shukran bezzef.*

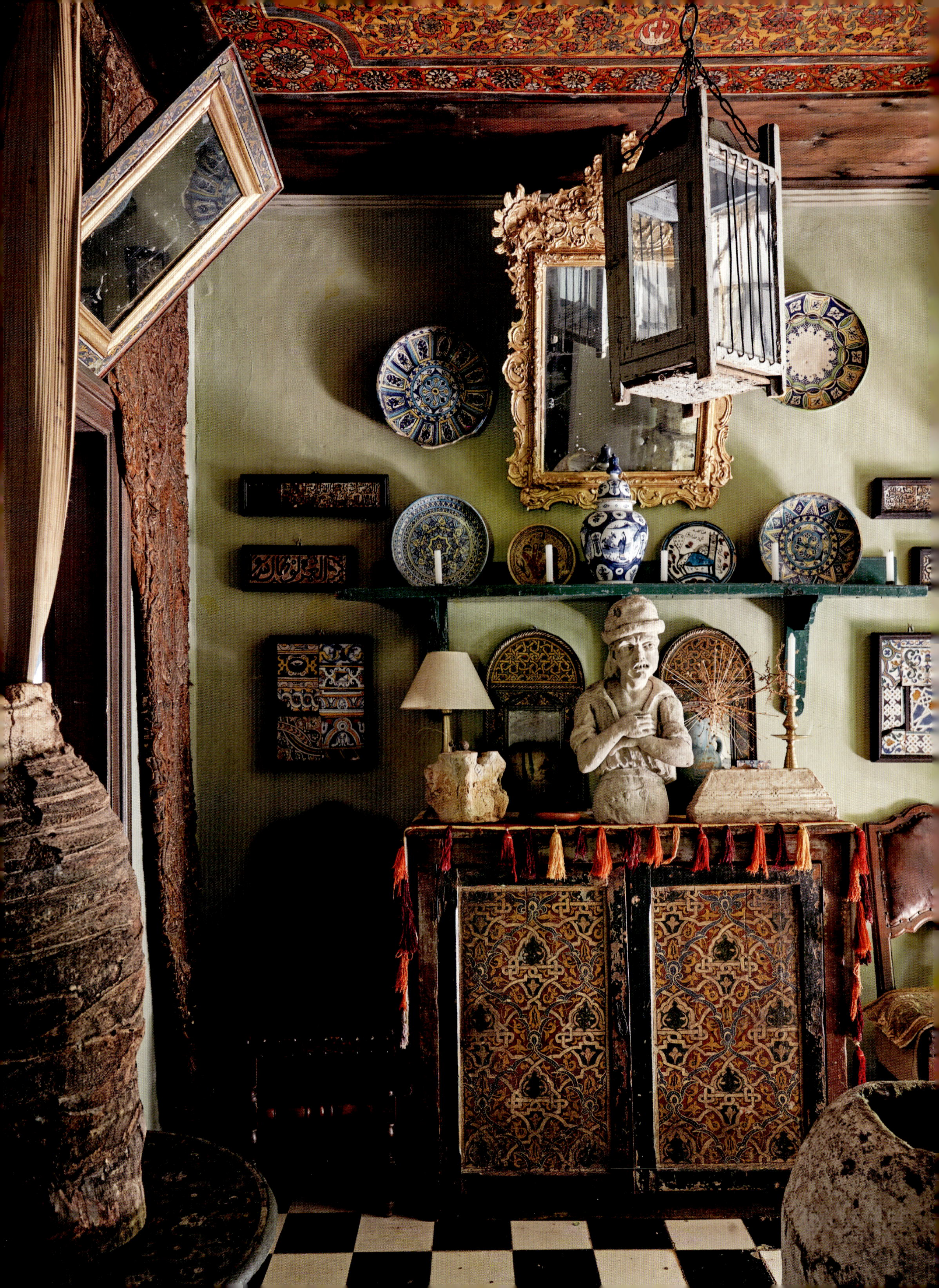

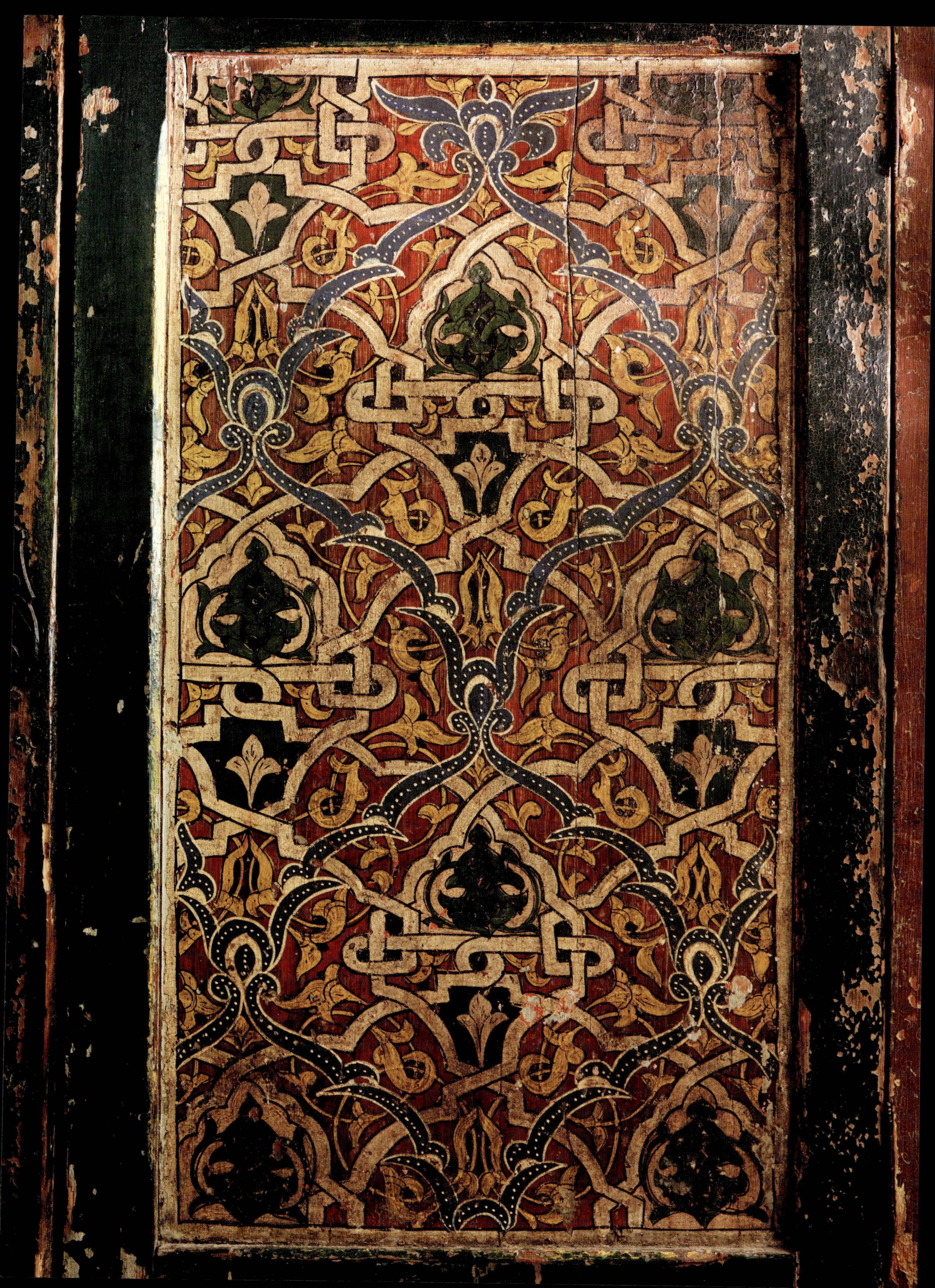

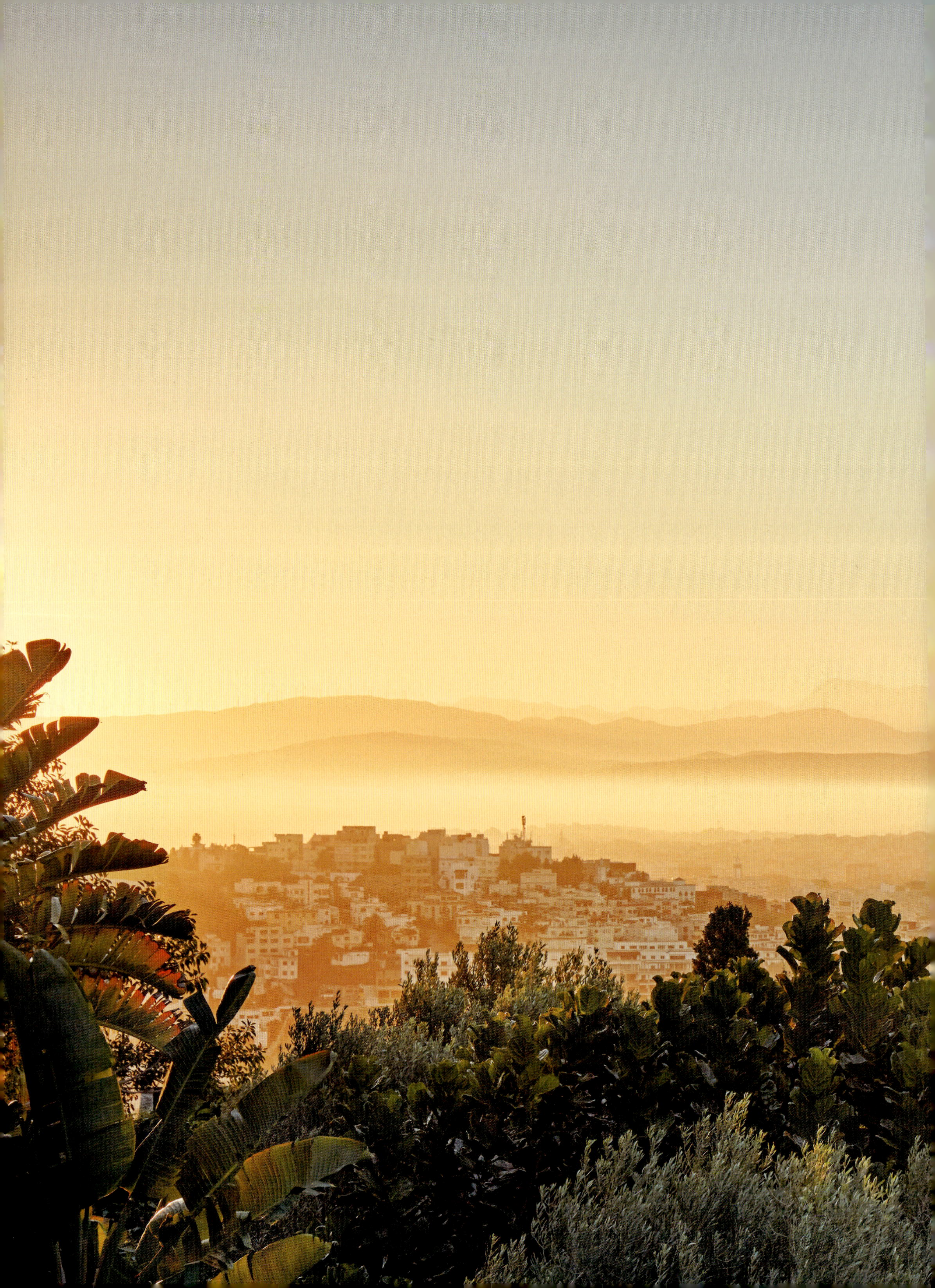

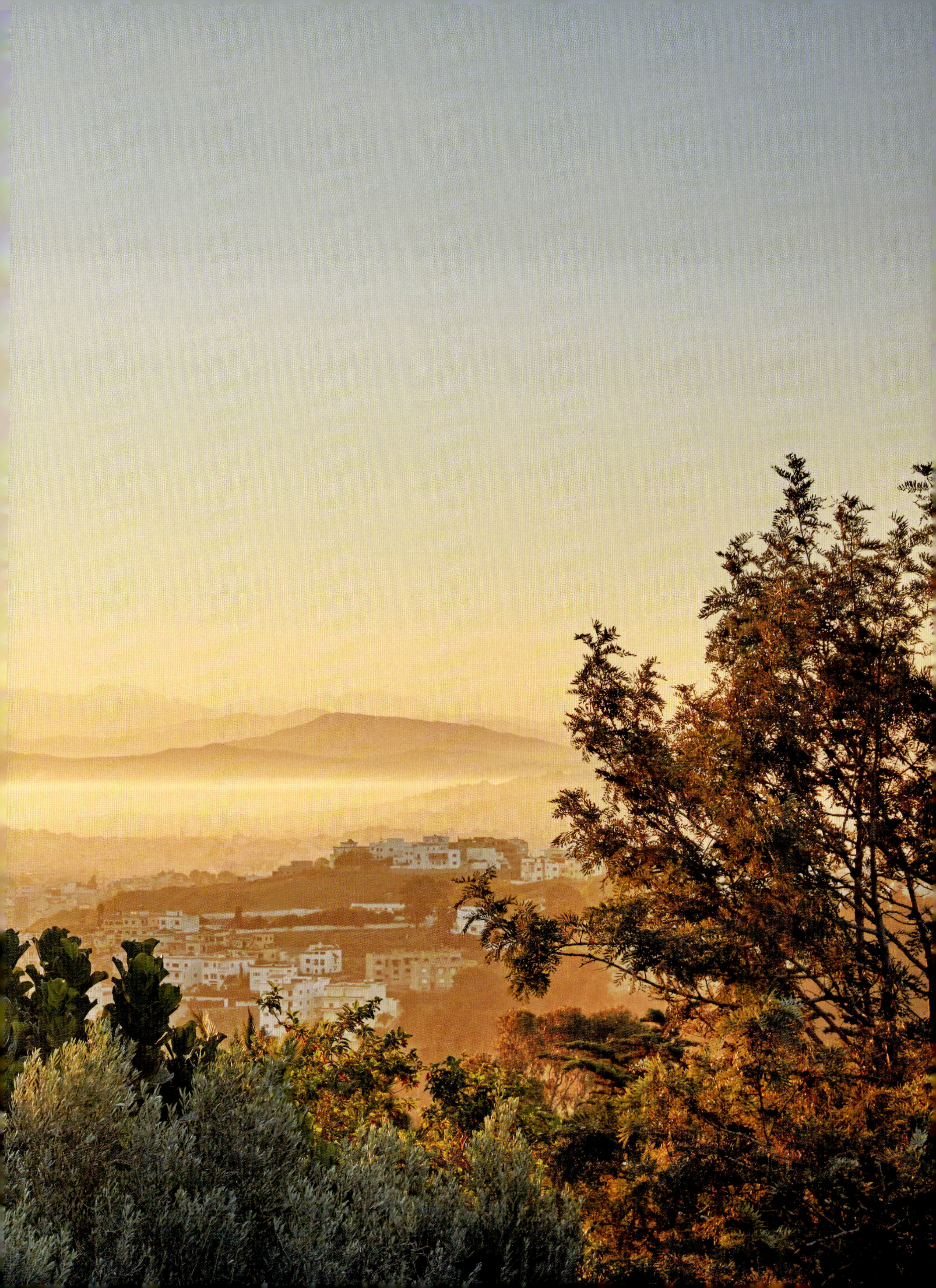

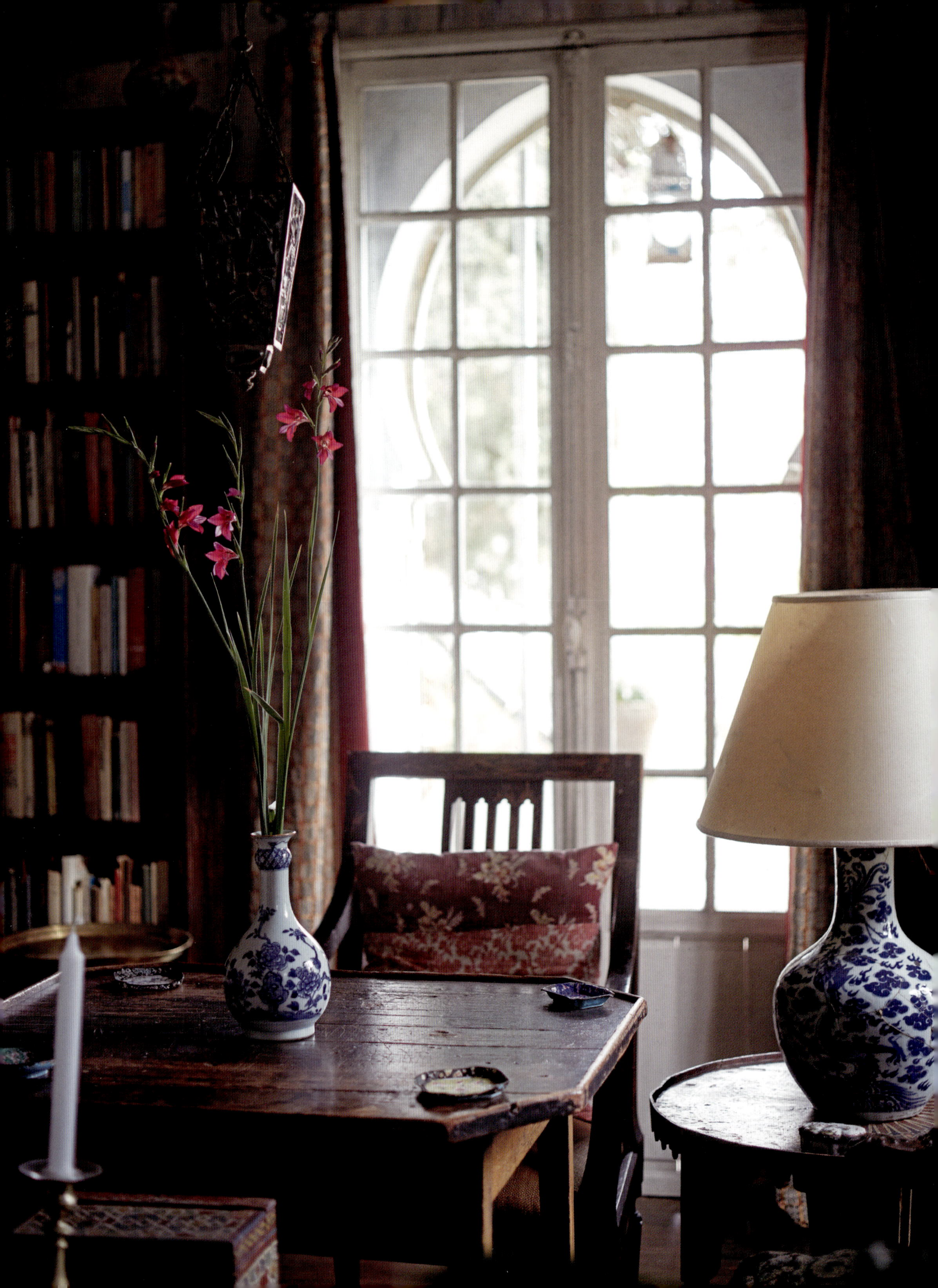

TIME REGAINED IN TANGIER

Why Tangier? Because we had taken the wrong road. It was the first time we had come here to the North, in December about forty years ago. We were fleeing Marrakech and its social scene in an old rental Renault 4. Shortly after the crossroads, we had found ourselves on a track that ran into a sea even bluer, even more silvery, than the shard piercing the horizon. We lay down among thousands of irises in bloom, among stems that swayed and danced like cobras to the flute of the wind. Removing some dirt from his sweater, Stephan said, "We're home."

The first house, which we rented a few weeks later, had belonged to the English art collector Jim Ede in the 1930s: a premonition. After leaving his post as curator of the Tate Gallery, Jim, convinced of the therapeutic power of beauty, had come to live here and had built Whitestone, later renamed Casa Azul. Tebarek Allah stands just below it, on the same side of the road that runs down from the forest of Armilat. We bought it after we had been coming to Tangier for six years in all seasons. We liked the white city, an old Carthaginian and Phoenician, Arab and Portguese town, on storm-lashed winter evenings, when there was no power and our new English friends vied to see who knew the most people who had been murdered ("Justin? They never found his head, did they?"), while the reflection of the candles transformed their faces into tragedy masks baked by vodka and the sun. We liked it in spring, when we would lie down to read in a clearing and were greeted by a falconer with hooded hawks on his shoulder, or by a shepherd who sang as he followed his sheep. And in summer... miles of Atlantic beaches guarded by young soldiers who slept in huts made of branches and idly kept an eye on the hashish traffic: they swam with us and invited us to share their grilled sardines and oversweetened mint tea. One of them called all of us in turn with the only words of French he knew, *Chéri* or *Bibi*. That was our nickname for him that August, and that's what we still call the beach where we spent those sunny days, even though the sand dunes of *Chéri Bibi* have been swallowed up by concrete.

With the house it was love at first sight. Tebarek Allah means *Praise the Lord*, the secular version of which could be *Time will tell*. Two Moorish-style pavilions in a parched south-facing garden; no view of the sea, but a panoramic outlook over the fields and forests that surrounded the forgotten village that the International City had become after three decades of annexation to Morocco. The house belonged to a teacher with the American School who had inherited it from a compatriot. He was asking far too much for it and resolutely rejected our counteroffer. But a couple of weeks later, having returned to Italy, we couldn't get it out of our heads. I waited for Stephan to go to dinner with friends. I had put enough money aside. So I called the owner. Then I opened a bottle of red wine (we don't like champagne) and called Stephan. He came back out of breath and I was afraid he would give me a telling off. "Tell you off? I'd jump for joy, but since the stuffed crocodile arrived there's no room even in the hallway."

Tebarek Allah was a construction site. We lived camped out in our pavilions, amid the comings and goings of friends. Bricklayers, blacksmiths, and carpenters shared our banquets, and often enlivened them by using a paint can as a drum or taking from the tool bag the violin owned by a grandfather who had played in the cabaret of a Hungarian madame famous for her poodles that danced the cancan. Among the mats, carpets, lanterns, cushions, and hundreds of other objects unearthed at Casa Barata, the local flea market, or in the sleepy bazaars of the medina, we felt we were living in sybaritic luxury, to which disorder and precariousness added a note of gypsy conviviality. One evening thirty of us were eating sardines beneath the new pergola, around an immense oleander table on which a street vendor had been trading underwear until only a few hours before. The following evening, lying on Berber blankets found in the port of Larache, next to a bed of dahlias and zinnias blooming for the first time, the party was on the lawn, where with harmless wax and the help of Mohammed I had fixed dozens of candles to the backs of tortoises that strolled among antique painted cabinets from Tétouan (I had always detested Montesquiou and Des Esseintes, I simply wanted to emulate my beloved Mouradgea d'Ohsson Tosunyan, the eighteenth-century Armenian historian who adopted the best habits of the Ottoman aristocracy, but I hadn't found enough tortoises for the effect to be truly fairy tale). Mohammed was the deaf-mute gardener who had always lived in a lodge inside the grounds. His wife, Ftoma, was the queen of the *tajine*, and Shousha, their eldest daughter, a doe-eyed girl who seemed to have emerged from a Persian miniature, would give a hand serving; her luxuriant dark hair falling over her pastel pajamas aroused the admiration of foreign guests and the amazement of the Muslims. Tebarek Allah, dubbed Sissinghurst-sur-mer by a friend who was a fan of Vita Sackville-West, was a seraglio. I recall, one evening, an American poet and opium addict disguised as a dragonfly (his wings of straw and wire so cumbersome that he had to eat standing up) asking a captain of Italian industry: "Do you think angels exist, treasure?" And the latter, adjusting the knot of his necktie and saying to me in a strong Bolognese accent: "So, did you invest here in expectation that property values would take off?" In the meantime Doudou got to his feet, impatient to begin his striptease (nothing orgiastic, he did it for amateur pleasure); São adjusted her emerald tiara and took a puff on a joint rolled by her Egyptian gigolo; old Josette from the bookstore, under the pretext of looking for her clutch bag, disappeared among the shrubbery with a retired general hoping to publish his memoirs; David and Richard reached an agreement on the percentage received from a merchant in the bazaar for the sale of various carpets to the "sucker" they had served up on a silver plate; and while someone went back to singing "The recipe for perfect happiness" ("Pour a thimbleful of milk of baboon / into a chamber pot under the full moon") and someone else took a shawl to cover Paul, who by now was snoring even though the French journalist hadn't stopped bombarding him with questions about Bertolucci's movie, Alfonso, a former pizza chef from Seville who reigned over the casbah and said he was a descendant sometimes of Montezuma, other times of Atahualpa, bent over me and whispered: "We are pillars of society, after all." And, after a big sigh: "Even in Marbella, my dear boy, they can only dream of evenings such as this."

But that Tangier was disappearing. There were some last suppers in the houses on the Vieille Montagne, some last masked balls, and the operetta was a swan song. The old foreigners were dying off. Real estate speculators and property developers were arriving on the scene. I read everything I could about northern Morocco and its inhabitants, the Jbala Berbers. I walked the trackless roads of the country, discovering its flora, fauna, customs, and traditions. Sometimes I found myself in a remote valley when darkness fell and spent the night in a farmhouse, welcomed with princely delicacy into the only room, which smelled of curdled milk, daffodils, and feet. I was getting better and better at the local dialect. In Chaouen, Asilah, Ouezzane, Tétouan, and in many remote villages of the Beni Ghorfet and the Beni Aros, among steep mountainsides and valleys covered with pink heather where the ocean's salty breath seeps in, I began to collect traces of the life and traditions of the land I already loved madly. That civilization and that mountain art, remote legacy of the Andalusian courts, were about to be devoured by bulldozers and stupefied by the din of televisions: I transcribed nursery rhymes, recipes, wrote down legends and life stories, and in the meantime I collected painted bridal chests, jewelry boxes, blankets, textiles, water jars, containers for grain and honey, mortars, and beautiful Sumerian- or Minoan-looking unglazed, all-purpose pottery decorated by women using terebinth tree resin. I was putting Jim Ede's lesson into practice: the identity of a people is founded and expressed through its artifacts. Then, in the story of Tebarek Allah, two things happened that were of decisive importance: in the medina of Tétouan, in a friend's secondhand store, I found a crate of sixteenth-century Spanish tiles; at the same time our French neighbors put the land beneath ours up for sale. The discovery of those mudejar tiles from Triana, which came from the collection of a Spanish pensioner who had died without leaving an heir, made me understand that by now many precious antique objects centrifuged by modernity were ending up on the market. Some years before that when redoing the paths and flower beds of our garden I had found among the stones a pair of provincial Roman capitals, bought goodness knows where by one of the previous owners. Around here no one had yet thought of saving the fourteenth-century Merinid friezes of the palaces demolished by the bulldozers, or of studying Moroccan tiles, not even the splendid later ones with their geometric and floral decorations; in any bazaar, from any secondhand dealer, treasures hidden among the junk awaited their buccaneers. Around Tebarek Allah, in the place of the ruined houses beneath the creepers once owned by foreigners, or in those of farmers surrounded by the fruit trees under which I had so often had tea, concrete and glass villas sprouted like poisonous mushrooms. To avert the danger of finding one of these in front of us, we decided to buy the land with the idea of planting a rose garden and a few almond and fig trees. The happy years were over; those of the resistance had begun. *Le développment* had wiped out everything: places, monuments, trees, animals, kindness, elegance, and trust. The population of Tangier trebled, increased tenfold, there was no place even for the indigenous irises, the ones of our first encounter, which had been everywhere until a few years before. The Atlantic dunes were swallowed up by cement mixers to become substandard concrete, the forests gave way to golf courses watered around the clock, while countrywomen still had to trudge along carrying heavy cans filled up one by one at the wellhead. When I am desperate, I throw myself into work: for the flora I built the garden of Rohuna in the middle of nowhere, and I used mules to carry all the plants and bulbs I could. For the history of man and his memory, I transformed Tebarek Allah.

Through a charity auction in favor of an association that helped the street kids in the medina, we got rid of many useless things. Our friend Roberto had persuaded us to build a third pavilion. He defines himself as a philosopher on loan to architecture and he designs and builds houses that look as if they have always been there. There were endless discussions. I took him and Laura, his partner, to see some places secretly dear to me: a sanctuary in a canebrake just outside Asilah, an abandoned villa on the Vieille Montagne, the little house above the harbor belonging to an old fisherman who occasionally gave me a basket of sea urchins. In those places Roberto found inspiration for the curve of an arch, for the projecting edge of a cornice, the moldings of a door, or the fretwork of an iron grille. From junk dealers, in dusty warehouses full of cats, we found marble slabs for the floors, window shutters, handles, fountains, and many, many stones (I think you can never have enough of them in a garden). But the country garden in Rohuna took up most of my time. I remember the day when, after an absence of more than a month, I saw the pavilion finally finished: my heart sank. It was too new, too arrogant, yet another offense to the yielding mellowness of the world, and this time I was the guilty party. Roberto armed himself with a ladder and a chisel, and oblivious to the rain, he began to hammer at the arches and edges to wound the surfaces. After a few hours I saw the flesh appear. I am a strong believer in appearances and even more in apparitions. The building breathed and asked to be loved. My treasures, amassed in garages and warehouses around the city, would find their place by themselves.

More than twenty years have gone by, and despite the time and passion I devote to Rohuna and its garden, I have never stopped adding to the collections in Tebarek Allah. Nothing "decorative," I just put the objects I like in the rooms and when it comes to arranging them I pander to their wishes—as with plants, I only put in the ones I love, both in my own gardens and in those I make for others. I dream of small, peaceful worlds suspended in time. The play of a fountain, frogs croaking at sunset, the light that caresses the ultramarine blue of old carpets… this is what counts for me in a house, in a life. I hope that, when we are gone, Tebarek Allah will live on, and tell a little of the history of Tangier and of those foreigners who at different times have chosen it—a city humiliated and wounded but still unique in the world, for the light that enchanted Matisse and fooled so many crazy people into believing they were happy, for the two seas it overlooks in amazement, for the east wind that transforms stray dogs into hippogriffs and little girls into fairies, and above all because the past still breathes in the insidious charm of its inhabitants.

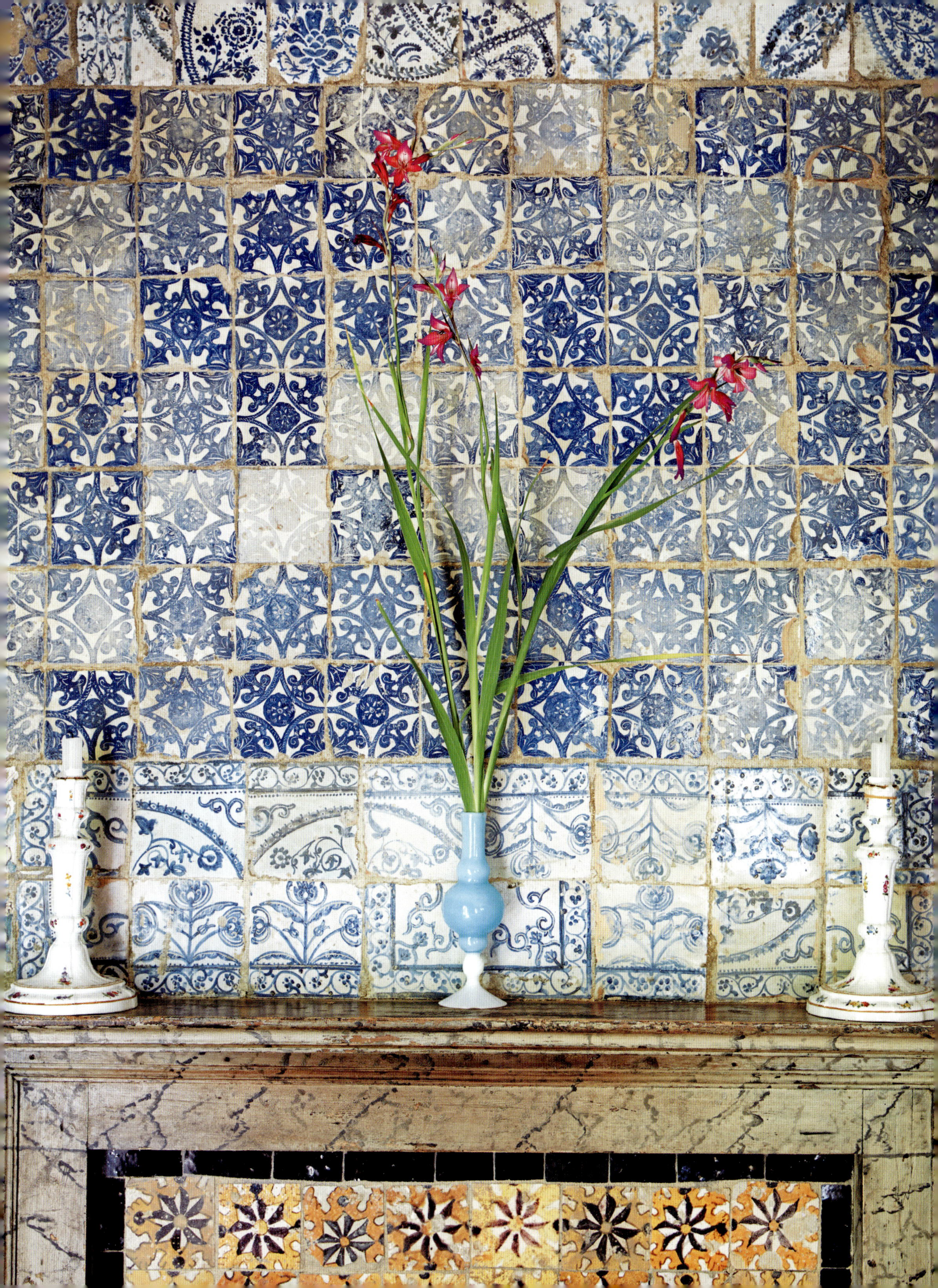

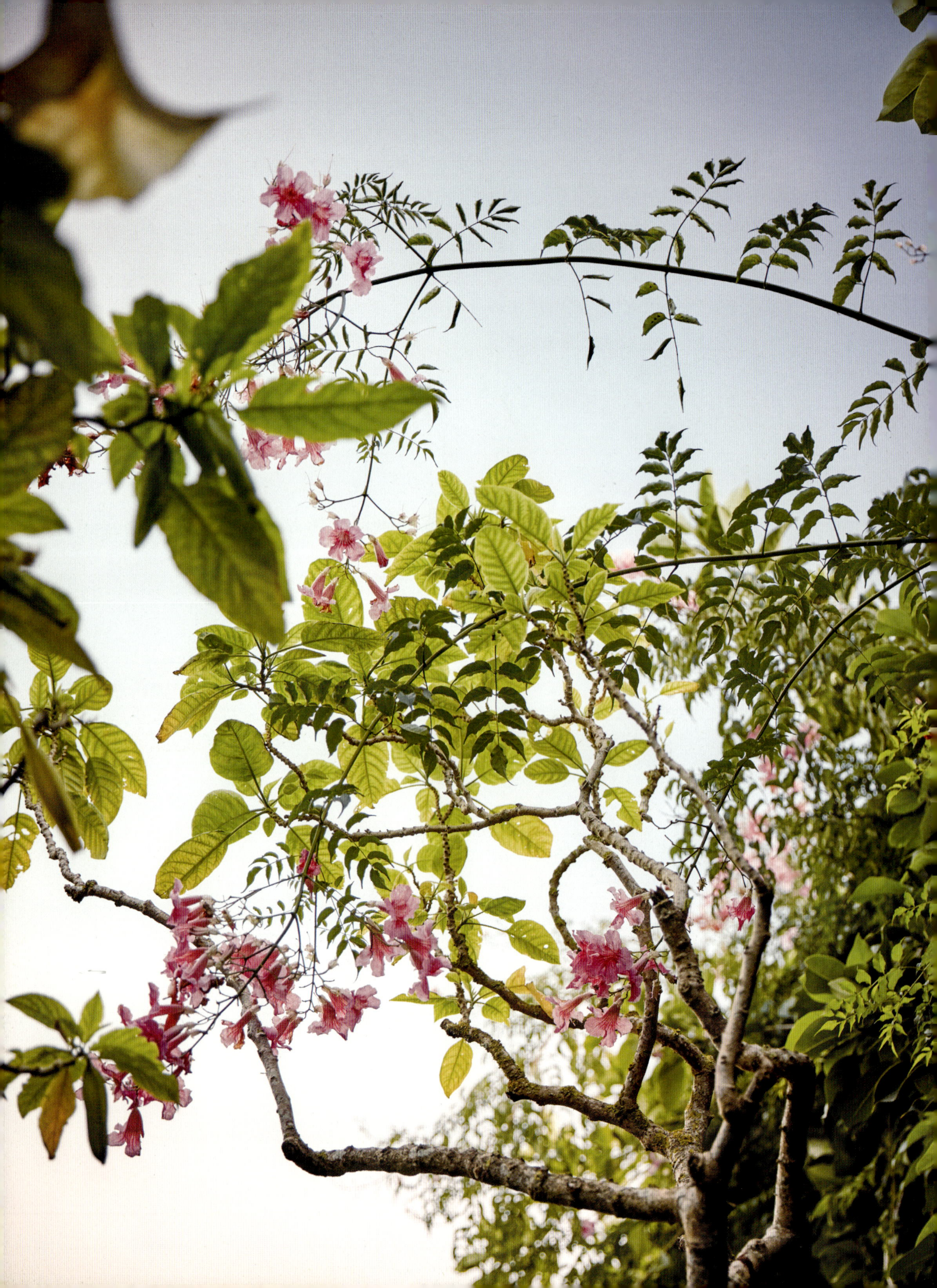

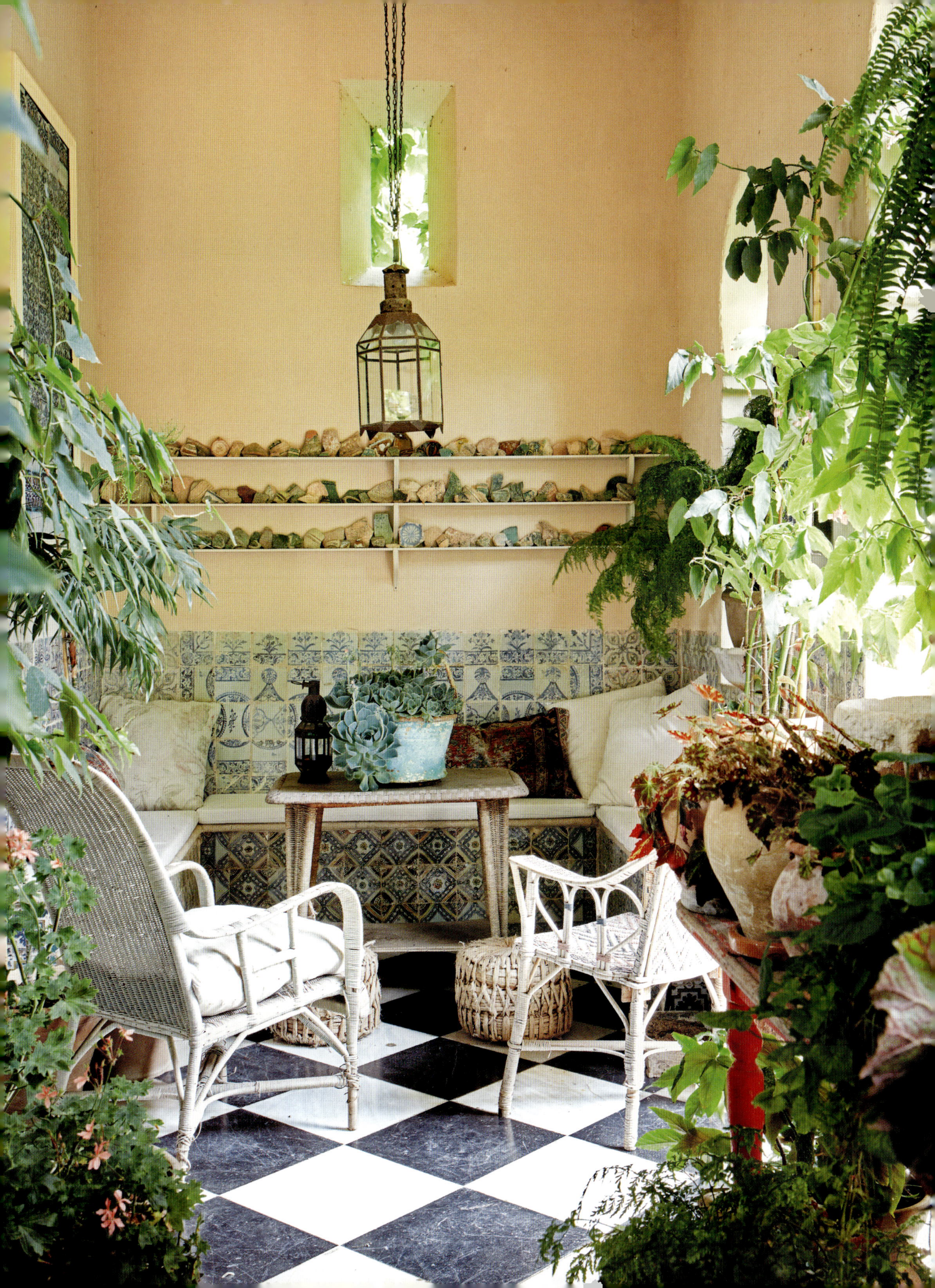

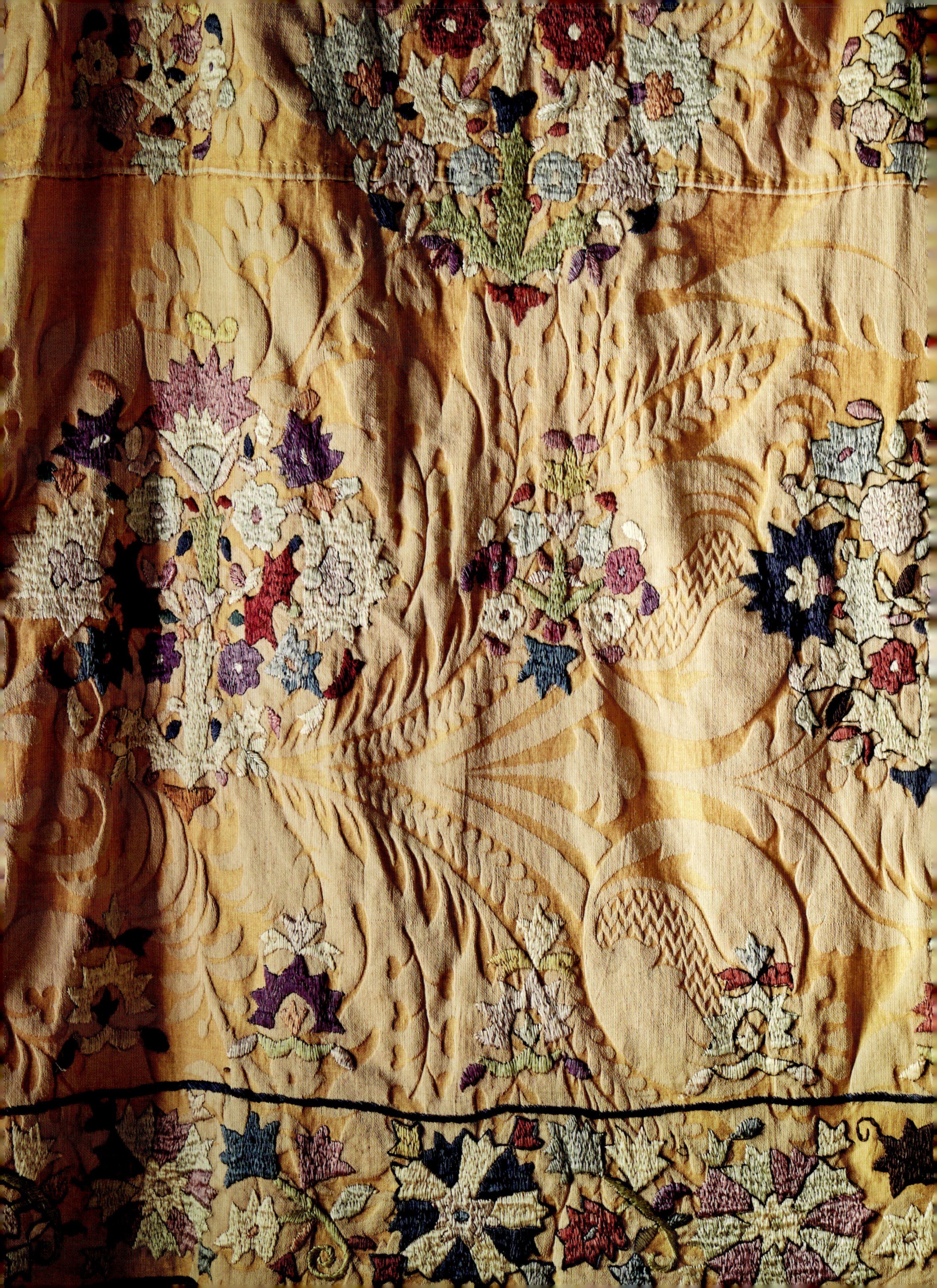

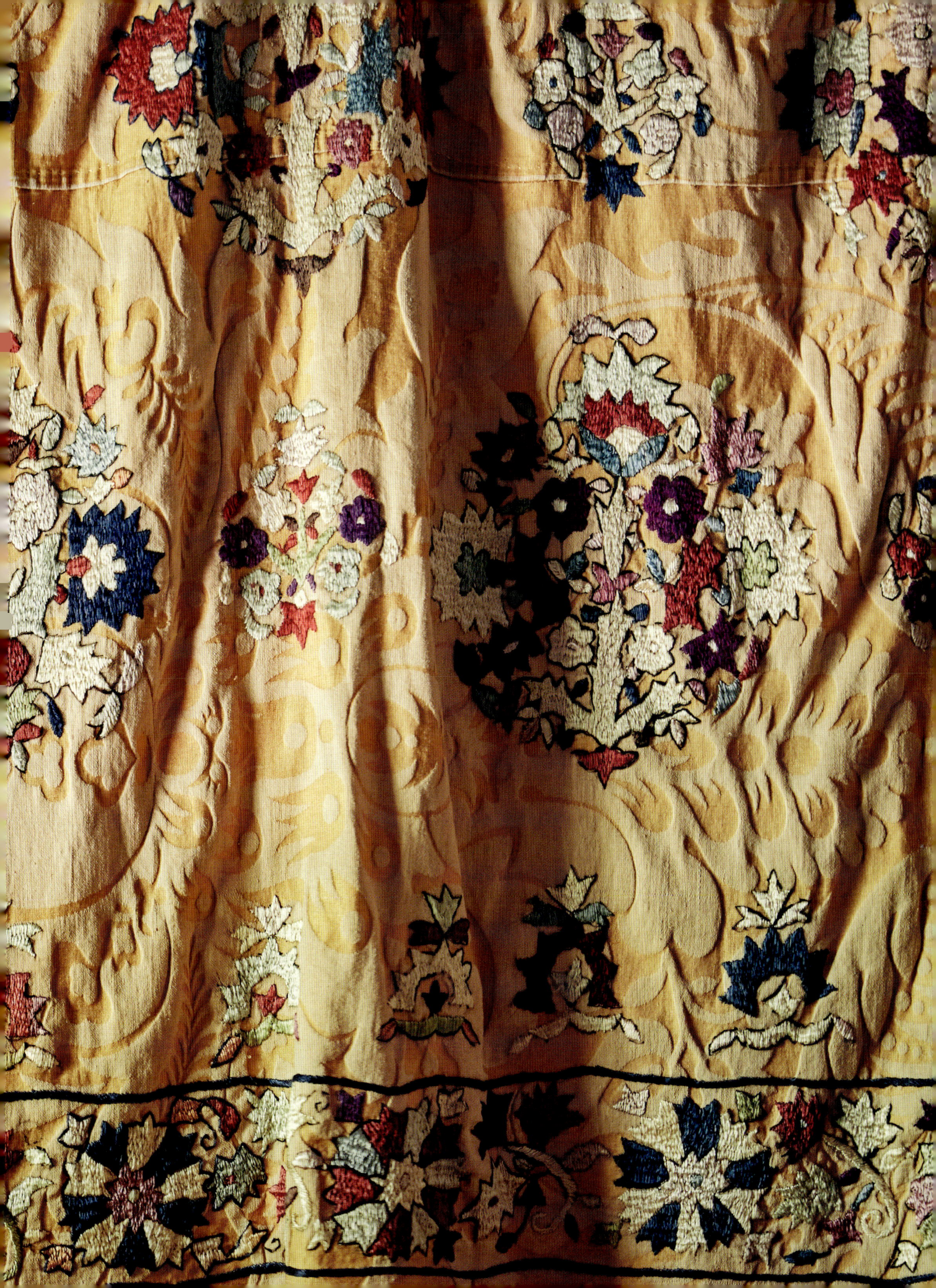

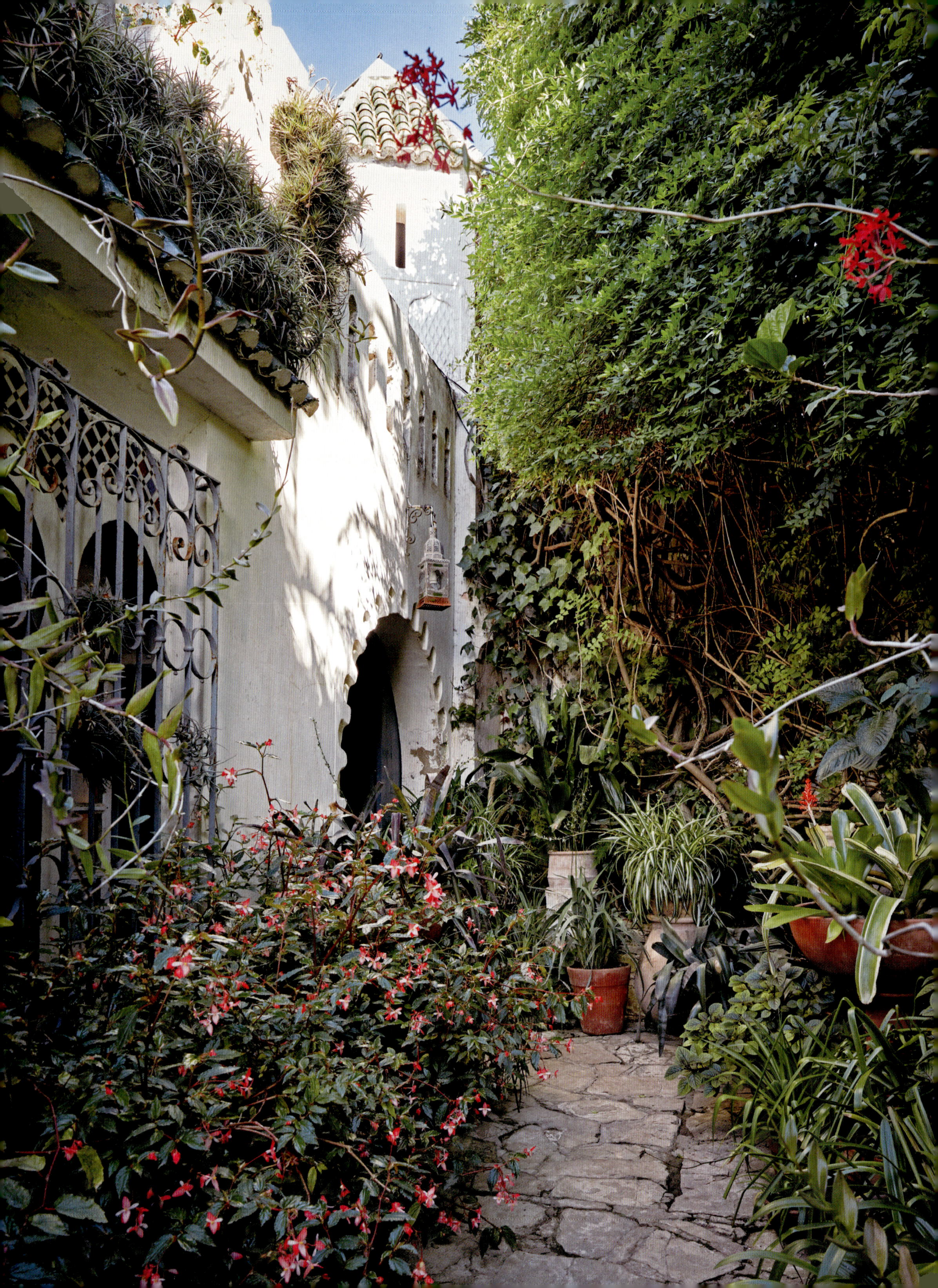

THE UPPER PAVILION

"Mozartian" was how it was described by an opera-loving Italian writer with a French *r* who influenced my youth "with a faint echo of *Der Rosenkavalier*." It was on the third or fourth night we had been living here. With its chessboard castle tower inspired by a minaret and walls crenellated like a fortress in a puppet show, with its lanterns that sway in the breeze making the ceramic mosaics glitter and its blind arches that print shadows on whitewashed surfaces, the pavilion is a nice little orientalist folly where a turbaned field marshal's wife might live among parrots and monkeys in tailcoats. In the late 1950s, Ottilie Cannon, the wife of the American ambassador to Rabat, bored by diplomatic life, had retired here with her donkey, which slept in what became our room while she contented herself with the cramped adjacent area that is today a study almost entirely occupied by the Sicilian desk my mother gave to me. The old English people who welcomed us with open arms—at last a bit of fresh meat amid that everyday social round of interchangeable vices!—often talked to us about her and her habit of dressing in lace and wearing strings upon strings of pearls like a great Edwardian lady: thus decked out, with the donkey on a leash and wearing her silk slippers, every afternoon she would walk miles over the scorching stony ground that separated Tebarek Allah from the Hotel Minzah in the center of town. The waiters would serve her tea on the cool Andalusian patio—but my experience of local habits makes me doubt this version, and I furtively pour a few glasses of gin into the teapot—while her companion was given a bucket of water and a bag of fodder beneath the dour gaze of a couple of baronets with a murky past, and the indifferent look of some beauty with no future.

Our marzipan mosque was designed and constructed around 1940 by a Spanish artist who lived here alone. The first time he came to visit me... No, even though he has kept me company and tormented me ever since that faraway night, I cannot speak here about my little ghost, the pale Andalusian Don Juan always in jacket and tie, with hair I suspect is dyed, as much in love with northern Morocco as I am. The novel I am currently writing is devoted to our adventures. His name is... his name was Diego, Diego Mullor Heredia.

He was born in Spain, near Cadiz, at the end of the nineteenth century. Since childhood he drew all the time. Then his family moved to Melilla, in Spanish Africa. Standing at the foot of the Rif, Melilla was the city that Gaudí's pupil, Enrique Nieto, was transforming into the cradle of Moorish art nouveau. Inhabited by Andalusian farmers and small traders impoverished by the dictatorship of Primo Rivera that burdened them with excessive taxes, Melilla seemed like a typical sleepy seaside city, but it was a powder keg ready to explode. The Rif war, the defeat at Annual, the atrocities committed by the militiamen, were among the bloodiest pages in the history of a century that ran with blood. The Spanish cultivated their traditions with the timorous tenacity of those who live on the edge of an unknown world. The young Mullor was fascinated by that world, so, although his compatriots could not mingle with the natives because outcasts and pariahs were separated by an invisible wall, he began to explore the forbidden mountains that faded into the horizon. The barefoot, snotty-nosed village kids, the whitewashed shacks, the prickly pears and goats were the same as those he had known since childhood; likewise the way of living cheek by jowl with others, for protection and to give one another courage. But these Berbers were warriors, ready to defend their fields with their lives. With rifles slung over their shoulders they would leap into the saddle and, spurring the horses on, set off at a gallop for a raid. When they were sick, they were treated by a witch doctor. Their women had faces tattooed in blue and fiery hair dyed with henna. At night, in houses just outside the villages, teenagers with bistered eyes kidnapped from neighboring tribes danced for their masters until they collapsed in exhaustion. Having lived among meek, God-fearing countryfolk, Diego fell in love with a people proud of their independence, who made their faith a battle flag and lived on those peaks wallowing in their isolation like a mule in the dust. Diego delved into a dream, tore off the veil, and entered myth. He explored iron mines dug by the Protectorate and towers erected on cliff edges in an unknown past, crystalline ridges, and cedar forests, Friday souks and paths where vultures tore at carrion; he came to know the mountain folk, slept in their houses, listened to their stories, disinfected their sores, and ate their olives. And he persuaded them to let him draw them. He filled sketchbooks. He had begun to contribute to several magazines, specializing in caricatures. Newspapers vied for them. A publisher bought the rights to make them into postcards for sale in bookstores and markets. He was earning good money and began to make a name for himself. He became a member of the Melilla Academy of Fine Arts.

In my rounds of the junk dealers of Tangier, the market of Casa Barata, bazaars full of carpets and lanterns, and apartments where even the bathtubs were a cornucopia of dime novels, illustrated magazines, and school textbooks in all languages, I bought all the postcards I could find. On the backs, printed in old-fashioned sepia italics next to the square for the stamp, there are titles such as "Types from Northern Morocco," "Shepherds of the Rif," "Moors in good spirits." The drawings, in Indian ink or black and white, convey affinity and participation, without the vapid condescension that in humorous drawings is a sign of intellectual torpor or fear—two shepherds in djellabas and Turkish slippers board a plane with their chickens in crates, old men with beards like those of biblical prophets play billiards, and a big strapping fellow with a scimitar at his waist and his ear glued to a transistor radio. Rather than the inadequacy of the locals, the real targets of the caricatures are the knickknacks of modernity.

By then Mullor was famous, he took part in exhibitions, traveled, and visited the United States. Then he committed an indiscretion, slipped up, did something unforgivable. The Special Commission for the Repression of Masonry and Communism convicted him of generic crimes against the regime. He was sacked from the school. Newspapers were forbidden to publish his cartoons. He was forced to leave Spanish Africa and take refuge in Tangier, which at that time was designated as an International City. What had happened? In the novel I attempt a theory, but the facts are shrouded in mystery.

He had some savings in the bank, and a couple of friends in the city. Since the end of the nineteenth century, Tangier had been a babel of exiles and refugees from dozens of wars who had landed there in rags from countless different countries, butchers with scales rigged to gouge a few cents on a packet of ground meat, wives kissing the cross around their necks while tormenting the *fatimita*, the maid, local doctors who prescribed egg yolk and glasses of milk, Balkan clerks, petty officials of the Austro-Hungarian empire, money changers from Thessaloniki and Livorno, milliners from Galata, Indian pastry cooks, Spanish prostitutes, stateless artisans, all attracted by a mirage born of hunger. In this seaport it was easier to go unnoticed, but the artist had to watch his back. Fascists and spies were all over. In the property deeds to Tebarek Allah, in a yellowing folder studded with illegible dark blue or fuchsia stamps smeared like the lipstick of an old canasta player in the Casino Judio, Diego prudently signed himself as Heredia, his mother's patronymic.

In addition to the courtly style of this small house—more than a mosque it might be a *kuba*, the tomb of a saint, and resembles the buildings he had discovered in the Rif and scattered in the backgrounds of his drawings—Mullor's love for Morocco is revealed in the choice of the place where he decided to build it. A decade earlier, Jim Ede had moved in next door, in his modernist refuge, where he and his wife welcomed the soldiers stationed in Gibraltar and comforted them in their homesickness by showing them his Ben Nicholsons, shells, and Hopi dolls. Later, he was to move his collections to a couple of cottages in Cambridge, making them a kind of museum open to all, where students could borrow an African mask or a cubist watercolor and hang them over the bed, hoping their beneficial influence might help them pass the exam they had flunked the first time around. In the 1940s this southern side of the mountain that dominates the city, far from the center, was still countryside; that parched Moroccan countryside where only prickly pears and dwarf palms grow and goats graze on thistles. A little further down stood Jamaa el Mokra, a village of huts and shacks built by families fleeing the famines of the Rif. Jessie Green, the eccentric granddaughter born in Tangier of one of Queen Victoria's ministers, lived in a shack full of dogs and surrounded by apricot trees. And if you continued along the path that leads to the spring at Lalla Laayoun you came to the canebrake where Jack Sinclair, another Englishman who had previously been an official in Madagascar, had just built a house. Unlike the English—incorrigible isolationists—the Spaniards all lived in the center, in their apartments furnished with heavy pine furniture and their stores selling contraband goods, amid stuffy Sunday *paseos* and an afternoon visit to the cinema in Socco Chico just to liven things up. Only a few families of richer and more eccentric merchants or bankers had built villas surrounded by a vegetable garden on the plateau next to the casbah, the Marchane. Diego had taken refuge up here, perhaps as a precaution, but certainly also because this was a world he liked. Even though he had to tighten his belt (buying the land and building the house had meant biting off more than he could chew), he did not succumb to nostalgia for the grandeur in which his fellow expatriates wallowed. During his time in Malaga, Alicante, and Madrid, he had frequented politicians and writers, painters and poets: he was a man of the world, conscious of being an artist. Besides, he had already been in this African elsewhere, where he had gotten lost in these windswept valleys, just as happened to me years later. After portraying his beloved Berbers by squashing their features into the mask of caricature, he was to live like them, in a house that in many ways is a boiled down version, a caricature, of their temples. The name invoking and thanking Allah was a fairly explicit statement when his fellow countrymen were naming any old alleyway or basement after the Blessed Virgin. In Tebarek Allah they did not drink the bitter wine of Galicia or Andalusia, but mint tea; they did not play briscola, sitting on leather Savonarola chairs printed with the aquiline profile of Don Quixote and Sancho Panza, but listened to Andalusian music lying on cushions and carpets while passing round the *sebsi*, the kif pipe; Diego and the few friends he had left did not sleep between starched (and patched) sheets but wrapped in blankets of goat's wool.

He worked in what is now our room, where the *gringa* Ottilie's donkey later slept. Of the two bedrooms, it is the only one large enough to spend the days in—in addition to the monumental canopy bed from Salé, I was able to arrange the series of furniture and objects that Stephan calls "the obstacle course for the nighttime pee," and there is a fireplace for the winter. The long entrance hall and the present dining room, which still have the original Sevillian cement tile floors, were presumably once a living room where Diego received a few friends, a passing actor, an exile like himself, a mountain man who would come at night carrying a basket of eggs for his old smoking and horse-riding comrade. Other comforts of the house were the bathroom and the kitchen, which have remained almost unchanged over the decades, the well, the room with the bathroom built into the buttress of the surrounding wall, and above all the turret-minaret that is merely the shell of the spiral staircase leading to the terraced roof.

    A couple of visits to Melilla have made me suspect that the architect Nieto had a hand in the design of Tebarek Allah. The various buildings he constructed in the city (the Grand Mosque, the Benchimol Synagogue, the facade of the "La Reconquista" Department Store) conceal revealing clues: the merlons—that set of little teeth that transforms the roofs into mouths gaping wide to fill with sky— crouching on top of the walls like snipers, the lunettes in ceramic mosaic that frame the arches of doors and windows, and the arches themselves, both inside and out, horseshoe-shaped in the Moroccan style but slightly elongated, almost like a gothic sigh that slipped out through habit. Even the iron lanterns are identical to those of Melilla, evidently coming from the workshop of the same blacksmith. It is an aesthetic that links Liberty-style vines to Moorish arabesques and intertwines Art Nouveau leaves with those of palm trees, heralding that rationalist modernism that was to find one of its sources of inspiration in the Berber houses of unbaked clay. The Spanish orientalism of this pavilion is different from that of other European countries: the model is closer, both geographically and culturally. Centuries earlier, Andalusia had been one of the beating hearts of Islam, and life in a *douar*, a village in the Rif, still looked a lot like that of a sunbaked pueblo between Seville and Granada. Nonetheless, Diego's pavilion, as Stephan and I call it, couldn't possibly have been designed by a Moroccan: only the detachment of a foreigner, allied to a precise, firsthand knowledge of the buildings that inspired him, would make it possible to select, domesticate, and amalgamate all these exotic details one by one to finally transform them into a home. These walls, these merlons, these arches, these niches, unlike many of their fellows scattered around the Mediterranean that chat in a rehashed version of classical Arabic riddled with mistakes, talk with garrulous naturalness in *jaquetia*, the ancient jargon of North African Jews brimming with words from different languages and dialects.

    Diego Mullor was a hard worker, apparently able to produce five caricatures a day. Even now, as I write at the desk in the study, he's there in the next room, restless, obsessed by the profiles of his shepherds. His drawings, as well as abounding with jutting chins, aquiline noses, thin legs and arms, deform his subjects, as if he sketched them from reflections in water. His caricatures conceal and reveal a powerlessness that is food for thought, like a joke between prisoners during yard time—this is why, despite a humorous intent, his mountain men betray sorrow and melancholy. I haven't found out much about Mullor's family; while still a young man he had married a first cousin, requesting ecclesiastical dispensation, but I don't know if she followed him to Tangier, nor what happened to their only son. This is the house of a man alone. Socially he belonged to the circle of the Spaniards and the Sephardi—the Orellanos, the Laredos, the Cenarros, the Toledanos, the Nahons, the Parientes—who went to the last parties at the Teatro Cervantes, organized charity receptions, and danced until dawn in the Kursaal on the seafront. His credentials as an artist exiled by Franco could have given him access to the closed world of the Brits... "Those *cabrones*?" he yells at me from the other room, "with their boar hunts in their Diplomatic Forest and their endless cricket matches? Always putting on airs and complaining about the sun, they and their ladies wrinkled as the prunes of Sanlucar de Barrameda..." There is no way to silence my cartoonist; he always manages to snatch the pen from my hand. "And their small talk, as they call it, that in order to loosen up a bit at cocktail parties they first had to make a trip to old Manolo, where they each had their *chico morito* or *patrón morassón* who would see to pulling down their pants and extracting the broom handle stuck up their asses..."

On the rare occasions when I am alone, we spend the day together. We sit down, one in front of the other, around the mahogany table from Lady Scott's dining room, on the nineteenth-century American chairs lacquered in black that belonged to Patrick Thursfield (I bought them from Ahmed, his sole heir), beneath the Portuguese gilt chandelier sold to me by the widow Amati, under the gaze of the Elizabethan lady in the portrait Lawrence Mynott sold me—with the objects in this room you could reconstruct the last decades of the history of us foreigners in Tangier, the arrivals, the departures, the hasty flights, the deaths. Usually, Diego and I argue about the arrangement of the furniture: he insists on having the earthenware vases from Granada on the mantelpiece, and to irritate him I say that this is a peasant habit. I point out that the vases prefer to stay in the middle pavilion, whereas here I like the glitter of the opal glass, and besides I am now the master of the house. Then we continue our argument in the entrance hall: he adores the painted ceiling in the Tétouan style that strikes him as a flower-patterned shawl, but he disapproves of the German rococo mirror hanging above the shelf with the ceramics from Fez; he would like a Moroccan mirror here, too, like the one above the butler's pantry door. And here we are, amid the English, Chinese, French, and Italian plates and trays I have been accumulating for decades, myself and an abstemious ghost who wouldn't know what to do with a *famille rose* plate, or a Wedgwood Etruria sauceboat, or a crescent-shaped salad bowl from Sarreguemines. At the end of the corridor whose walls are cluttered with *marfas*, the painted shelves of the Jbala, we argue once more in the guest room that Stephan and I use as a dressing room. Diego approves of the big early nineteenth-century Venetian wardrobe that Christopher gave me, has nothing against the Lisbon bed with the petroleum-colored posts, tolerates the small white folding table I got from the lifeguard at Briech with the aid of smiles and endearments, but he can't stand the chromolithographs on the walls. How come, I protest, they are Islamic religious subjects, printed in Egypt, Tunisia, and Algeria! Then I get it: in his day these colored testimonies to Maghrebi syncretism, with its sects, saints, and fabulous bestiary, used to adorn barbershops and grocery stores. And if I object, to my snobbish ghost, that today these popular images are being studied, that an illustrious professor came here from the United States just to see and photograph our collection, he looks the other way. Luckily, he likes the overflowing bouquets of wildflowers that I arrange everywhere—on the Berber chests, on the Georgian tables painted in black and gold, on the Victorian bureaus, even on the corner cabinets from Tétouan with the fragile heron legs, forcing the guests into contortions like bayaderes to move in already narrow spaces.

To end the arguments, a little while ago I suggested that he accompany me to get bread at the *baqqal* on the corner, him panting as he trotted along beside me (recently we have let ourselves go a bit). Around here, the countryside is no longer visible: these ugly villas with streetlamps and all the rest have sprung up in its place. In the square the watchmen no longer light the fire, Aziz who hangs on in his little house at the end of the street is no longer allowed to graze the cows in the municipal park, he was forced to sell them. How long has it been since I heard the manger-scene sound they used to make by rubbing against the wall of our room to seek relief from the horseflies? Evening was falling. "Smell," Diego told me all of a sudden, "listen." The tip of his statuesque nose quivered. A rooster crowed, then silence.

I looked at him in puzzlement, he had suddenly grown sad. Perhaps, I thought, the tragedy of his life was that, like all cartoonists, he would have liked to be a painter. He wasn't, he wasn't good with colors. What about me, then, I who can show colors only with words? But suddenly the picture was before our eyes: old northern Morocco with its brown precipices, its black-painted backgrounds, its green valleys, its clearings in a paler shade of that color, the lightning flash that reveals shepherds lying down amid fields in bloom, the dancing women with faces aglow, the whiteness of boys diving naked in the streams, the ocher and fawn of its goats, the bay of its horses, the deep brown of its mules, the gold of the straw and of the incisors that sink into the bread . . . Well, I said to myself, we'll keep cultivating our dream of ink until a colored bud appears, then we will leave our orientalist pavilion and return together to the Rif, and finally we will paint.

THE PAINTED FURNITURE OF THE JBALA

The Jbala Berbers live in the mountains of the western Rif and in the valleys that flow into the Atlantic plains of northern Morocco. The men wear short brown djellabas and carry leather saddlebags over their shoulders, the women have their heads covered by a wide-brimmed hat made of dwarf palm fibers decorated with woolen ribbons; to carry the children, the wood for the oven, and household things, they tie a piece of striped fabric called *mendil* around the waist or shoulders. There are about sixty tribes. Mostly Arabic speakers, they don't like foreigners. But the Semitic profile of an old man, the Pasolinian prognathism of a boy, the blue gaze of a woman, the tow curls of the little girl who trots next to her father on his way to the souk, reveal at a glance that in their veins runs the blood of all the people who have passed through this region: Carthaginians and Phoenicians, Romans and Vandals, Visigoths and Byzantines, and perhaps some hippies who got themselves accepted, earning blissful years of diving into the clear streams and nights under the starry sky. In the city, my archaic Jbala are not at their best. *Jebel*, mountain, gives us the word *Jbala*, the singular of which is *jbli*, which in these parts is synonymous with hillbilly.

They are xenophobic, perhaps because, being fervent Muslims like all converted idolaters, they have had to put up with contact with the *Nasrani*, impure Christians, for centuries. On the top of Jebel Alam, their sacred mountain, from where, standing on tiptoe, you can comb God's blue beard while listening to the call of the Barbary apes, you can see the sparkling of the Mediterranean and the ocean. The mountain holds the tomb of the Jbala's favorite saint. After having traveled to the East and meeting the most important writers and mystics of the time, at the end of the twelfth century Moulay Abdessalam Ben Mchiche, the light of the West, returned to meditate and die where he was born. Everything here—the steep terraces of steaming earth plowed by oxen, the strawberry trees with their scarlet fruit, the blue and black coniferous forests, and the herds of opal-eyed goats scrambling up the cliffs—is the backdrop to a desperate old fable.

Perhaps the choral hallucination induced by the clouds of kif and by the chants and prayers is the flesh that surrounds and protects this sacred place, hard as the pit of an apricot and sharp as obsidian.

Or maybe it's parochialism, or snobbery. For a poor Jbala, visiting the tomb of Moulay Abdessalam can however substitute for the pilgrimage to Mecca. Every time I come up here, I have to make my way through a crowd. Cars parked and traditional clothing hastily donned, the Jbala of today jostle toward the sanctuary taking selfies and tossing a coin to the second cousins and great-aunts huddled among the acorns, who invoke the protection of the saint while mumbling his name, murmuring old magic formulas and making vague gestures of blessing in the air, but maybe they just want to go back home to watch the Egyptian soap opera broadcast at lunchtime on Channel Three.

Greedy for the honey of which they are expert producers, and for the youngsters they used to kidnap from neighboring tribes, sensual and introverted, lovers of gambling and terrified by the *jennoun* (the spirits who live where water stagnates and watch over buried treasures), my Jbala have first and foremost the cult of the home. They live in large houses made up of several units with Roman-tiled roofs, closed exteriors, and internal courtyards that house the bread oven and give access to the barn, the stable, and the main room. The rooms are swept daily by the women, who on religious feast days expose mattresses, mats, bags of grain, and provisions to the sun's rays and touch up the whitewash on the floor and the walls.

It must be thanks to this love of home that here in the North of Morocco the Berber art of painted furniture, one of the most original artistic expressions of the entire country, has flourished. Around here people have always had a strong feeling for decoration, which is expressed—where traditions have died out or lie dormant and noble materials have disappeared—in the garlands of plastic flowers that frame the windows, as festive as those of dried figs that until a few years ago hung from the ceiling beams; in the posters of alpine lakes hanging above synthetic damask banquettes (formerly made of goat's wool woven beneath the loggia); in the color of the buckets and flowerpots; in the celestial harmony with which even the tiniest objects are arranged... A visit to a Jbala home, always a pleasant experience, can become breathtaking. An elderly lady acquaintance of mine had filled her garden behind Ketama with old refrigerators standing wide open among the blossoming almond trees, and on the rusty shelves she had put a menagerie of multicolored animals in plush and plastic, as well as dolls, some naked, others dressed in all sorts of ways, among seashells, broken alarm clocks, remote controls tattooed with decals, a record player, and a pair of miniature souvenir clogs from Amsterdam given to her by a nephew who was dealing drugs in Holland. Led by her deaf-mute youngest son wearing a white djellaba along the terraces of broad beans and artichokes, together with a botanist friend, we visited that daydream while our hostess boiled up some water for tea. Sitting beneath a fig tree, I thought that paradise must be strewn with refrigerators full of things people don't eat.

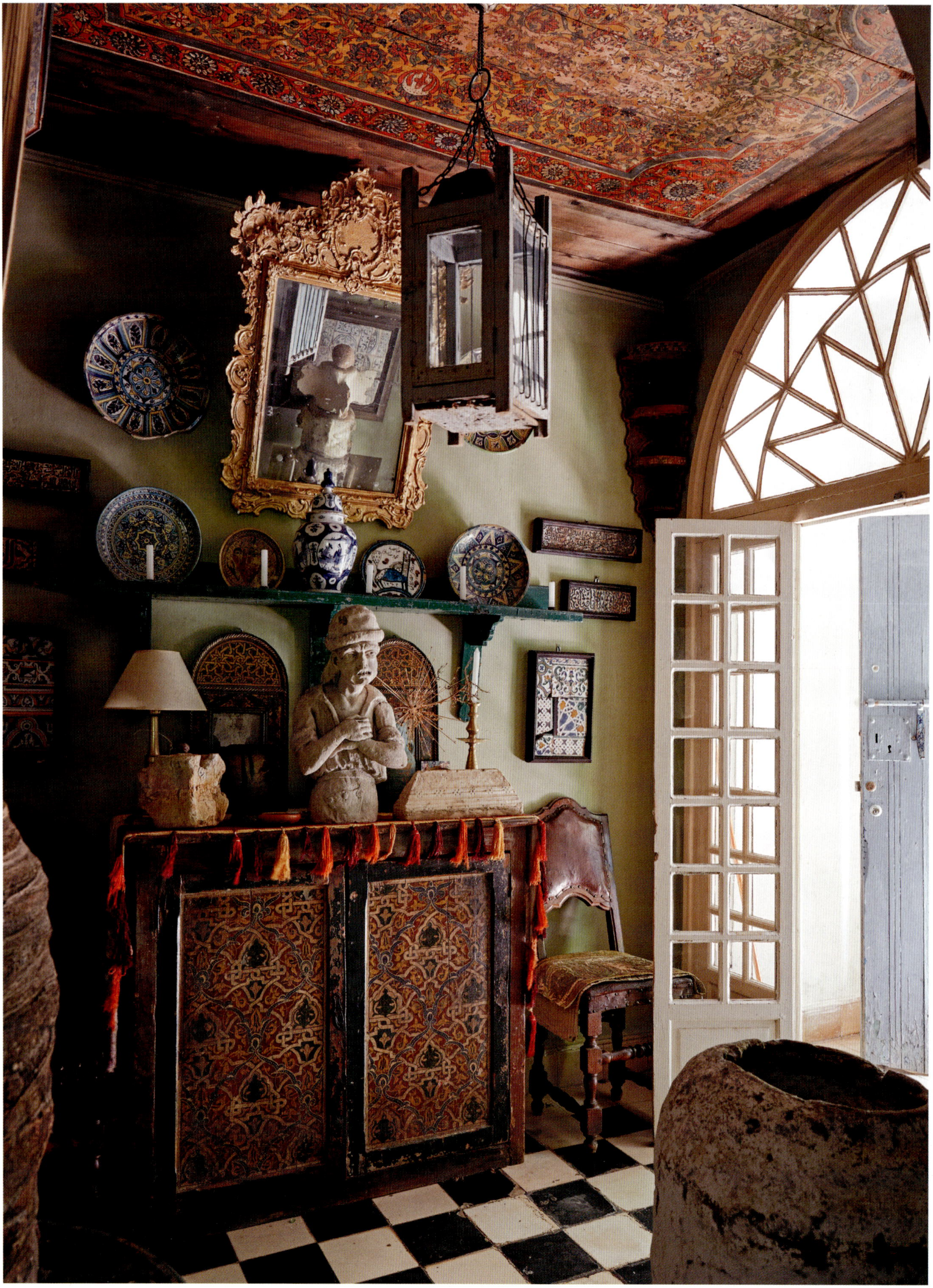

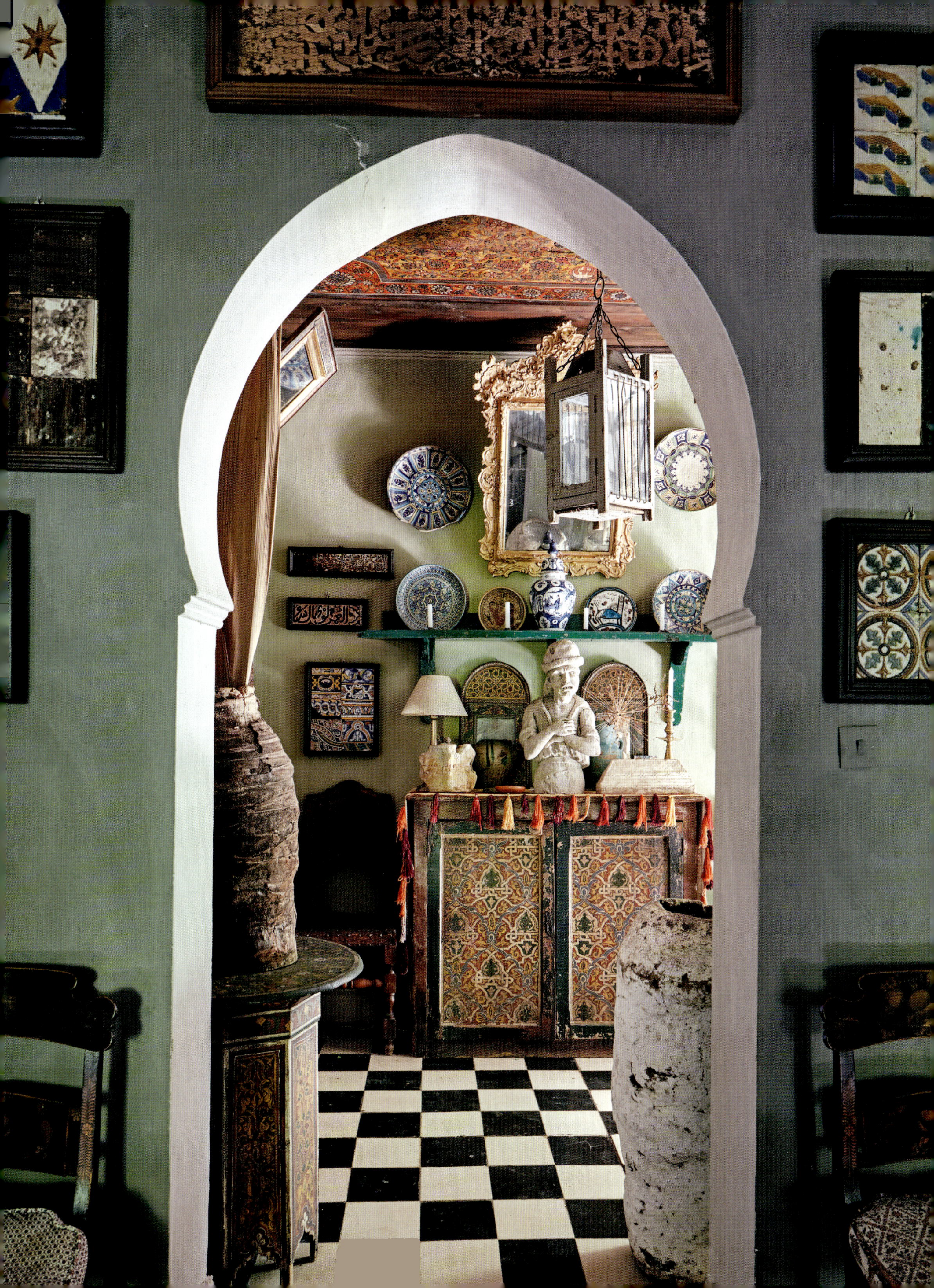

PREVIOUS SPREAD: *In the entrance, an eighteenth-century marble monster from Veneto protects us against evil spirits. The quiet, unassuming chairs are from eighteenth-century Lombardy, and the painted drawer from Fez. This kind of furniture did not exist in traditional Moroccan houses; constructed using existing pieces of ceilings, doors, and shutters, it was made for colonists' homes.*

OPPOSITE: *I found the whale bones in villages on the Atlantic coast, where shepherds picked them up on the beach and used them in their homes as occasional tables or stools. The eighteenth century hanging tiles are from Fez. The big pot on the floor is made of cow dung; it's very light and I can lift it easily, and everybody thinks I'm very strong.*

FOLLOWING SPREAD: *In the dining room, a nineteenth-century Tétouan wedding trunk (*sunduk de l'arousa*). These hope chests for brides from well-to-do families were made and painted in northern Morocco, where the Moriscos, driven out of Spain from the sixteenth-century onward, brought with them a tradition of wood painting that had been developed in the Alhambra and the great centers of the Andalusian courts. On the top, a jewelry box from Chaouen and two containers (*mayda*) for sweets, also from Tétouan. On the walls, sixteenth-century Spanish tiles and eighteenth-century Moroccan tiles. The lacquered chairs are American; the early Victorian table, English; the gilded luster, Portuguese—our Tangier is a cosmopolitan town.*

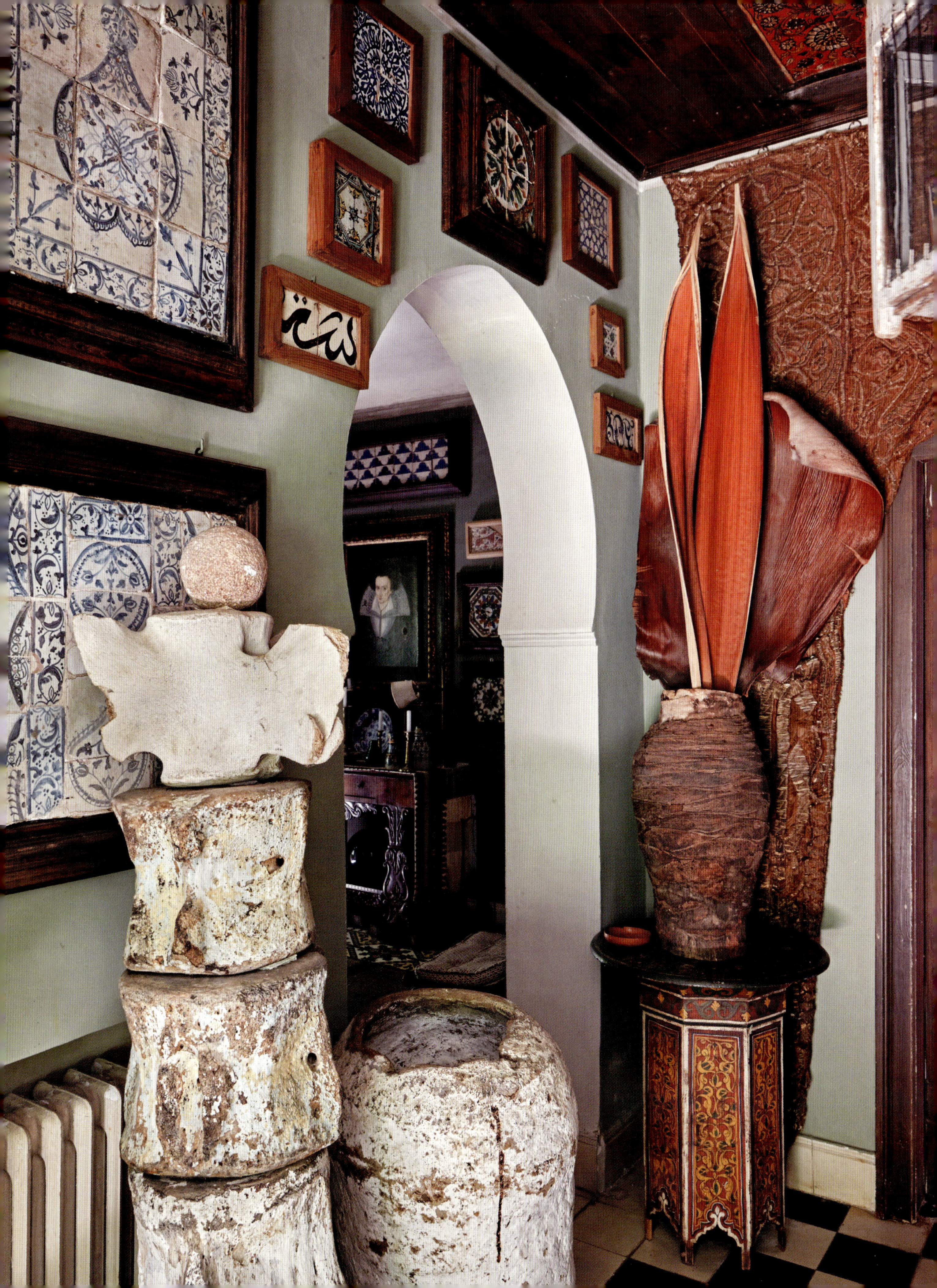

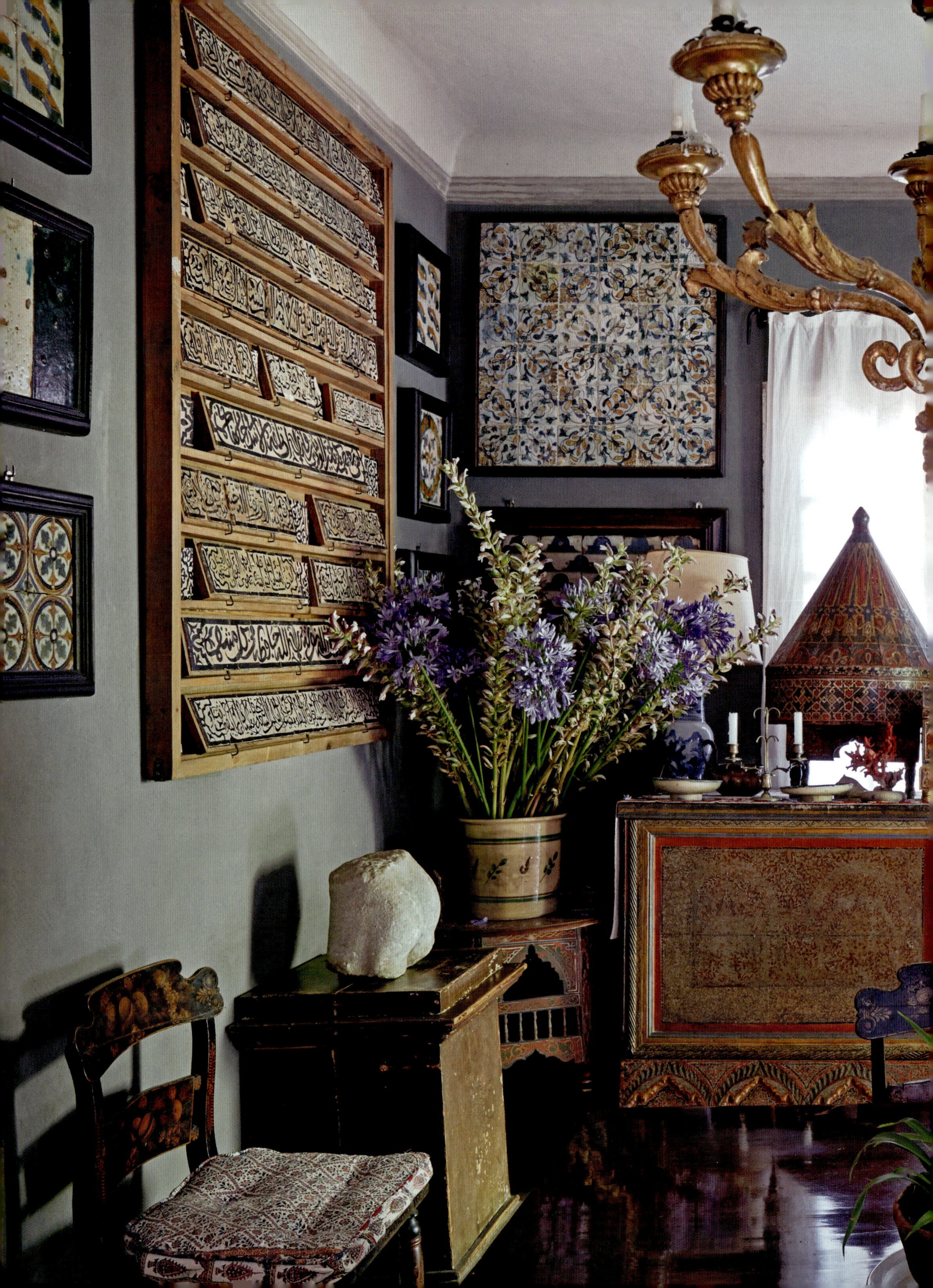

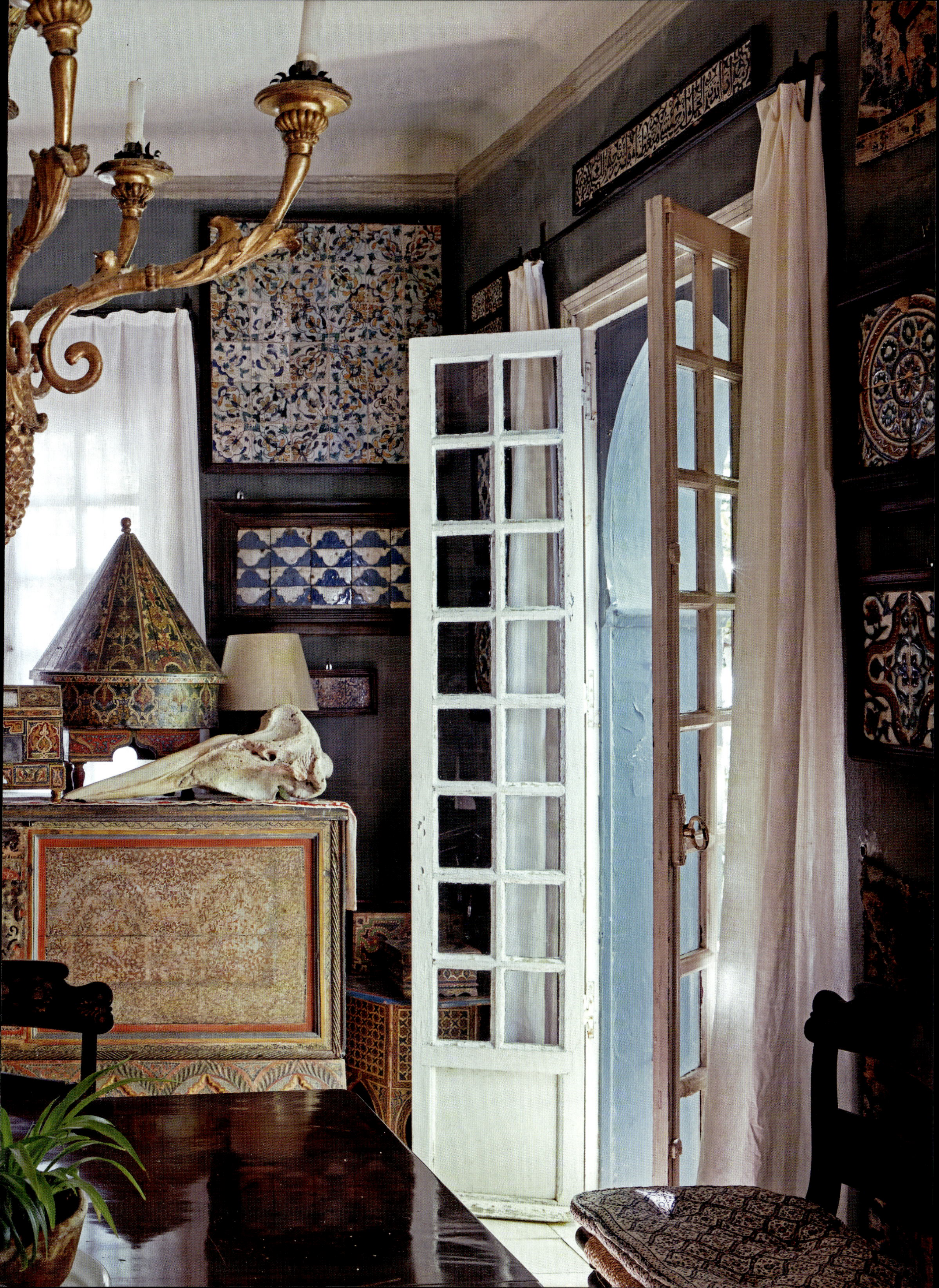

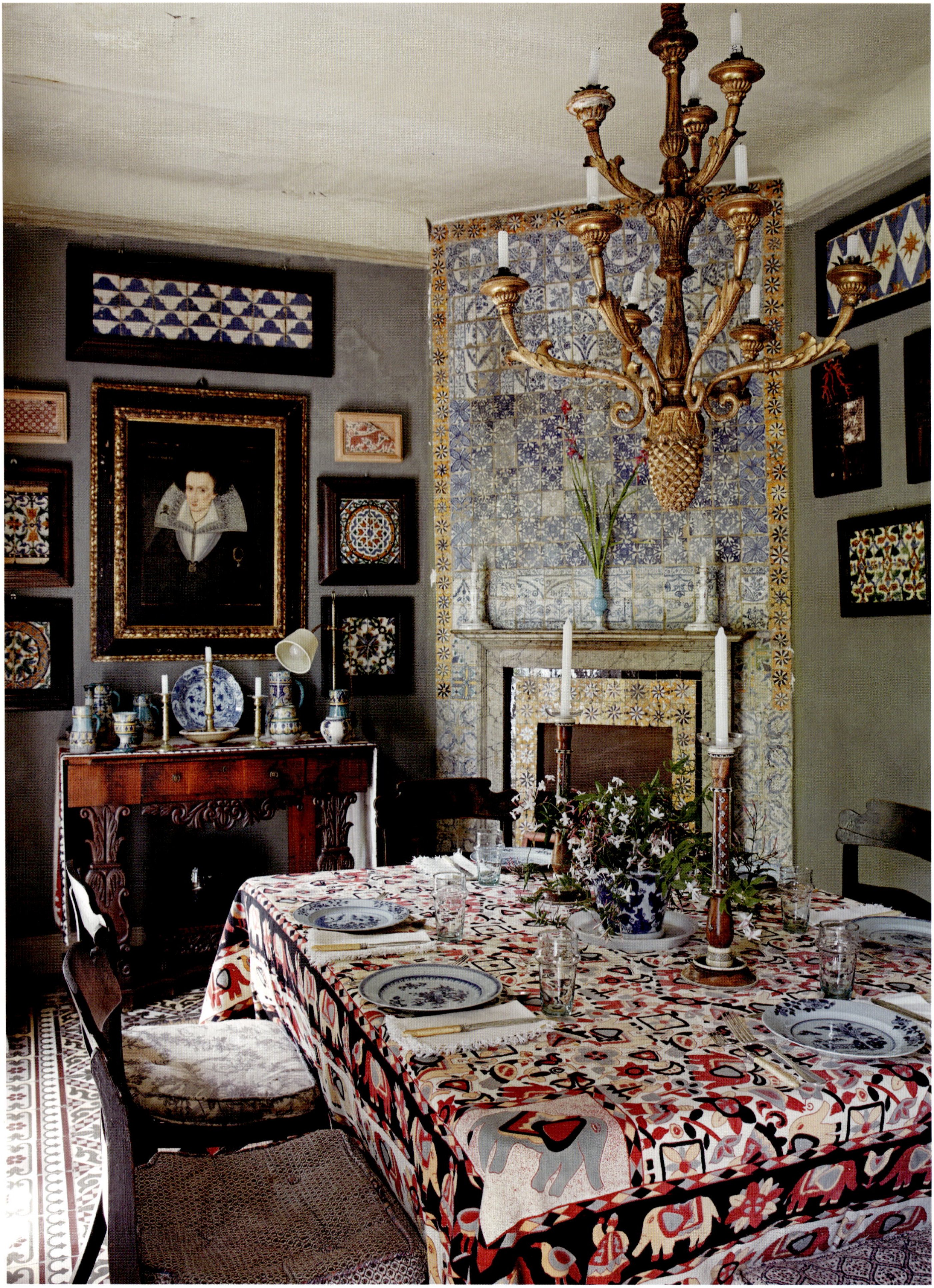

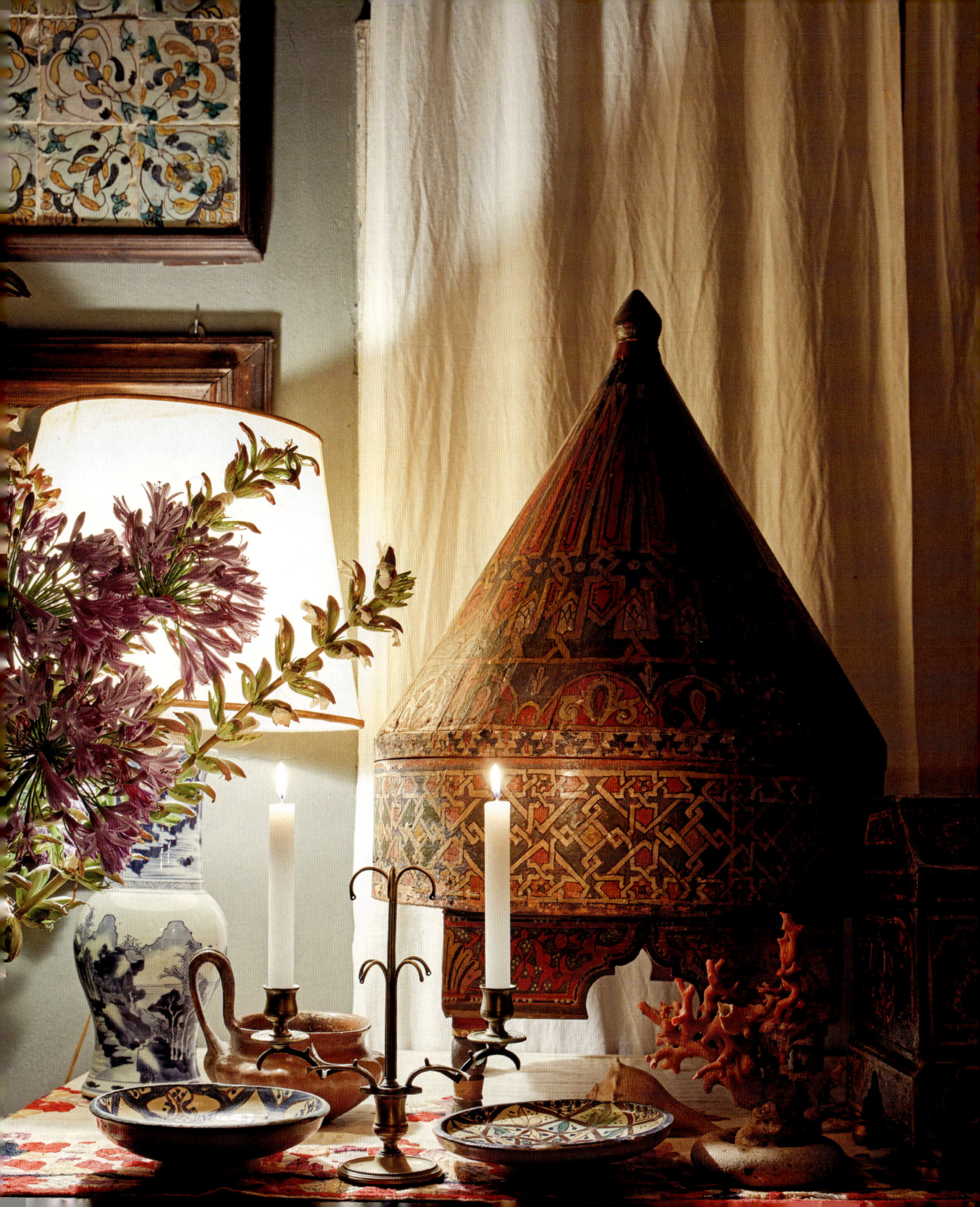

شفشاون 23 رجب
1367 موافق لسنة
1948

PREVIOUS SPREAD, LEFT: *The little Piedmontese Louis XVI wooden fireplace is surrounded by old tiles from Fez. The Ugly Lady is a Jacobean portrait in a seventeenth-century Spanish frame, and the Italian console is packed with Fez pottery.*

PREVIOUS SPREAD, RIGHT: *The best* mayda *in the family—a beauty.*

OPPOSITE: *The jewelry box from Chaouen, from the gallery of my friend Khalid, is one of the few pieces of Moroccan furniture I ever found bearing both the Muslim and the Gregorian calendar dates—certainly the only one in Latin script. Chaouen! How exciting it can be to read the name of this holy city that non-Muslims were forbidden to enter until the early twentieth century! Throughout northern Morocco, the ancient local tradition of painting on wood flourished in the early twentieth century, encouraged by the Spanish who, during the Protectorate (1912–1956), promoted crafts and opened the Escuela de Artes Indígenas in Tétouan, where young people learned the arts of ceramics, metalwork, embroidery, leatherworking, and the weaving and knotting of carpets, as well as that of painting on wood.*

FOLLOWING SPREAD: *These medieval* sgraffito *tiles from Fez benevolently watch over The Bottom, a fragment of an archaic Greek marble* kouros *that Christopher Gibbs bought from Bruce Chatwin and left to me. The sgraffito technique is one of the most original inventions of Maghrebi potters. It consisted of patiently removing the monochrome glazing from the face of the tile to leave only the enameled motif, which stands out against the brownish-pink background. Applied mainly to epigraphic friezes, it reached its apogee under the Merinid dynasty (1248–1465), when the magnificent inscriptions that adorn the interior of the madrassas of Fez were built, but it continued to be practiced until the second half of the nineteenth century, albeit with less musicality and excitement. The cushion on the chair and the tablecloth are Persian Kalamkar, the ivory cutlery is Indian, the blue and white dish is from the East India Company—it may have been from the table of a Jewish merchant living in town at the time of Delacroix's visit, a gentleman trading with China via Livorno and Gibraltar.*

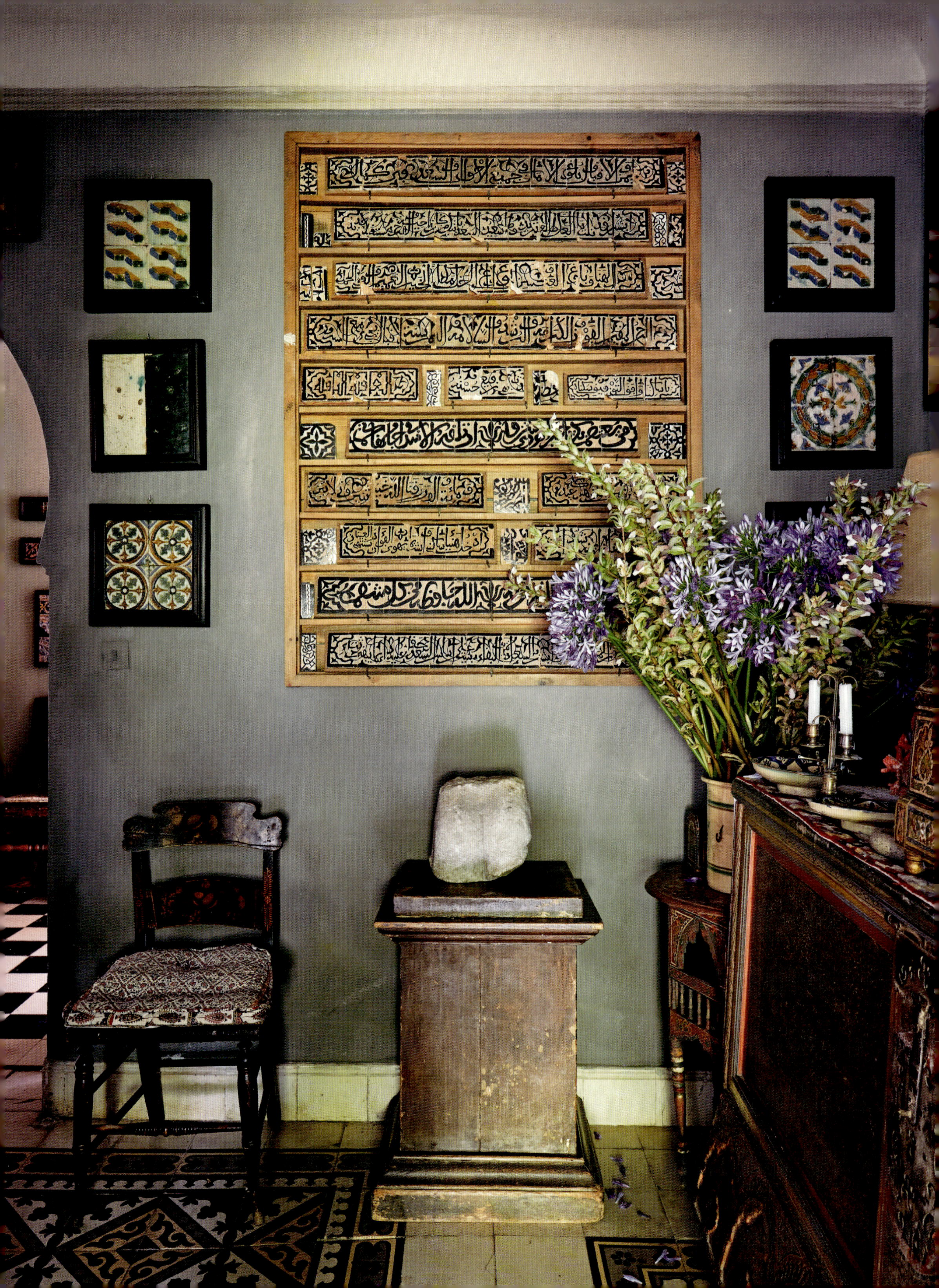

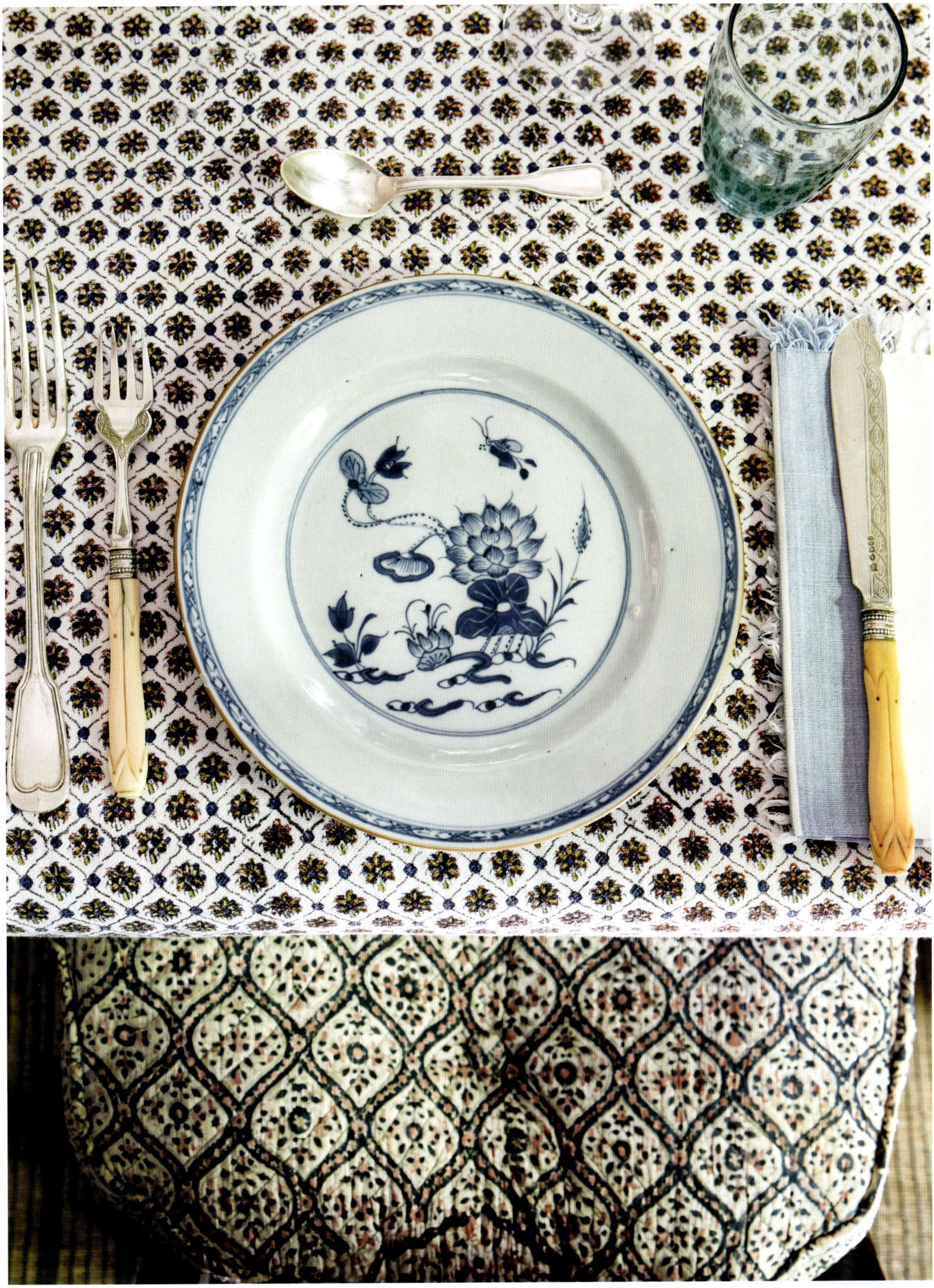

A BIT OF HISTORY

They say that in Chaouen, founded by citizens of Granada expelled from Andalusia, the exiles used to hang the key to the house they had had to leave at the entrance to the new home. The same happened in Tétouan, the regional capital at a time when Tangier was only the seat of capitulations and legations of foreign powers, where infidels were left to cool their heels before being received by the sultan in Fez, the capital. Certainly, for more than a hundred years, these North African coasts have witnessed an enormous increase in population. Together with the house keys, and the nostalgia that still torments them, the Moors brought with them jewels, silks, books, skills, and knowledge: music and millstones, poetic canons, sciences, names, words, the art of embroidery and that of painting wood, of which they had become masters after having decorated for centuries buildings that already had running water and air-conditioning. Their arabesques and intricate tangles of plant shoots are so similar to the Andalusian ones as to suggest that the painters had the necessary stencils to make them with the dusting technique, where the pattern is formed by pigment deposited on the surface like face powder, falling from little holes in the piece of wood or cardboard skillfully manipulated by the craftsman. What I would not give to see this cautious, gentle ballet!

Unfortunately, even in the most important buildings of Tétouan there are no traces of the early age of painting on wood—but since there has always been a passion for novelty in these parts, sumptuous decorations spoiled by damp may still lie smothered beneath coats of whitewash. I tried to find out but got nowhere. Once, some bricklayers kindly lent me their ladder on which, however, very high and shaky as it was, I did not feel at ease; on another occasion, in an abandoned religious building, I dared to climb the equally unstable, creaky ladder—covered in pigeon droppings, moreover—of an old *minbar* from which a muezzin used to preach; I even tried letting a gentle giant boost me onto his shoulders, but my cell phone light was dead, he didn't have a phone, and by setting fire to the notes I had in my pocket we very nearly turned ourselves into a human torch. So I have to resign myself to the fact that these doors, windows and ceilings of mosques, madrassas, palaces, and tombs of saints only date from the end of the eighteenth century—moreover, in the semidarkness and several meters up it is difficult to tell the original parts from those retouched later. The first certain date is 1832, the year when Eugène Delacroix returned from the journey that was to lead to the myth of orientalism. Every time I go to Paris I pay a visit to the Musée Delacroix where I can get a close look at those two chests and, with the management's permission, even caress, open and close them, smell them inside and out, and if necessary, as my friend Fathi the grave robber used to do to check if a bronze was forged or not, give them a little lick to see if there are any traces of acid in the patina.

The nineteenth and early decades of the twentieth century in Tétouan and Chaouen marked a boom in workshops specializing in *zuwak*, painting on wood, where anonymous masters produced their decorative masterpieces: *sunduk de l'arosa*, chests for bridal trousseaus; *marfa*, multitiered shelves on which stood tea glasses and Bohemian opalines; *taifur*, small tables that would appear at the first hint of hunger and disappear into a closet at the last belch; and also jewelry boxes, frames, mirrors, and other objects. In the rest of Morocco houses were almost completely devoid of furniture except for mattresses, carpets, and sofas, but northern homes boasted metal four-poster beds (first imported from England, then from Andalusia) flanked by tall bedside tables; on the Spanish chest of drawers and on the boxes covered with embroidery work stood lamps, clocks, and other objects, and on the walls, over the local silk drapes and the appliqués in French damask and velvets, hung Imari plates that came from Japan via Gibraltar and Louis XVI mirrors inlaid and gilded in Castile and transported to Algeciras by mule.

Of all places, it is no coincidence that I ended up in this land of Cockaigne.

In the years of the Spanish Protectorate until the conquest of independence in 1956, Spain tried to encourage this tradition of painting on wood, while the French did the same in the South for carpets. The new masters made an inventory of old buildings, carried out archaeological digs, studied the crafts, folklore, flora and fauna, geology and geography of the country, and although they did this to make their possession more desirable so they might enjoy it even more, they preserved the evidence of a past that, given local neglect, was already on the verge of disappearing.

In Tétouan they opened an Escuela de Artes Indigenas headed by Mariano Bertuchi, famed for his elegant little paintings in the orientalist manner and his devouring passion for the picturesque. Under his leadership, the last great *mellemin* introduced youngsters and children to this art from the Alhambra. The Moroccan Pavilion at the 1929 Universal Exhibition in Seville, an authentic showroom for this production, proved that the investment had been profitable: on observing the photos of Spanish interiors I bought from a bookseller in the old ghetto, La Luneta, I realized that in those years arabesques had enjoyed a return to fashion. Not long afterward, however, the country's treasures were to end up in the clutches of Europe's youngest general, Francisco Franco, who as chance would have it was stationed right here in Tétouan. Happenstance, too, comes in the form of an arabesque.

I was lucky enough to come across these objects right from my first visits to Tangier. *Escuela*, pre-*Escuela*, Jbala atelier, city shop… At that time I was still unaware of the doubts and questions regarding attribution that were to obsess me for years. I had fallen in love with those forms, which seemed to have come intact from antiquity, and with the decoration that reminded me of the panels and frames of a polyptych in tempera and pastel from our Renaissance; the same grace, the same wit, together with the poet Angelo Poliziano's leaves and flowers that had ended up here goodness knows how or why.

In those blissful years I was buying everywhere, from junk dealers, in tourist bazaars, flea markets, and dusty open spaces in the souk where instead of sheets and woolen drawers the chests contained chickens and rabbits, from barbers and grocers… Every time that, in the half-light, I recognized one of those little floral frames from which an image of the old king peeped out, my heart would skip a beat. I found them in exchange for a fortune in a local restaurant and in a pretentious riad transformed into a boardinghouse; a lady I had known for a quarter of an hour gave me the finest of my boxes, a shrewd antiques dealer sold me his gun cabinet after a siege lasting months, and a kind perfumer settled for my vest in exchange for a shelf that held men's colognes. Back home, I cleaned them for a long time with a damp rag, spent hours injecting insecticide into the woodworm holes, wiped them with the rag again before waxing and rubbing with a woolen cloth. Gradually, I realized that a city tradition that I knew well by now was accompanied by another, more mysterious, tribal, country tradition, whose production centers—it took me years to identify them—were the region of Asilah, the district around Larache, and the mountains of Beni Aros and Beni Ghorfet. They were objects of simple and sometimes coarse workmanship, and from a later period (it takes luck to survive in certain incandescent latitudes), but their very clumsiness, and the vitality of the rustic decoration, excited me to the point that on certain evenings this handling and those therapies turned into caresses of another nature. I have never been a wholesale collector: every one of the objects that I save interests me for its voice, skin, and musculature. I sensed that the great Hispano-Moresque tradition must have acquired new lymph, new turgor, from the blood of the people among whom it had spread after having died out in the capitals; I had before my eyes, in my hands, against my heart, the last exemplars of a popular Islamic art—they conveyed the habits, the flavor, and the breath of a life that, thanks to them, flowed back into me.

For some time I had been wandering in the mountains in search of flowers. I also began to hunt for old furniture, and I found some in the back of some stables where they were quietly moldering away; I found some already loaded on the backs of donkeys or on carts heading to the baker's where they would serve as fuel for the oven in exchange for a few cents; I found some in dilapidated huts two days' walk from the end of the last track, but also under everyone's nose, at the side of the provincial highway, half buried under the blocks of quartz and the desert roses of an offended fossil trader. I bought them intact and broken, rickety, gutted, and even in pieces, rescuing even the fragments, down to the last tiny slat, to the humblest splinter, as long as it retained a trace of paint: a few centimeters of a certain pink or a certain blue served to continue dreaming of other eras for hours and hours.

In a mountain souk, among dark boulders watching over a lunar landscape of mica slabs, I met the last itinerant painters. Those old down-and-outs were now haunting markets like this, where there was still a remote chance of ensnaring some rustic without a television set. They answered my questions in great detail, running their gnarled fingers over the decorations reproduced on my photos, spitting, arguing among themselves, snatching them out of one another's hands, contradicting themselves and cursing at the barefoot children hovering around us: this is the palm leaf that welcomes you, that flourish is the snake that keeps Satan at bay, the superimposed *V* motif symbolizes the ears of wheat and barley, and that square with an *X* inside is the *amaria*, the wooden structure loaded onto a mule in which the bride is transported from her house to her husband's on the last night of the wedding. When I hugged them and kissed them on the cheeks they looked at me in bewilderment.

I gleaned some other precious notions from a junk dealer more curious than his colleagues, from a city matron who showed me her grandmother's bridal chest and described in detail the outfits of each of the guests invited to the wedding (here wedding parties last three days, and every day the ladies change at least twice), from a countrywoman who insisted on the importance of *zahtar beldi*, wild thyme, in the preparation of the rancid butter couscous the recipe for which she had just dictated to me (but to which of the native species was she referring, I wonder, to *Thymus caespititius*, *T. cephalotos*, *T. membranaceus*, or *T. broussonetii*? Over twenty varieties grow in the region and each one has its own scent and flavor!); she remembered with infallible precision every detail of her life, starting from the visits to the souk with her father while still a girl to choose the coffer for her dowry ("The year when it finally rained … the year before the pear trees died … when Ahmed fell ill … when Aysha had an accident …"). In exchange for a shred of bibliography on my beloved painted woods, even a single text, I would sacrifice, I confess, a couple of shelves in my library devoted to monographs on carpets, embroidery, ceramics, and the jewels of this country that has made Berber art its patent of nobility. But, evidently, experts in the minor arts are blind. As well as lazy.

ATTRIBUTIONISM

My oasis in this desert was Nadia Erzini, a neighbor and art historian who has dedicated her life to the study of Tétouan, her paternal family's hometown. An academic, she knows everything about her city and nothing escapes her. Although committed to the daunting task of putting together collections for a new government-sponsored museum, she has always found time to encourage my rescue work. She has shown me old photographs, pointed out unobtainable publications dating from the Protectorate in which a few skimpy notes are devoted to painting on wood, helped me sift through letters and lists of names, dictionaries and tourist guides, persuaded me to venture hypotheses and then forced me to refute them and formulate new ones. Internal chronologies, supporting data, stylistic comparisons... but above all she has taught me to observe, to look closely, to understand whether the cedar or pine plank has been smoothed with a gouge or a plane, hand- or power-sawed ("Look in that register to check the year in which Suk el Khamis was hooked up to the grid"), whether a nail was forged by a blacksmith who had hot-wrought a piece of iron, or whether it is an industrial product—and in which case if it is a Spanish, English, or Moroccan nail. She is amused and perplexed by my tendency to give stores names; she calls it my "côté Bernard Berenson." But when I detect the same structural and formal characteristics in several objects, in short, when I discover a *style*, I get very excited. After bombarding her with phone calls, she finally humors me, and she is barely in the door—"I can only stay for a few minutes, I have to hand in the article tomorrow morning"—when I grab her hand and lead her to the storehouse where, on the lawn (there's no room inside) I have been studying three *marfas* for days, one recently purchased and two that were hanging in the lower pavilion. "Can you see anything odd?" Patiently, Nadia bends down, kneels on the grass, turns them over one by one. "I'd say they've been made out of old crates..." And running her finger over the blue letters printed on the back of the new shelf and comparing them with those on the other two, she spells out: "DON... GIN... GOR... Ah, Gordon's Gin. Hmmm... I'd guess a date after 1950, when they began to import this brand of liquor into Morocco..."

"But what about the decoration?" I ask, trying to restrain my impatience.

She shrugs. "I wouldn't know... Geometrical, it's geometrical all right... These poor-quality colors look synthetic..." And now she's back on her feet again, observing my three *marfas* from the height of her knowledge: "But perhaps I know what you're getting at... the artist seems to have been inspired by a specific model..."

"Do you mean to tell me that these rectangles and lozenges don't make you think of seventeenth-century English portraiture? The scrolls with the names of the people portrayed?"

She looks at me in astonishment.

"See how they simulate the consistency of paper. Don't they remind you immediately of the ovals and friezes of the boiserie in those chilly manor houses? Hardwick Hall, Bess of Hardwick...? The connection is blindingly obvious!" And finally I get to the point: "I've called the artist the 'Master of the Jacobean cartouche!'" Nadia nods, then seems to reflect. And with a glint in the ice-colored eyes she inherited from her mother, a good gardener who was my friend: "Maybe 'the alcoholic housepainter' would have been sufficient... Are you sure you're getting enough sleep? I'm cold, offer me a cup of tea because then I have to hurry off to work." Despite her puzzlement, she still encourages me, so, proud of my nomenclatorial verve, I can give vent to all my enthusiasm for the artistry of the "Workshop of the

Taifur table with the star-shaped crosspiece" of the "Workshop of the naturalistic tulip," of the "Master of the Ottoman slat" and of the artist whose profile is still uncertain, whom for the moment I have dubbed the "Master of the *rocaille* arabesque on a black background" ("He must have liked the lacework of Spanish dolls," comments Nadia, "or maybe he had seen Lucia Bosé's house in a magazine"). I am no longer lost in the desert, but I struggle to find my bearings, I wander in a no man's land with few points of reference: I certainly cannot afford to take them lightly. Luckily it is a flowery land.

PAINTED FLOWERS

Since time immemorial my Jbala have cultivated a clump of scented carnations in a pot on the windowsill, the rhizome of which must have arrived in a backpack on a ship. But as local painters portray them with the same crested profile as those found on Iznik tiles, they must have been looking at a Turkish product, maybe merely a towel from a hammam or a xylographic copy of the Koran bordered with those carnations. The same goes for tulips, which probably came to Tétouan from Algeria when it was a vassal state of the Sublime Porte, in the weave of a length of damask or embroidered on the linen of a turban cover, and immediately became widespread because few fevers are as contagious as tulip fever: two or three flattened petals, but slippery as a fish, fleshy as a pinup's thighs, streamlined as a vial full of nothing, and hypnotic as a viper spitting a kiss.

But while, in the fabrics and ceramics of Asia Minor, tulips are always red like most of the hundreds of varieties that flourish between the Altai and Epirus, here in the North of Morocco the native species prevails: *Tulipa sylvestris*, which, according to the botanists of the Protectorate, grew in the mountains around Tétouan until the first decades of the last century, has now taken refuge in some clearings in the hills north of Moulay Idriss. It has yellow golden petals. Thus, on the oldest shelves and chests, the little wildflowers ruffled by the wind are not the cheeks of a cold child blowing soap bubbles in a wintry park on the Bosphorus, but the hard beaks of birds with necks more sinuous than those of swans swimming in the pond in which wooden domes are reflected among cypresses and weeping willows where the call of a nanny from Languedoc rings out: "Kanoum Effendi! Kanoum Effendi! *Rentrez donc*! *Vous allez attraper une grippe*!" As I have finally understood, stylization in art always starts from the observation of nature; the flowers among which you lie down to take a siesta move and influence you more than those woven into the carpet on which you pray five times a day.

But on tribal artifacts, devoid of Turkish influences, the species that drew me here—and, I hope, will see me die here—flourish above all: irises and narcissi. On the shelves from the Beni Ghorfet, the *Iris tingitana* of our first fateful trip to Tangier are self-important, thick-skinned: stems straight as broomsticks end in large corollas without a trace of naturalism, graceless. But the flower is there. It has the emotion of the painter hypnotized by that naked genital organ, it has the scandal of beauty, the same thing that to this day amazes me when I wander among them at Rohuna, where after titanic effort I have managed to persuade them once more to make their camp—of beggars, saints, hawkers, pimps, jugglers, and legionnaires and dancers and hermits and whores—irises that used to bloom for miles and miles around the white city and today have vanished forever. As for daffodils, they are always depicted on the coffers and boxes of the Jbala, given that between October and March, one after another, a good three species carpet these blessed mountains: *N. obsoletus*, *N. elegans*, and *N. papyraceus*. They form snowfalls that would make a depressive mad with good humor. After all, with their six petals and trumpet, already stylized by nature, daffodils recur in all the artifacts of Mediterranean man, from Cretan vases to the cornices of the Italian Renaissance, in the hope, I suppose, of managing to capture in ceramics, stone, wood, and gold their perfume of love. The narcissi of the Jbala are white six-pointed stars, with a swelling in the center: the kind of flower children draw when they want to draw a flower. But on these pieces of furniture, often fluttering at the edges like makeweight ornamentation, separated from the others that all together make a pattern codified over centuries of efforts by my mountain dwellers determined to capture the mystery of the world, another flower of the same family appears. It suffices to be mildly familiar with the surprises of the seasons in these parts to recognize the tiny *Narcissus cavanillesii*, the earliest of the native narcissi, and the oldest. With no corona, naked, this yellow daffodil—reiterating its color is the only way to describe it: yellow, yellow, yellow—is the survivor of a flora millions of years old. Perhaps this is why, every time I find it before me on ground lashed by rain or on the front of a chest, it triggers in me the mysterious prehistoric memory of a little girl killed by a mammoth's tusk and buried by her mother in the cave of Achakkar: having closed the little girl's eyes and painted her face with ocher, she had crowned her with a garland—a natural thing which for the first time acquired a symbolic meaning, the beginning of our ordeal as mammals sick with beauty, loss, and nostalgia. Perhaps as she wailed, certainly as she wept, these were the flowers that woman had woven together.

In almost forty years here in Tebarek Allah, I have collected over three hundred pieces of furniture and objects, and several hundred fragments. I hope that the collection will remain intact even when Stephan and I are gone. Around here I am known by the countryfolk as "the flower Christian." But junk dealers, carpenters, bazaar traders, and collectors—as well as the many unfortunates who have been the targets of my most urgent questions—could also call me *el nazrani di el zuwak*, "the painted wood Christian." Because basically nothing moves me more than my wildflowers as depicted by an old artisan.

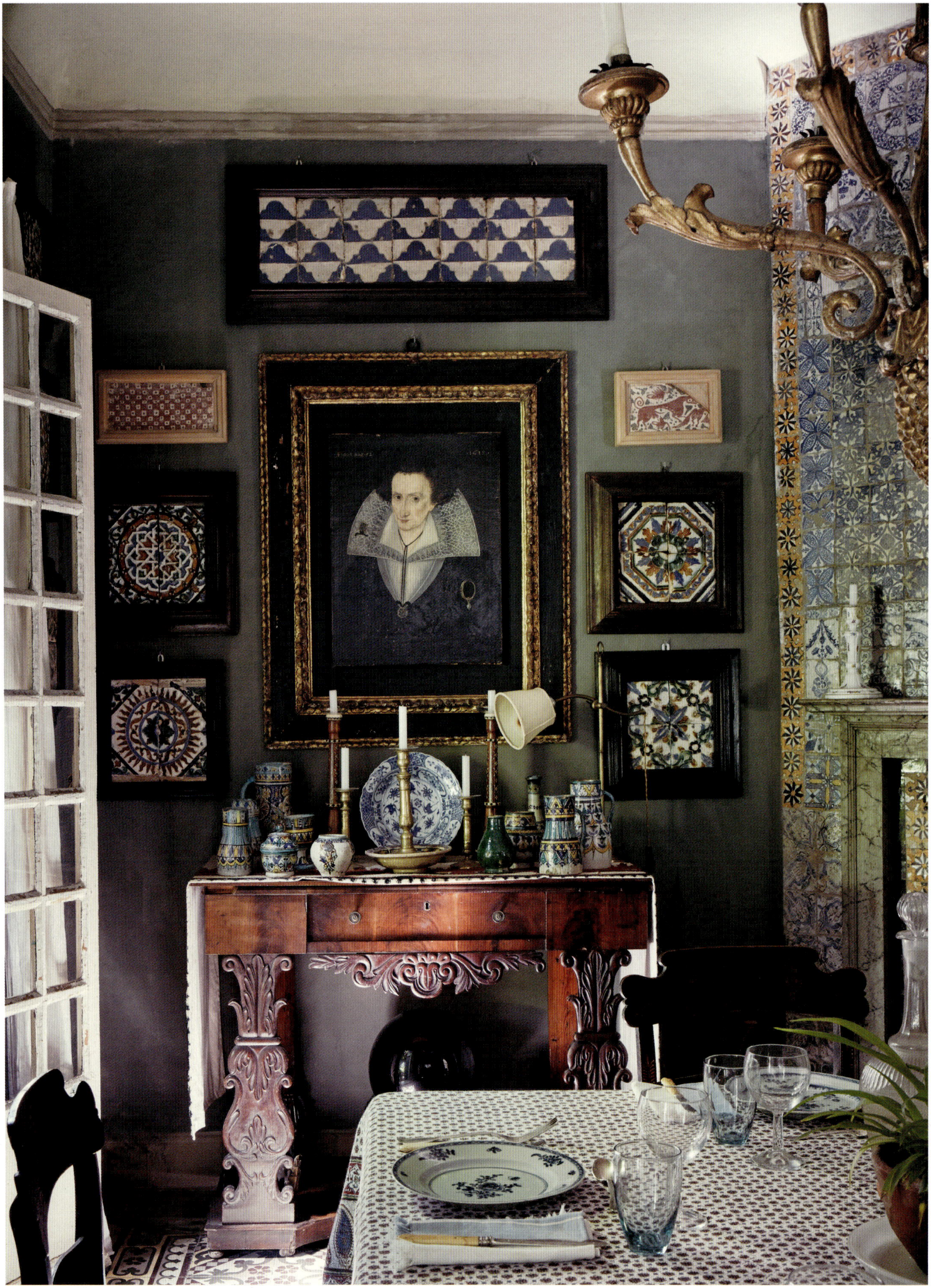

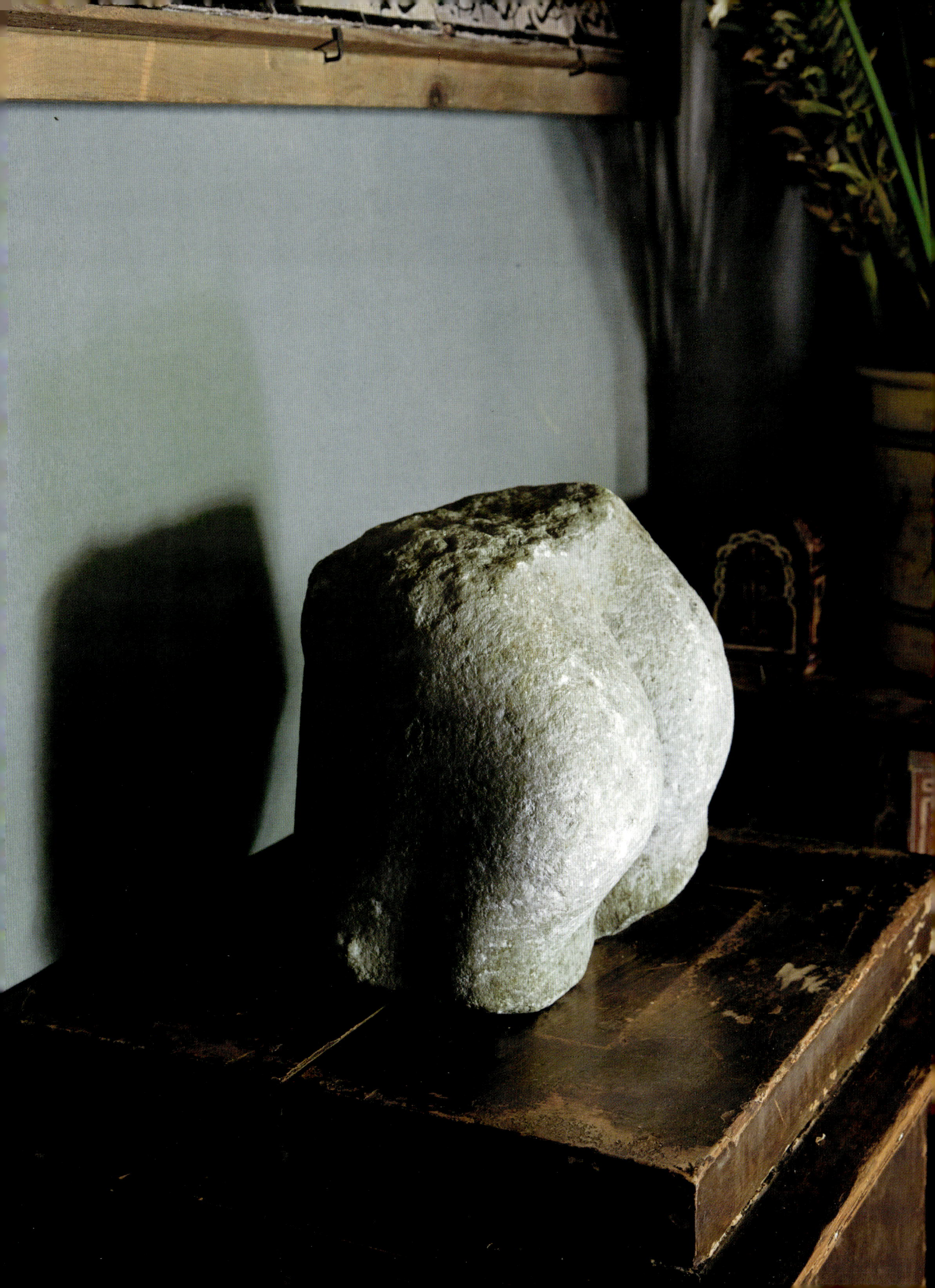

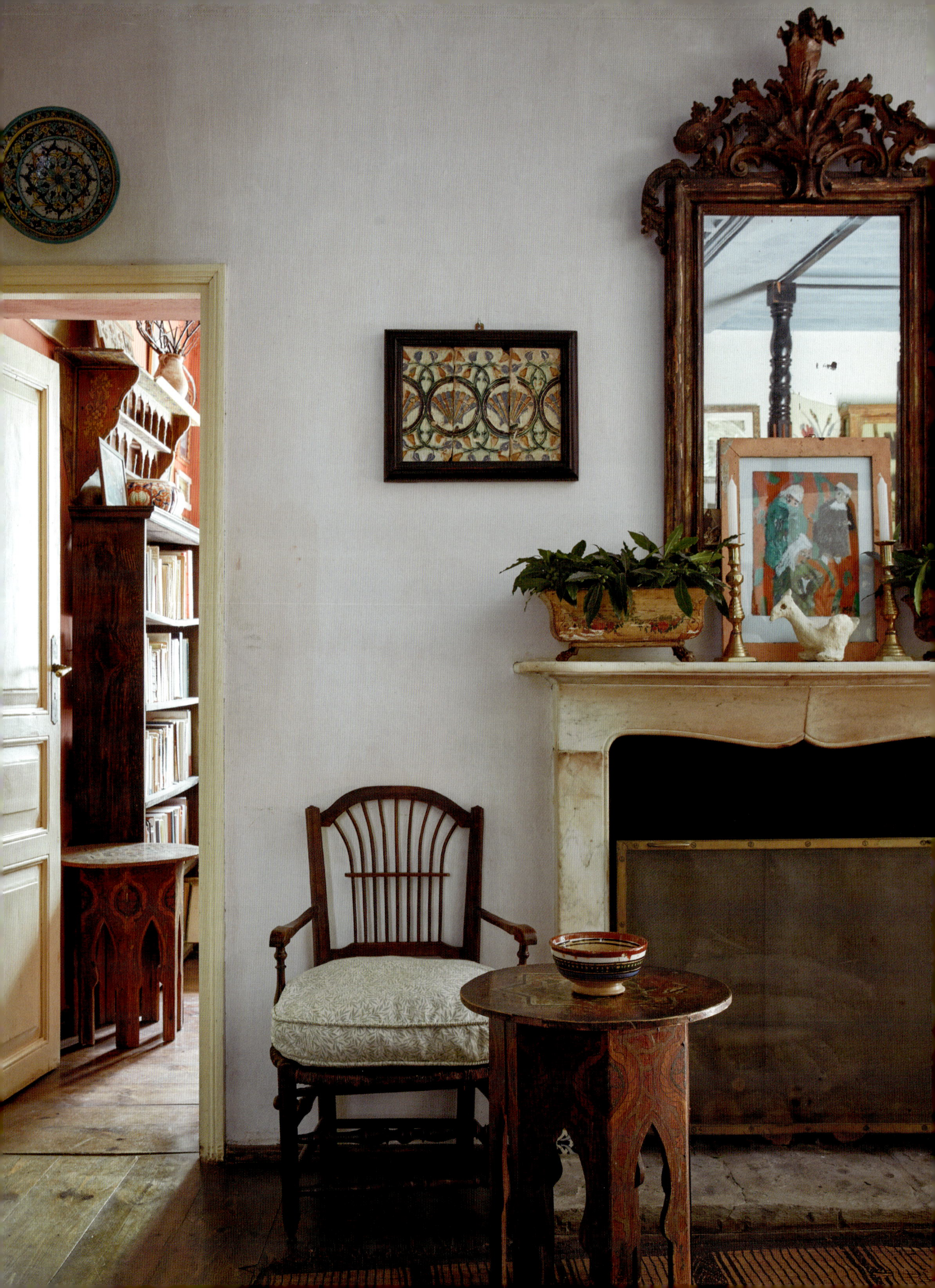

PREVIOUS SPREAD, LEFT: *The Ugly Lady surrounded by an Invincible Armada of Spanish tiles.*
PREVIOUS SPREAD, RIGHT: *I think The Bottom is smiling, and in my imagination I reconstruct the body and the face of the young man sculpted from a block of Parian marble in the sixth century BC—art historians have defined it as an "archaic smile."*
OPPOSITE: *On the northern Italian fireplace in our bedroom: an Italian gilded mirror, a painting by Hamri, whom I consider the best northern Morocco painter of the twentieth-century, and a clay hen by Latifa Aimran—our neighbor in Rohuna—a peasant lady of fifty-five with seven children who has just discovered she is an artist. The late eighteenth-century chair covered in William Morris's Willow is from Provence. I found the* taifur *(a small occasional table that would appear at the first hunger pang and disappear after the last burp) in Larache.*
FOLLOWING SPREAD: *In my tiny studio, the painted wooden wall from a chapel in the Rif mountains that separated the area reserved for women from that for men. I bought it from a truck driver; it had already been sold to a bread oven where it was going to be used as firewood.*

It bears witness to the success of painting on wood in the areas outside the urban centers here in the North, in the mountains of the Berber Jbalas, and it shows how a refined decorative but rather anemic tradition developed in the courts of Andalusia drew new vigor and firmness from the blood of the mountain folk, among whom it spread. The prints are views of coastal Moroccan towns from a seventeenth-century edition of Leo Africanus's Description of Africa. *The painted frames are mostly from the Escuela de Artes Indigenas in Tétouan.*

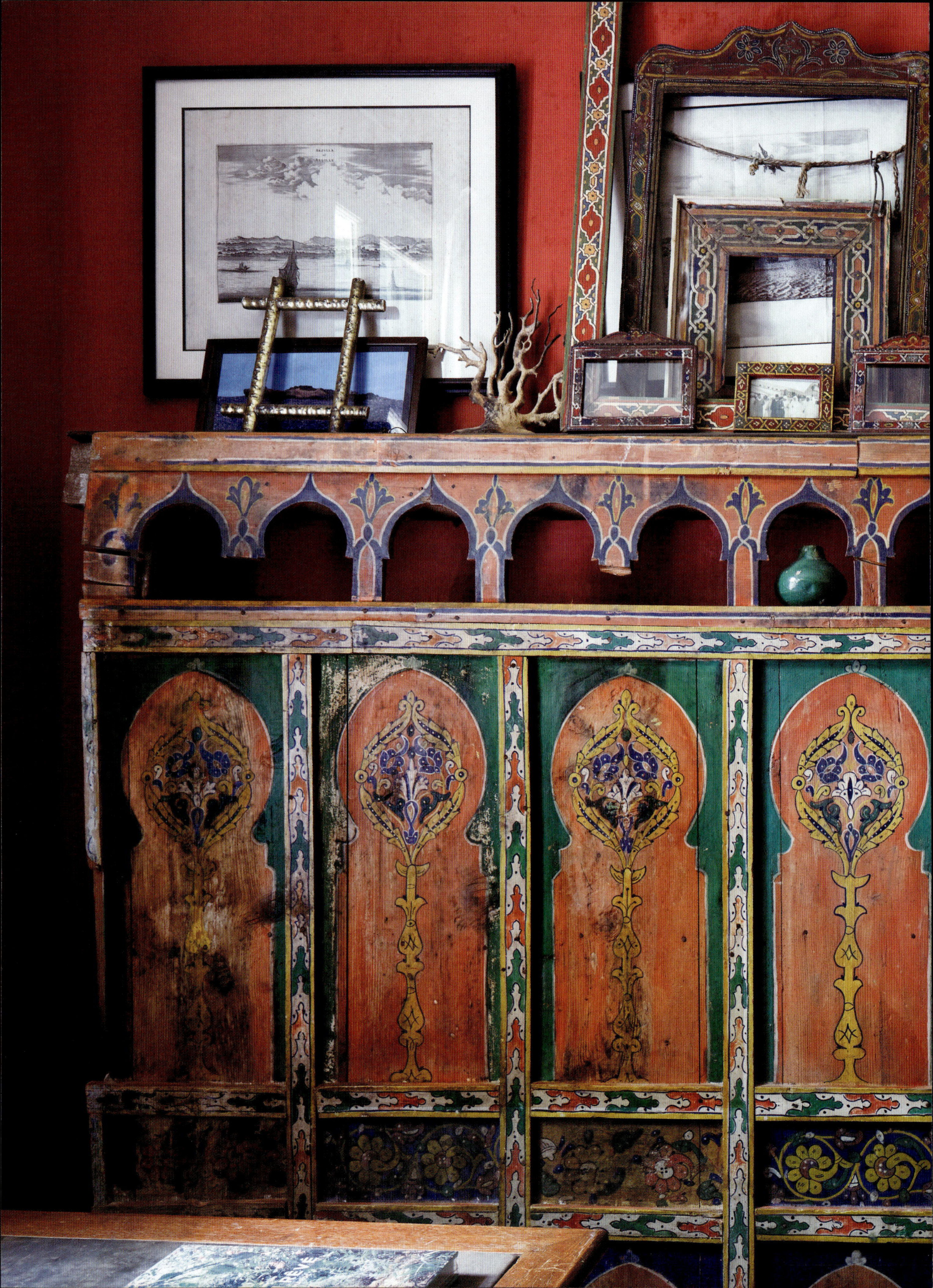

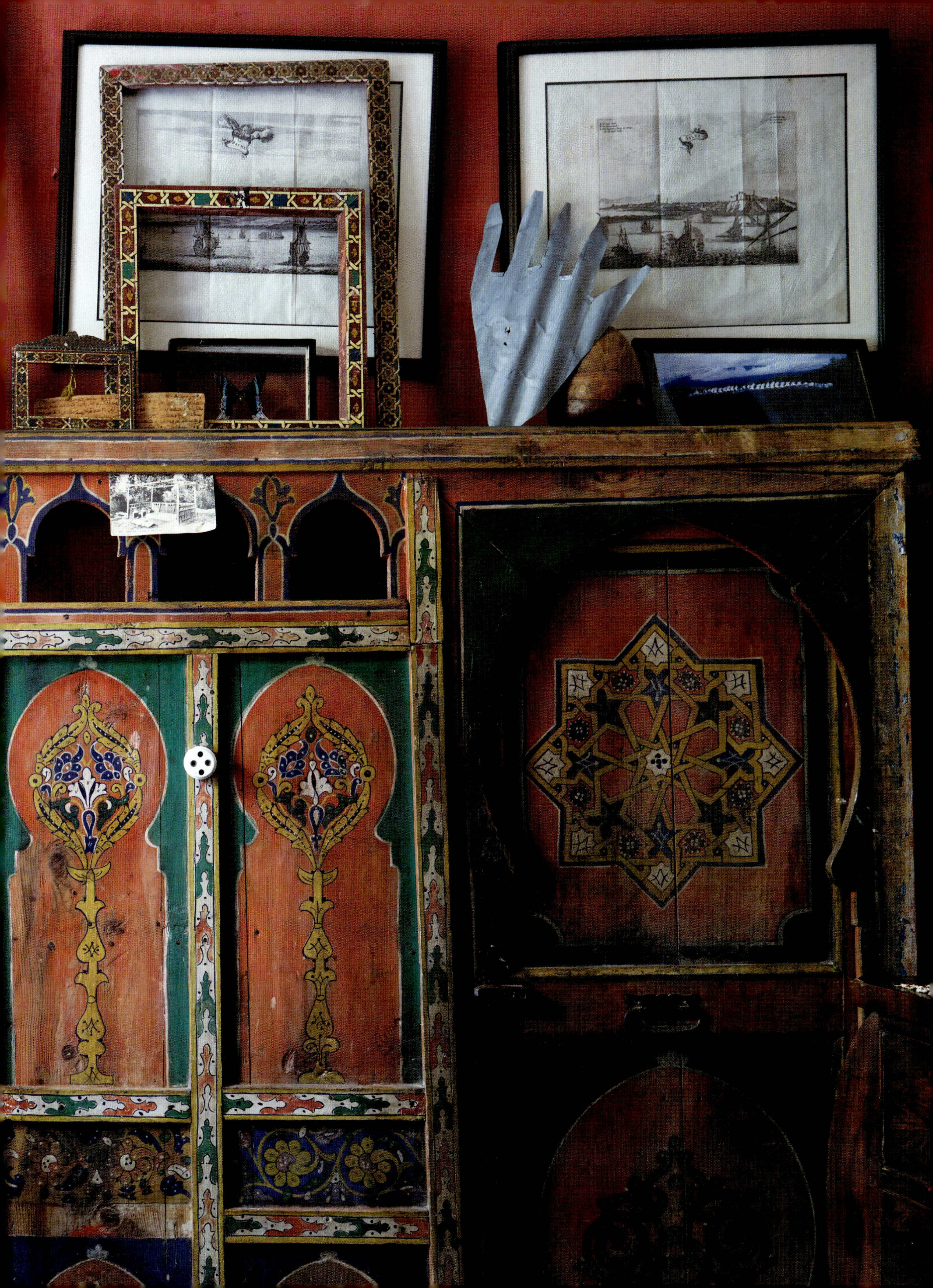

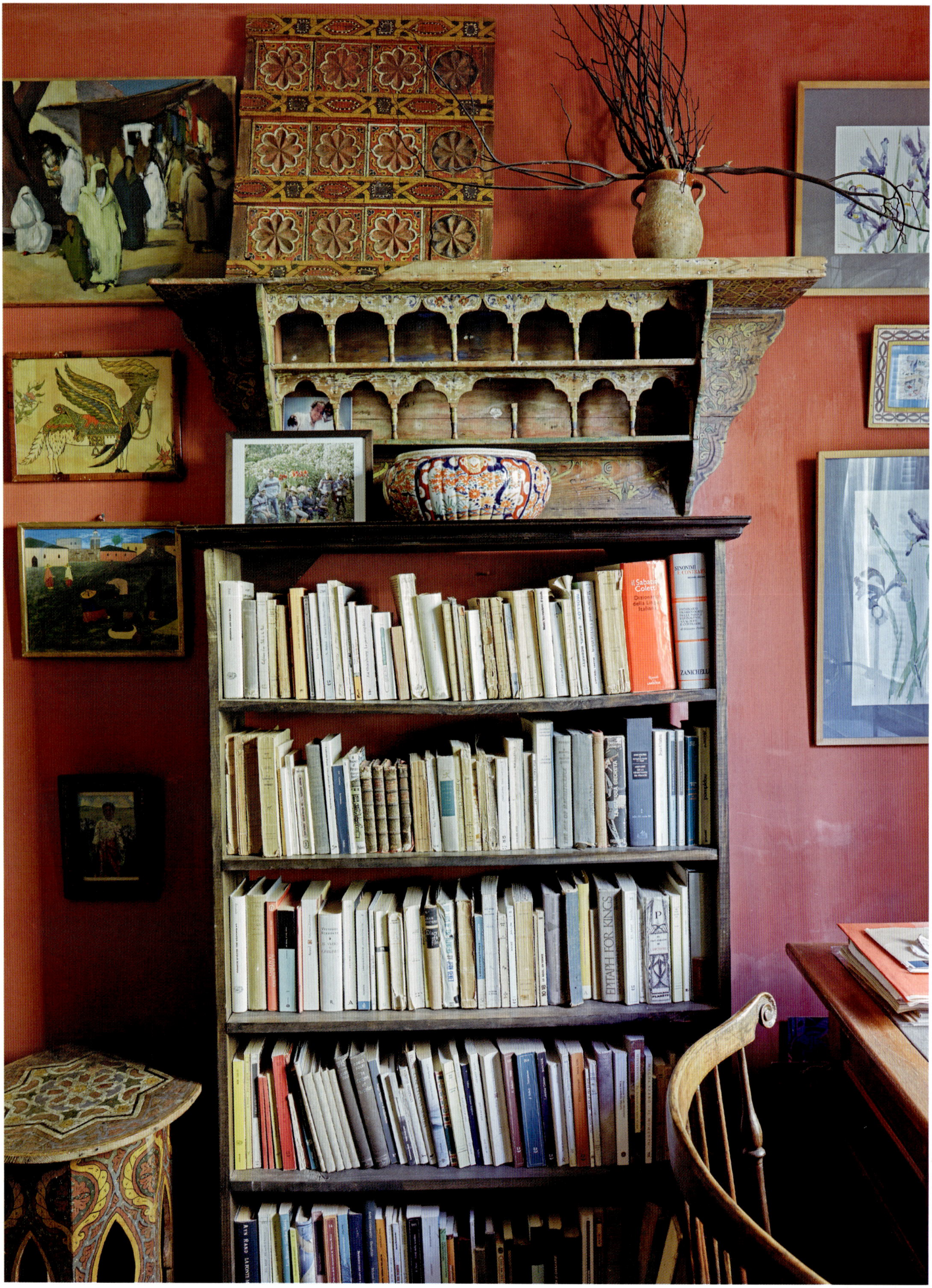
SINONIMI E CONTRARI
ZANICHELLI
EPITAPH FOR KINGS
AYN RAND

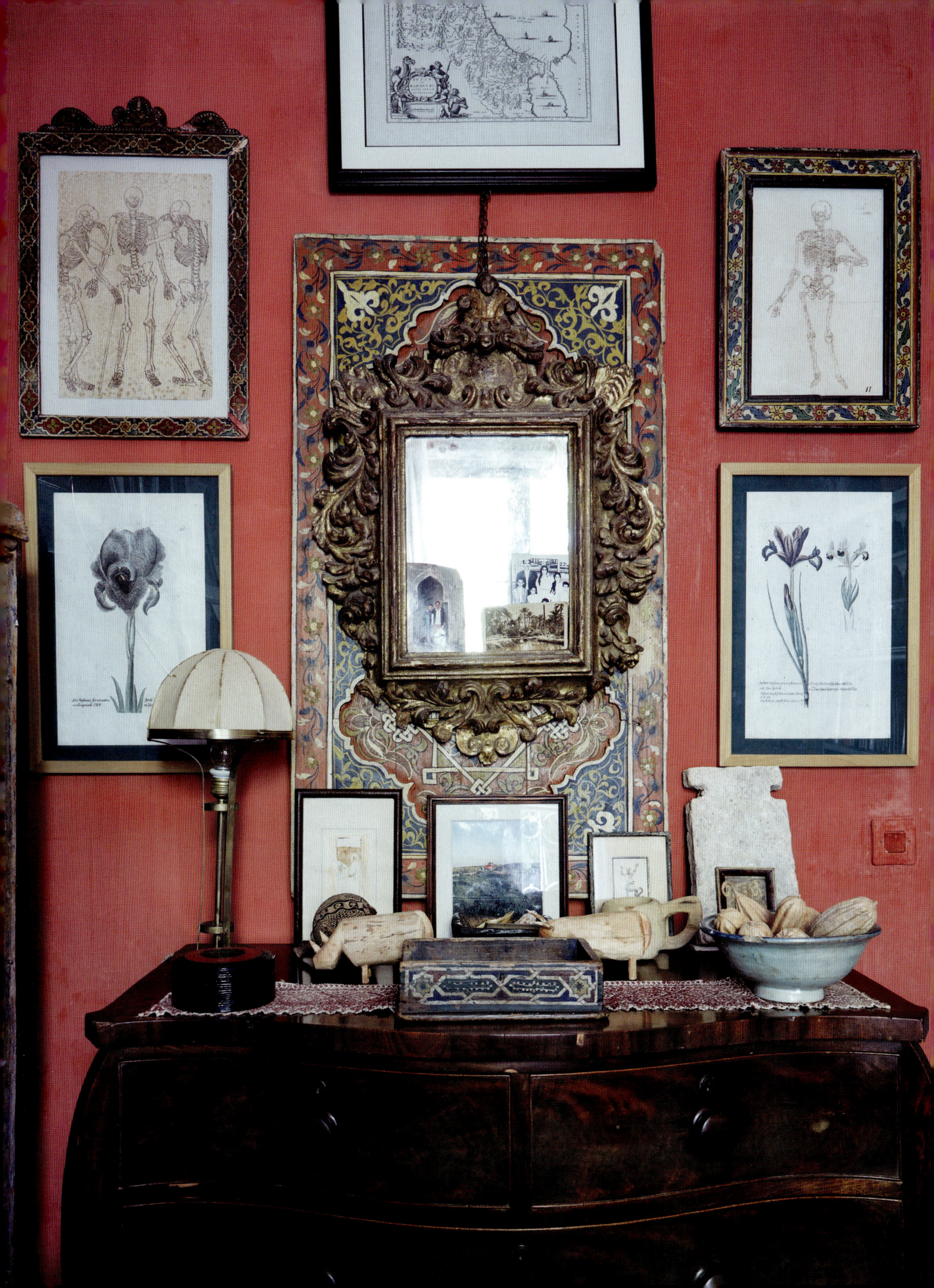

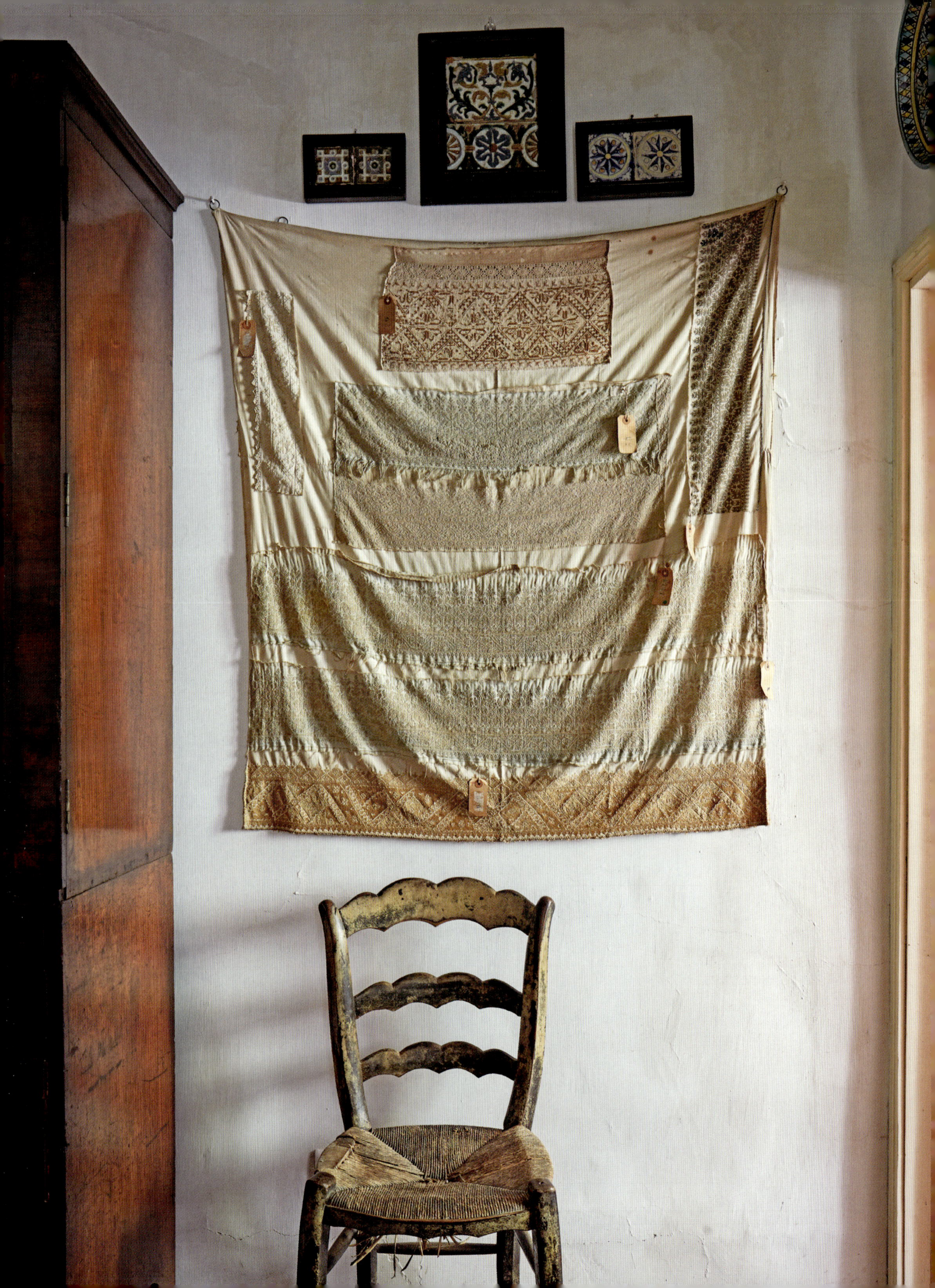

PREVIOUS SPREAD, LEFT: *On a shelf (*marfa*) from Tétouan, a fragment of a ceiling from the same town. Along with chests and occasional tables, marfas were the only furniture in Moroccan homes. Probably inspired by the cornices of wooden ceilings, and similar to both the* muqarnas *shelves of Mamluk residences in Cairo and the* kavukluk, *the Ottoman turban stand that enjoyed great popularity in rococo Venice, these shelves usually served to display Imari ceramics, Bohemian crystal bottles and glasses, opalines, and other imported objects popular in Morocco since the eighteenth-century. Almost all the interiors of stately homes, as well as those of religious buildings, had carved and painted wooden ceilings.*

PREVIOUS SPREAD, RIGHT: *Beside a gilded Spanish mirror, drawings of skeletons and prints of irises:* et in Arcadia ego—*death flourishes in Arcadia too.*

OPPOSITE: *The pieces of Fez embroidery work come from the Bernheimer collection, one of the most important European collections of old textiles, which was dispersed twenty years ago in a wonderful sale. I found the Andalusian chair, one of my all-time favorite pieces of furniture, in a coffee shop in a small town called Ouezzane, and I had to come back many times to convince the owner to sell it to me. I finally managed to coax him to make the deal in exchange for a plasma television set.*

FOLLOWING SPREAD, LEFT: *On our bed, embroidery (*futa*) from Chaouen. Behind, a bedcurtain (*taajira*) from Tétouan. Morocco was never ruled by the Ottomans; the appearance of their unmistakable flowers in embroidery from Tétouan is probably down to the large number of refugees who took shelter there when Algeria, which had been under Ottoman dominion, was conquered by the French in 1830. The painting on the left is by James McBey, the Scottish artist who came to live here in 1932 and married our friend Marguerite.*

FOLLOWING SPREAD, RIGHT: *The white table belonged first to the best butcher in town, then to the best flower shop, both in the Fez market. Like all collectors, I'm very keen on provenance.*

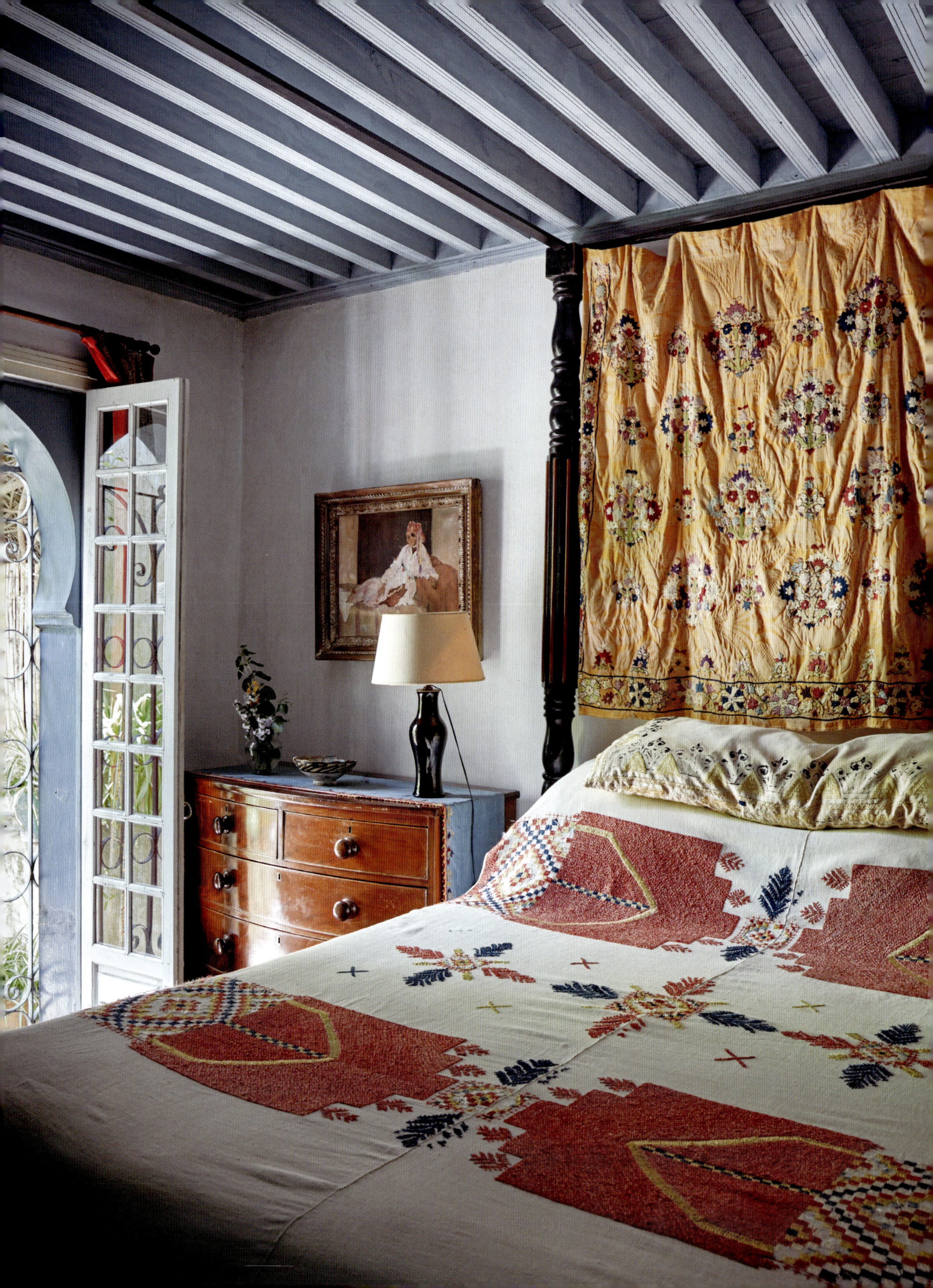

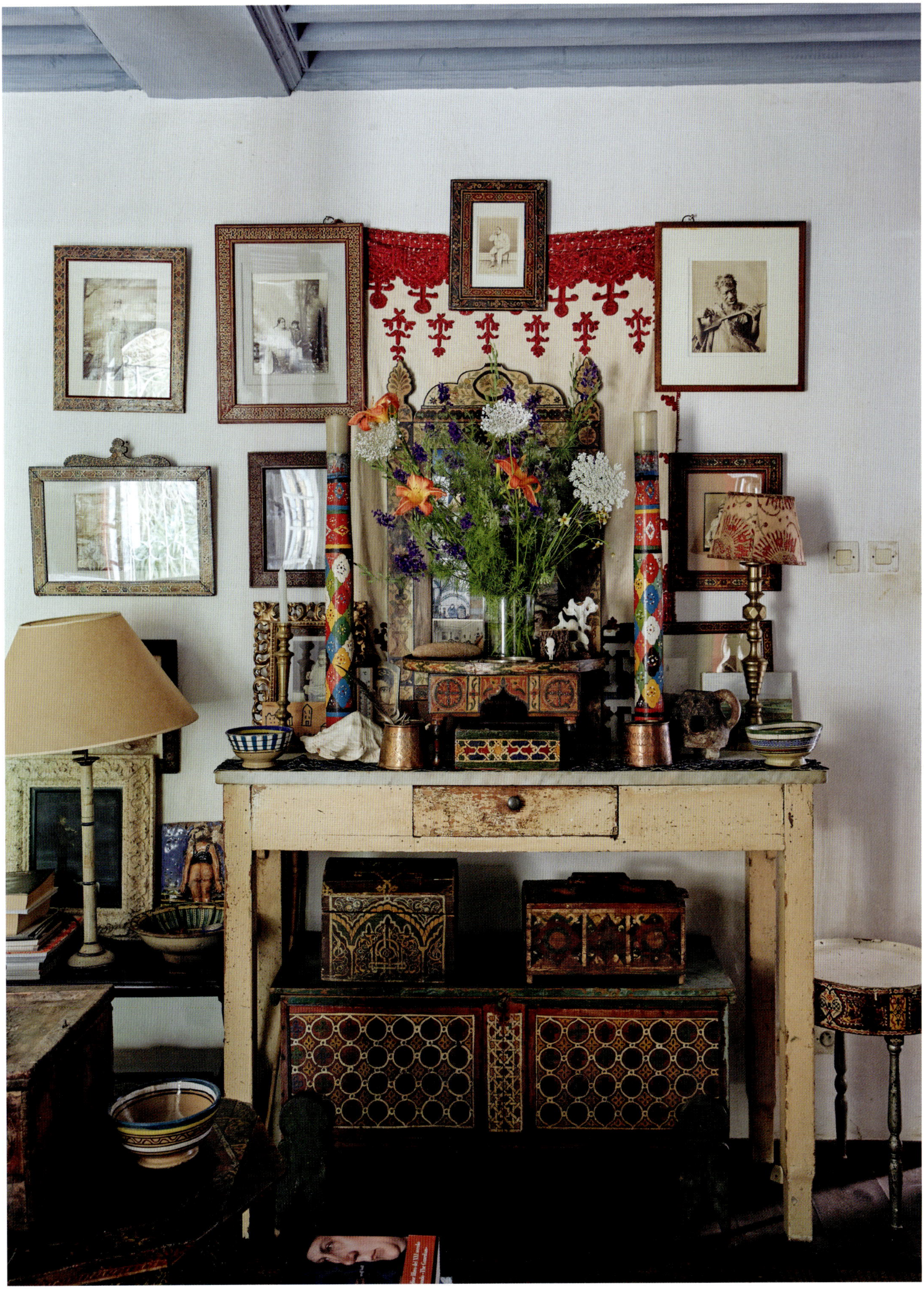

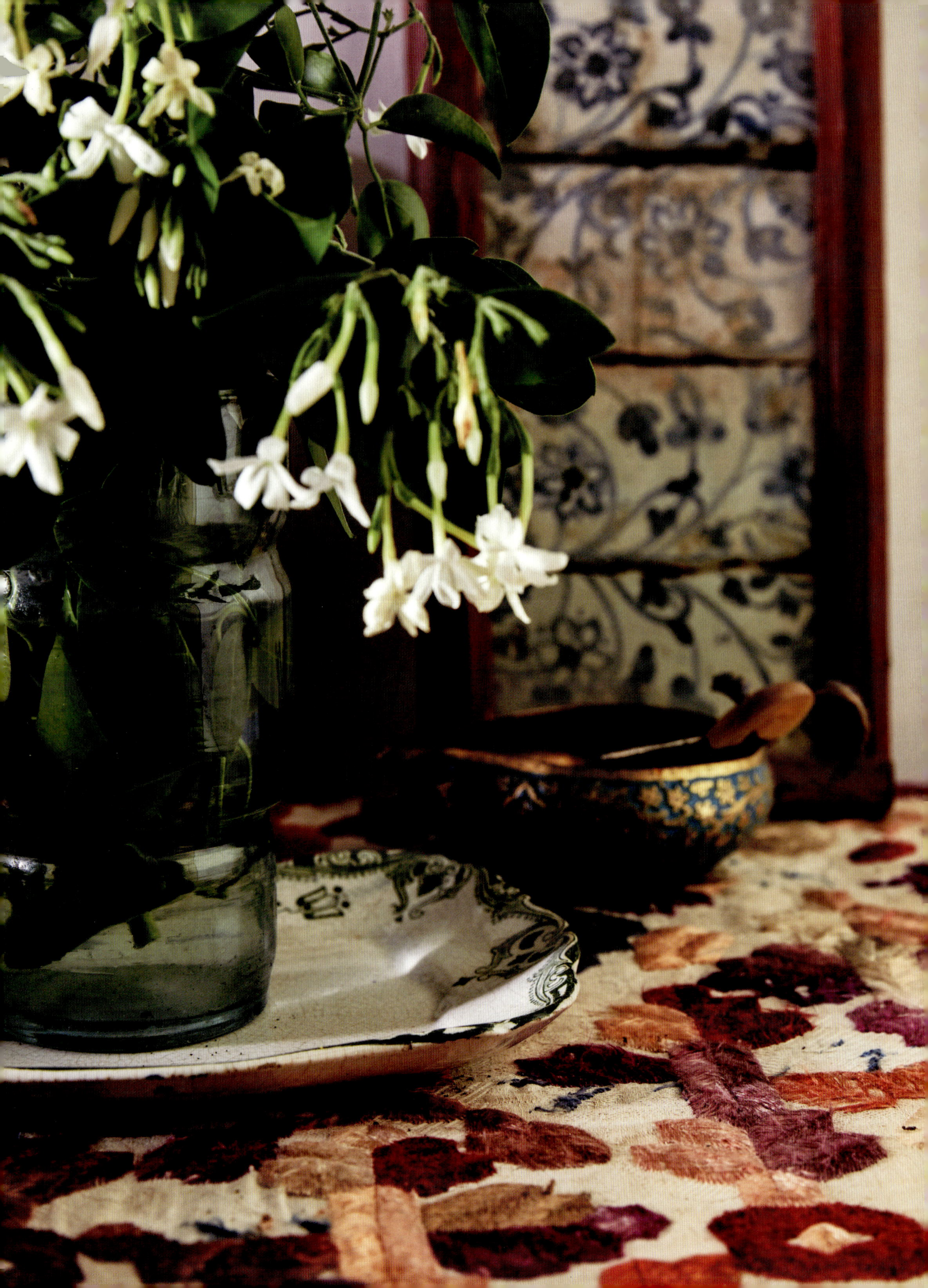

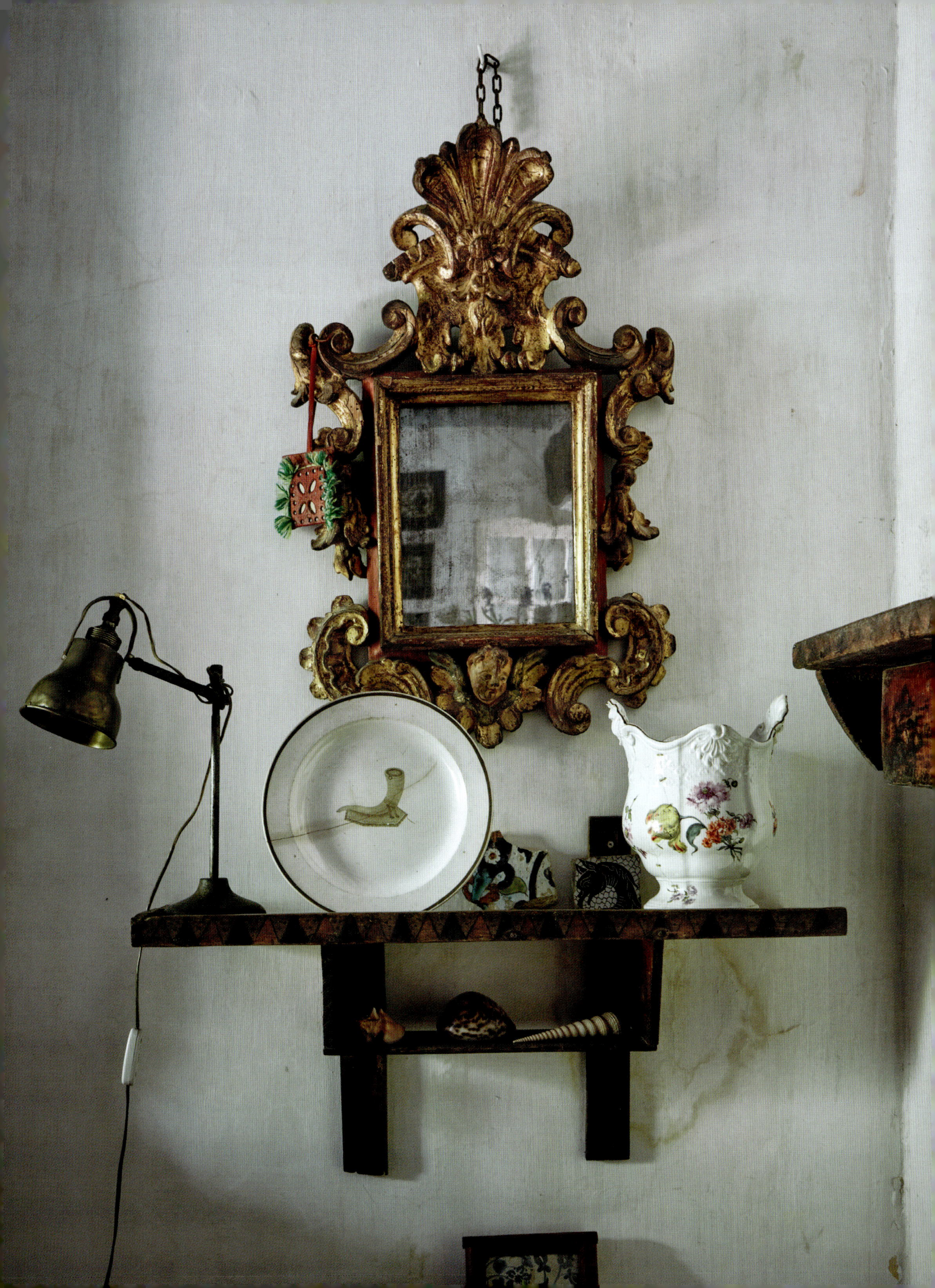

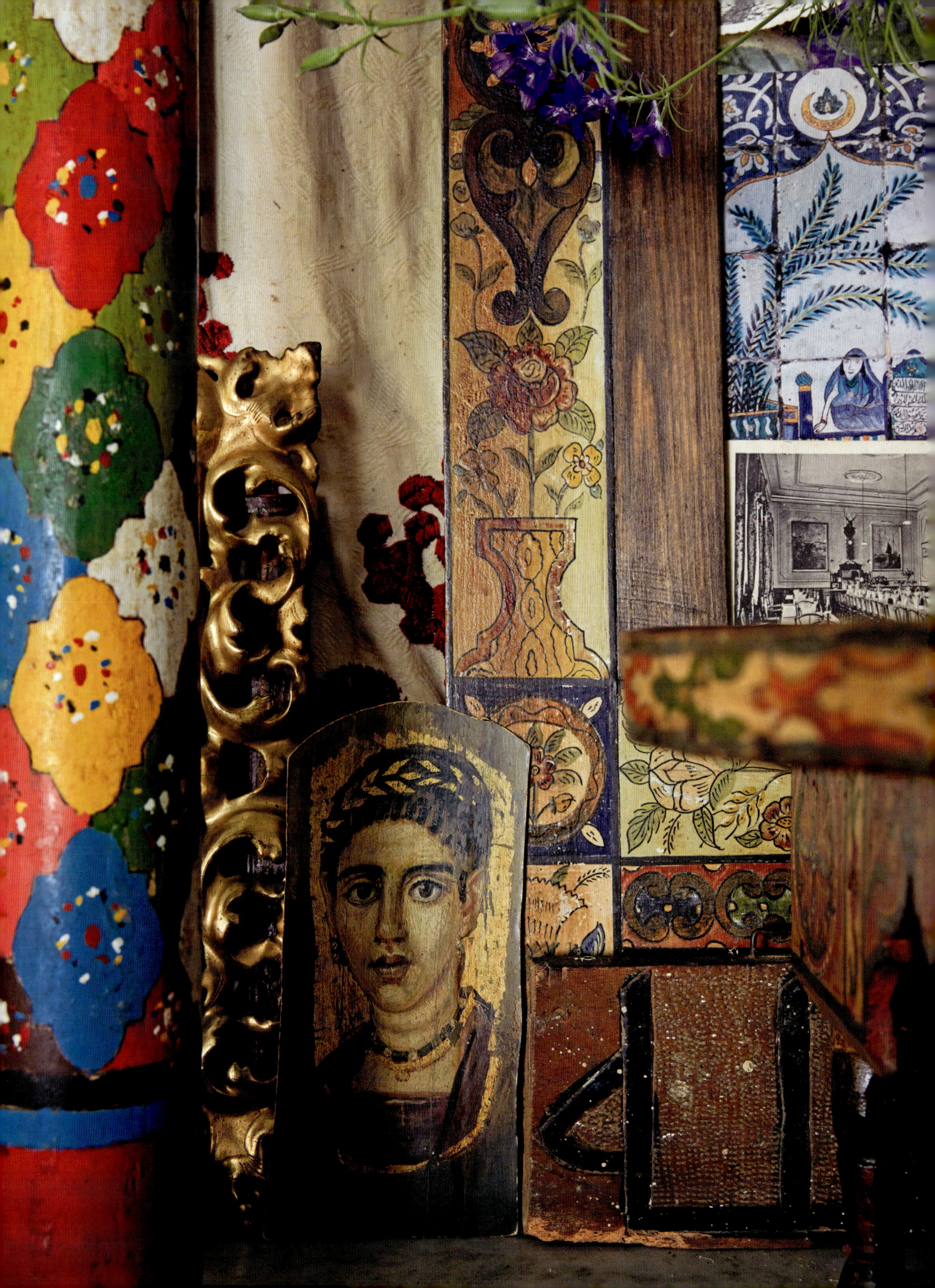

PREVIOUS SPREAD, LEFT: *A nineteenth-century embroidery from Rabat on a table.*
PREVIOUS SPREAD, RIGHT: *On a little* marfa *under a Spanish mirror, a flowery Meissen vase and a Wedgwood dish celebrating an important nineteenth-century archaeological finding.*

The candleholder in the foreground, in painted wood, makes me think of Matisse; I am sure that during his stays in Tangier he saw both this one and its twin, which is not in the photo.
FOLLOWING SPREAD, LEFT: *A ceiling from a Chaouen mosque in the blue corridor. It is sad to think that in the course of deplorable restoration works, elements like this, even if only slightly deteriorated, are removed and thrown away. These stylized flowers painted on hand-planed slats, these frames intertwined with leaves and branches, and these wonderful combinations of colors express the culture and identity of a people, while the new things that replace them are banal and devoid of character.*
FOLLOWING SPREAD, RIGHT: *More* marfas *from Chaouen.*

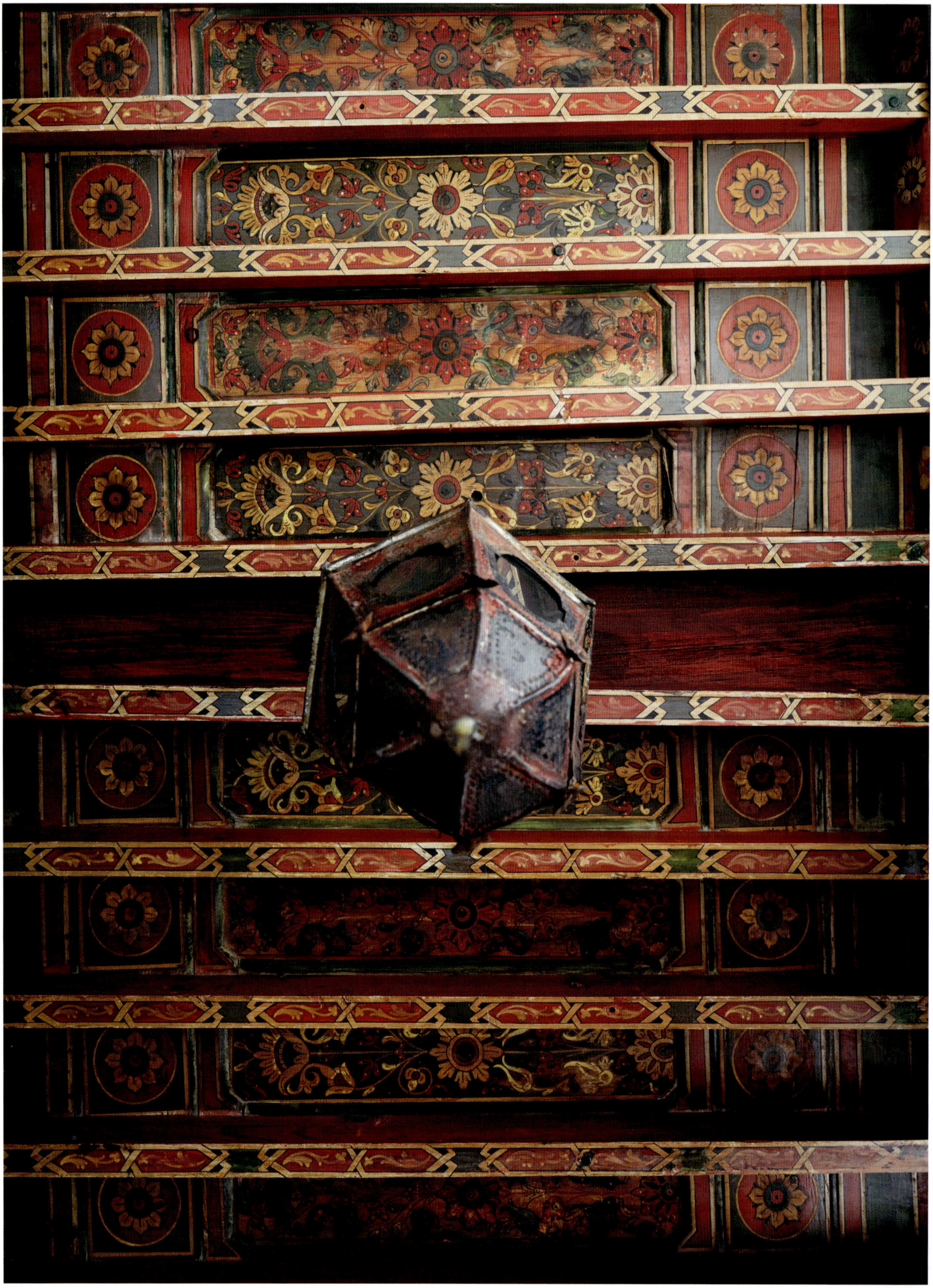

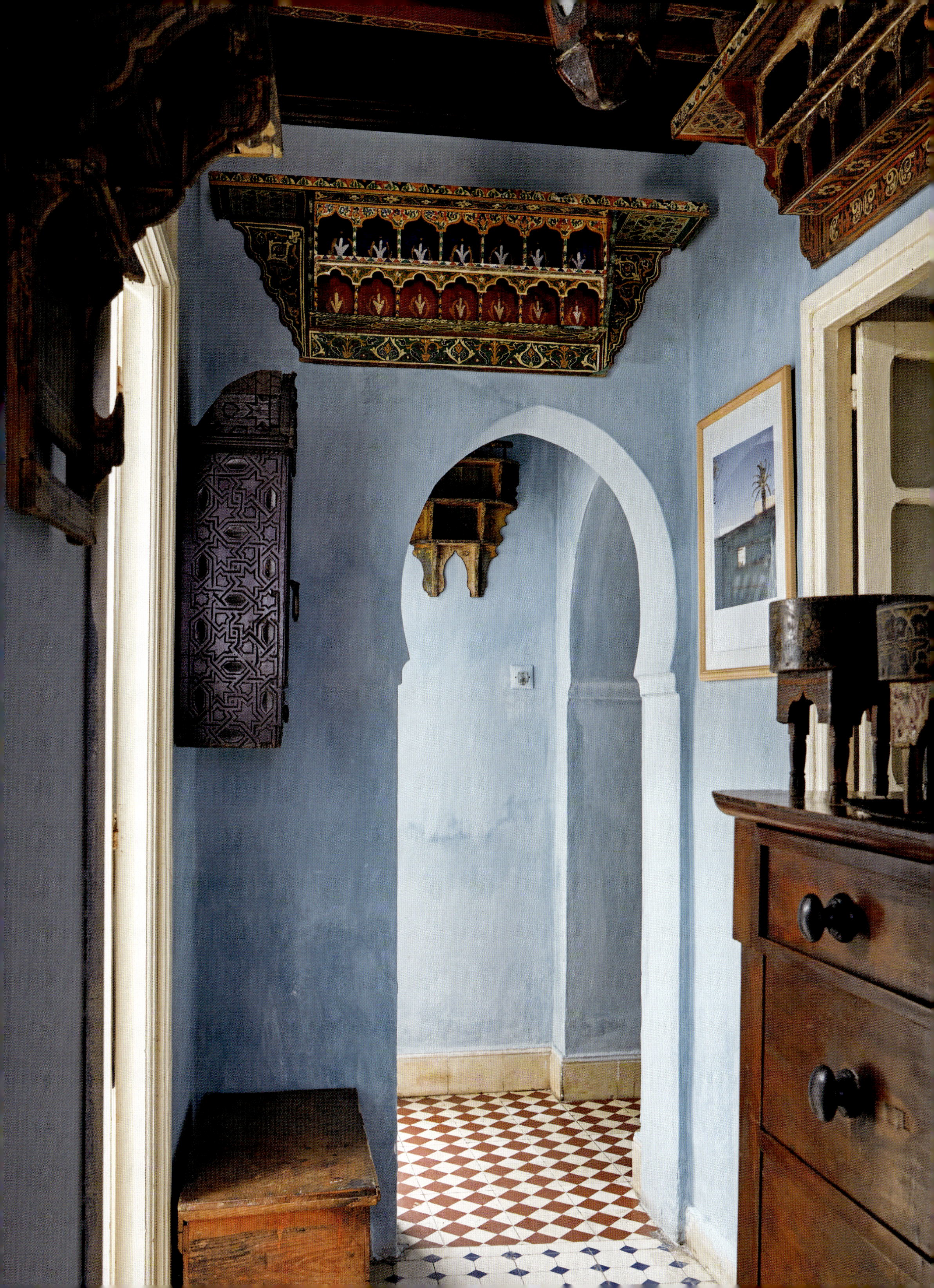

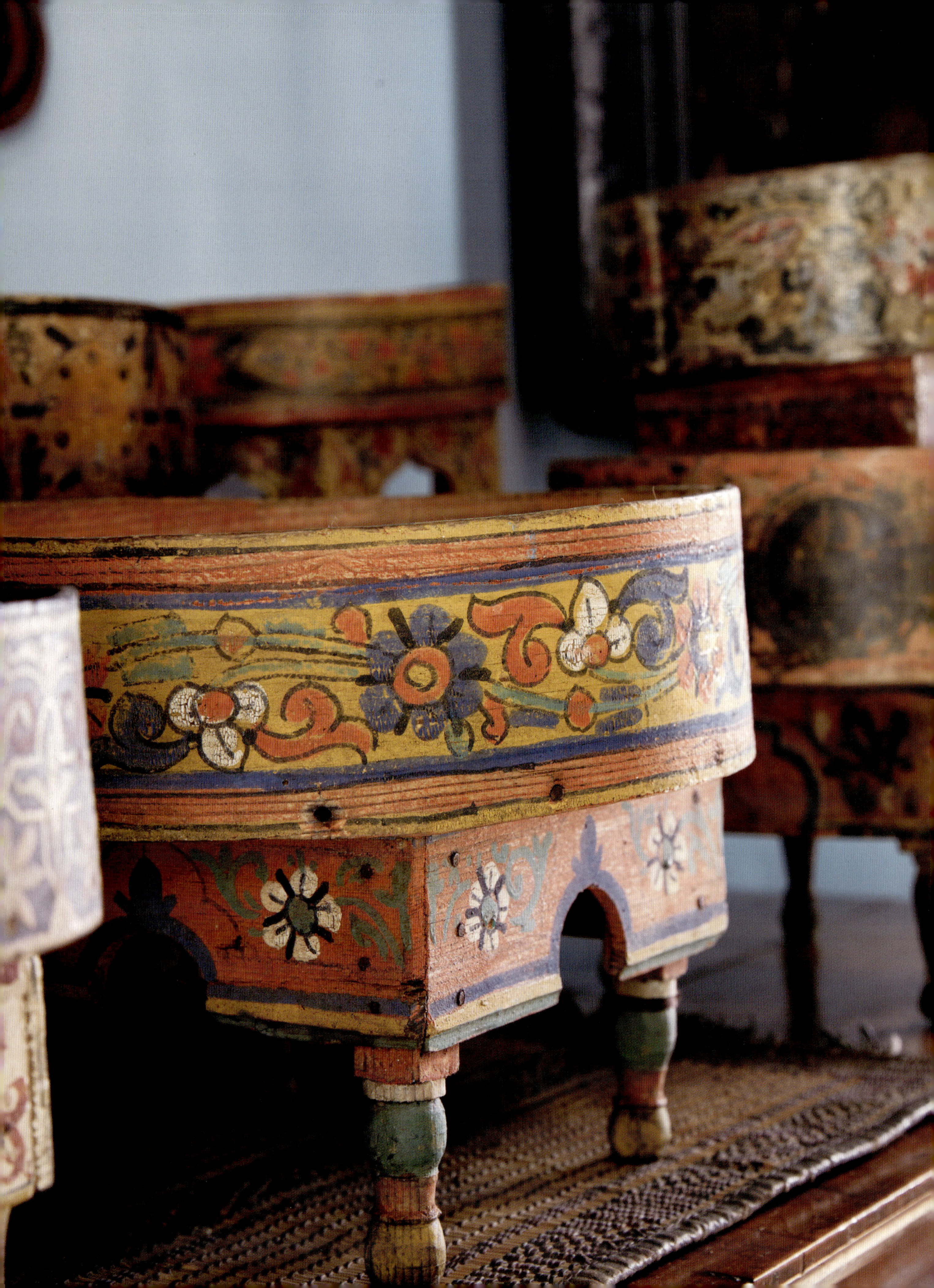

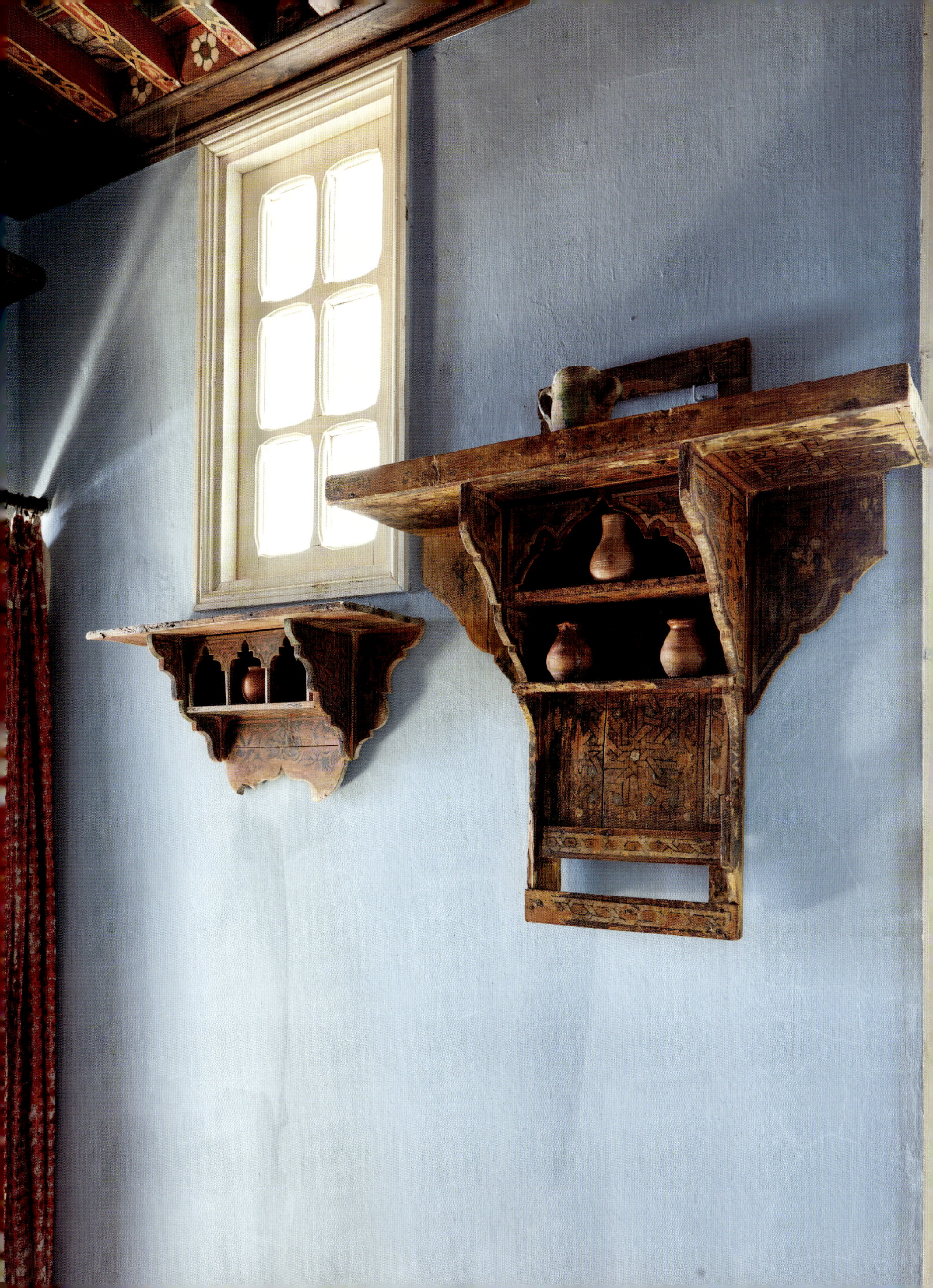

PREVIOUS SPREAD AND OPPOSITE: *It took me more than thirty years to put together this family of little* maydas *from Tétouan, Chaouen, and the Jbala mountains. When a neighbor died, custom forbade his family to use the kitchen, so the neighbors would send food over in one of those wooden containers. Made of thin bark that is much coveted by woodworm, their covers didn't survive, unfortunately. The gun holder is from Tétouan.*

FOLLOWING SPREAD, LEFT: *A sweet little* marfa *made in reclaimed wood by an anonymous Jbala master.*

FOLLOWING SPREAD, RIGHT: *A Gujarat silk embroidery hides the door.*

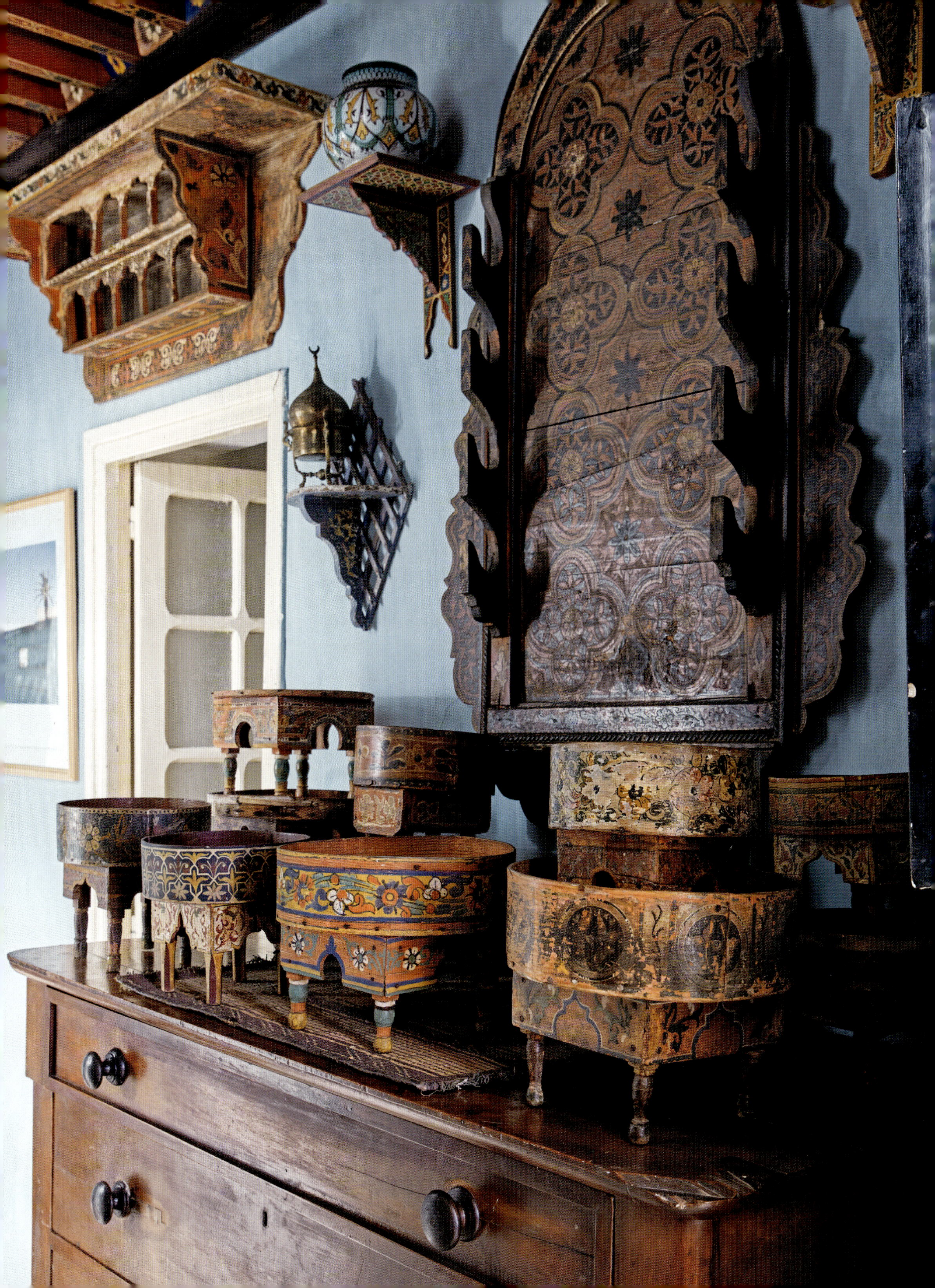

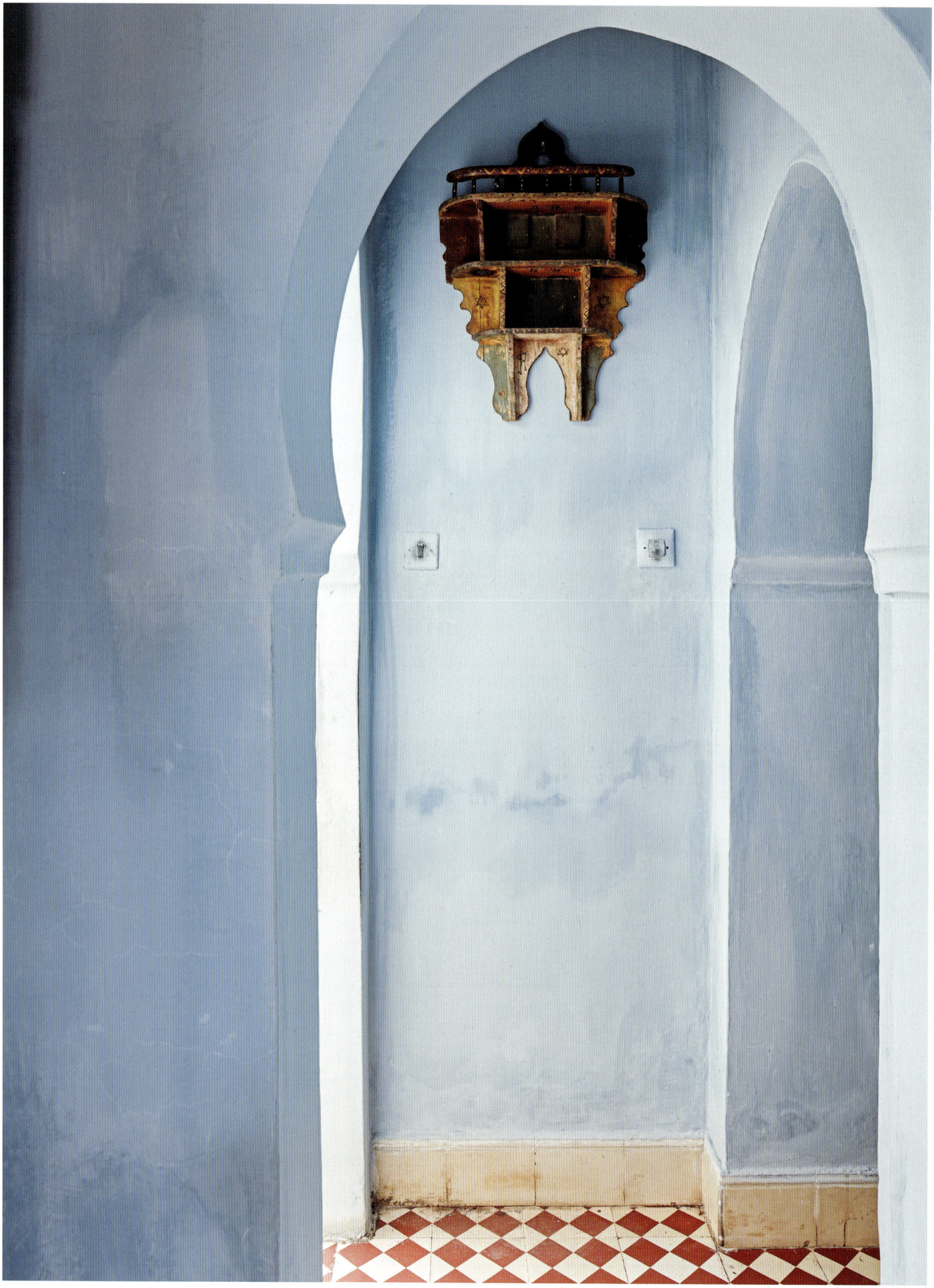

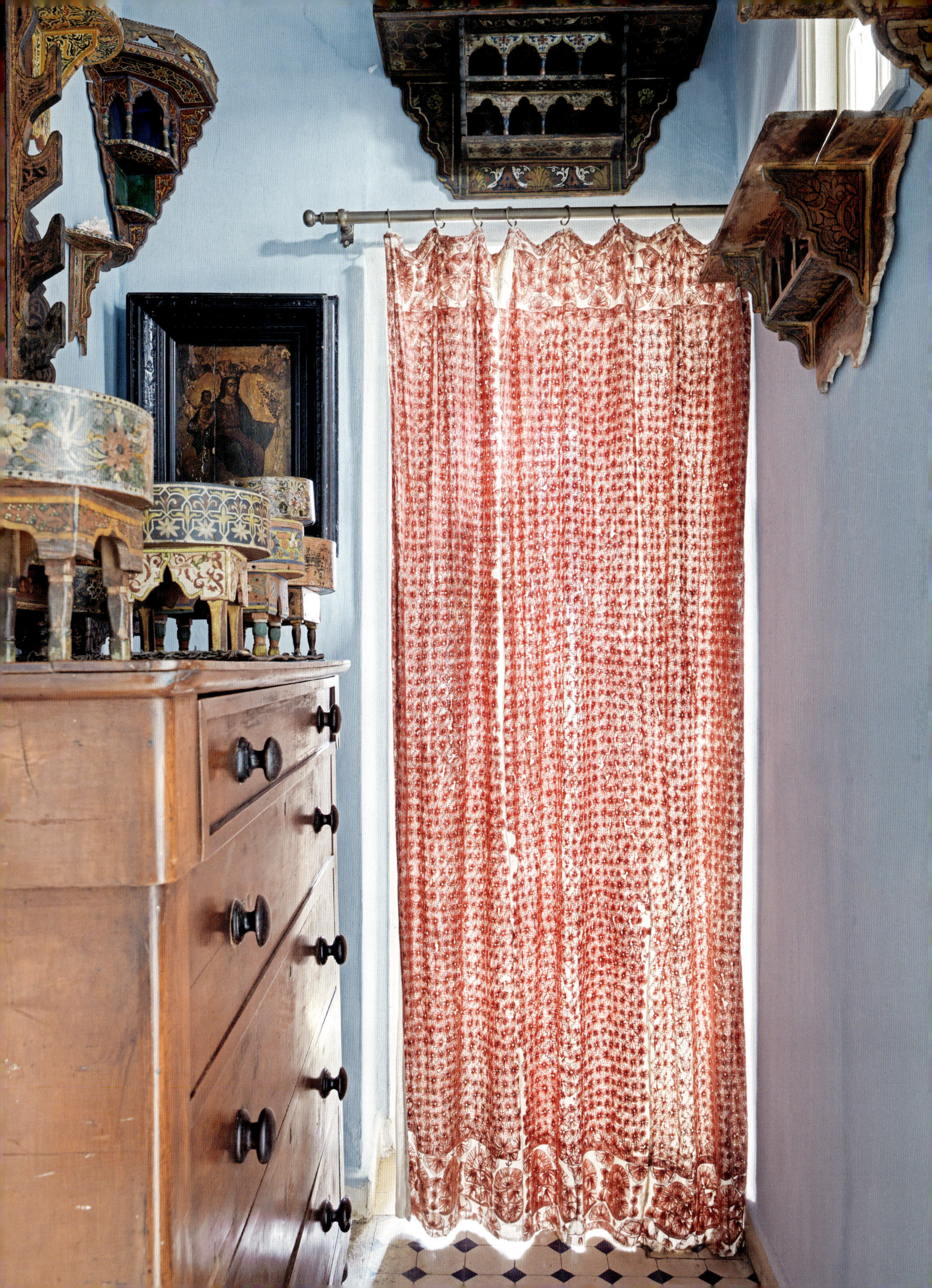

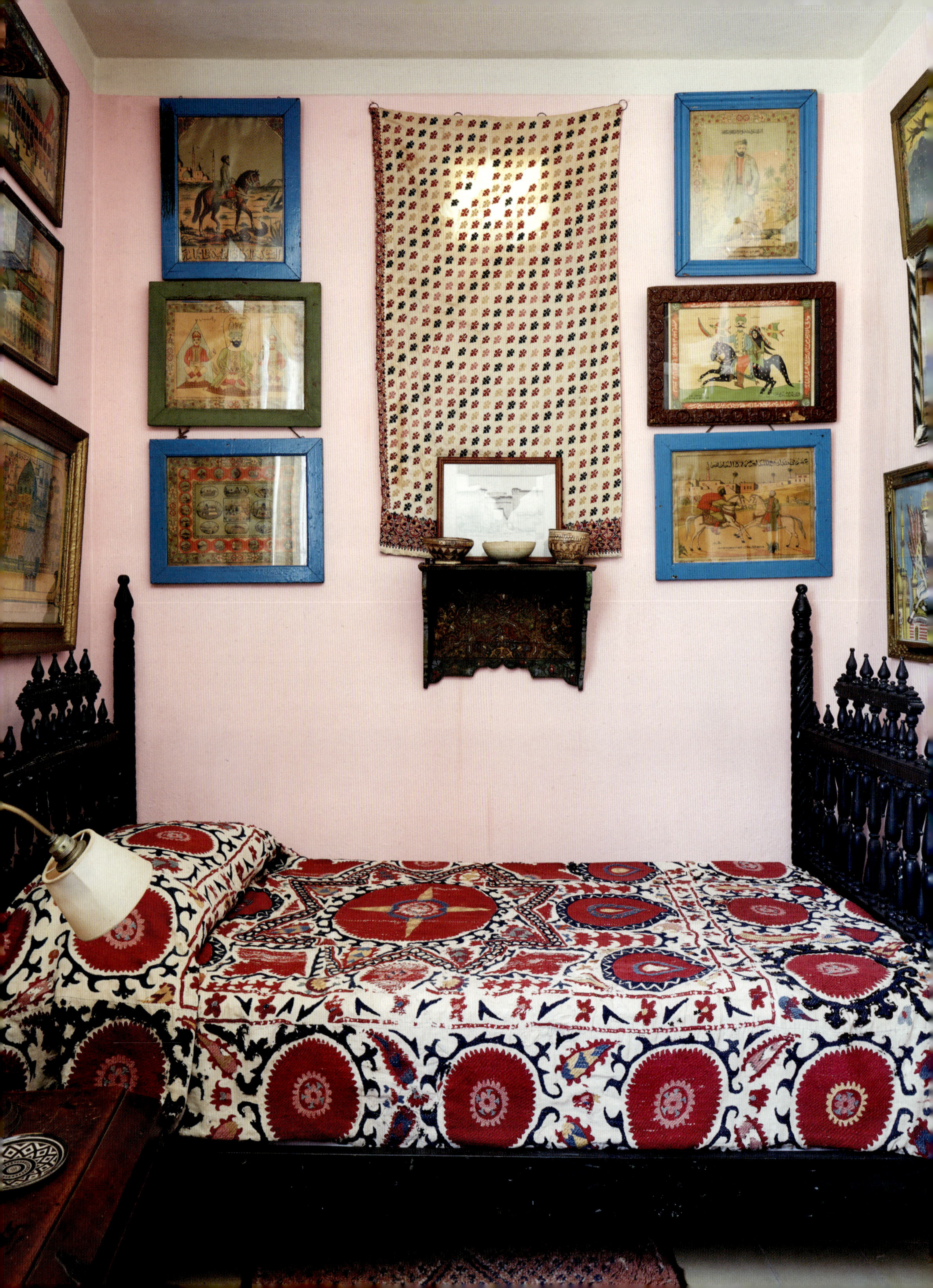

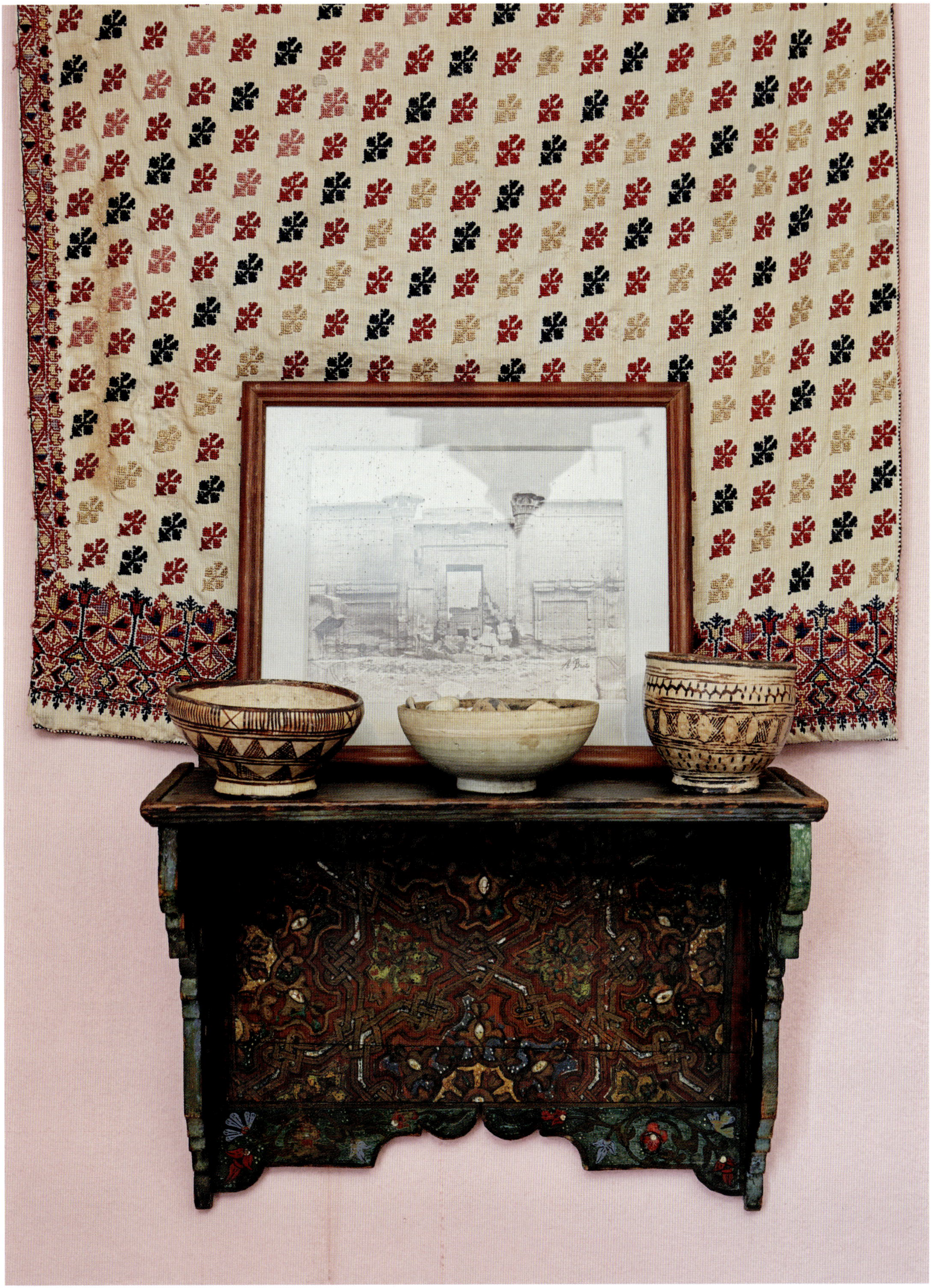

PREVIOUS SPREAD, LEFT: *Color prints featuring religious subjects were made in the early twentieth century in Cairo, Tunis, and Algiers, and until fifty years ago were hung in most Moroccan homes.*

Extraneous to the figurative culture of Orthodox Islam, these human characters, saints, dervishes, anchorites, and this bestiary of winged and proud horses testify to the presence in the Maghrebi cult of more ancient elements, derived from the pagan or Christian world. Until a few years ago, in the Moroccan countryside, religious sects such as the Hamadcha, the Aissaoua, the Heddaoua, the Tijani, and the Jilali venerated saints and lions, eels and cats, demons and caves, with rites that suggest both the world of the Phoenicians and that of the ancient Egyptians as well as that evoked by the Neolithic engravings and cave paintings of the Sahara.

On the nineteenth-century Portuguese bed, an old Suzani embroidery from Bokhara.

PREVIOUS SPREAD, RIGHT: *The embroidery is from Meknes, which Stephan found in Saint Tropez. The small pots come from the Rif.*

OPPOSITE: *The big* marfa *in the kitchen, painted in the seventies, bears witness to a local tradition that was alive until recently.*

FOLLOWING SPREAD: *On the dining room terrace, we eat amid ferns and aspidistras in summer.*

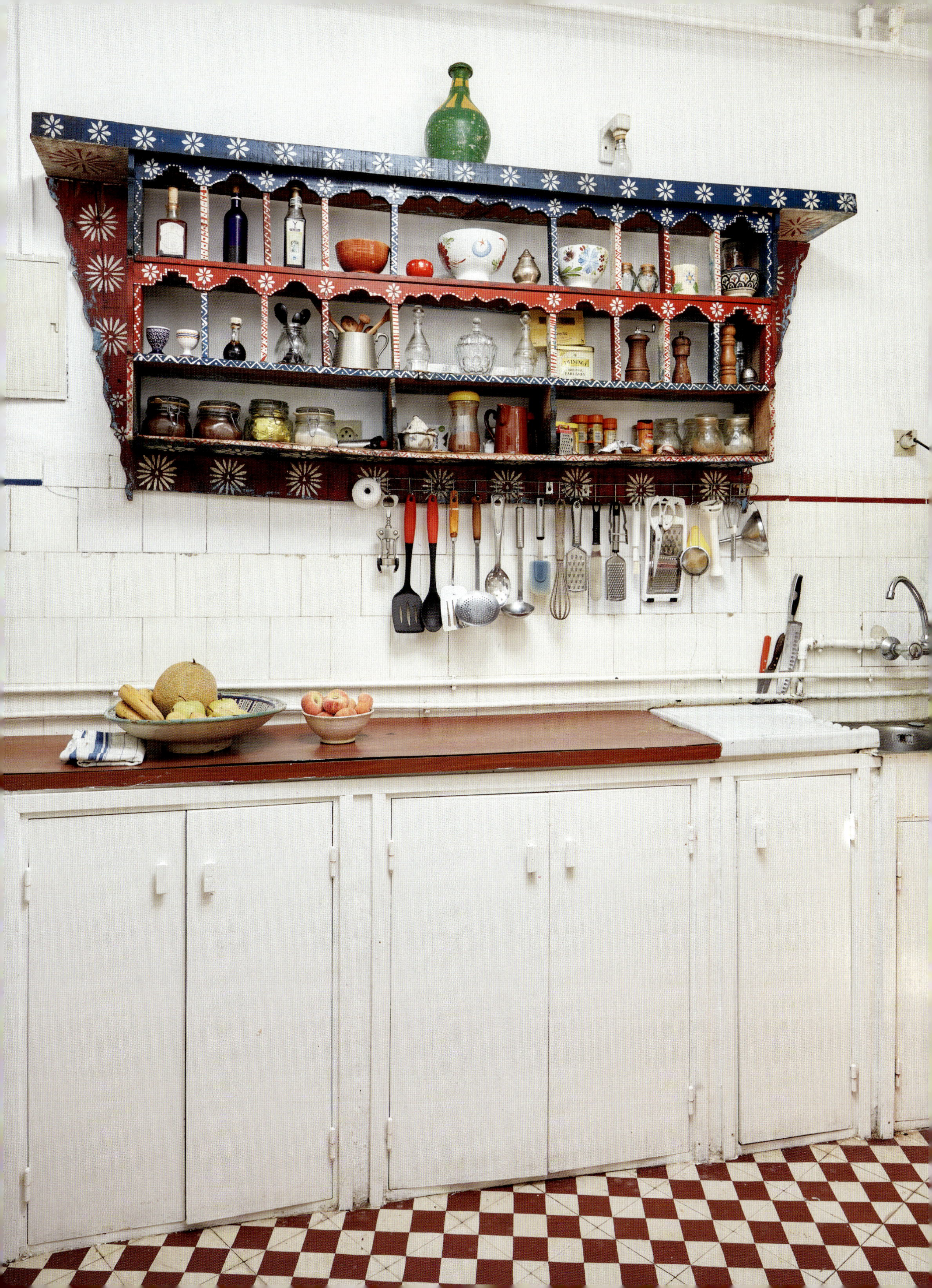

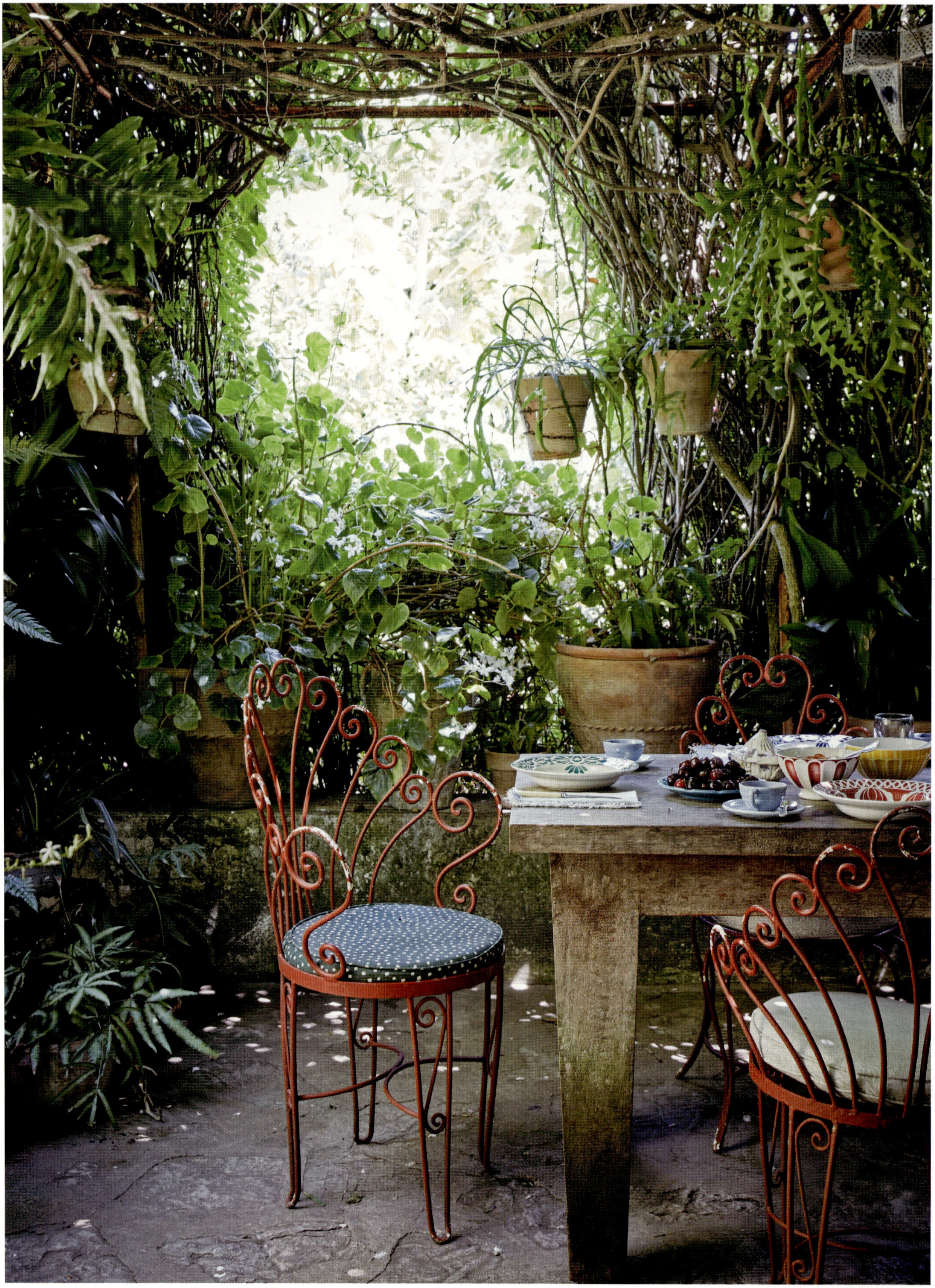

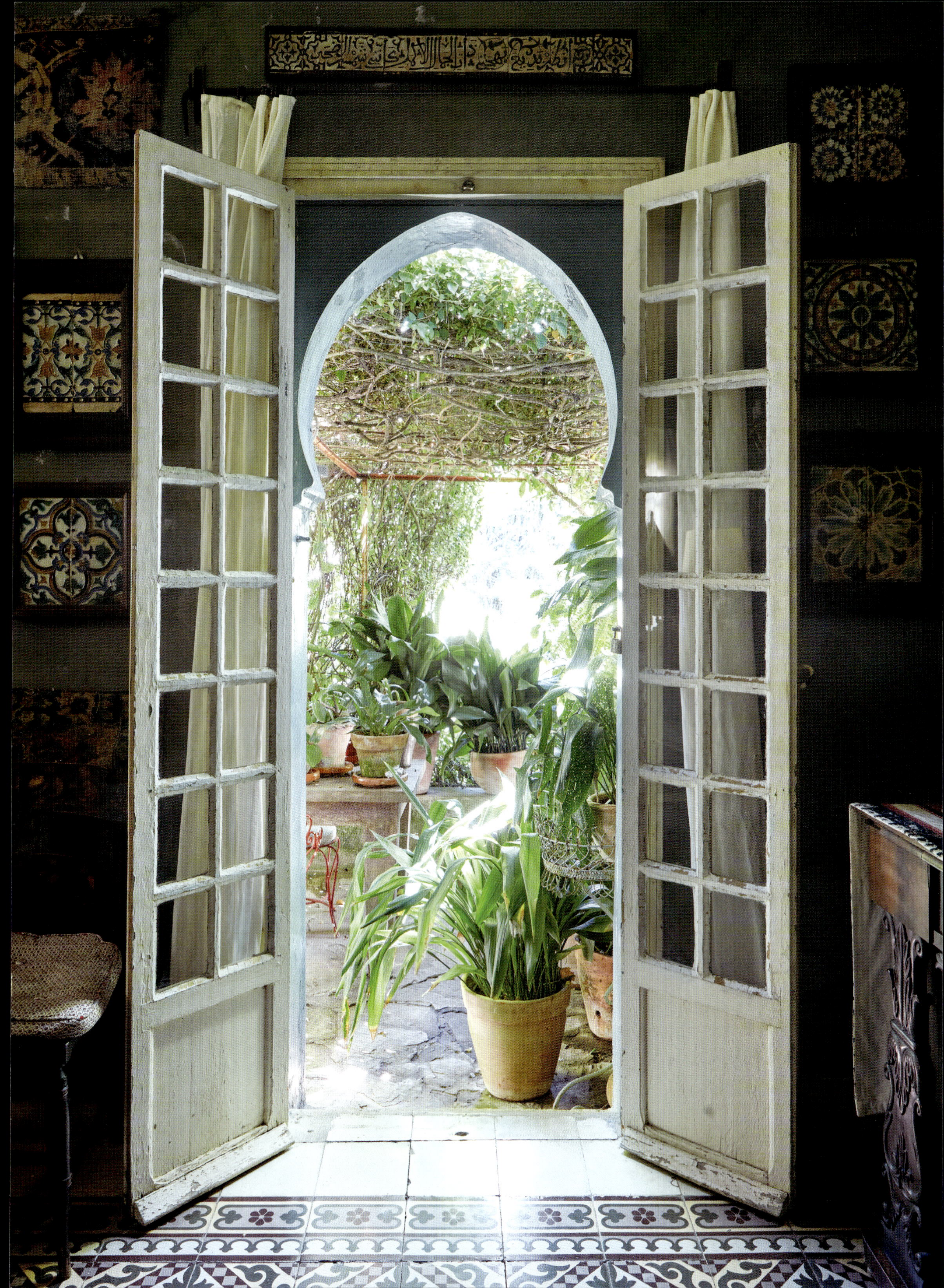

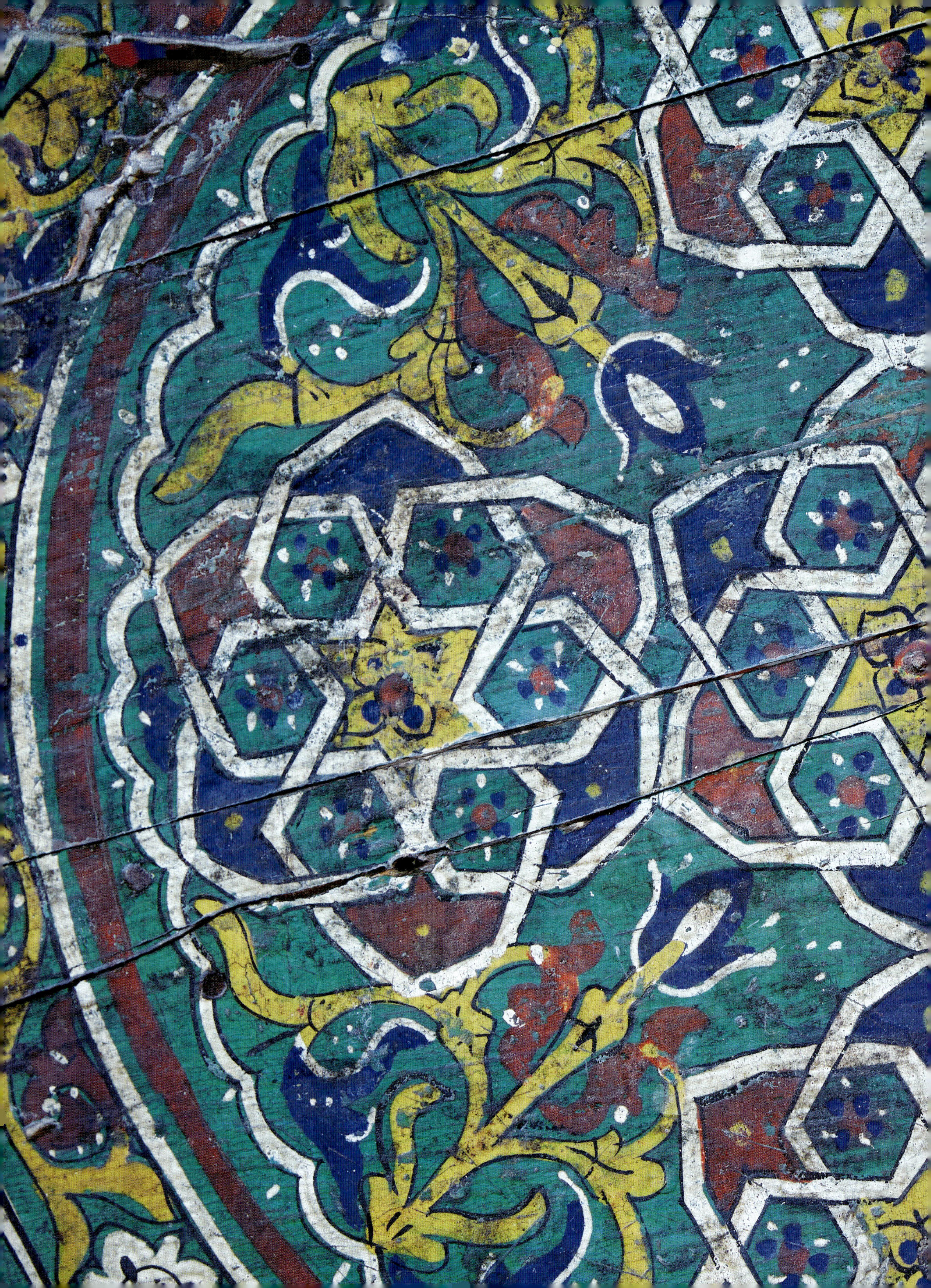

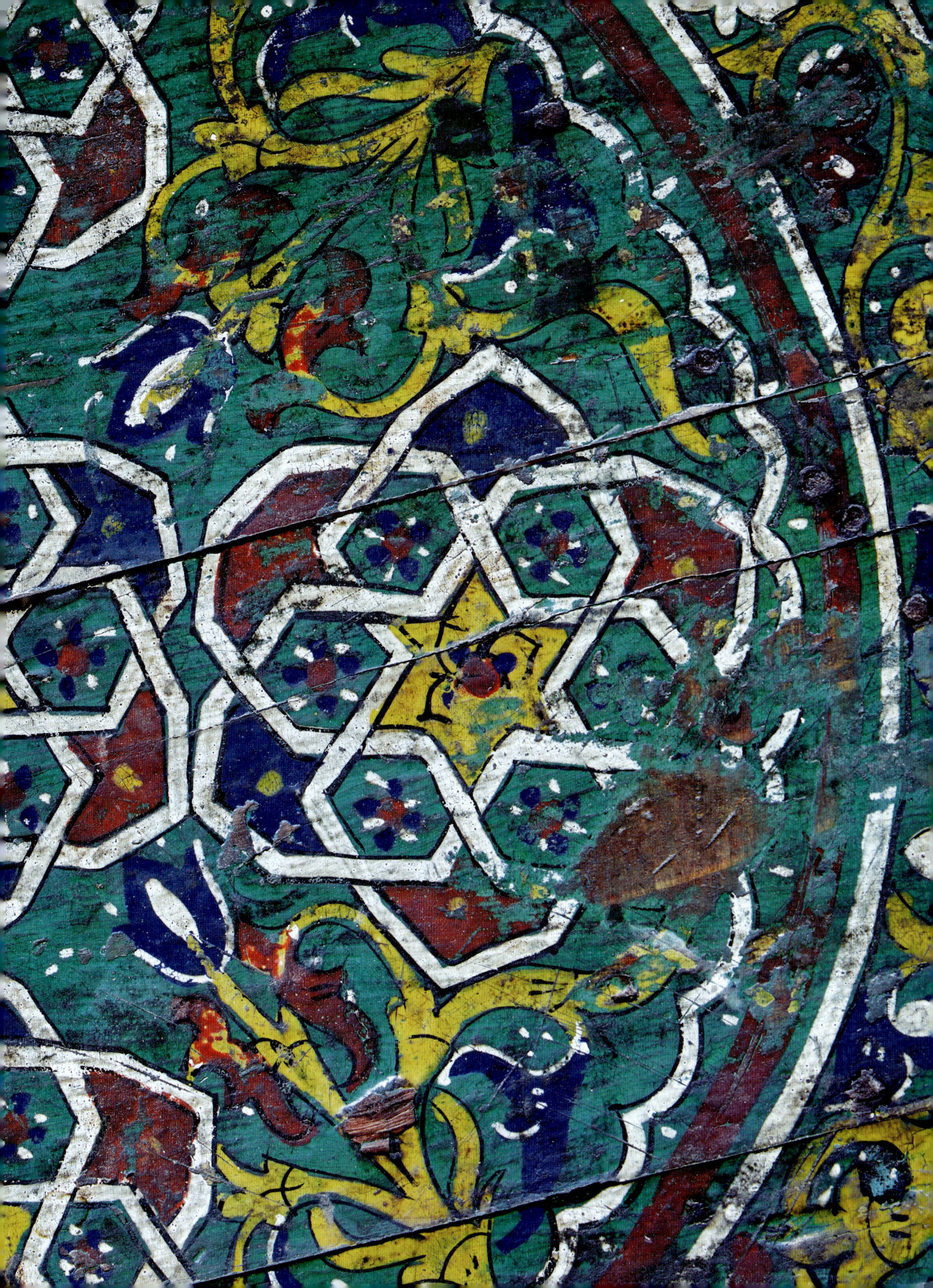

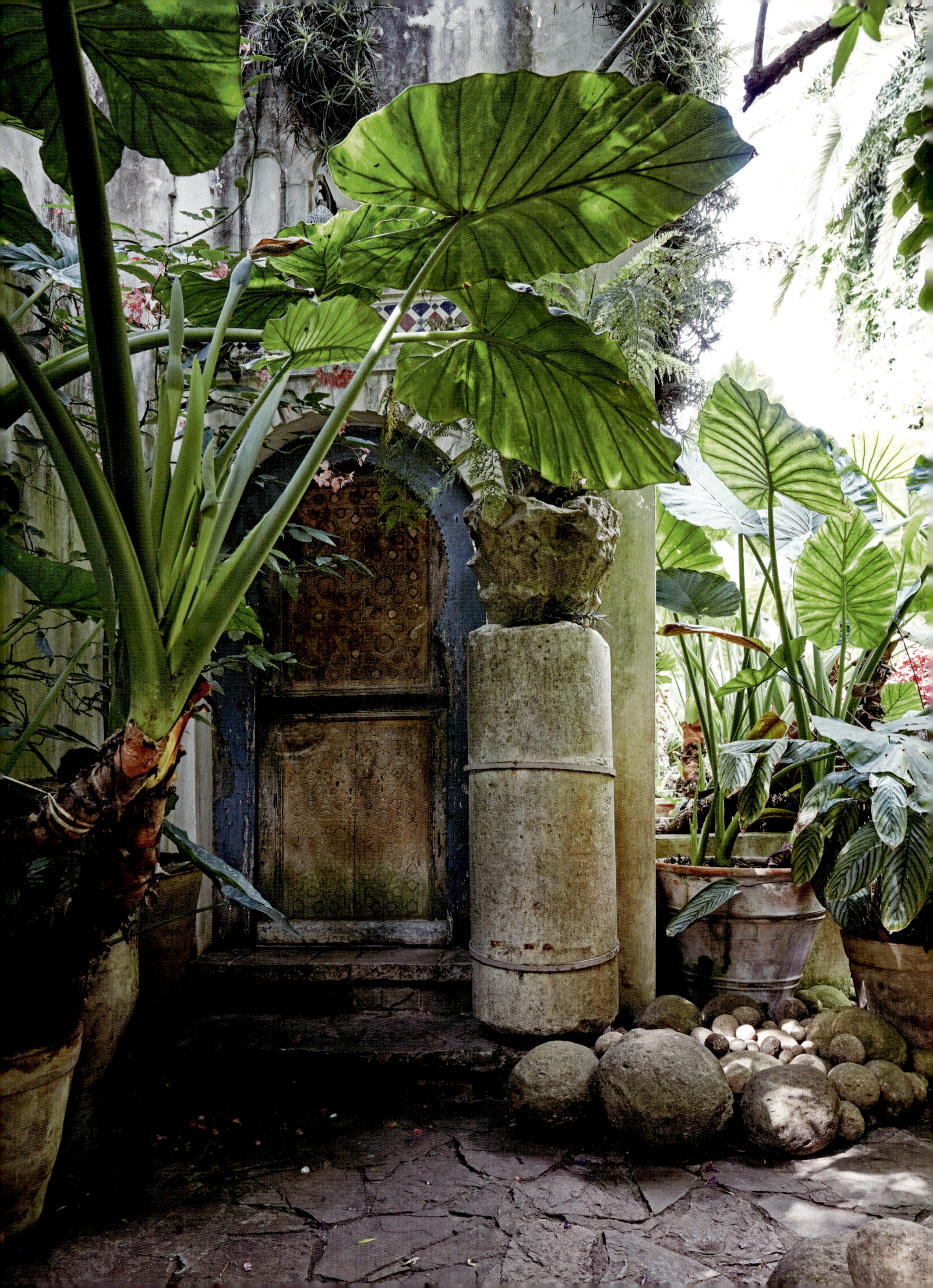

THE CENTRAL PAVILION

Standing near the main entrance of Tebarek Allah, this pavilion was built in the late 1960s for Sanche de Gramont and his wife Nancy's two children: a tiny entrance, kitchen, breakfast room, study, and two bedrooms separated by a bathroom with a kerosene stove. Before coming to Tangier, the couple, who lived in the United States, had been living in Rome. From a few watercolors by Eugene Berman (a melancholic neo-Romantic painter who had turned his hand to scenography), from some fine Iranian terracottas dating to the beginning of the first millennium that could have come from the "Obelisco" gallery of Gasparo Del Corso and Irene Brin, from many issues of the literary journal Botteghe Oscure and books of Italian poetry, anthropology, sociology, and psychoanalysis, all found in these rooms, I guessed at the circles they moved in, she an American and he about to become one, in that Hollywood on the Tiber of Cy Twombly and the old princess Caetani. Like Alberto Sordi in a famous movie, albeit for different reasons, Sanche wanted to be an American with all his heart, he who had studied at Yale. Perhaps also on account of the trauma of the Algerian war, where he had served as a noncommissioned officer in a regiment of Senegalese infantry and had seen the horrors his French compatriots had been capable of. Shortly after leaving Morocco he abandoned his glorious name and took its anagram: Ted Morgan, a "Mister Nobody" who inevitably makes you think of Ulysses—and nails you to the fact that sometimes the only way to free yourself of the cyclopes of disgust is to blind them without further ado. The grandson of the haughty Élisabeth de Gramont, one of the models for Proust's duchess of Guermantes, he was to have himself filmed by CBS with wife and children in a fast-food restaurant, just like any other happy family into the American way of life—he had made it!

It was immediately clear to me that among the successive owners of Tebarek Allah there had been no bibliophiles or tidy people: stacked on the shelves of the library of this pavilion there were papers of every kind, but among the invoices, typescripts eaten away by mold, packages, bundles of letters and pamphlets devoured by silverfish, I found first editions (some miraculously well preserved) of many works by the Beat Generation poets, with bookmarks in the form of mimeographed leaflets hailing peace in Vietnam printed by anarchist collectives.

But why on earth had the young couple come to live here, in North Africa, amid a climate, a people, and a light that must have inevitably reminded Sanche of the hell of Algeria? And why did they leave like that, out of the blue, with the children, leaving behind so many valuable things and so many memories, without even asking the next owner to ship them all to them? Nancy was a poet; in the only photo I found she is a beautiful girl who looks a bit like Ali MacGraw in *Love Story*: is she the key to the mystery? I had exposed all the sheets and notebooks to the sunlight. They were nearly all faded and almost indecipherable, crumbling in my hands, or had stuck together to form bricks that bent and cracked. A folder had emerged containing yellowing articles from English, French, and American daily newspapers. They all dealt with the hijacking of a plane in July 1972. Some Black Panthers had seized a DC-8 jetliner between Detroit and Miami and ordered the pilots to take it to Algiers. Anyone rummaging through the remains of an old archive and coming across what they take for a clue will know what it means to suddenly feel like Miss Marple. Eagerly, I read every detail, from the cheese sandwiches requested by the five hijackers on their first landing in Boston—one was even dressed as a priest—to the gun hidden in a hollowed-out Bible, to the three children who were with them (three, that couldn't have been happenstance), and I learned that following the final landing the Algerian government had set them free, merely sending the plane, crew, and passengers back home. What was the truth behind all this? I felt I could see Nancy, her face disguised by big sunglasses and wearing her long floral skirt, sneaking into the corner *baqqal* with her Afghan purse full of coins—the home phone was certainly under surveillance—to get news of a certain friend from another friend who had studied with both of them in California. The attempted assassination of Hassan II occurred on July 10, 1971, in Skhirat (it was the king's birthday, therefore a national holiday): from that day on the Moroccan secret services began monitoring all foreigners, especially intellectuals and progressives like the Gramonts, with an effectiveness that was the result of their training with Hoover's FBI. What if the Californian friend wasn't just a friend but an accomplice? A fellow cell member? Or perhaps, believing she was making a donation to a movement against racial hatred, Nancy had unwittingly found herself financing a terrorist group. Given his head, Miss Marple—yours truly—went on to imagine the Moroccan police raiding Tebarek Allah with submachine guns leveled: all those suspicious books, the butts of two joints tossed into the unlit fireplace, a photo of Jean Seberg with dedication . . . there were several compromising clues, only the occupants were missing. A providential tip-off from some well-informed anonymous person had saved them in the nick of time, and while the cops proceeded to search the property, the family was already safe in Paris, where the hijackers were arrested only years later. And what if . . . But then, after one glance at our glorious garden, the detective's spirit promptly abandoned me.

While still very young, Sanche had won a Pulitzer Prize for recounting the last minutes of the life of a baritone who collapsed on the stage of the Metropolitan while singing *La forza del Destino*. At the wheel of their thirdhand station wagon, Nancy drove the children to the American School every morning. Those pamphlets and those clippings, proof of an evident interest, certainly did not mean they were even remotely involved in the hijacking. I, too, happen to keep folders on heinous news stories. But mythomania, as I have learned after years in this gossipy and scandalmongering city, is one of the most widespread local ills, a virus that travels through the air like the smell of kif. The Gramonts were a couple of pacifist intellectuals who arrived here in the wake of Paul and Jane Bowles, like many other kids of the Beat Generation. Why here? For the myth of the excellent (actually terrible) climate, for the lifestyle, for the cheap joints, and for the relative freedom enjoyed by foreigners, especially if they have a few dollars in their pockets, in a region where the tolerance and helpfulness of the locals dates back to the time when it was an International Zone (in those years the English Queen Mother asked a courtier where her friend Cecil Beaton had got to and was told that he was in Tangier, but it was a secret. "Tangier is no secret," she remarked pithily).

One of the most picturesque Beats, the Englishman Brion Gysin, became great friends with Sanche and Nancy. He made his debut as a painter in 1935, in a surrealist collective in Paris, with small watercolors of meticulous workmanship, which evoked both imaginary deserts, à la Dalí, and the backdrop of an aquarium into which a child wants to put all the pebbles and seashells he has found.

Expelled from the group by the poet André Breton, who reigned over his acolytes with the arrogance of a despot, he ended up in Tangier, where he sure made a hash of things! Infatuated with Hamri, a big fellow from the nearby village of Jajouka, he taught the guy to handle a brush, turning him into one of the first Moroccan painters; with Hamri he rented a wing of the ramshackle Menhebi palace and opened a restaurant, the 1001 Nights, where traditional dishes were served to the accompaniment of the music and dance of certain musicians, heirs of Pan hailing from the same village as Gysin's protege, who a few years later were to arouse the enthusiasm of the Rolling Stones. Gysin wrote, painted, invented devices he called "dream machines," took drugs, and partied a lot (he was a sort of link between the world of the old expats and the newly arrived Beats, especially if they were good-looking) and on afternoons of tedium—between parties Tangier can be a deadly bore—armed with scissors and glue and surrounded by piles of newspapers he invented the technique known as cut-up. Another victim of the mirages of the medina, his friend William Burroughs, was soon to appropriate it to compose his most famous novel, *Naked Lunch*.

In Burroughs's biography published in 1988, Ted Morgan relates that one evening after dinner, on getting up from a sofa upholstered in blue linen, Gysin left "a round bloodstain the width of a teacup," the first sign of the colon cancer that would kill him—he died in Paris, but his ashes were scattered by a group of friends into the sea at Cap Spartel, near Tangier. Ted Morgan locates the incident in the home of "those arrivistes of the Montagne called Sanche and Nancy de Gramont." In short, he defamed himself. Forget hijackings and Black Panthers disguised as priests! It is not the Atlantic that separates Ted from Sanche, and not even ten centuries of history, but a mysterious, ancient, and profound ill. Who knows what witchery Proust's Duchesses had woven around that babe in arms, their aquiline faces adorned with diamonds as they bent over the cradle, while licking their chops and staring at him with that big eye... To blind his Cyclops, my Oedipus had to go as far as painting the world in stars and stripes.

Ted Morgan was a prolific writer, he published other biographies (Somerset Maugham, De Gaulle, Churchill, Roosevelt), books of history, articles for newspapers and magazines. According to David Herbert, the younger brother of the Earl of Pembroke, who tyrannized the foreign community with relentless frivolity, "he had no revolutionary sympathies at all: he was too unsympathetic"—and as always when he was gossiping, he who "adored" everyone, the Honorable Mr. Herbert would emit a brief neigh and adjust his toupee with a hand glittering with amethysts while Pearl Gray, the parrot he kept on his shoulder, flapped its wings menacingly. Sanche was reserved, a hard worker, little inclined to local pleasures, "an immense bore." Goodness knows how bored he was with the rituals that punctuated expat life, from picnics on the Atlantic beaches in honor of the occasional passing legend (Truman Capote, Marina of Greece, Tallulah Bankhead, Tennessee Williams) to pompous evenings at York Castle, when hundreds of carpets were laid out in all the alleys and in the square of the casbah. How out of place this clerical intellectual must have been, amid a motley swarm of creatures in caftans chasing after a shepherd boy in the dunes, or in a tuxedo, bowing and kissing the hand of the heiress to a department store chain covered in the emeralds of Catherine the Great and seated on a replica of the Peacock Throne. His idea of fun must have been a Sunday family barbecue in the garden, a double whiskey or a ginger smoothie with a retired history professor, at most a swim in the icy waters of the bay followed by fried fish in the *chiringuito* of an exile from Francoism—you don't rename yourself Ted Morgan and get away with it that easily.

Cynthia Munroe, the wealthy American who was the next owner, was too taken with a self-styled Andalusian hidalgo to bother with a house she lived in less and less. The purchase of a *finca* that was immense, and maybe nonexistent, along with hundreds of horses that her Spanish lover had managed to launch at a gallop but only in his imagination, had bankrupted her; a brother of hers who lived in Marrakech paid her debts and began to come here in the warm months, but the pleasures of Tangier could not supplant those of the small court of young boys he held at the gates of the desert. Instead, George Staples, the American School teacher who had eventually inherited Tebarek Allah before selling it to us, was an ascetic—he would offer you a glass of water insisting it was from the faucet, just as a more hospitable host would tell you the vintage of the brandy he was about to offer you.

Stephan and I found ourselves dismantling one by one the elements of a functionalism that was senseless even when it was still in fashion: away with the walls that enclosed already cramped spaces, away with the horrible low wall for passing dishes from the kitchenette to the dining corner, away with the dining corner and the study, the bricks supporting the shelves of the famous bookcase, the shoddy floor tiles, the suffocating stove, away with the lot. From all that dust there emerged a cozy living room with fireplace, a kitchen, and a bedroom preceded by an airy bathroom. Thanks to the new boiserie made from scaffolding planks, and to the addition of a bow window with a green tiled roof like those of the old houses in Fez (my design for it was inspired by the first owner, the pale Diego, another flowering of the orientalist sapling we cultivate together), all traces of that punitive past have disappeared. Once the town house, the spirit of Ted Morgan, and the fried egg smell of the American way of life had disappeared, we began to enjoy life, and my collections were able to take up all the space they wanted. When the huge bowl, full of the opercula of shells I had been buying from children at the Reine Mère beach (a less sedentary way to earn a living than begging) decided it wanted to sit on the low table from the barber's in Moulay Abdessalam, I heaved a sigh of relief: it weighs almost one hundred kilos, obviously it is not autonomous, and before being moved it thought twice about it. As if on an agreed signal, a crowd of furniture and objects that are particularly dear to me followed it: the console table from the Marché de Fès with the marble top on which Anwar the butcher sliced the best steaks in Tangier and on which Hassan, the stammering florist, had later displayed bunches of daffodils, lupins, and calla lilies (when buying flowers was still a party, and what a party it was); the lean late-eighteenth-century Boston chairs Stephan discovered in the Hôtel Drouot; the Directoire vases in painted tin that stood on the top shelf of a grocery store on the outskirts of Rabat; my lantern made of fragments of Roman glass that a painstaking tinsmith had worked on for months; the shell that the muezzin of a mosque in the Middle Atlas used as a megaphone to call the faithful to prayer (every time I try it out I am stunned, invariably someone comes running and I have to invent some excuse); the pine cones given to me by a soldier from Jebel Tazekka that have scales like the claws of the extinct cave bear; the fearsome Leyla's bronze mortar that still smells of garlic; and the fragment of Mamluk carpet; the toolbox once owned by the mechanic from Tamghrout who was obsessed with Sylvie Vartan; the beautiful ammonite; the Giustiniani tile with the gorgon, and so on.

The last time I heard of Nancy was at Christopher Gibbs's place. Having recently bought Marguerite McBey's house on the Vieille Montagne, he had found a folder in the attic: *property of Nancy de Gramont*. "Terrorists on the run? Come on, they were just a couple of slobs." Tracking her down was a challenge, but in the end he had been able to call her and make her a generous offer—yes, they really were

Eugene Berman's watercolors. Nancy had completely forgotten about them. She lived wrapped up in her shawls, probably still in that flowered skirt, in a village in the Highlands of Guatemala; with the money for the paintings she would have warmed her freezing little house under the volcano for the whole winter. How many were there? Six? Really? At over eighty, she concluded, she was very, very lucky.

TILES

Since boyhood I have had a passion for Islamic tiles. I learned much of the little that I know by losing myself among the red tulips of Iznik tiles and the carnations of their siblings in Damascus. Later, I got interested in Spanish tiles, in which the flowing, musical legacy of the courts of the Andalusian caliphs stiffens and congeals on contact with the rigidity of the late Gothic style of the Reconquista: a naked houri in the starched, coarse habit of an abbess. First painted with the *cuerda seca* technique, then printed with that of the *arista*, the hundreds of thousands of tiles fired in the kilns of southern Spain, of Catalonia, and of Toledo were used to line the interiors of churches and monasteries, halls and loggias between the Algarve and the Rio de la Plata, the Yucatán, and Liguria, spreading throughout the Christian world the symbols, coats of arms, and emblems of the conquistadors derived from heraldry and Muslim decorative motifs: suns and stars, swords and clover, shields and acanthus leaves, artichoke flowers and lilies, rampant felines, spheres, iguanas, dice, towers, and scallops. In the nineteenth century, while the neo-Gothic style born in England conquered all Europe, with the onset of historicist and orientalist fashion, tiles began to be collected by romantic explorers of the Alhambra, and then by the followers of Prosper Mérimée who discovered the thrill of flamenco and pursued their Carmen amid the crowds of the *Feria* in Seville.

I bought my first panel of Triana tiles in Paris; according to the antiquarian, it came from the home of Anatole France, the nineteenth-century best-selling writer who, like many contemporary artists and dandies, loved the Troubadour style and millefleur tapestries, lace fans, and mother-of-pearl boxes. For the frames of all subsequent panels, I always drew inspiration from the first one: the dark, large, and heavy profiles—made by Abderrahim, my carpenter from Fez who can do everything—enhance the golden highlights of the enamels and emphasize the intricate patterns. Tiles like these were even used to cover the ceilings of religious buildings, turning them into chocolate boxes within which the dazzled faithful knelt, trapped like rum truffles inside a glittering wrapper: hanging on our walls, they become windows opening onto another world.

TUNISIAN BEAUTIES

The only Mediterranean ceramics that are almost as widespread as Iznik's are the tiles made in the kilns of Qallaline, on the outskirts of Tunis, starting from the eighteenth century. These small tiles have traveled as far as Sicily, Provence, Catalonia, Libya, and Egypt: in Muslim countries, following the collapse of the Ottoman Empire, they have taken the place of Iznik tiles. They are the timid Western response to them: a later, more modest and manageable product, they seem to bleat like sheep where their Turkish forerunners roar like steppe tigers, but in reality their melancholy song is that of the end of a world. While their forebears had proclaimed the absolute dominion of the Sublime Porte over even the remotest province, these are the testimony of a lingua franca founded on trade and commerce: wheat, oil, textiles, slaves. Even here in northern Morocco, in Tétouan, the ancient capital of the region, which was never under Ottoman rule, they adorned minarets, the portals of mosques, and the courtyards of palaces before they were swallowed by hasty coats of whitewash, or worse, before infelicitous restoration was to shatter them or stack them up in the back shops of ignorant junk dealers. Some of those I collected come from local traders, but I found most of them thirty years ago in Pau, in the Pyrenees, at an auction where treasures from the palace of a French governor of Algeria were being broken up. I remember the car trip in the snow with Roberto, the cold, and the revelation of Mediterranean colors (cobalt blue, soft olive greens, honey) on that gray winter day, I remember the bouquets and garlands of flowers with their gauche, peasant grace, and the thrill when I managed to secure a crate of tiles—at a glance it seemed to me that they made up a single design, a large two-handled vase amid a row of cypresses—and my excitement at the idea of reassembling it whole or almost whole near the place it came from, on the sunny coast of North Africa... Of course, they were poor relations of those Turkish sultanas whose slipper they were unworthy to kiss, yet the language they spoke—provincial and full of foreign words, but confident and heedless, even of mistakes, with that scent of orange blossom on top of a hint of fried fish—was the same as the speech that resounds in the alleys of the cities I love.

EPIGRAPHIC TILES AND TILES FROM FEZ

Since the Middle Ages, epigraphic tiles have been manufactured in Morocco using the "sgraffito" technique. The surface was glazed entirely in a shade of brown tending toward eggplant, which the *mellem*, the artisan-artist, scraped away with a little chisel, removing most of the glaze with small tweezers and leaving on the pinkish terracotta base and thereby laying bare only one dark letter—or a part of it—with which he would compose a text by placing it next to the others on the wall. Reduced to thin strokes and scrolls, in slight relief against that somewhat faded mass of flesh, the color of the glazing shines with a markedly black light, like lacquer. And here, every time Islamic art takes your breath away, one might wonder whence comes that procession of Uighur women on camelback, their thick raven hair gleaming with yak butter contrasting with the powdered white of their almond-eyed faces ... In traditional Moroccan interiors, these inscriptions were placed above high wainscoting made of multicolored ceramic mosaics, just below the engraved stucco panels that ended in the wooden frieze of the ceiling. They were at just the right height to be observed standing with one's head slightly bowed, as when meditating. Every time I incredulously handle one of these tiles, I wonder how it is possible to make such a patiently complex work without jeopardizing the fluidity of the result. In Islam the name of God *is* God. And an inscription, in these parts, cannot merely say something: it must run and dance, its most profound meaning is in the air that it moves. The result of so much dedication, these fragments of meaning seem to spring from a hand imbued with divine inspiration. They are touching because they are an expression of the freedom won by craftsmen as a result of the extinction of self through their work.

Tebarek Allah has a small collection of these thirteenth- and fourteenth-century tiles, and their more lethargic, plumper descendants up to the seventeenth century, where the awkwardness of decadence is already looming. Most of them are in the dining room, on thin shelves in natural pine aged by Abderrahim—to smooth the edges he beat them with the chain of his motorcycle, and now they are worthy of a room in some dusty provincial museum where a cat snores blissfully in the sunlight streaming in through the window. Unusually in Islamic art, the inscriptions are not religious but celebrate life, hospitality, friendship, the home, and the coolness of the garden. The same formulas for greetings and the same poetic compositions adorn the princely rooms of Andalusia, where even before the year 1000 while reading Plato and Aristotle and listening to the music of the lute and the song of frogs, fondling gazelles and drinking pomegranate juice, African boys who had just taken off their chain mail before washing off the dust and donning a silken chlamys lay down their scimitars in favor of quill pens to become humanists *ante litteram* who breathed new life into poetry, medicine, botany, and astronomy.

Only after living here for years did I discover that the local production of wall tiles continued throughout the eighteenth century and for much of the century after that. Just for a change I was in a junk dealer's warehouse, in Salé, bent over a stack of dusty tiles. I observed them one by one, incredulous, uncertain, pouring water over them from the bottle I had filled in the courtyard. And as I went on, and as they thanked me gratefully for having given them back their life and skin, my doubts were confirmed. I had read all the books on Moroccan ceramics, in which amazingly no one had deigned to mention these tiles, beautiful as they are and easy to date thanks to the decoration and glazing they share with the vases, bowls, and plates from the same period. Why had they been forgotten? Only because they were humble extras destined to "play the wallflower"? The deep grayish blue is the well-known "Fez blue"; the straightforward yellows, browns, and greens are the same as those of the widely studied and published containers sought after by collectors since the nineteenth century. The dark outlines, the stripes, the flowers, the *boteh* motif of leaves with a curved upper end, the toothed trim, the flourishes, the circles—all were taken from imported Persian fabrics. When I put four together that went to make up a single motif, and little by little—in a series of lucky breaks and disappointments, forced insertions and fateful reconnections—another twelve were added to those first four, and the pattern grew until it returned to the harmony of its original conception, the decorated and blank spaces were the same as those of the large, decorated vessels in which traditionalist families still eat *tajine*, couscous, and lemon chicken. Playing with tiles is the most rewarding of puzzles: when the poor junk dealer managed to get rid of me it was already night. But he was satisfied with the transaction, judging by the smile with which he helped me put all those sacks in the trunk of the car. Since that day I have bought hundreds, thousands of tiles, both in Europe, where they are generally mistaken for Sicilian or Tunisian, and around Morocco, from antique dealers who thanks to the "Arab telephone" knew of my interest (it is surely no coincidence that Virgil's famous allegory of Rumor flying from mouth to mouth spreading the news of the love between Aeneas and Dido is set right here in this land of legendary gossips), from junk dealers whose shop stood next to a small praying room under restoration, and even from warehouses of recycled materials, where they lay piled up among old bicycle frames, boxes of bazaar souvenirs, marble steps, and ripe yellow melons. Beneath an apparent naivete, the stylization of the plant motifs—my beloved wildflowers, irises and narcissi, dog roses, and *saz* leaves copied from Ottoman models—reveals a mastery and a sense of rhythm that becomes overwhelming when the need for speed gets the better of the devotion to the rules: the variations are infinite, lightning-fast, and the design felicitous even when limited to reinterpreting the bland overlapped polygons invented five centuries earlier by the artisans of the Alhambra—yet here, in Morocco on the threshold of modernity, they regain their original power.

    The feature that distinguishes Moroccan art from the grand, celebratory style that flourished under the other Islamic dynasties is its urban and bourgeois nature, as ordinary as bread and olives or the road to the store, an art that evokes houses and buildings overlooking alleyways where you walk taking care to avoid getting splashed with mud or stepping on mule droppings. There are many reasons for this: the precariousness of a central power weakened by continuous dynastic disputes and harried by the Berber tribes, the difficulty of collecting enough taxes to afford the aristocracy the luxury of developing and imposing a style, and vice versa the enrichment of the urban merchant classes thanks to contacts and trafficking often linked to piracy—and you could add more, including the absence of a palatine tradition such as the one inherited by the Middle Eastern world, and the mobility of the court itself, often reduced to an itinerant tent city in order to stem the flood of rebellions. In short, in Moroccan art, just when we would expect to be dazzled by the caliph surrounded by his musicians and cupbearers, or to chase breathless after the lord preceded by his falconers during the hunt, or to look up at the phoenix flying in the company of a pair of simurghs escorted by a herd of hippogriffs, we find ourselves among fat barefoot women bent over to wash the floor. The water is still running off and the guests are already arriving, removing their yellow leather slippers as with a satisfied sigh they sit down next to us on the low sofa covered with damasks from Lyon, among cushions embroidered by the daughters of the neighbor who has fallen on hard times; praises to God rise up, the musicians begin to play, jugs and bowls are passed around for hands to be washed, the aroma of onion fried with raisins spreads, and conversations die out in watering mouths... Selecting a fig from the large plate used for Friday couscous, arranging roses in a bowl for *harira*—the soup that breaks the daily fast during Ramadan—or wild gladioli in a bottle that contained orange blossom essence for sweets, allows us to get closer to a world, to enter it, to become part of it. And every time I lie with a book on my stomach in the loggia of the lower pavilion, and I contemplate the Fez tiles on the walls, I suddenly find myself waiting for the arrival of the garlanded donkeys onto which we will load supplies for the picnic to celebrate the *Ashura*: I must get up, make haste, I still have to make sure that the leather laces of the rolled-up carpets are good and tight, to ensure that the straw bags holding the bread and dates, the dried meat and eggs are closed, and that the tarred cap of the full water jug is firmly secured. This is what happens to me when I have supper by myself, and having lit all the candles in our dining room up to those of the topmost arms of the chandelier, I pour the soup into a small eighteenth-century *jobbana* where an overexcited theology student used to hide his supply of *majoun*, the candy made with hashish and honey: under the reflections the bowl glows like an African smile, the decorative red lead circles are red as poppies in bloom, the ancient wooden spoon caresses the edge of the bowl—and I am in my Morocco.

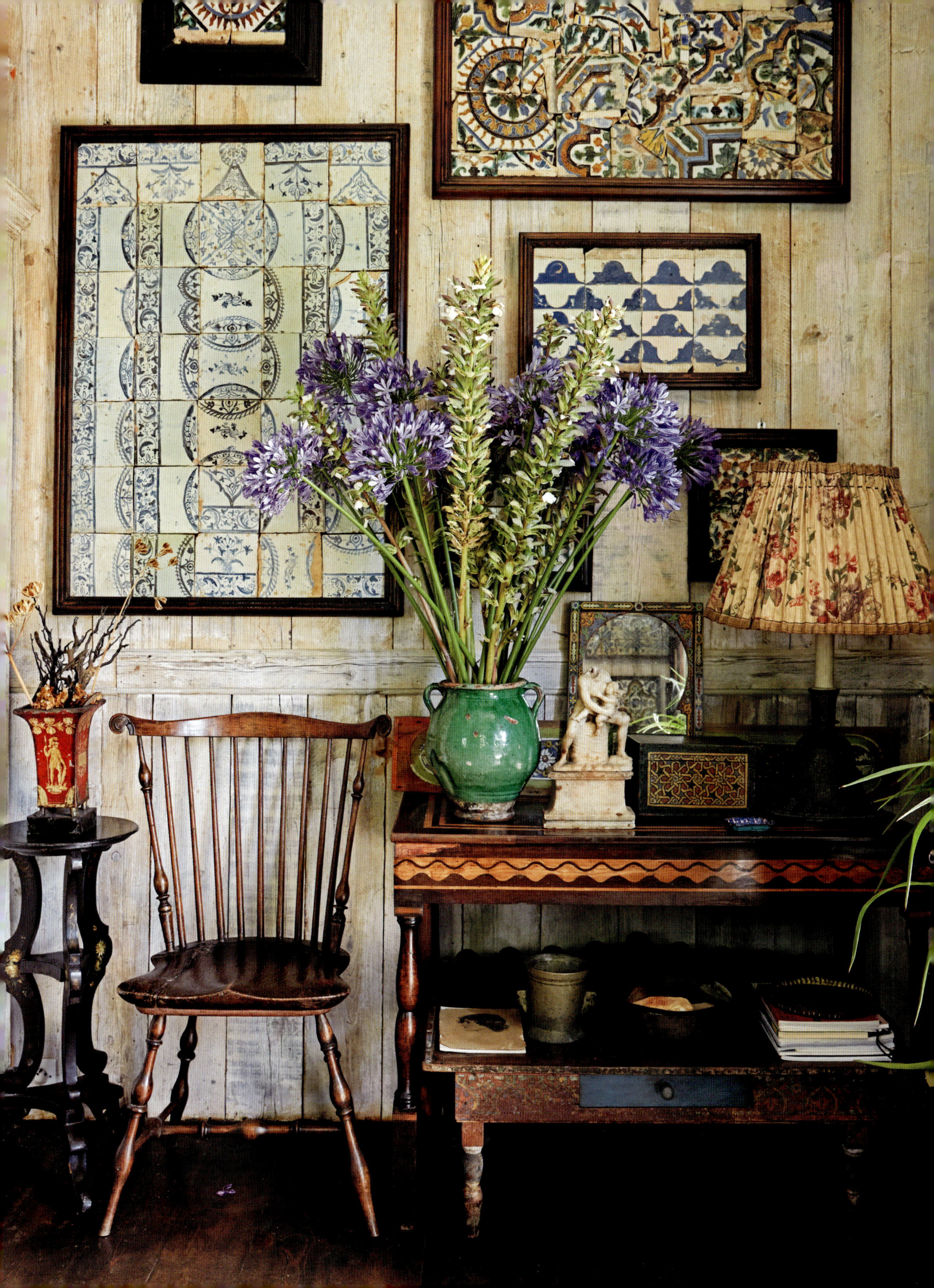

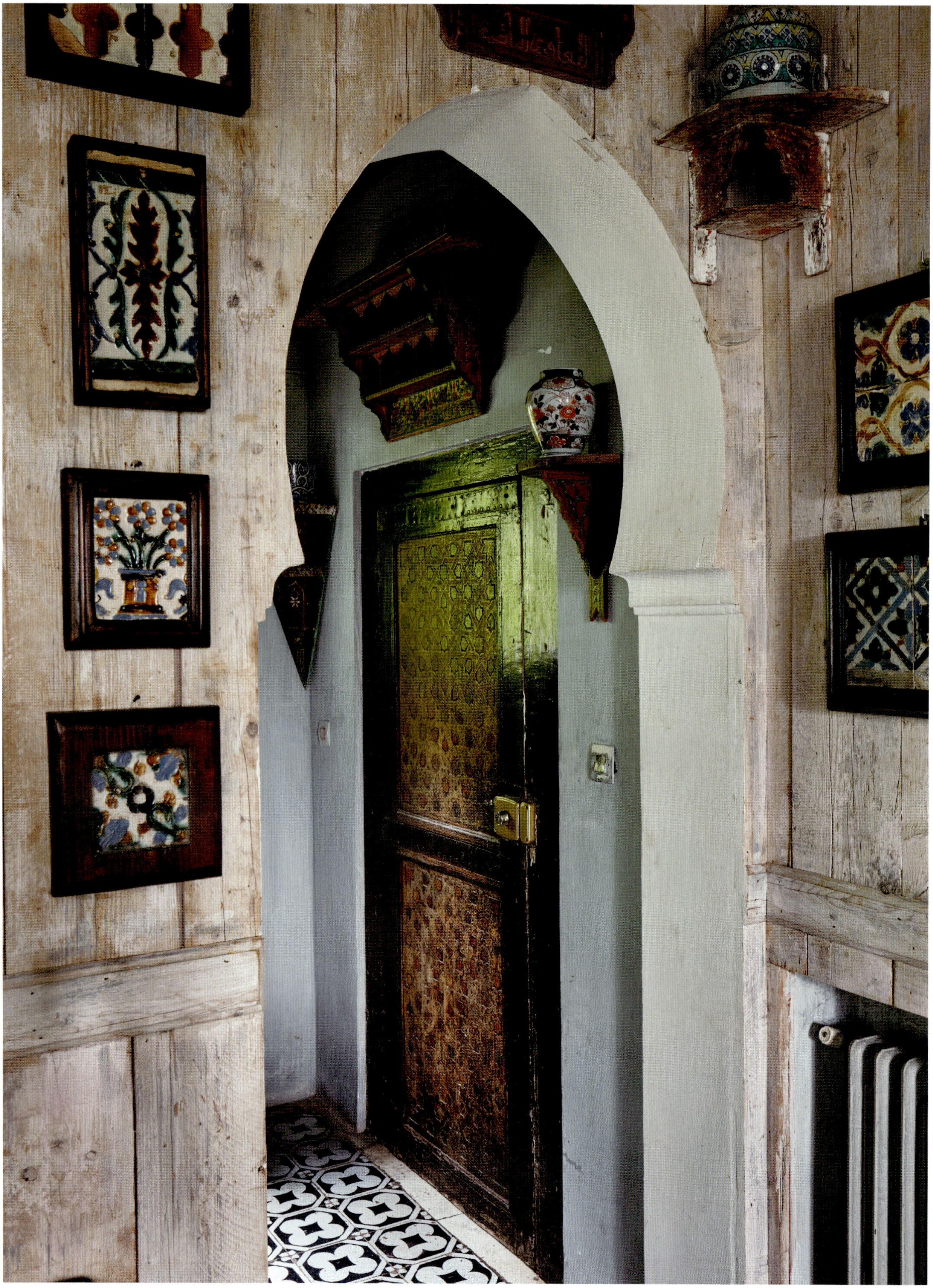

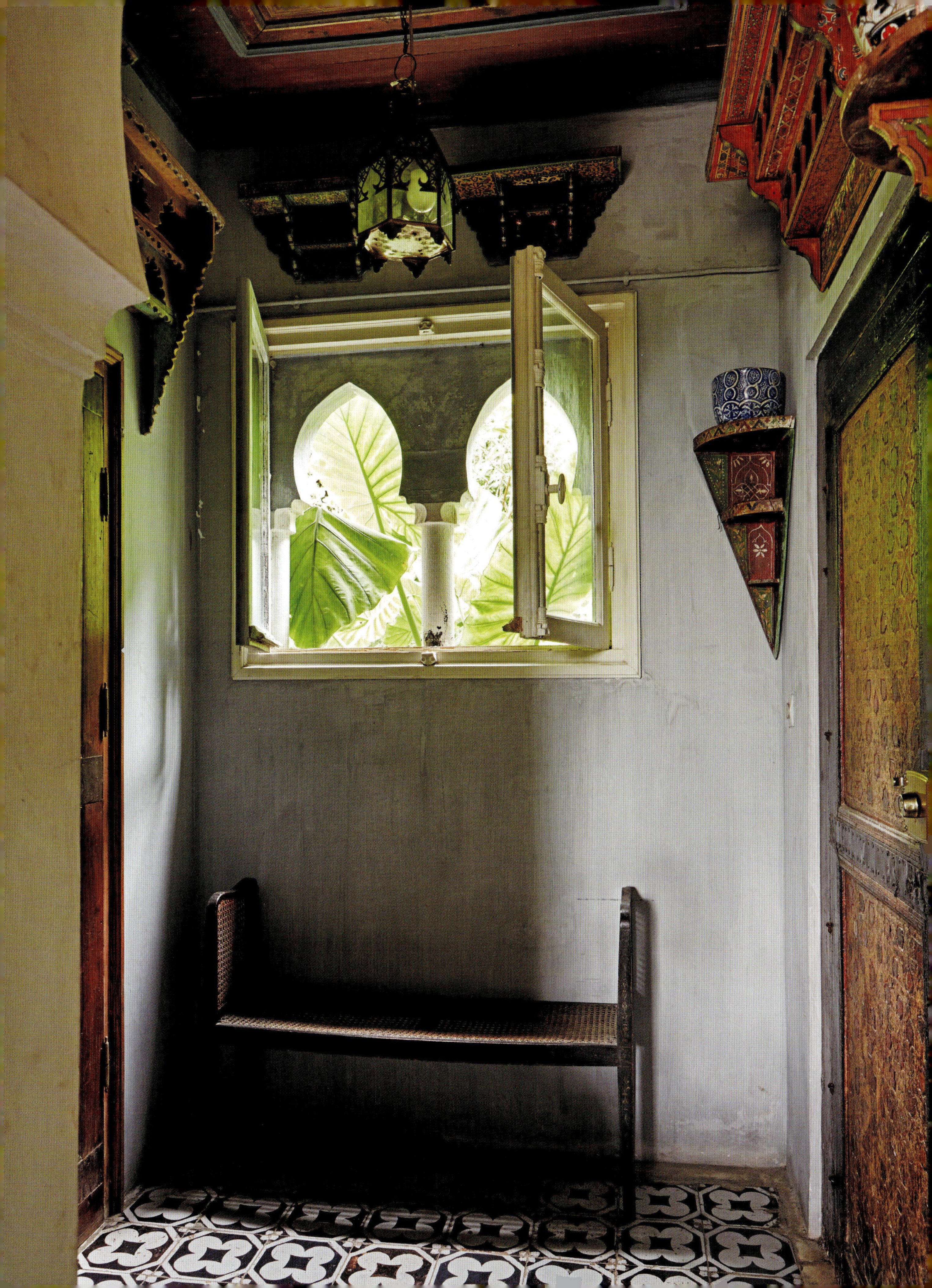

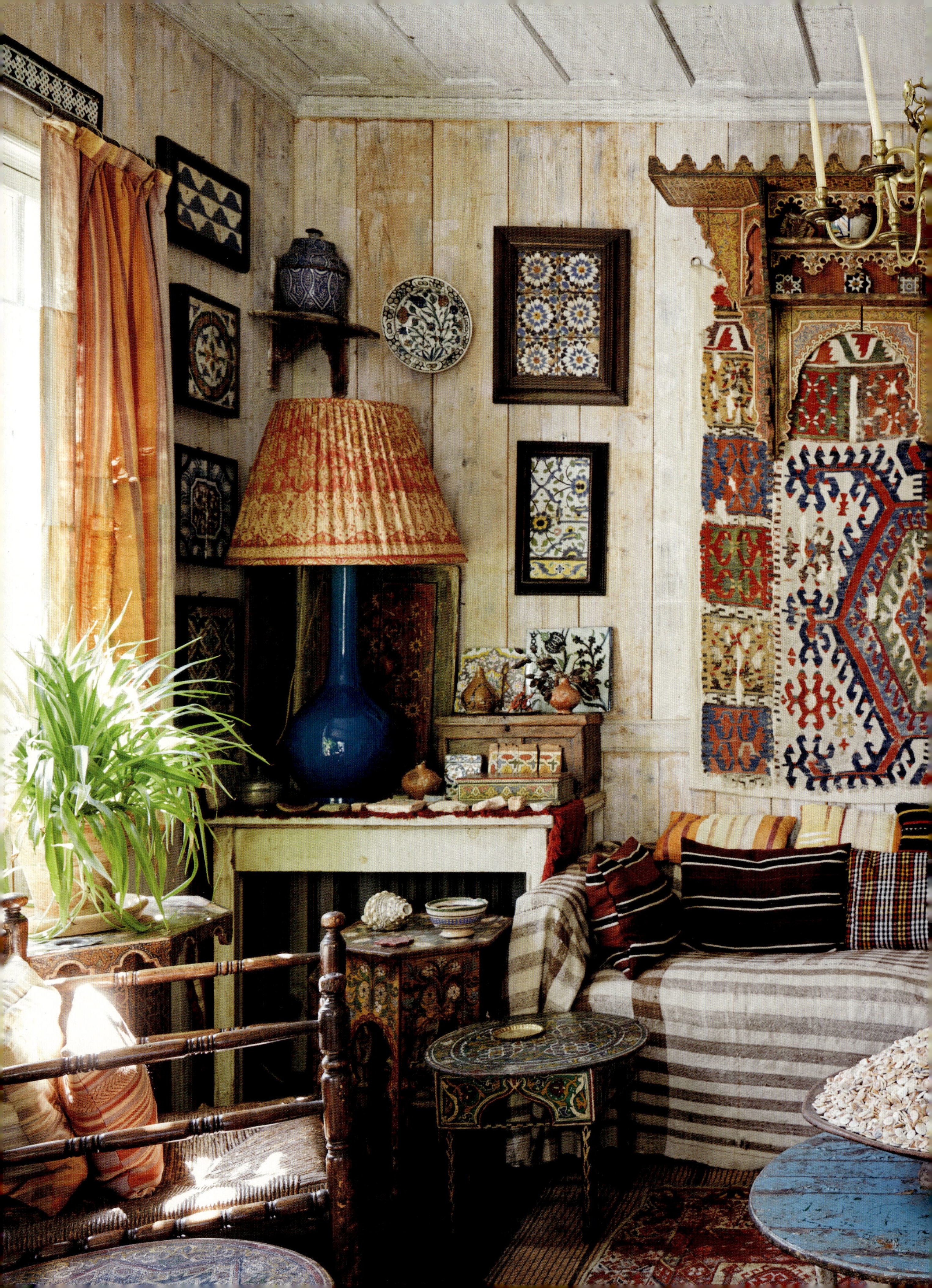

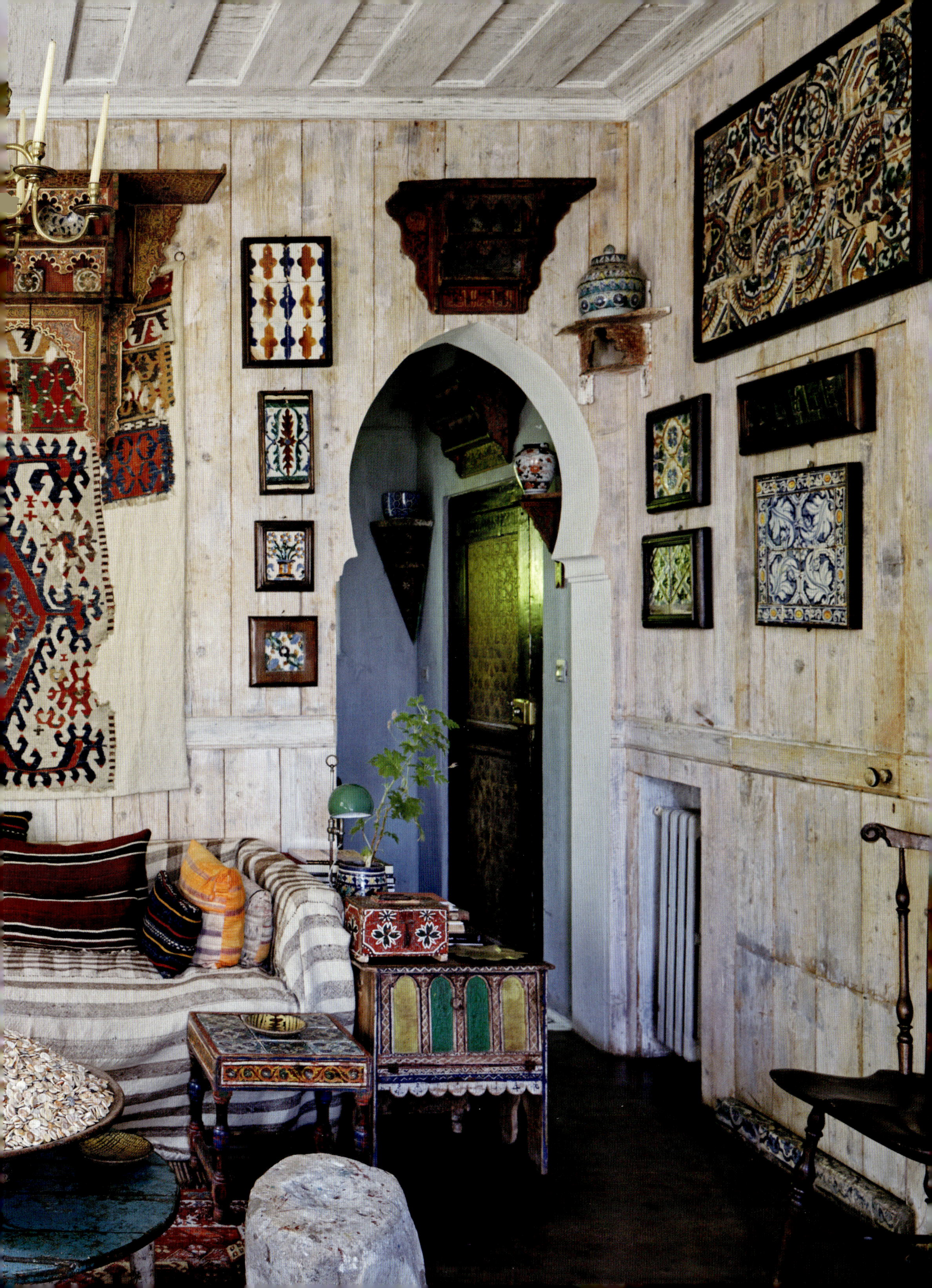

PAGE 92: *The* marfa *above the entrance door has a label on the back; it was bought in 1883 by a Spanish gentleman staying in the Hotel Continental by the port.*

PAGE 93: *The little bench is English Regency; it belonged to our friend David Herbert—the second son of the count of Pembroke who ruled the small world of local expats with a frivolity so steely it earned him the title the "Queen of Tangier." The tiles on the floor are Sicilian.*

PREVIOUS SPREAD: *The boiserie on the walls is made from wooden planks of the scaffolding used by the men who fixed the pavilion. The fragment of the early nineteenth-century kilim from Central Anatolia, a birthday present from Stephan, hangs below a* marfa *from Fez. The sofa is covered with a shroud I found in a Turkish village near Sivas. The little seventeenth-century luster is Dutch, bought in Florence.*

OPPOSITE: *The eighteenth-century northern Italian fireplace is lined with Qallaline "patte de lions" early nineteenth-century tiles and eighteenth-century Portuguese azulejos. In Qallaline, near Tunis, they made tiles since the eighteenth century that were hugely popular all over the Mediterranean; easily handled, cheap, and very colorful, they were used to decorate churches and buildings, pavilions, and fountains from Andalusia to Egypt, Liguria to Sicily. It was the last melancholy flowering of an international Islamic art that had triumphed first with the "arista" tiles of Seville, then with the Ottoman ones from Iznik. The two pottery vases are food containers from Italy's Puglia region. I keep them here even though most of their relatives reside with us in Milan.*

FOLLOWING SPREAD, LEFT: *The carpet fragment is Mamluk Egyptian from the sixteenth century, and the neoclassical tile with the gorgon's head was glazed in the Giustiniani kilns in Naples at the beginning of the nineteenth century, when archaeology became highly fashionable.*

FOLLOWING SPREAD, RIGHT: *A* taifur *(an occasional table) from Tétouan, with a Delft vase made into a lamp.*

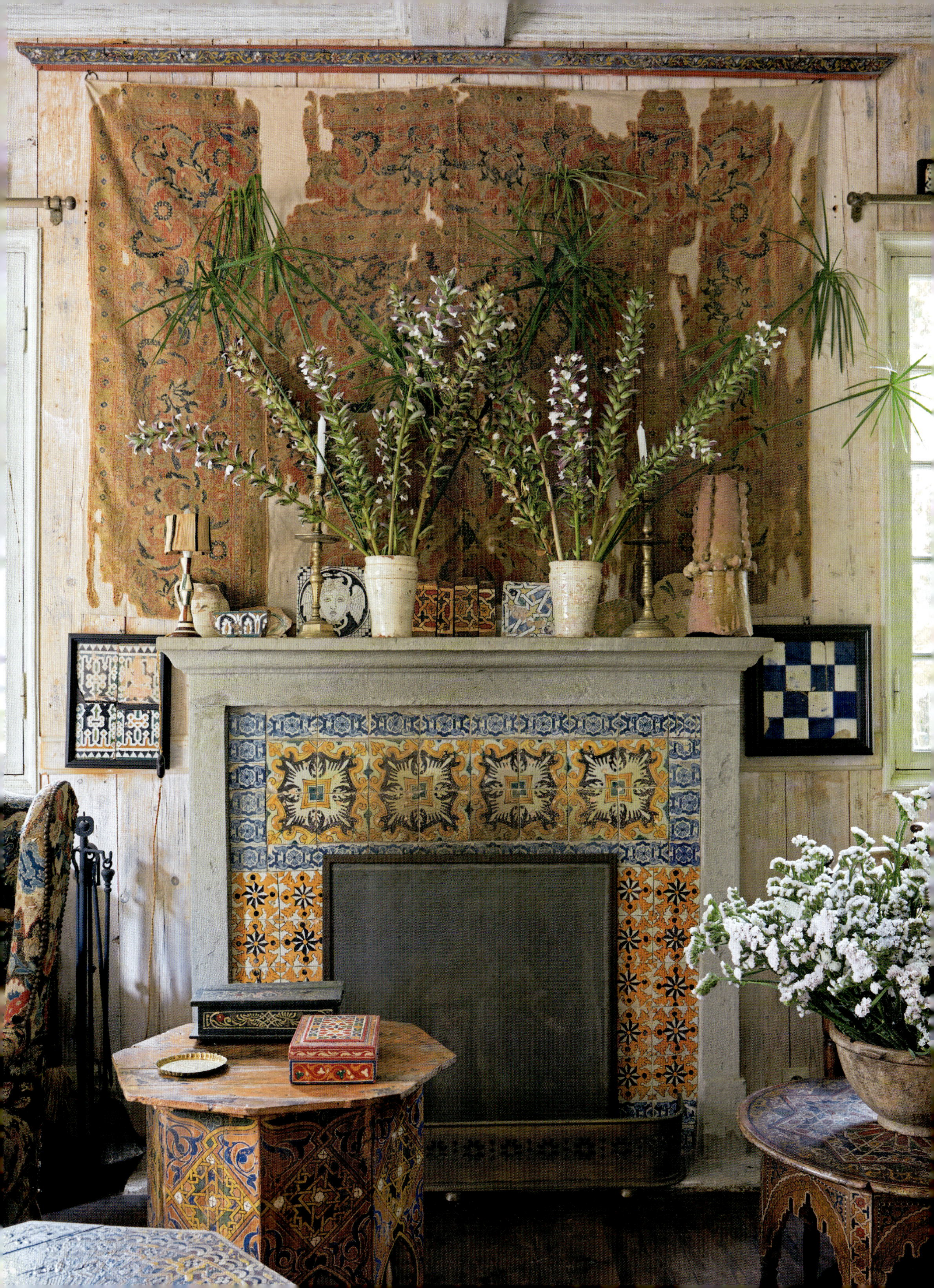

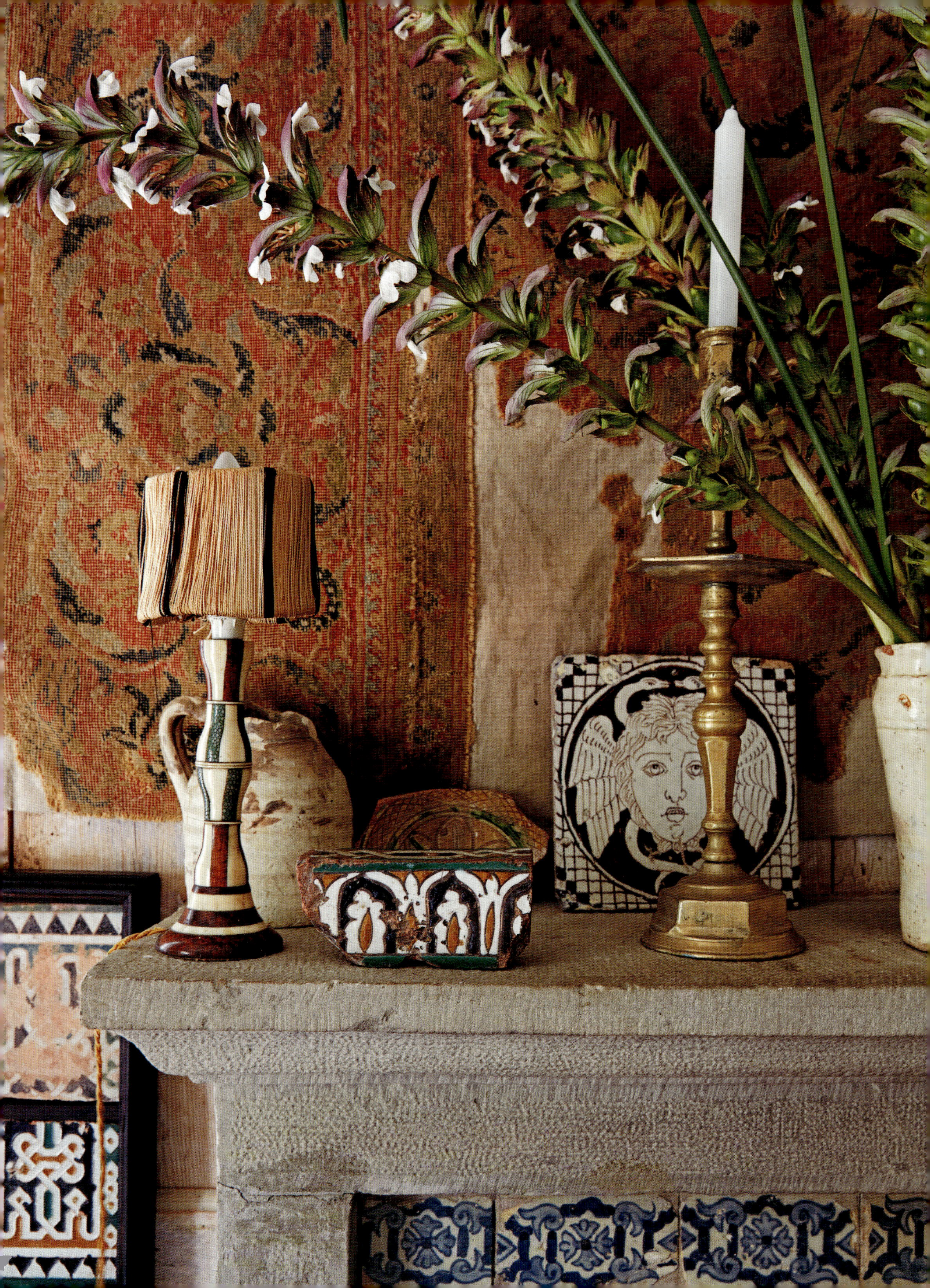

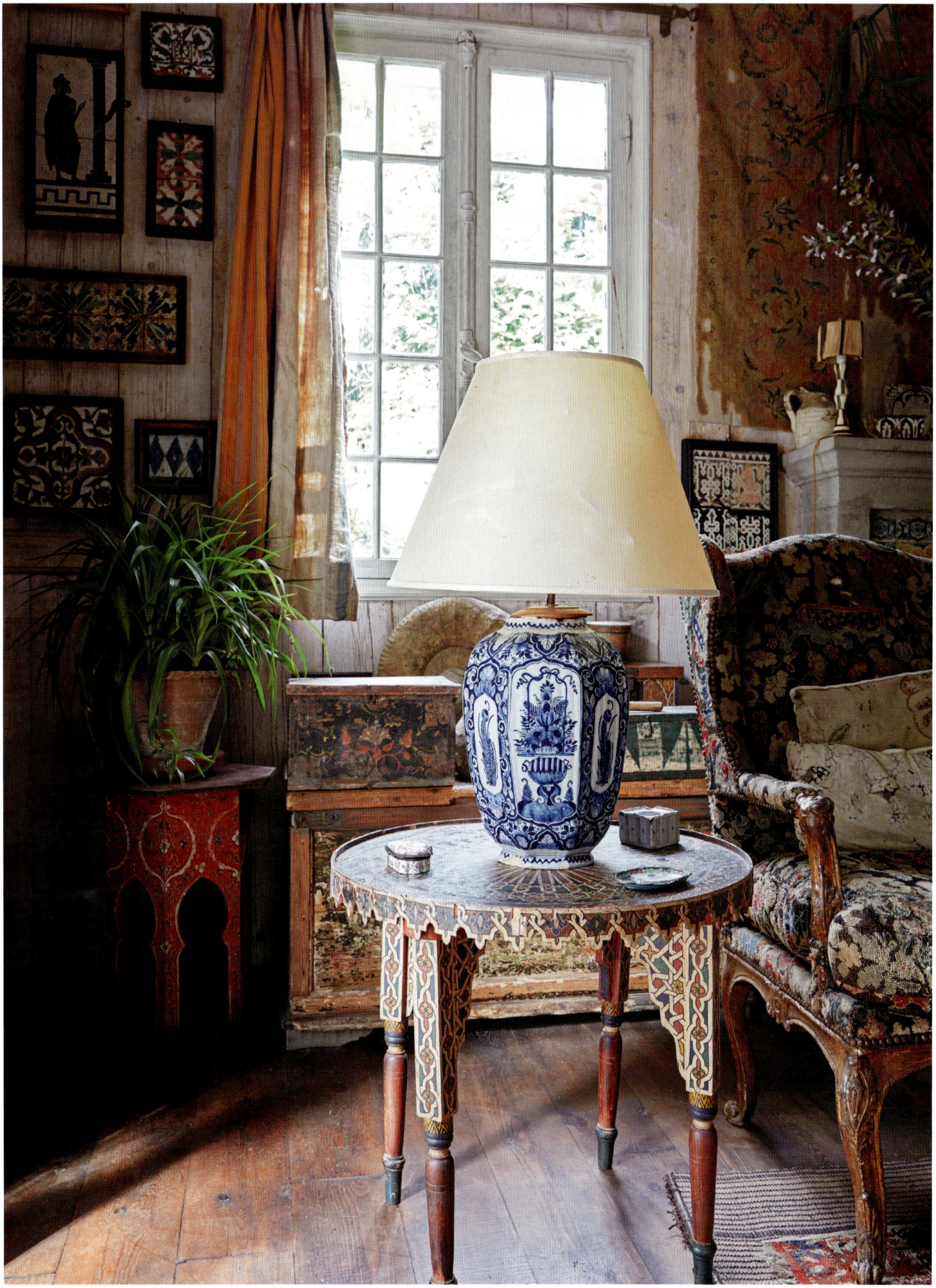

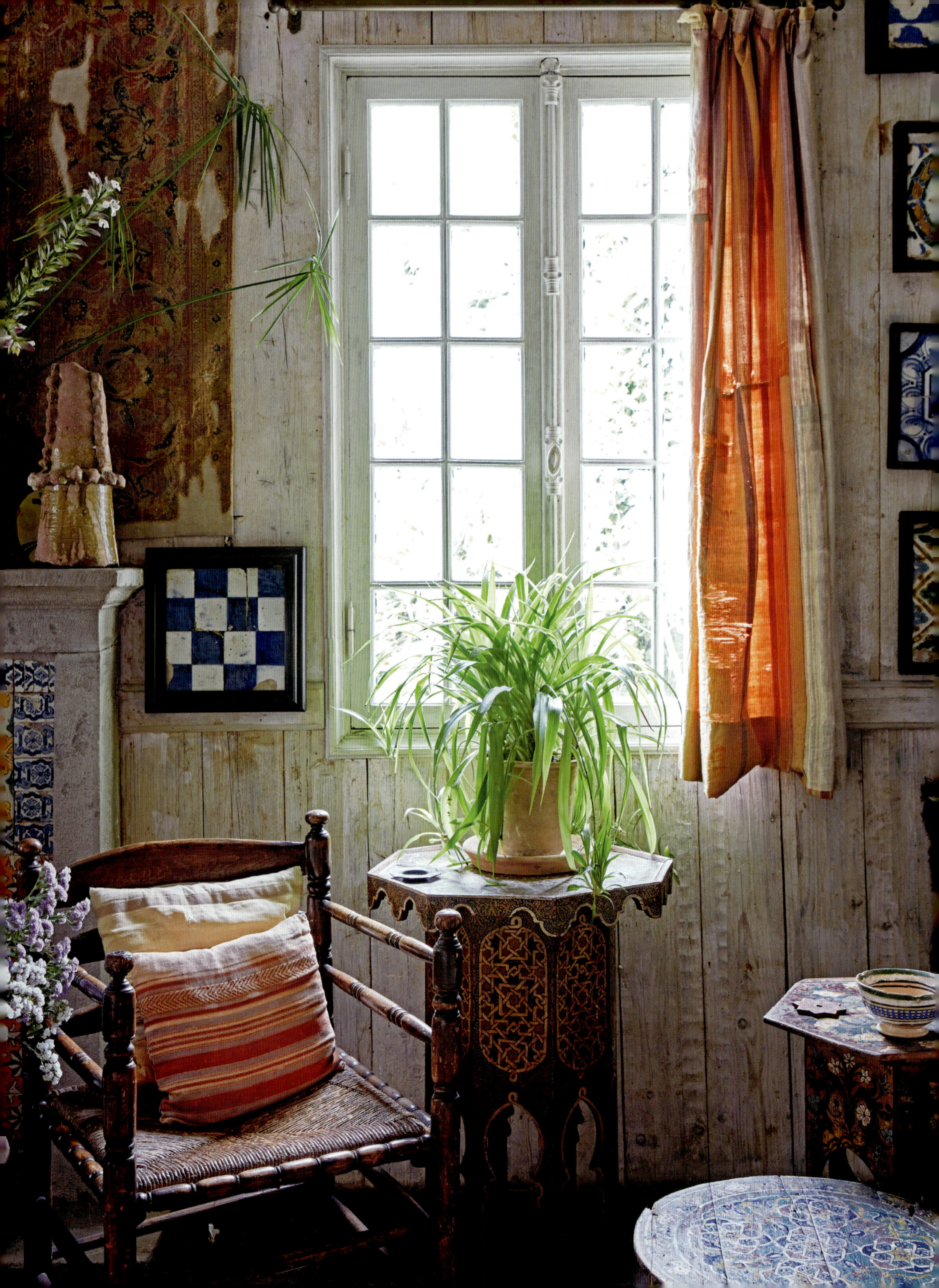

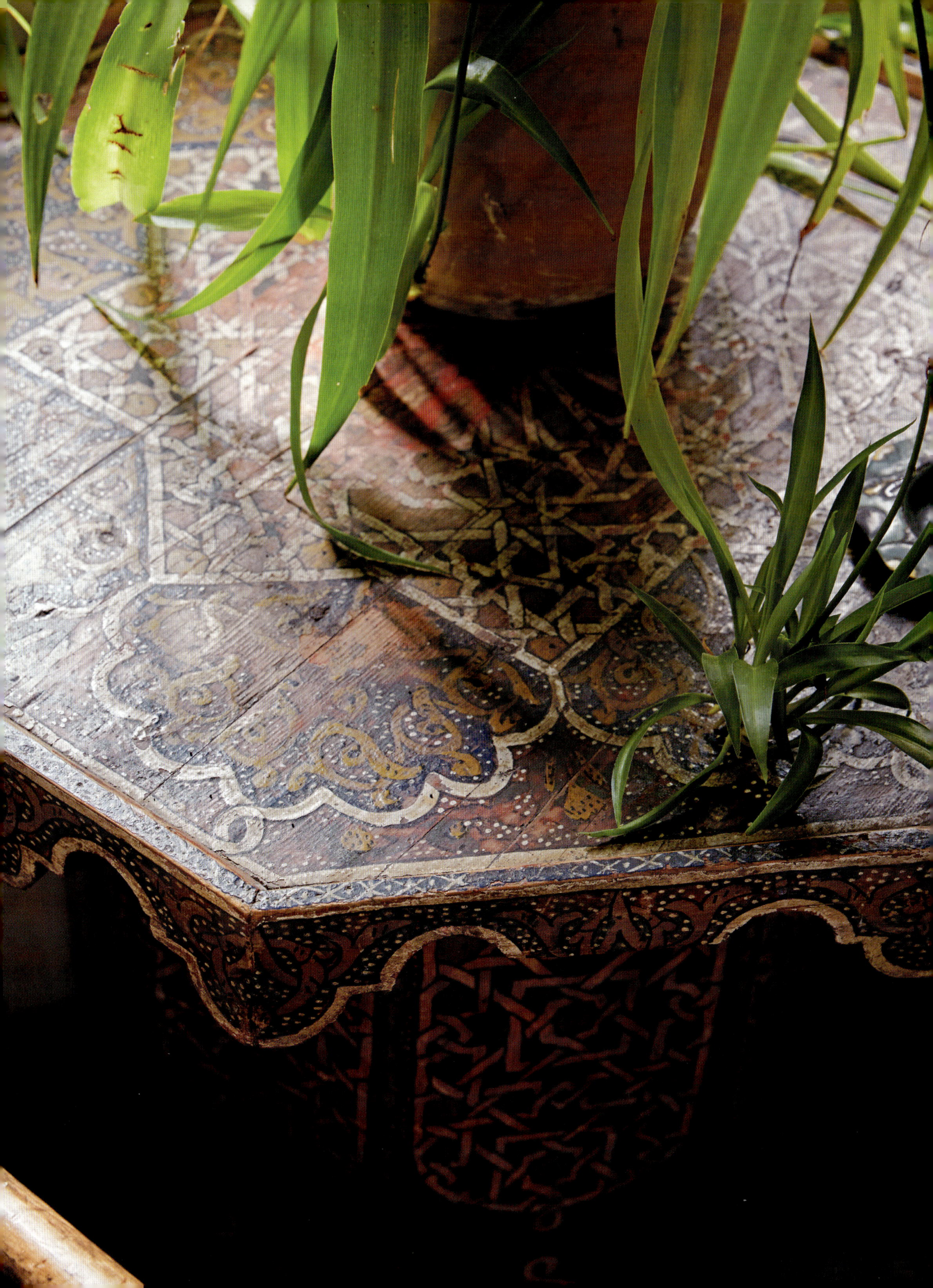

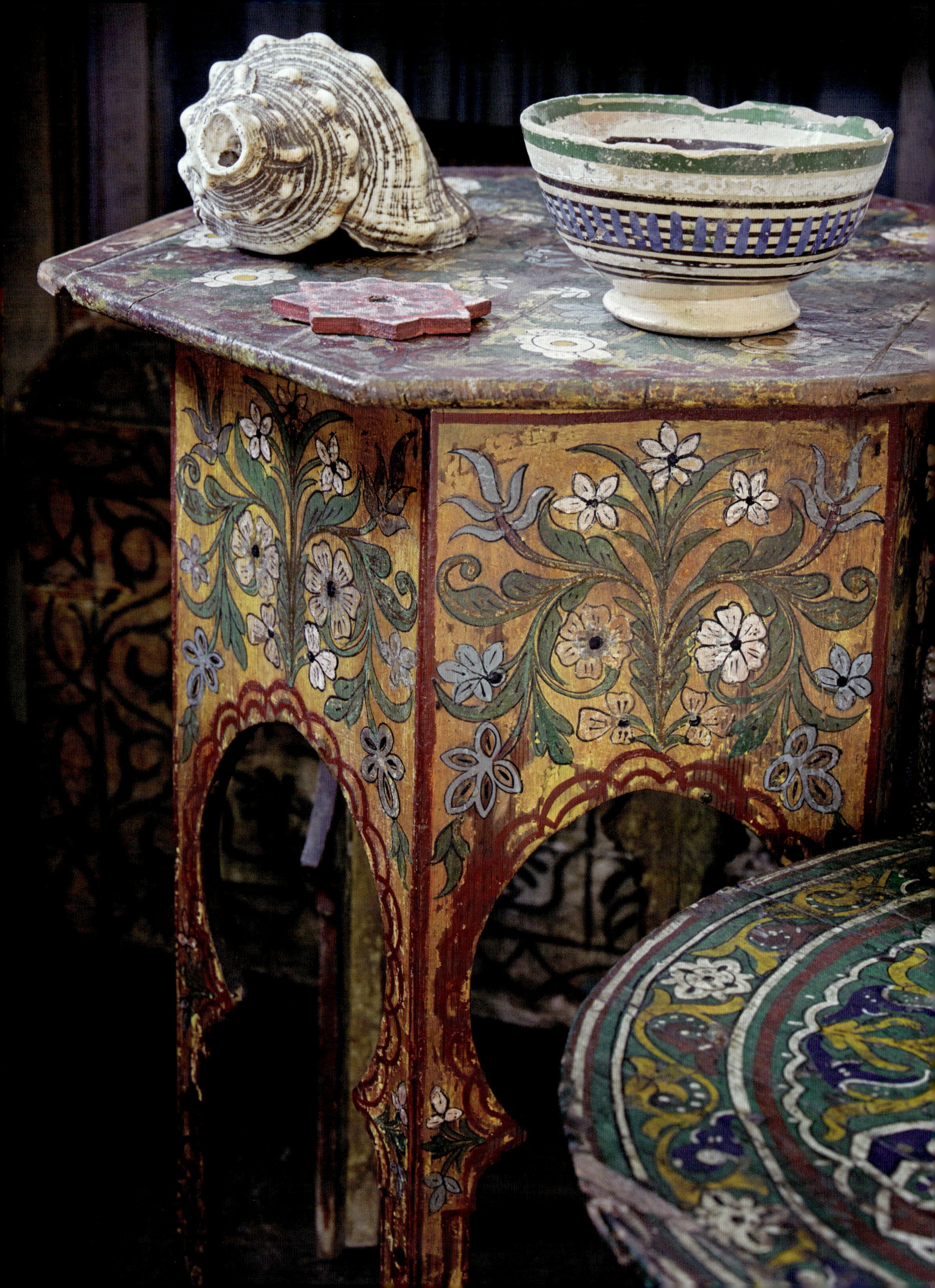

PREVIOUS SPREAD: *A Tétouan* taifur. *The curtains and most of the cushions in this room are made of silk woven in Tétouan. This privateer city—refounded in the seventeenth century by exiles from Andalusia and nearby Chaouen—was famous for silks with geometric jacquard patterns, heirs of those of the Spanish courts.*
OPPOSITE: *This shell was used as a megaphone by the* muezzin *to call people to the mosque for Friday prayers. Every time I try it, somebody rushes in— frightened by the sound—and I have to find an excuse.*
FOLLOWING SPREAD, LEFT: *The shells in the cup are actually the covers, or* opercula, *of a particular shell, and for many years I bought them from the children at my favorite beach.*
FOLLOWING SPREAD, RIGHT: *Fragmentary Almohad pottery, a late Iznik and a Safavid tile, jewelry boxes, bits of wood from an old ceiling—my recipe for perfect happiness.*

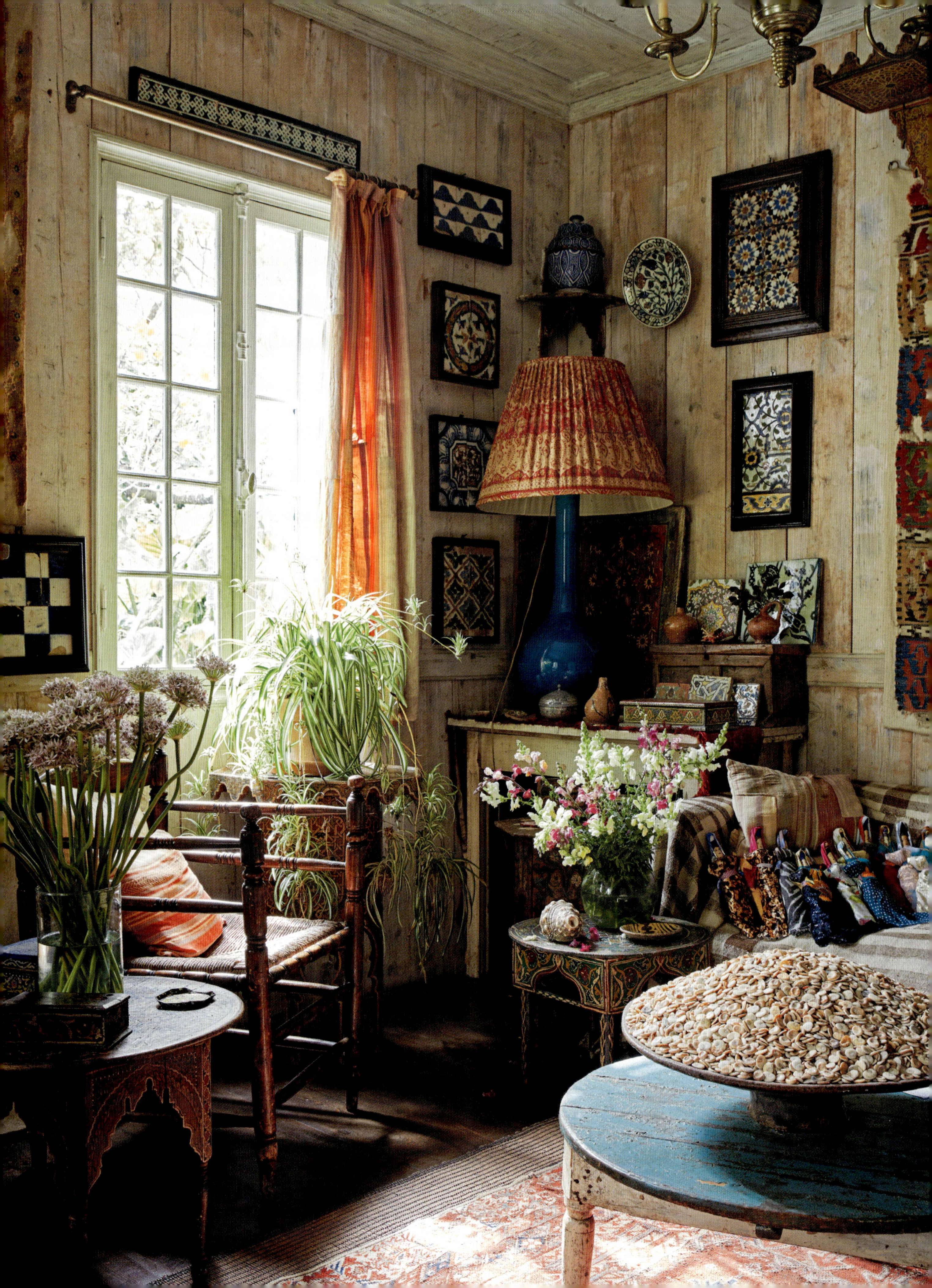

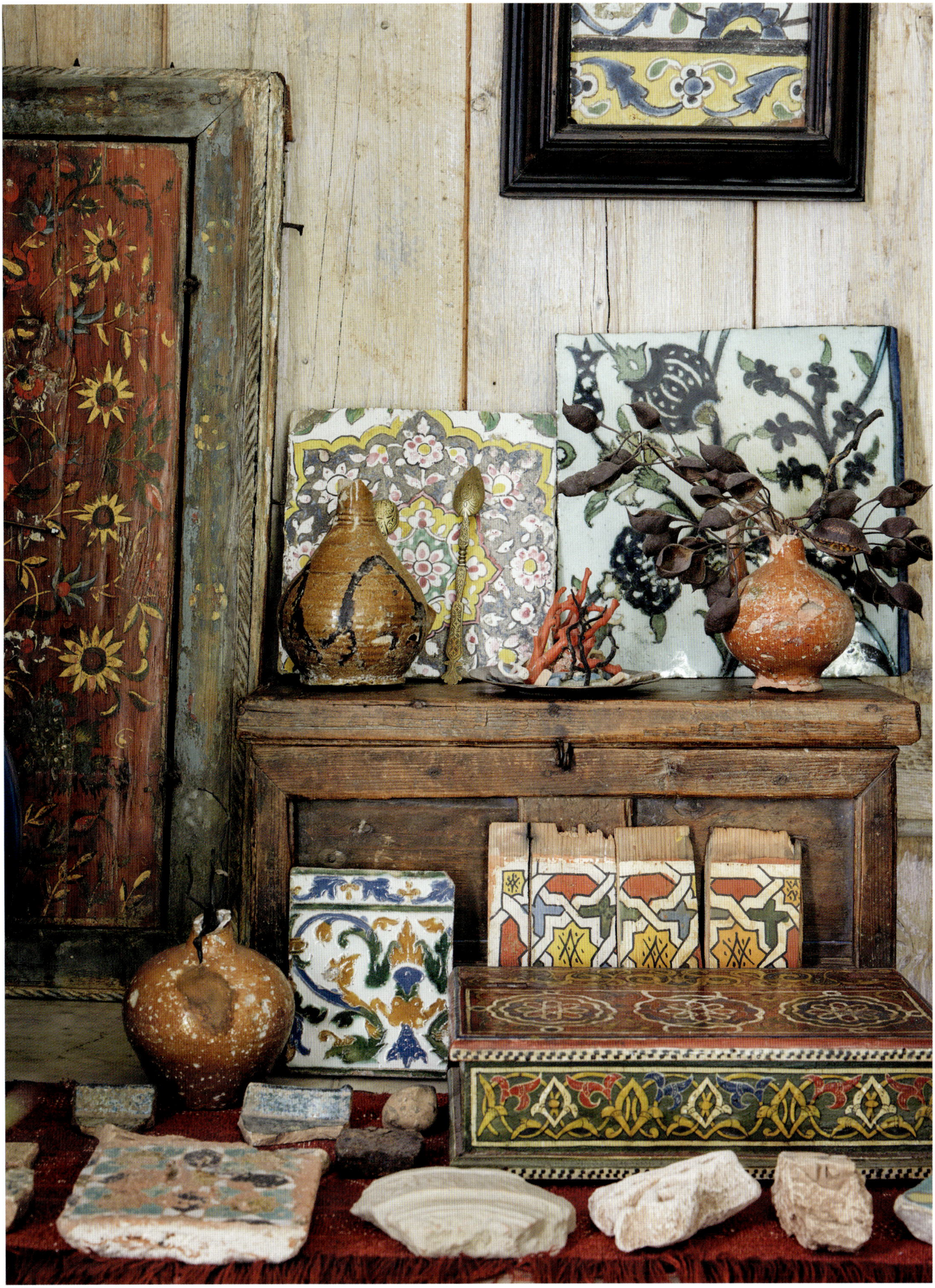

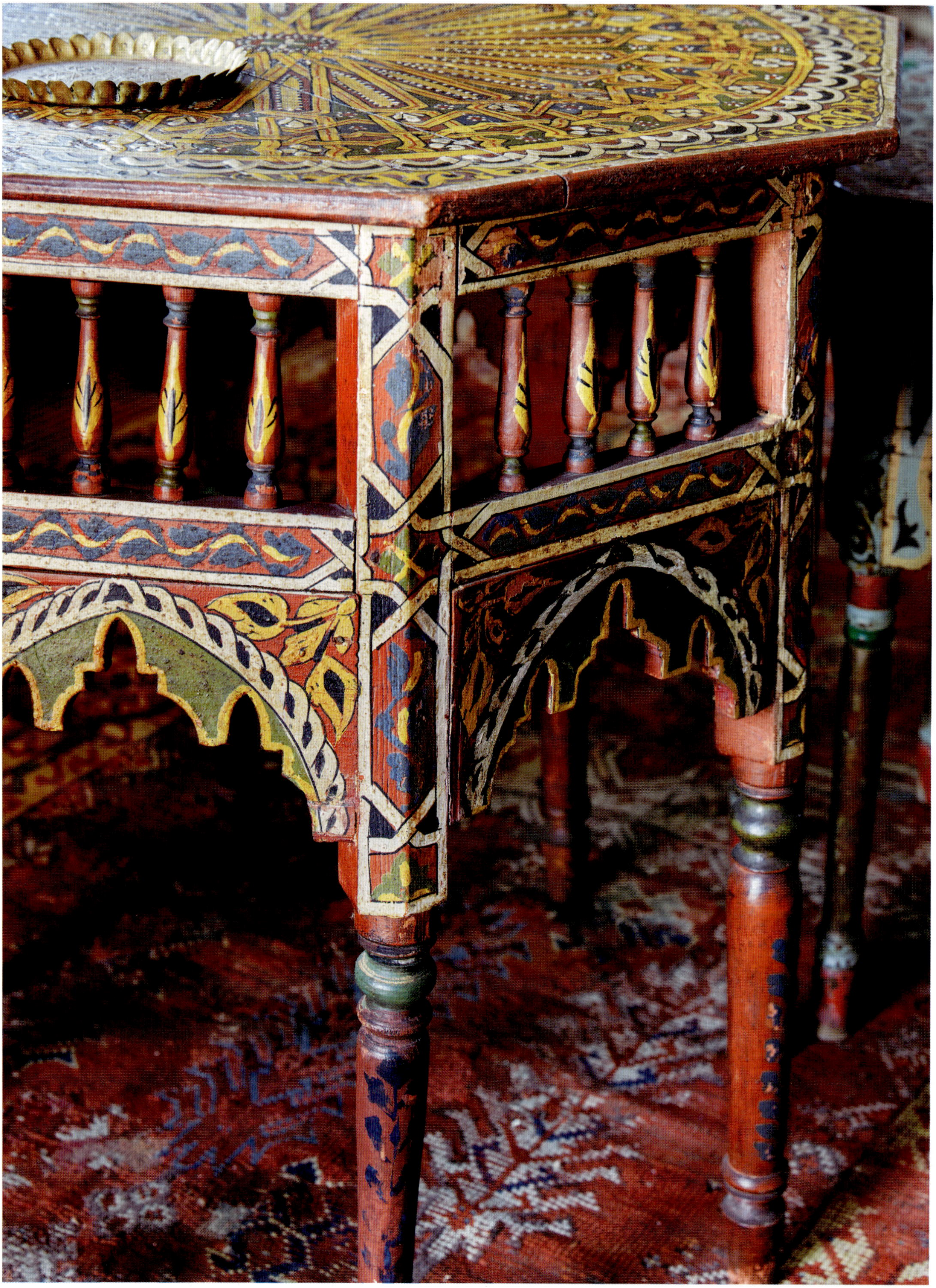

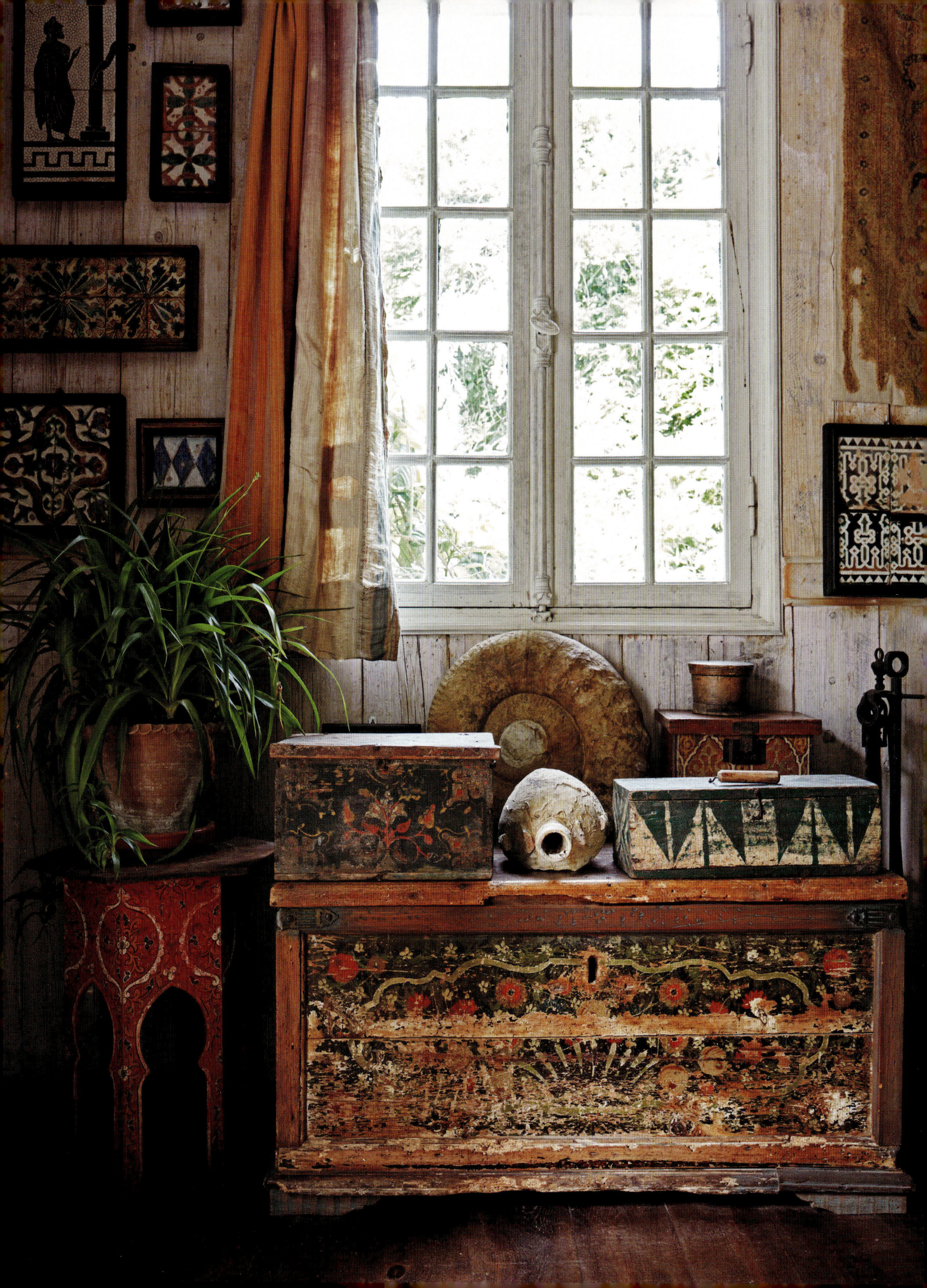

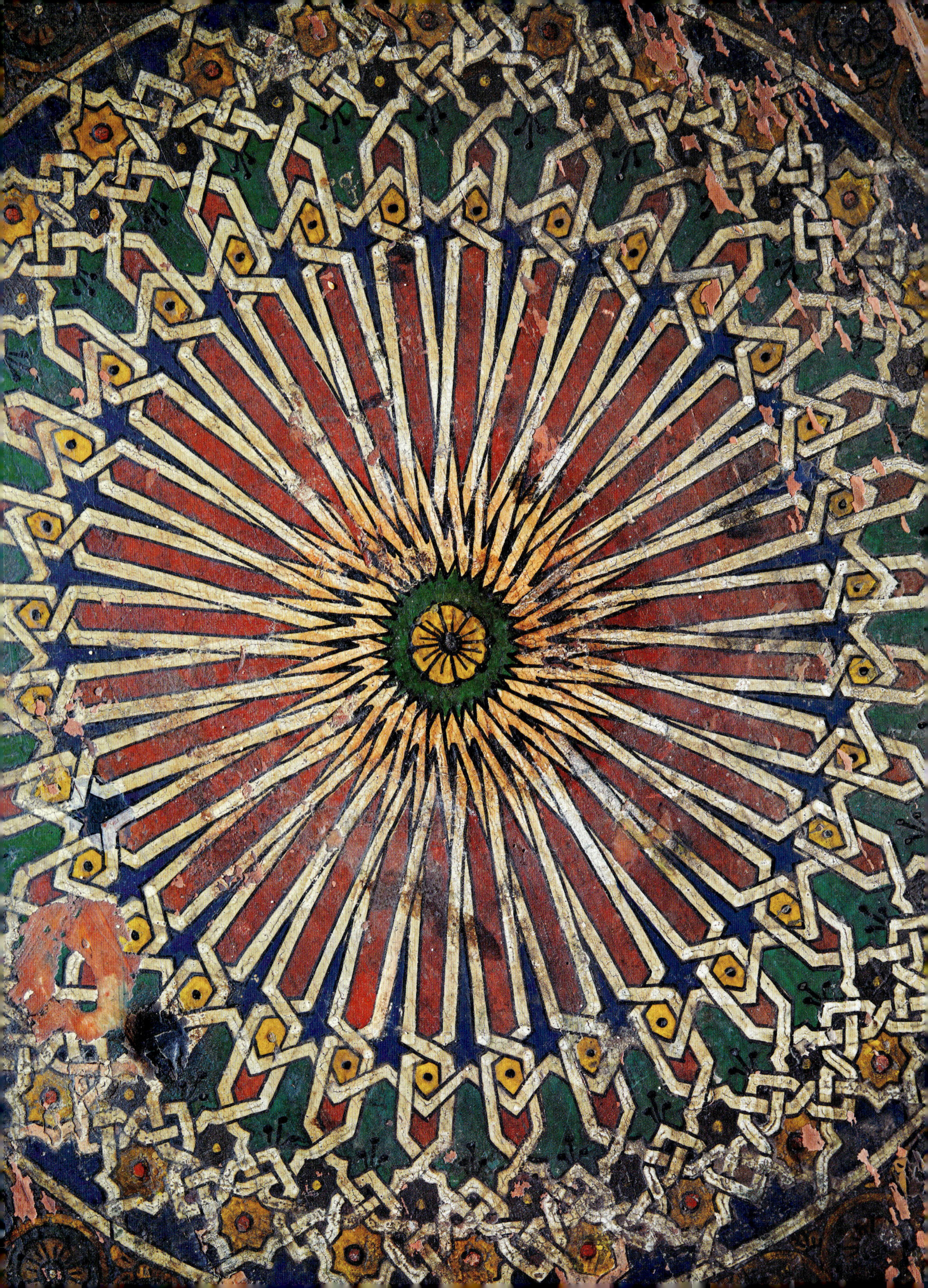

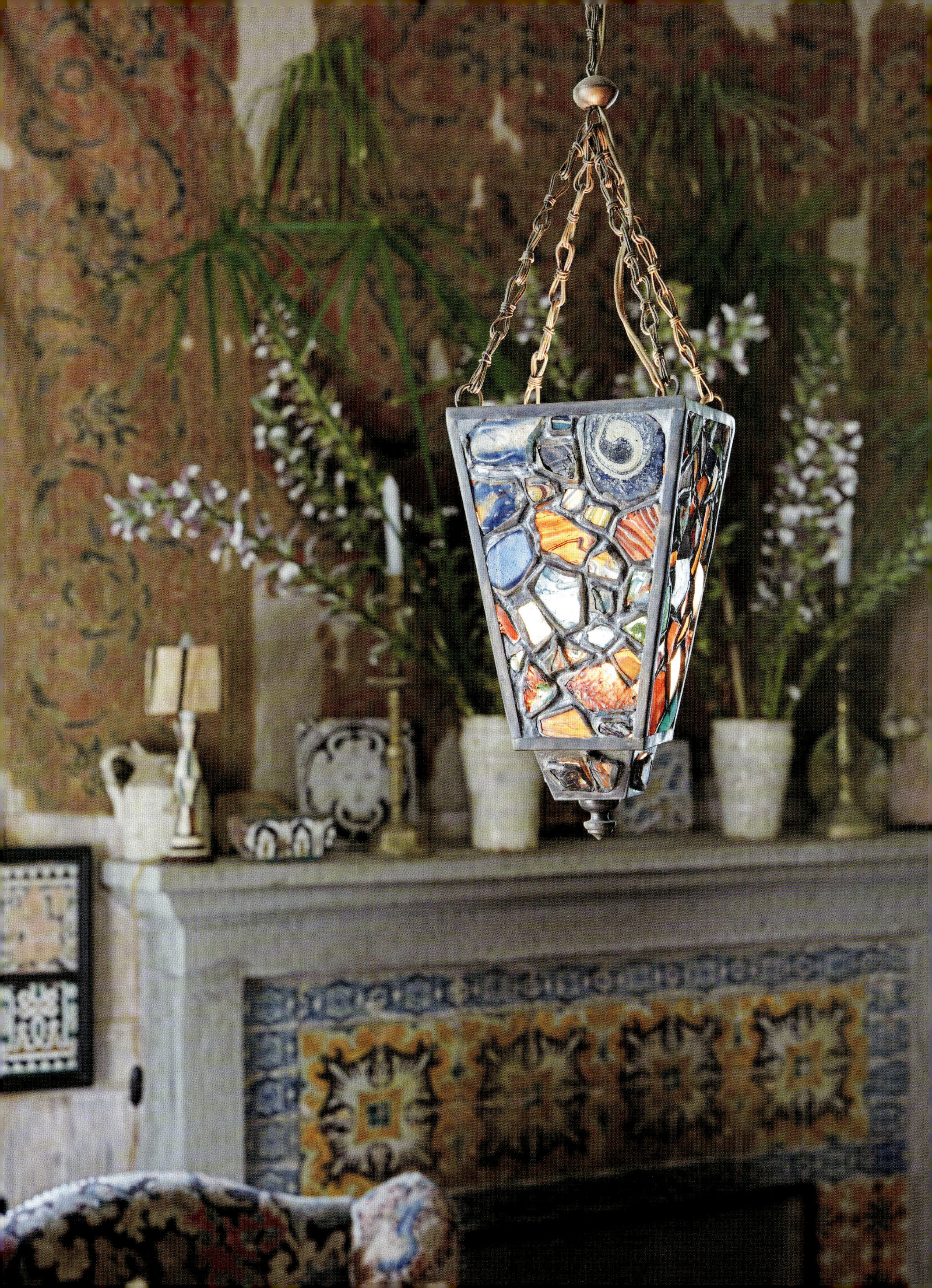

PAGE 106: *A nineteenth-century* taifur *made in Fez; I discovered it in Paris.*
PAGE 107: *Made in city ateliers or by simple country artisans, these "jewelry boxes" contained the most precious possessions: gold and silver jewelry, amber and coral, but also marriage certificates or the deeds to houses and gardens, coins, keys, talismans, and perhaps the black-and-white photo of the son who emigrated or died in the war. Some larger boxes held tea glasses, the fragile pride of every Moroccan house. Others, the keys to which had been lost, were gifted to a religious institution; by making a slot in them they were transformed into offering boxes placed above the altar of a chapel dedicated to a saint. They evoke a private, secret world, and that's why they make me dream. Part of their big family sits happily on an Algerian chest that I found in Tétouan, where lots of Algerians took refuge after the French invasion in 1830. The ammonite fossil looks on impassively.*
PREVIOUS SPREAD, LEFT: *Moroccan decorative arts have two trends: one geometric, the other floral.*
PREVIOUS SPREAD, RIGHT: *The little lantern made with dozens of fragments of old Roman glasses. It took a highly expert metalworker nearly two months to make this. Now, every time I go into his shop with a new idea, he yells at me to go away because he is busy.*
OPPOSITE: *A late example of the Moroccan floral tradition, in which the motifs of European origin are not assimilated, but merely reproduced in a mechanical way.*
FOLLOWING SPREAD, LEFT: *An earlier floral example, on a beautiful window screen from Fez. The disheveled little sunflowers, the rosebuds whose forebears adorned Iznik tiles, even the mysterious inflorescences in the shape of Persian* boteh, *are all* fleurs savants. *They share the self-assurance of those who have seen it all, and their scent comes to us even more powerfully because it is blended with the afflatus of history.*
FOLLOWING SPREAD, RIGHT: *The lantern hangs from a star that was in a mosque in Tétouan. The eighteenth-century Rabat carpet, one of the earliest I have ever seen, was found in California by my friend Giacomo Manoukian, one of the finest connoisseurs of carpets I have ever met. We spend exciting evenings wondering whether the woven flowers on a Ladik prayer mat are tulips or opium poppies, and speculating as to how the knotter in the "lane"—where the many yellow dyes were obtained from pomegranate peel—managed to get over such an overdose of the fruit.*

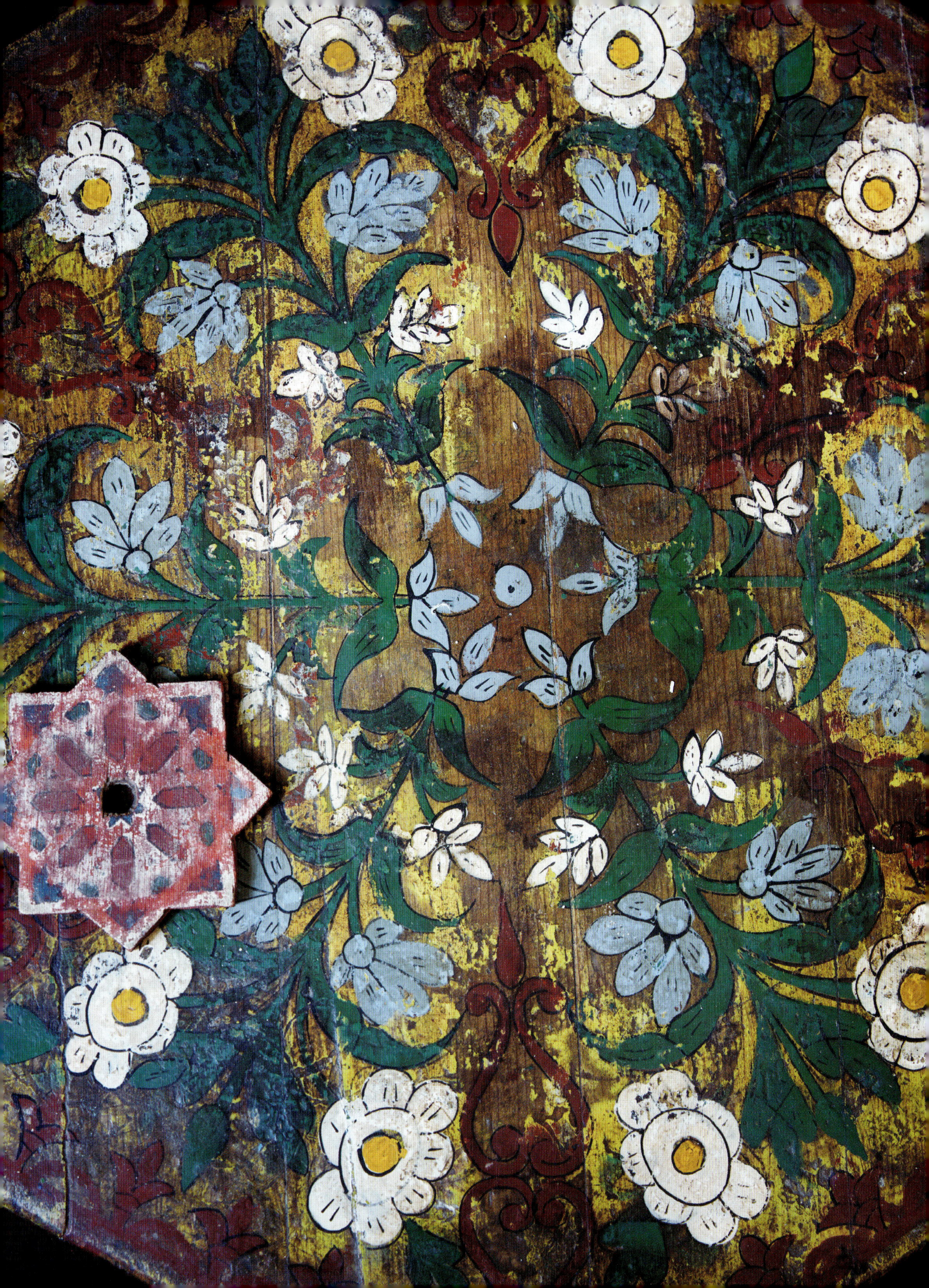

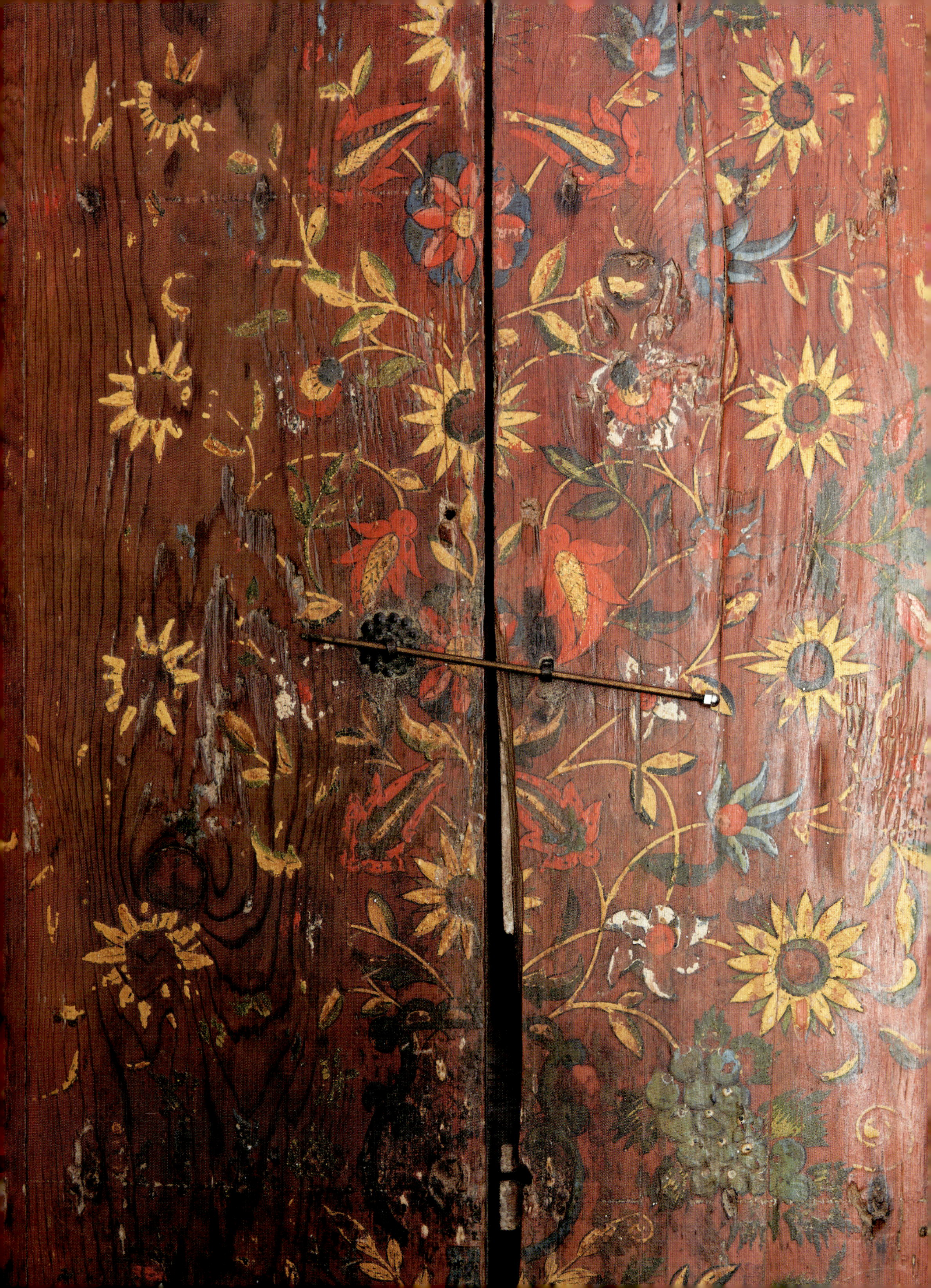

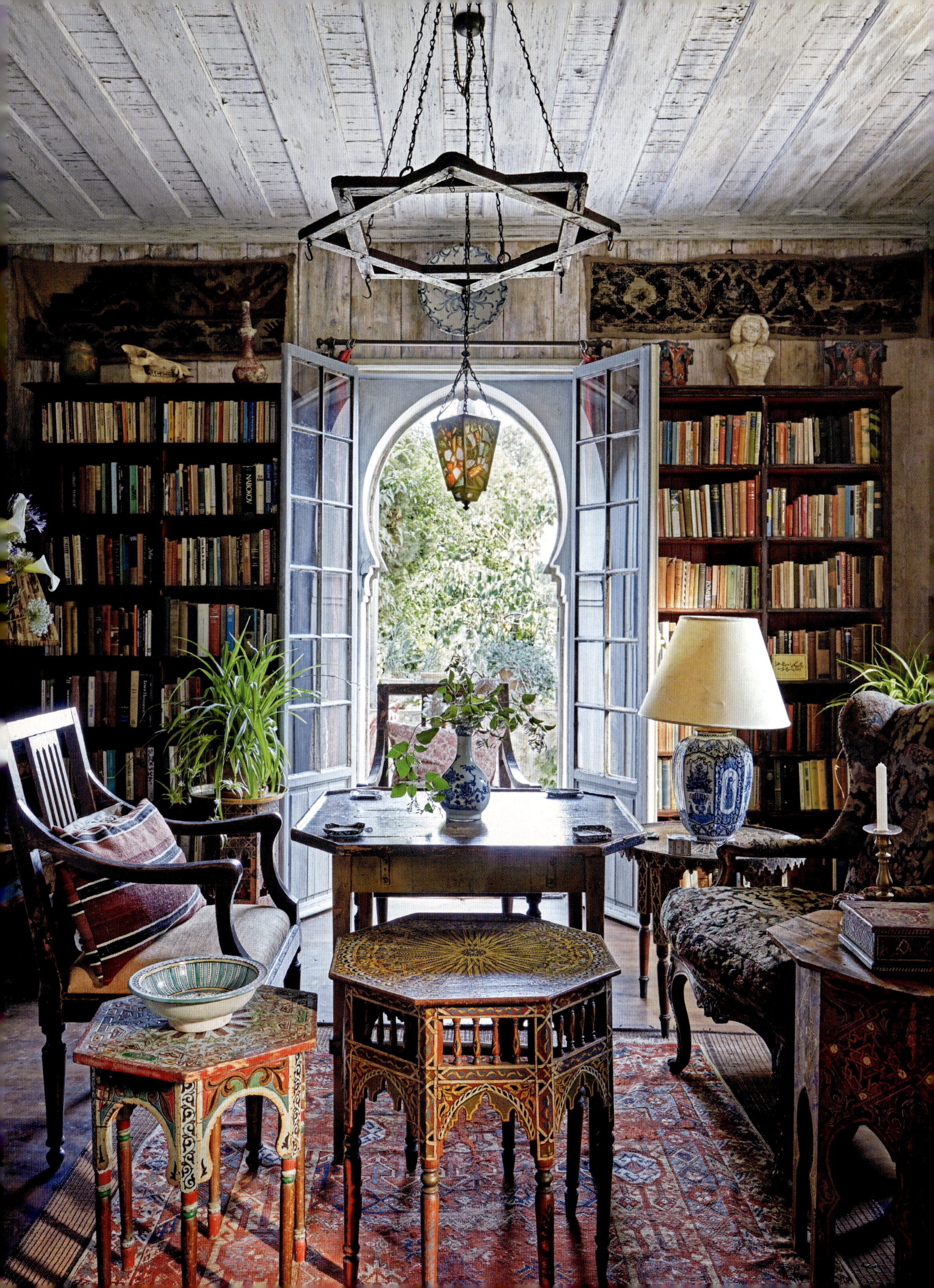
NABOKOV

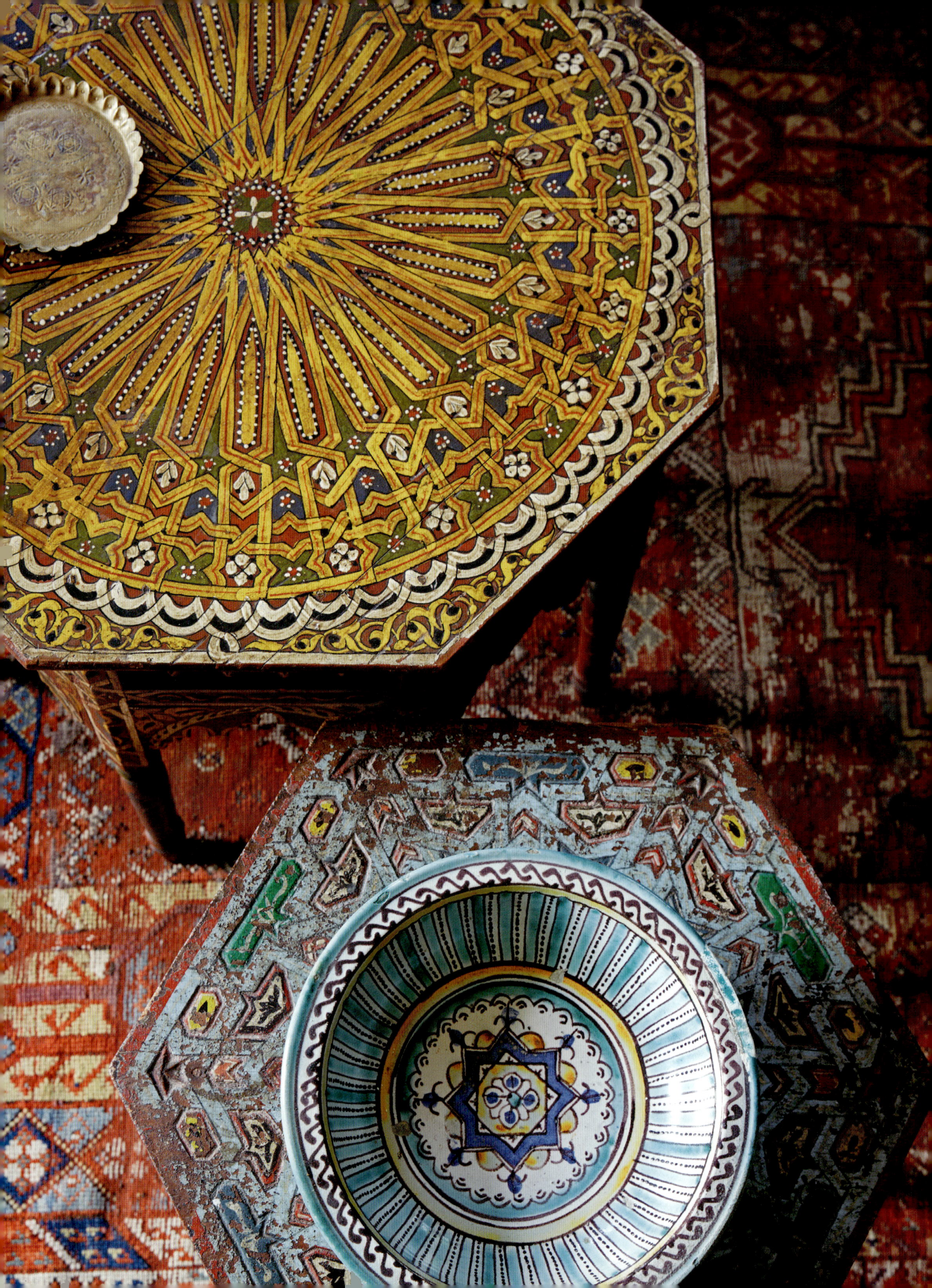

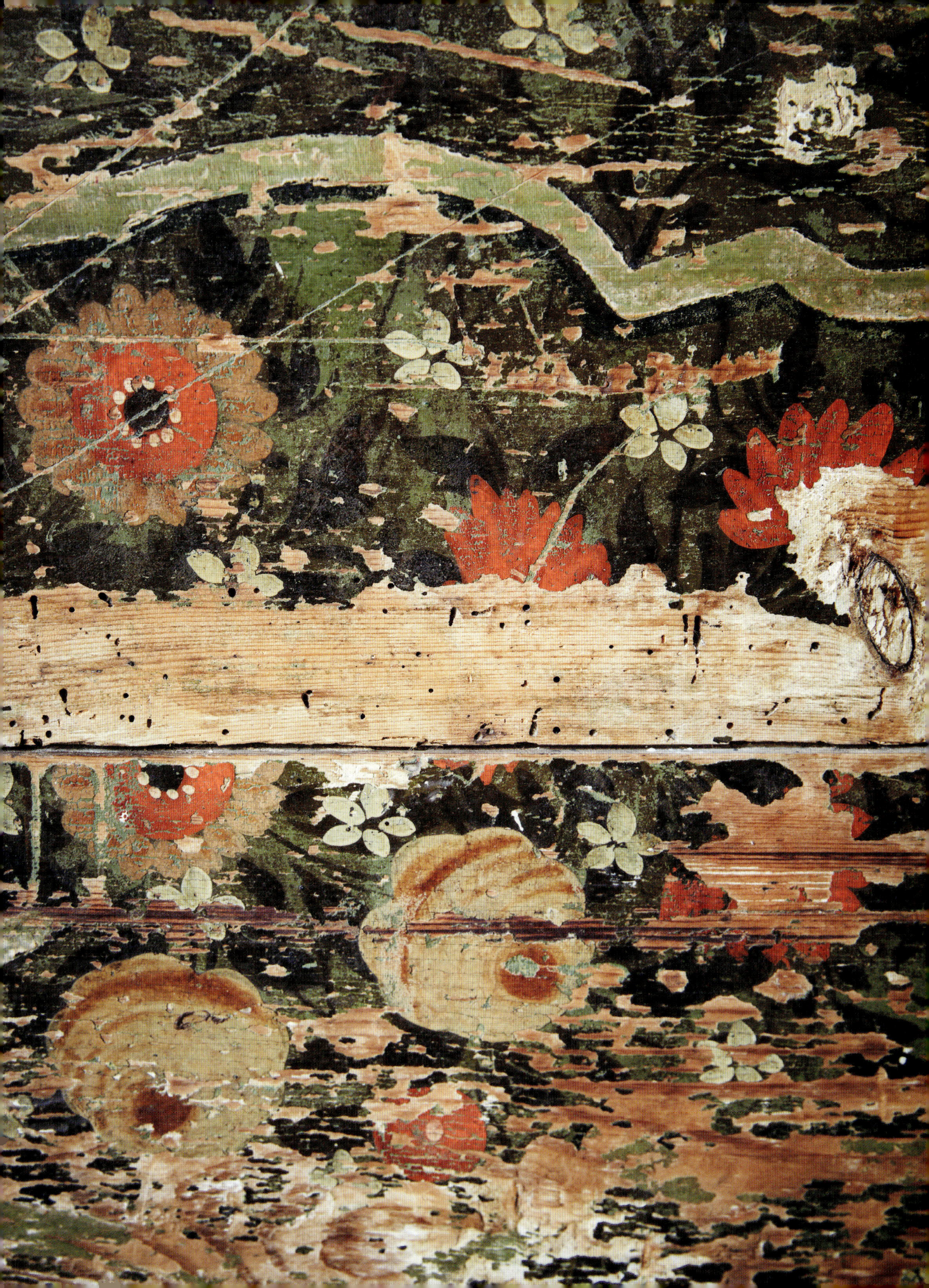

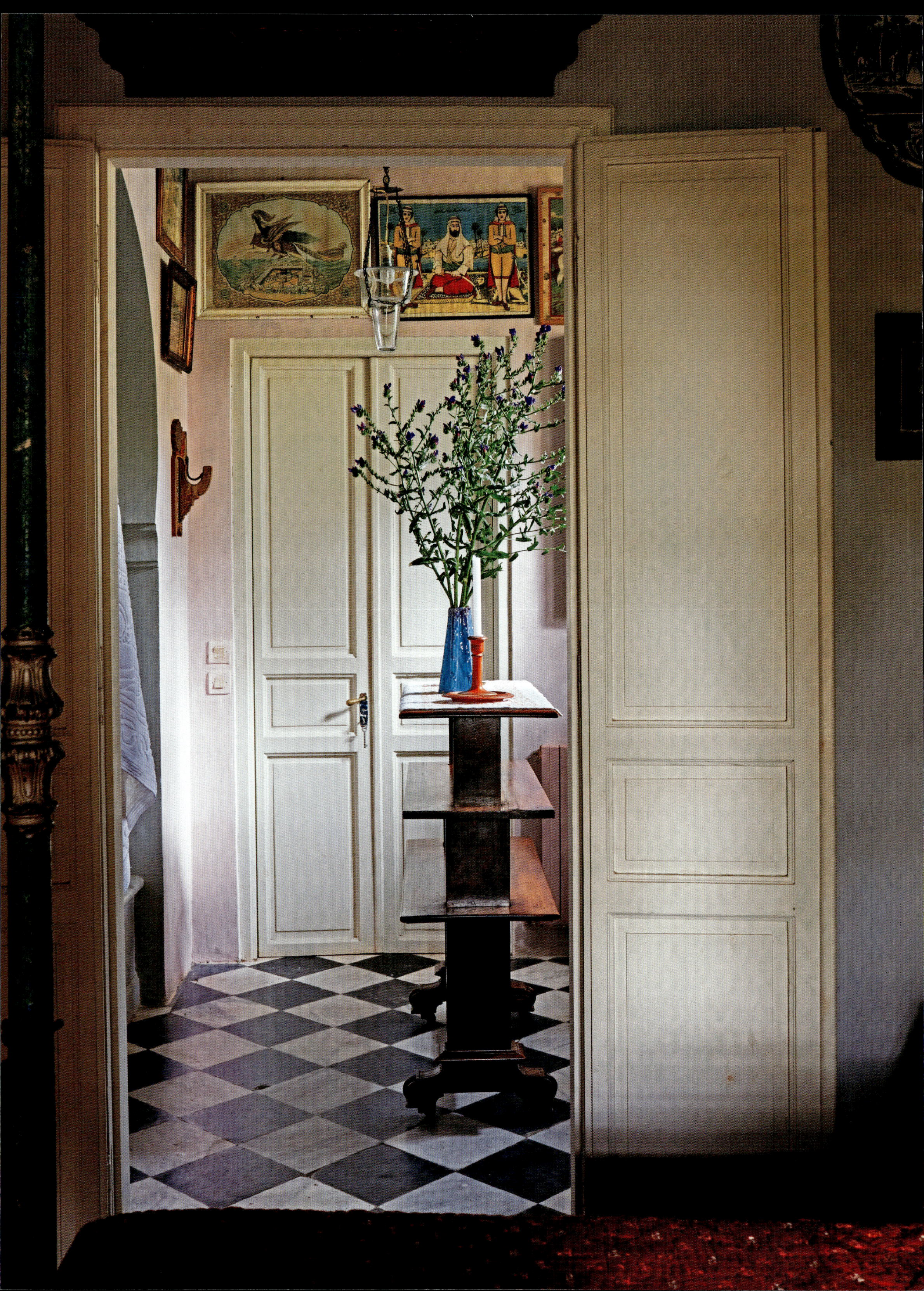

PREVIOUS SPREAD: *Trends, again: geometric (North African/Spanish origin) and floral (Hellenistic/Ottoman origin).*

FOLLOWING SPREAD: *This iron bed in the guest bedroom is the Andalusian copy of a prototype made in Manchester for export. Most of the beds in Northern Moroccan homes share this origin, and they have spread to even the remotest Jbala villages. My friend Gordon Watson gave me this gorgeous Safavid carpet fragment in exchange for my sorting out his garden. I'm sure he still regrets it. It's surrounded by paintings and drawings by the Scottish-Tangerine artist James McBey.*

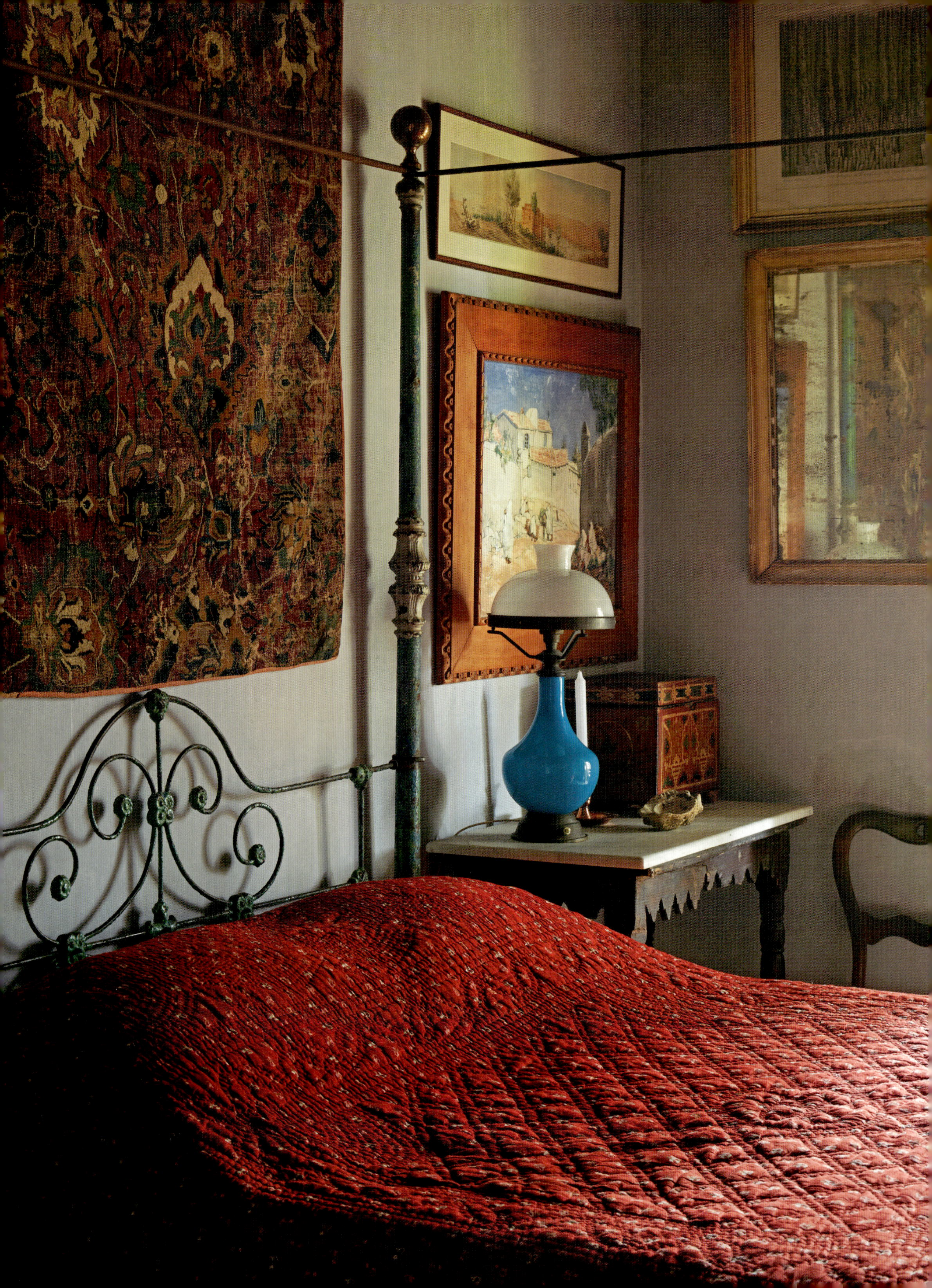

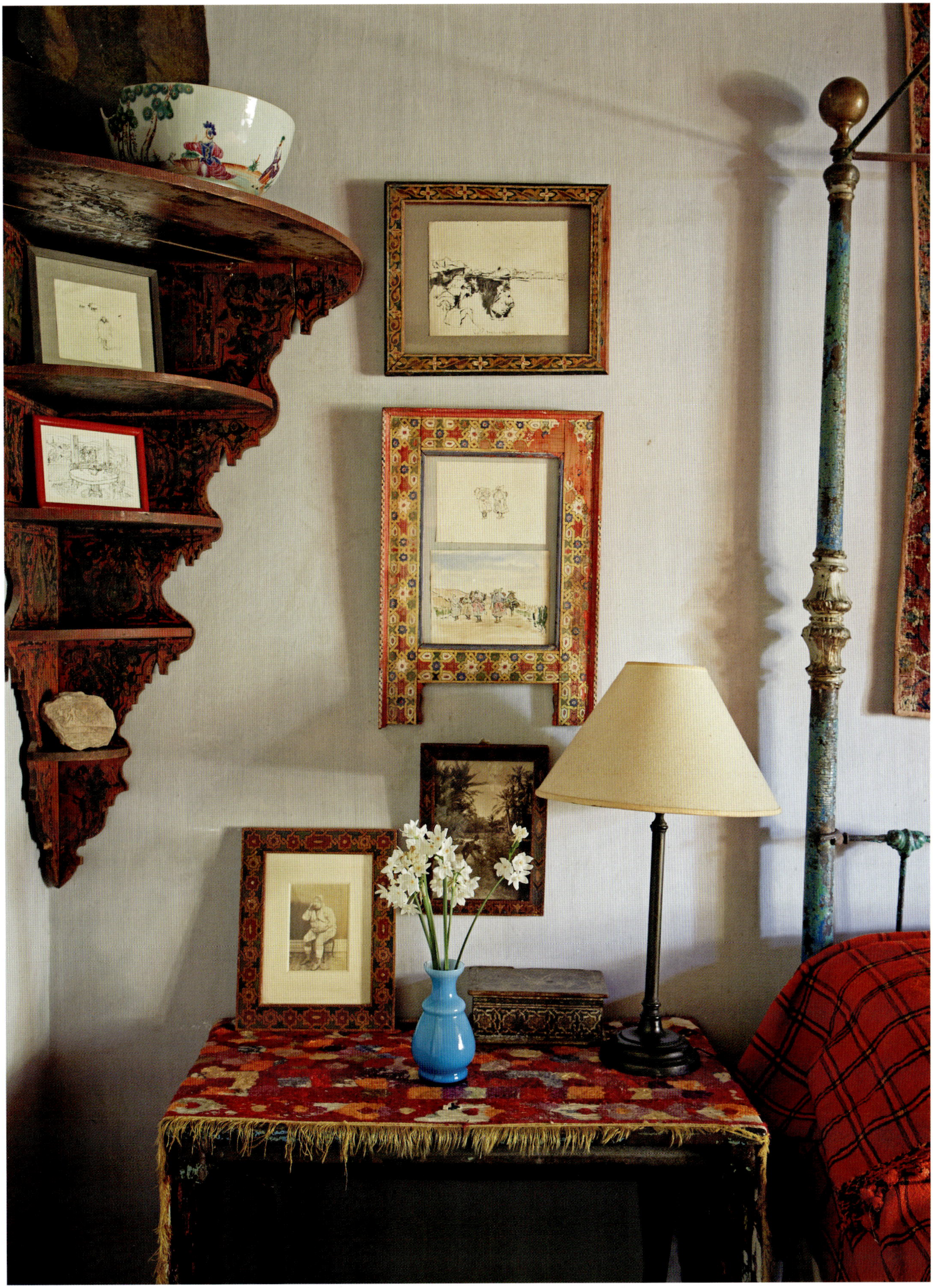

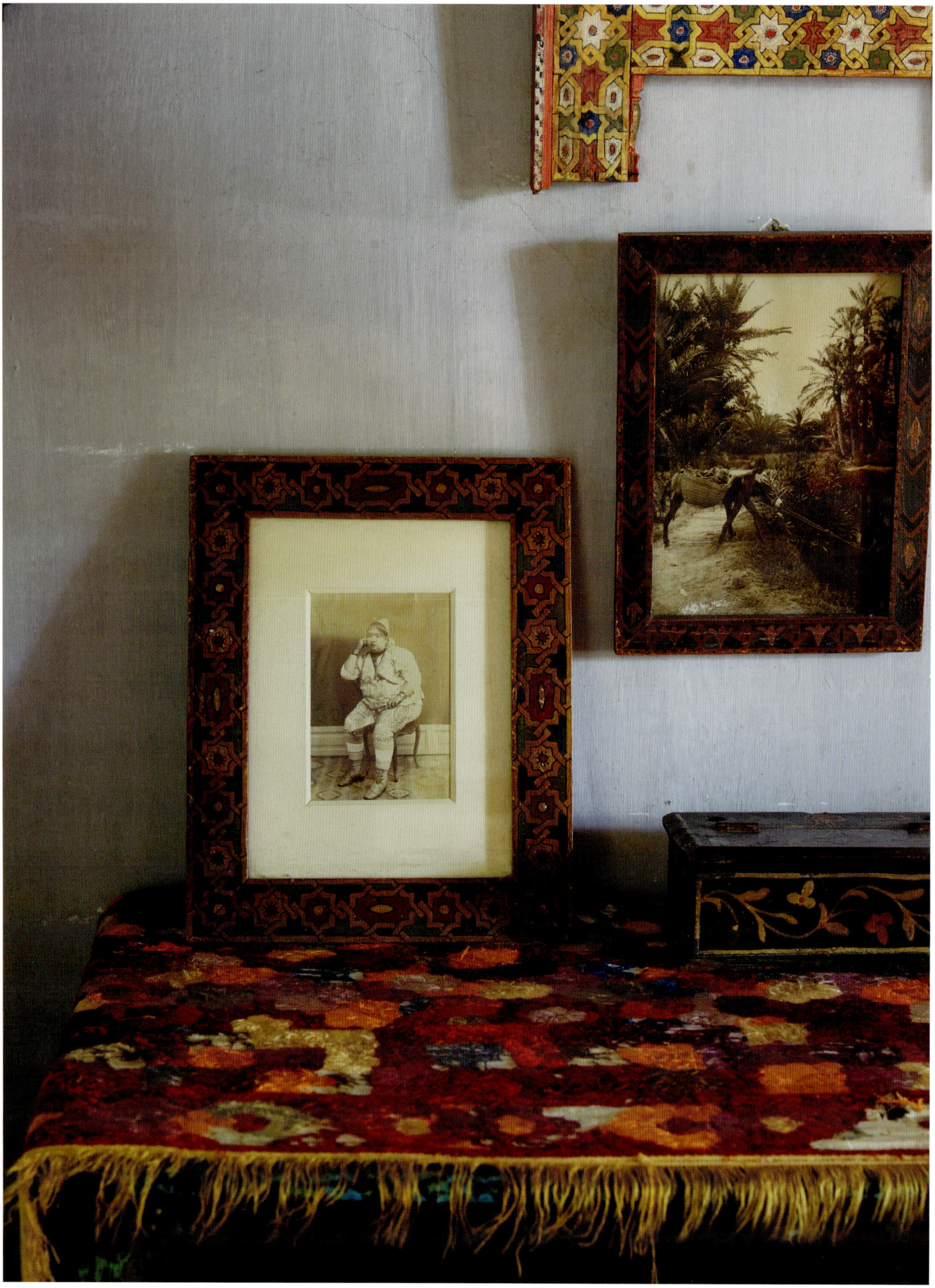

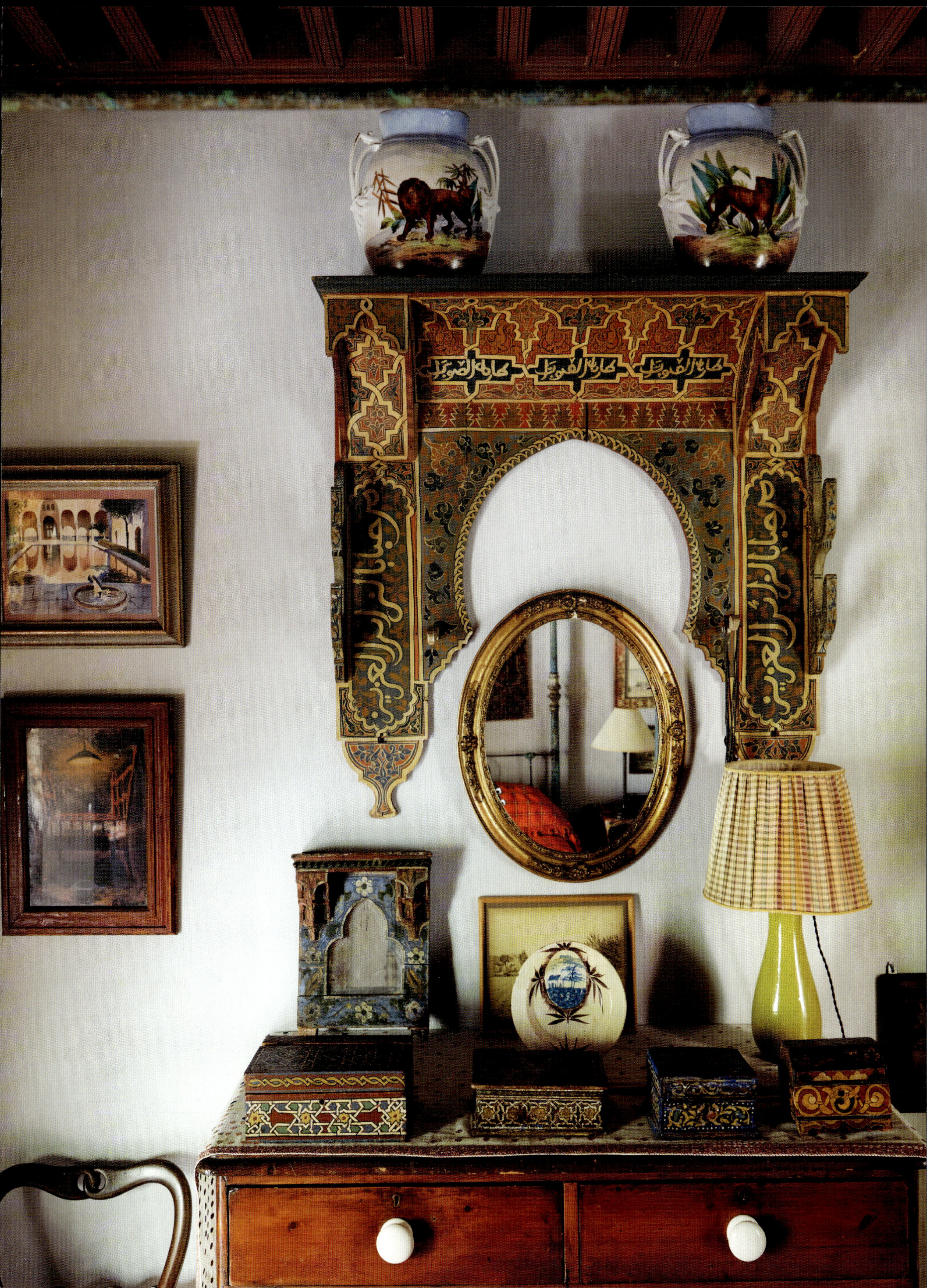

PREVIOUS SPREAD, LEFT: *I collect old photographs of Moroccan subjects.*
PREVIOUS SPREAD, RIGHT: *Above the Victorian chest of drawers found in Tangier, where the British brought their furniture from home, the gun holder comes from the house of Michael and Cherry Scott, which now belongs to the emir of Qatar. The two vases with the lions are French and were made for the North African market.*
OPPOSITE: *A nineteenth-century embroidered curtain from Rabat opens at the wooden bow window I copied from old houses in Fez and Cairo. How many times I rang the bell of those apartments and asked the stupefied tenants if I could take some measurements!*
FOLLOWING SPREAD: *The floor is made with sixteenth- to nineteenth- century tiles from Fez, Qallaline, and Seville. I had the idea of making the curtains out of my collection of* yasma, *the handprinted handkerchiefs favored by the women of rural Anatolia. I painstakingly put them together for many years but, alas, within a few months they faded under the Moroccan sun.*

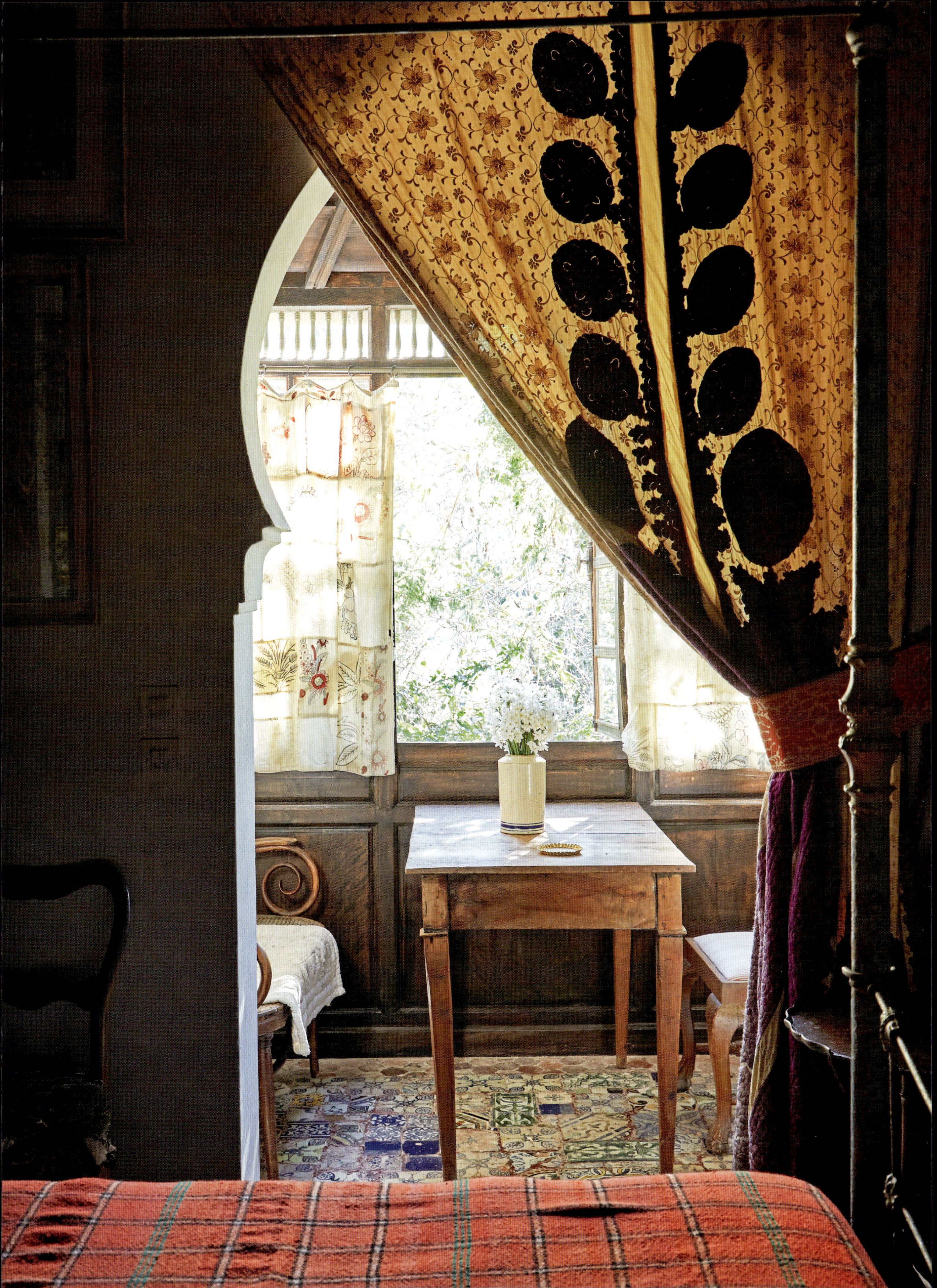

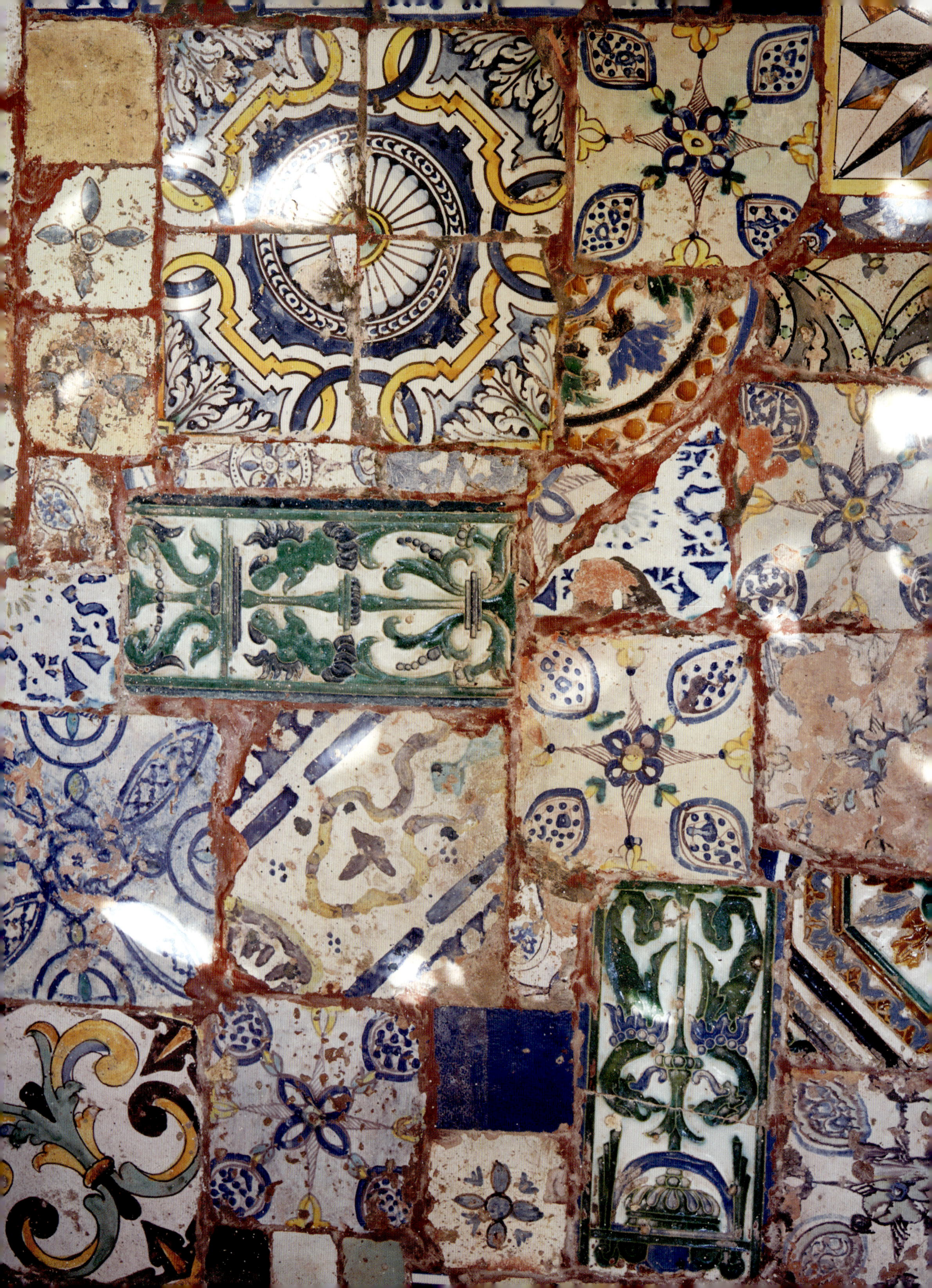

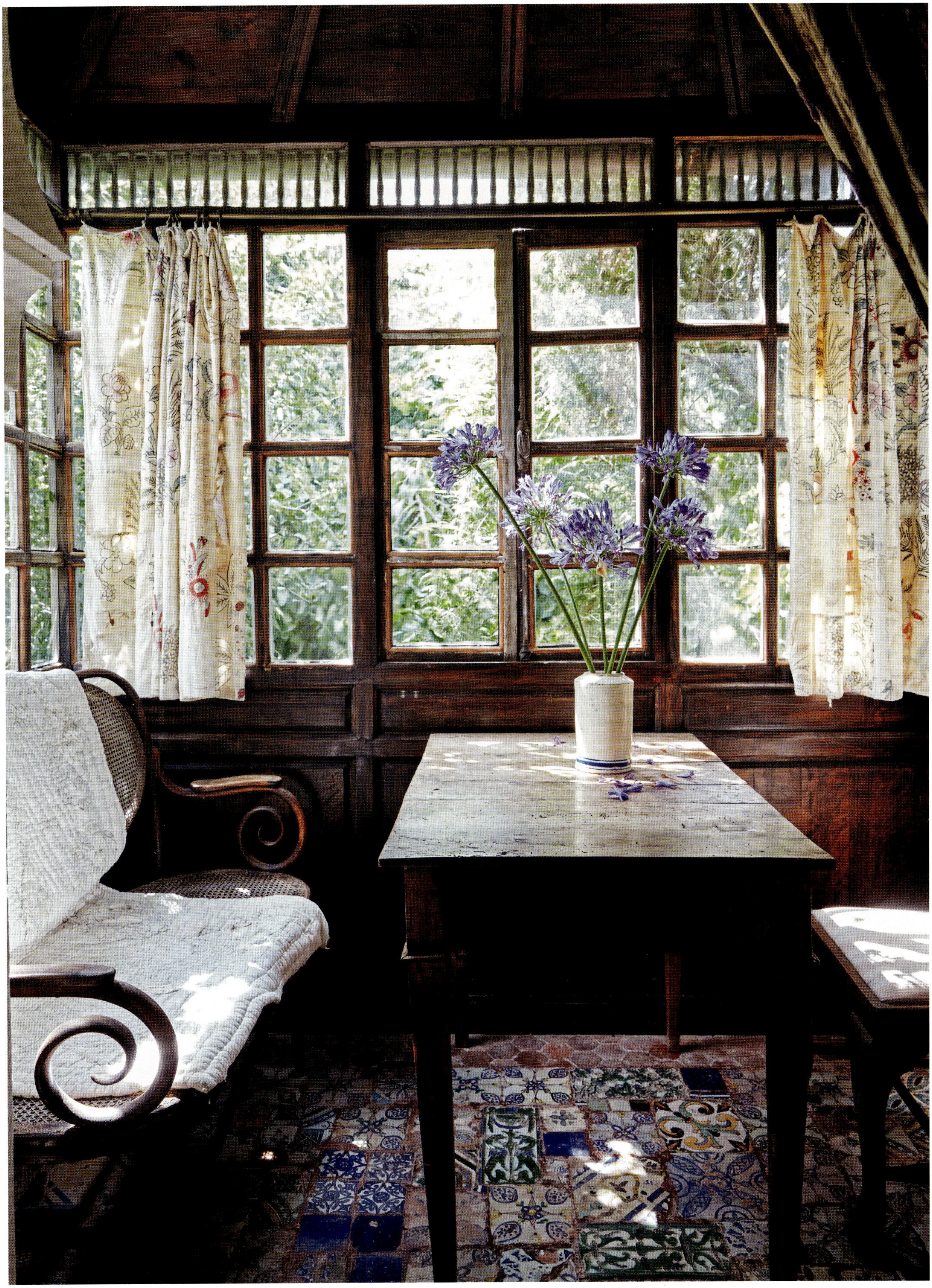

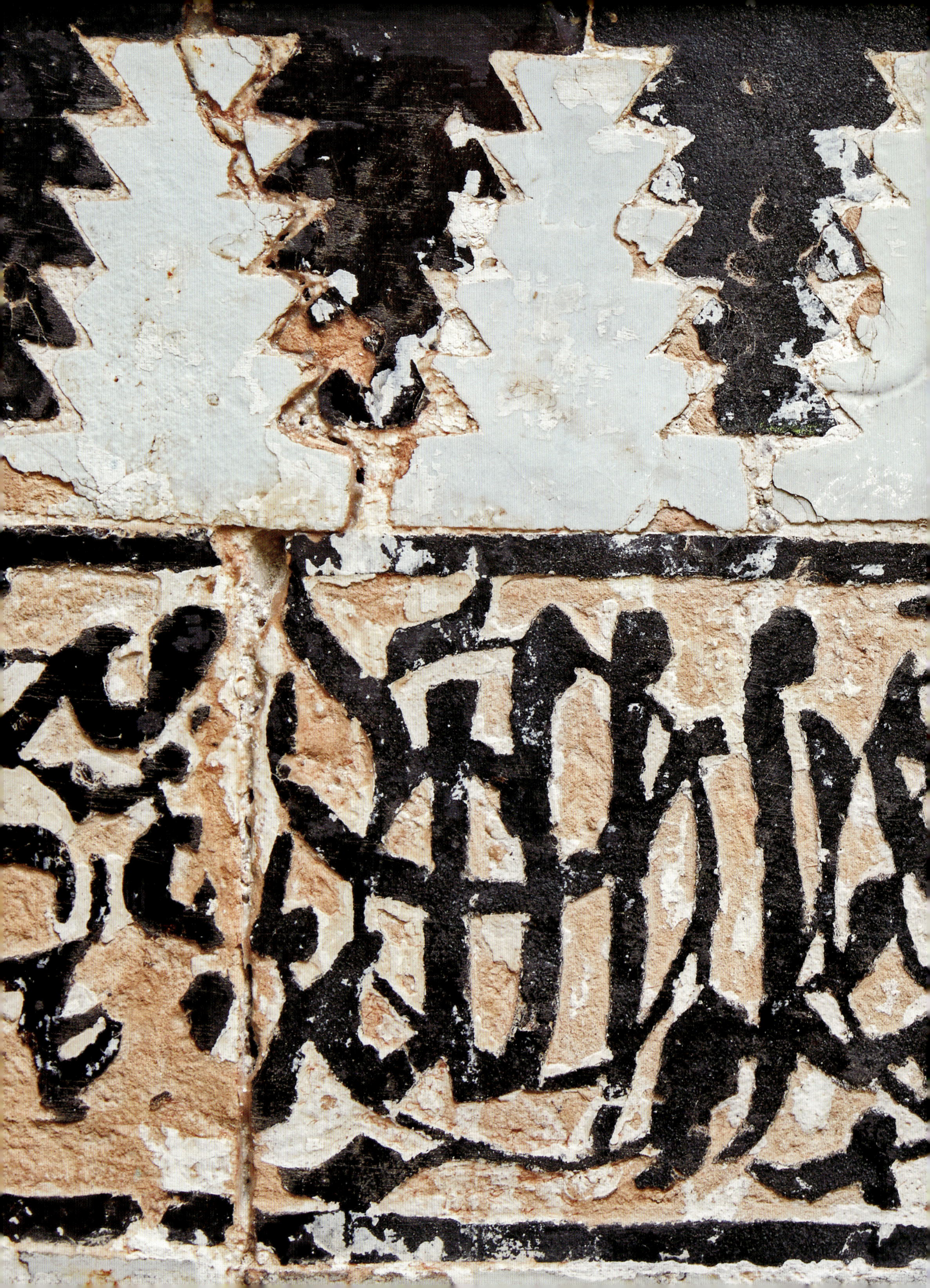

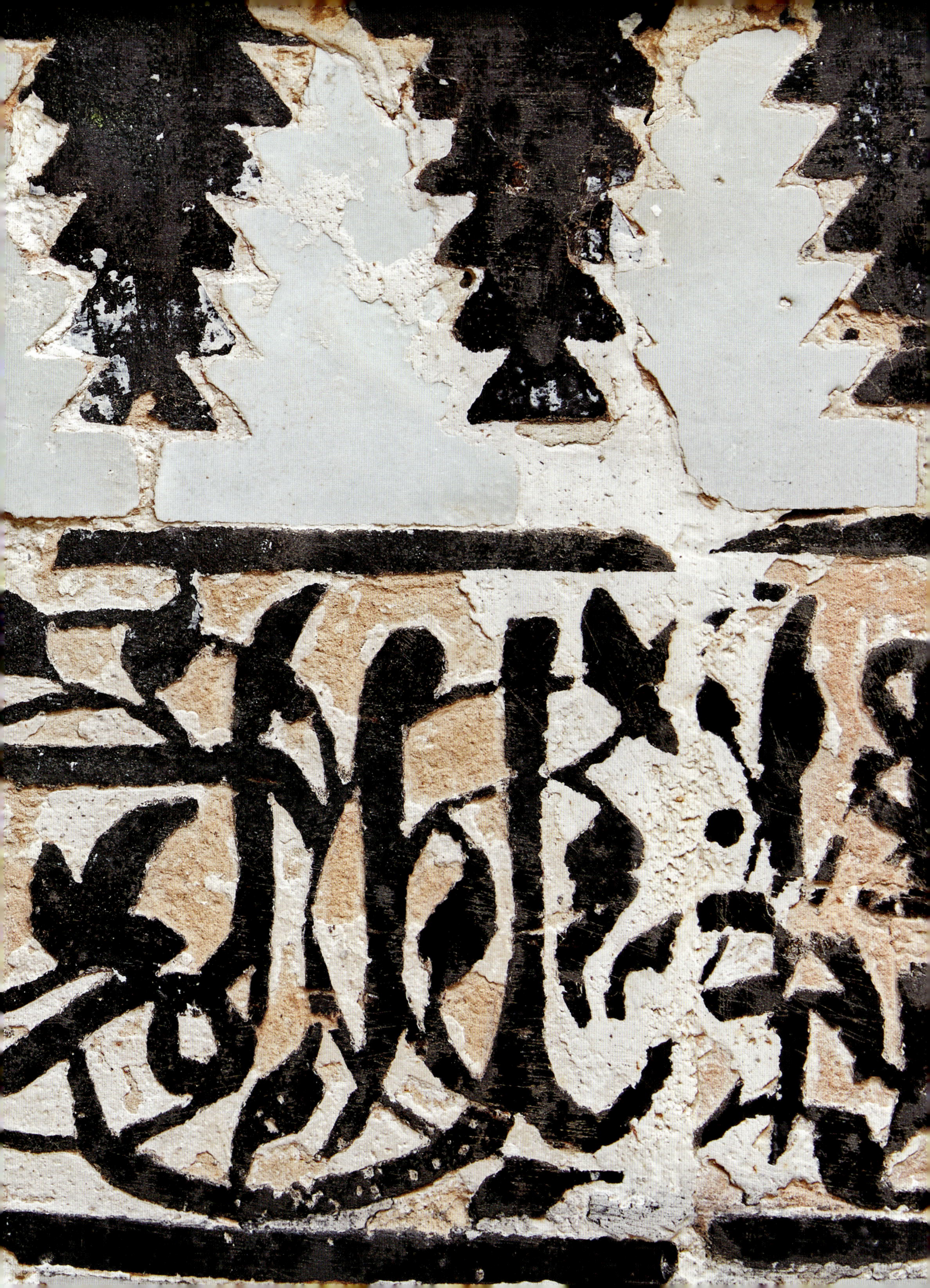

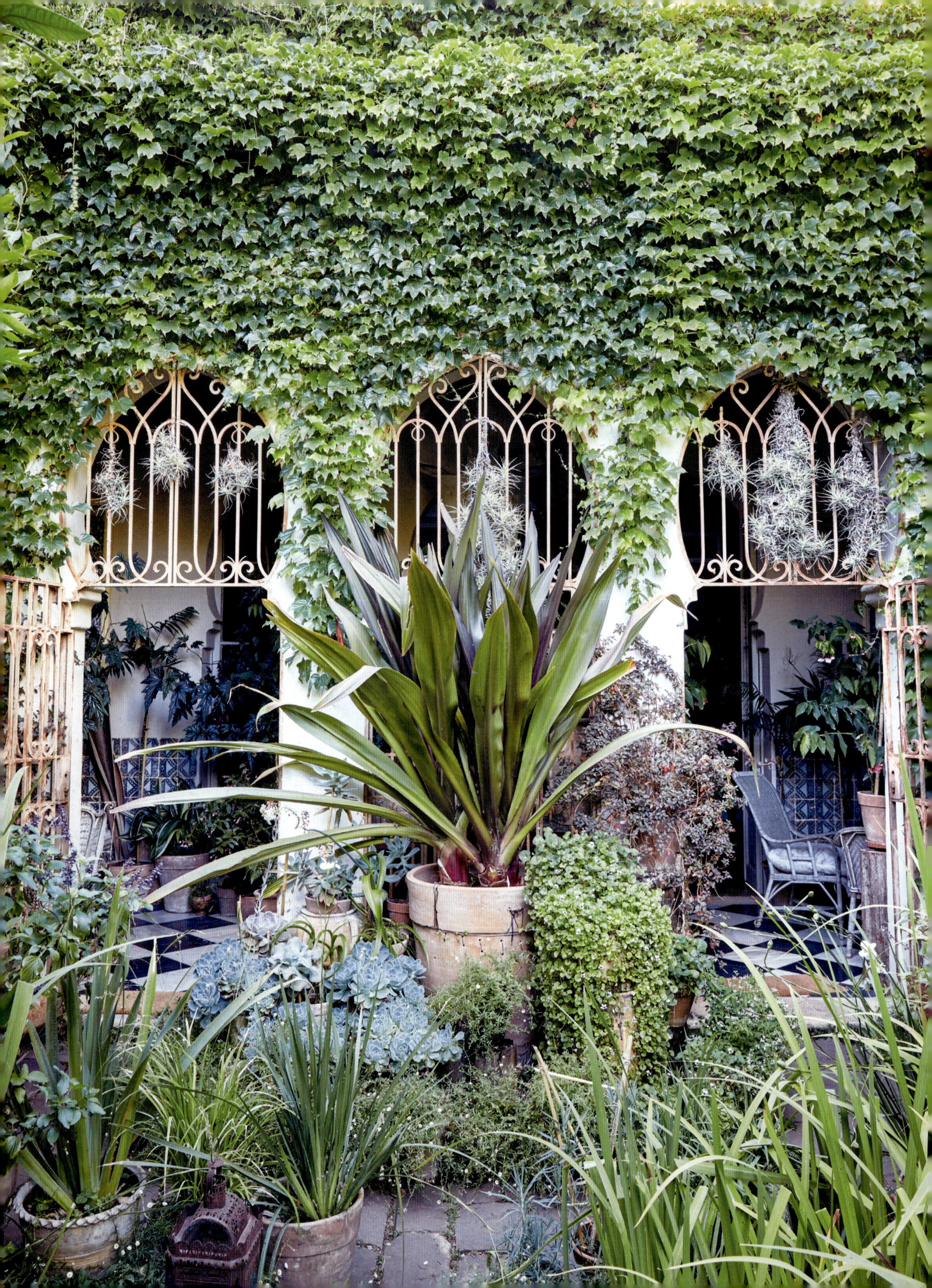

THE LOWER PAVILION

Twenty years ago, I thought building a house was immoral, especially if my furniture and belongings already had a roof over their heads. Thirty years ago, I would have found it useless: I preferred to surround myself with unusually shaped roots, colored berries, stones, and lichens, and sleep in the woods. Yet for Roberto, our architect friend, it only took a few months to convince me that in Tebarek Allah it would not only have been beautiful, comfortable, and pleasant to have a third pavilion, but that it was really necessary. He seduced me with a story: once upon a time there was the special pavilion, the one for housing my collections and chatting with friends, an airy living room from which you went up through the mystery of the garden to the candlelit dining room.

"Large wide-open windows with fluttering curtains … Your objects finally at peace … Deep sofas for conversation and siestas … Everything looking rather temporary, flowers everywhere, the light pouring down from a skylight …"

With his persuasive manner of speech, in which the vowels lengthen to melt French *r*'s so syrupy as to make me feel like a bee on the edge of a corolla, he conjured up an old house like the ones we were familiar with in Tangier, where the fragile elegance of colonial customs was diluted and coarsened in a life that was still rustic. By now, even the beaches were no longer wild: "A melancholy, shady swimming pool, similar to a reservoir for irrigating the fields, will wash away your tears." Stephan cleared his throat and began drumming on the armrest. Neither he nor I fully shared Roberto's vision, yet we agreed to it. Not that Tangier induces nostalgia, for time stands still here. The parade of mules on the boulevard, the noisy haunt of Phoenician merchants, the lion hunt of English soldiers with their golden helmets, all take place at the same time, namely now. Hooked noses, curved eyelashes, the smell of dung and charcoal smoke—this is what our Tangier is like, with two lubricious seas that sneak up on it like the old men who spied on Susanna while she was bathing. It often makes my head spin: when looking at the facade of a building I imagine the bedroom beyond the balcony, and instantly there appears before me a Greek currency trader running a comb through his pomaded hair, a new Andalusian mother lying on the bed with her crying baby, a Berber parking attendant placing two canvas bags full of magic dust on his wife's glaucoma-blanched eyes, and I feel dizzy. But the passersby, even if disguised, for who knows what reason, with tracksuits and sweaters and sunglasses branded Chanel and Armani, can't conceal what they really are: Vandals and Phoenicians, Romans and Jbala mountain dwellers—and that blonde girl in a miniskirt tottering along on platform heels is none other than a Visigothic vestal torn from the altar of some chthonic cult. The illusion of the so-called present—the custom of tapping on the keys of a gadget called a mobile phone and using the same gadget to produce instant portraits of oneself, driving noisy chariots, agreeing to live in concrete boxes with eyes glued to smaller boxes peopled by moving shadows—has never fooled any true Tangerine. But since, in the long run, the childish tricks with which the present tries to attract our attention—jostling, shoving, emitting its noises and its stinks—

can become frankly unbearable, I have succumbed to the temptation to enlarge our private world, to seal it off by barring the door to that pimply teenager obsessed with roundabouts. Furthermore, I had accumulated crate upon crate of tiles, and dozens of headstones, pots, jars, fountains, mortars of all shapes and sizes, stone tubs, pieces of columns, painted beams and ceilings: it was time to put an end to the diaspora of all those objects, to free them from the rented storehouses where I kept them and give us the pleasure of their company, and them ours.

    Like all talents, Roberto's feeds on precision. Realizing the things one has imagined requires accuracy. And you also need to be agile, because the dream changes as it becomes true. He is honest, on the skinny side but a good swimmer, and he makes his way splendidly up the rushing river, stubborn as a salmon. During the first phase, the search for architectural sources from which to draw outlines and sketches, we met up almost every evening. Endless discussions, first between all three of us, then him and me. Stephan was the first to give in and go off to bed. The plan, with the central sitting room and the two rooms on either side, had struck him as too symmetrical: "He may well be a philosopher, but as an architect …" I really liked the three large arches that opened onto the loggia, and I was thrilled with the truckload of Sevillian concrete tiles we had salvaged following the demolition of some houses in the Tangier of yesteryear. But I would have liked some differences in levels, worn internal steps cluttered with shoes and slippers, closets for storing mats and watermelons and the canaries' cage at night, and windows giving onto corridors with bunches of garlic and bay leaves hanging over the aspidistra tubs and walking sticks with shiny pommels standing there as if catching their breath—in short, at least something in common with the beloved houses of Tangier where you take a siesta lulled by cicadas and the click of the sewing machine. But Roberto always got the better of me. The honey of his rolled *r*'s was a trap, a spider's web: with my wings stuck to it, the most I could do was waggle my legs.

    Finally, the workers arrived on the site, a stony cliff over which for years the inhabitants of the neighborhood had been throwing junk too bulky for the bins in the square, but while the work was in progress my life was shaken up and blessed by the encounter with Rohuna. The sprites of a valley overlooking the Atlantic Ocean had ordered me to plant a garden in a background worthy of Piero della Francesca's most beautiful painting. By then I was spending very little time in Tangier, absorbed in a task that our architect friend, who does not like the countryside and deep down was jealous, called "a folly à la Fitzcarraldo." But his *r*'s, no matter how ravishing, entrapped me no longer. I had flown away, destination heaven. Since I was a child I have been a builder of huts, even in my bed, with pillows as walls and a central pile of books supporting the dome of sheets. The house at Rohuna, isolated, with no trace of human presence as far as the horizon, was the ideal hut. What was I going to do with a new pavilion in the city? But over the years a part of me had grown fragile, a creature of habit, fond of the neighborhood, and that part of me still loved Tangier and its suspended time, I can't deny it … Every now and then I would leave Rohuna and come to see how things were progressing. Sometimes I would eat with the workers. All country boys, they looked a lot like my friends over there. I remember one, in his underwear, washing himself while standing on a piece of cardboard. For face, hair, ears, neck, armpits, feet, chest, belly, and legs, he managed to make do with the water contained in a bottle of "Hawaii," a fruit juice popular at that time. He got dressed and joined us in a flash, as fresh and smiling as a young patrician leaving the thermae. I thought of the countrywomen in the village who could prepare a princely lunch for the whole family with two potatoes, two tomatoes, and two eggs, and if I passed by they would insist

I join them. Knowing how to make do with little is a form of trust in destiny. The elegance I admire is only good humor.

As his right-hand man Roberto had chosen Zerrya, a beast of a bricklayer reeking of Spanish brandy who could create frames and moldings with any small rocks that came to hand: his creations were alive and sinewy, not inert and "rubbery" like plaster moldings. They made an odd couple, our slim architect in his striped cotton jackets, with his refined speech, and the big man in his undershirt three times bigger than him, with tufts of hair on his shoulders, whose talk was composed mostly of curses, but they had a wonderful understanding. For my part, I had brought in the Boutiza brothers, two boys from Fez with doe eyes like those of the Al Fayyum portraits who worked on the *zelliges*, the ceramic mosaics that have adorned local buildings since the Middle Ages. It was they who put up the old tiles in the loggia. The youngest always had a flower behind his ear, sometimes a carnation, sometimes a sprig of jasmine. We spent our days trying out the tiles, making up designs on the floor that were always new; we were fascinated by the possibilities offered by those polygons and those tangles of branches, and we usually agreed on the solution. It was so much fun that I persuaded them to stop sleeping in town, where they would have to waste money on a boardinghouse. During our dinners for three they told me about their life in Fez, the difficulties that had arisen when their father died, and how hard it had been to learn the trade. When they talked about their little sister, their faces lit up. Then they went to bed in a room in the new pavilion, where I had laid out mattresses and blankets. Thanks to the friends I was making, and the confusion of the construction site, I felt as good in Tebarek Allah as I did in Rohuna.

I am obsessed with colors, and I was afraid that when the time came to paint the walls I would make myself detested as the worst kind of pain in the ass: after seeing Roberto at work, I realized I was an easy-peasy sort of fellow. Impeccable in his usual jacket despite the ferocious heat, freshly creased trousers, loafers barely dusty, he stood in the center of the room waving his arms like a traffic cop at a difficult intersection. He was explaining to two boys in Bermuda shorts, who gazed at him in astonishment from the tops of their stepladders, what was wrong with the thirtieth sample of paint they had just finished producing. The pink had to be "lighter ... as if a moth blinded by the light, its wings loaded with color, had crashed into the freshly plastered walls ..." The paint had to be applied "irregularly, but not with mechanical fortuitousness ... silences are required ... a room cannot be petulant ..." The grim executors, accustomed to decorating the villas of drug traffickers with paint rollers, shook their heads as soon as he turned his back or made comments that fortunately he did not understand. But if by chance, by pure chance, the color sample ended up resembling what our friend had in mind, the handshakes, the smiles, and the compliments he bestowed turned them into two schoolkids who had just been awarded gold stars. They would get back to work. "Robi, Robi," they would bark loudly in imitation of me (in construction sites all over the world workers address Roberto with his proper title), "*te gusta daba*, do you like it now?" He, who had gone off for a huddle with his Zerrya, would come back, take off his glasses, give them a wipe, and put them back on: "No. I don't like it at all." And after a silence, while I seemed to see tears shining in those two pairs of eyes (or perhaps they were beads of sweat), Roberto, as abstruse and merciless as the penal code recited to two urchins caught stealing an apple from the tree, in a cascade of rolled *r*'s that were about to overwhelm the two stepladders and send them tumbling down to Gehenna: "*Per piacere, ragazzi*, you can't apply the paint here in this amateurish way, it loses innocence!" The poor souls nodded, accustomed to swallowing bitter pills, but immediately started all over again with threefold energy, secretly galvanized by the challenge of satisfying him. When, taking advantage of Roberto's momentary absence, I invited them to forgive that excess of perfectionism, they gave me a contemptuous look: there was nothing to forgive, if this was the way the Nasrani painted it was fine by them, and besides they were learning a new trade (in fact Khalid and Jawad are now among the decorators most sought after by foreigners who buy homes in Tangier). As the results gradually emerged, we understood that Roberto was right. His aristocratic idea of home rules out the automatisms of any abstracted norm. For him, between the mind that conceives a design and the hand that makes it there must be a direct connection, through which apprentices like them were able to build the Taj Mahal, the palazzi of Florence, and old farmhouses. It is one of the qualities I admire in him: he respects a good artisan more than a good architect.

When my father died, I inherited some furniture, and I also bought some at a couple of auctions. Moroccan law allows foreigners to move house only once, no second thoughts or supplements are allowed. So, regarding the shipment from our home in Milan I could not afford to forget anything: not, for example, the lacquered chinoiserie bench from Lucca that Stephan had given me for my birthday, nor the Anglo-Indian fish cutlery, nor the shards of obsidian collected on the slopes of Mexican volcanoes. And then there was the routine management required by any move: the books, prints, watercolors, fossils, flowerpots, closets, sleigh beds and four-posters, armchairs, screens, stools, the large sofa upholstered in kilim, bureaus, the stuffed platypus in its case; ditto for the Victorian iguanas, the two mirrors, a few boxes of shells, the fragments of Roman frescoes, the Ptolemaic terracottas, dried pods, exotic seeds—and the African baskets, branches, lampshades, some cushions, some antique blankets, a little monster figurine in Vicenza stone for warding off the evil eye, the Tuscan high chair, an easel, a sideboard, a couple of plate racks... in short, all that was needed for my collection of Moroccan items to be welcomed into the arms of a home. But there were other Moroccan artifacts, too—mostly embroidery and textiles, pottery, painted wooden furniture, lanterns, two magnificent Tuareg cane structures for holding the wooden bowls from which the camels drank—which I had purchased over the years around the world, and which finally had the chance to reunite with their brothers and sisters who had remained at home. I anticipated that agnition with delight and impatience.

When the trailer truck came rumbling out of the belly of the ferry that it filled practically from bow to stern, it was immediately stopped by the customs officers. Two hours later it was the only vehicle left on the quay, an old queen bee with an abdomen deformed by too many births, abandoned to its fate. My list aroused the officials' suspicions. Amid shouts, calls, and insults, the shipping agent's workers were forced to unload crates and packed furniture until for a hundred meters the quay was cluttered with my belongings, just as the rain began to fall. After several phone calls, the trucker and the customs officer locked themselves in the latter's office. No, I was not a theatrical impresario, I replied dryly to the irritating uniformed customs officer who kept lifting cardboard flaps, risking exposing objects to the rainwater, and, no, I wasn't a circus owner either.

The trucker emerged from the office with a look that did not bode well.

"They don't believe us. Nothing doing."

"Why? It's all on the list."

"The problem... You must forgive me. They don't think anyone would want to import this stuff."

"Too valuable?"

"The opposite! The officer claims that no one would pay for shipping all this old junk. If you had added a couple of plasma televisions, a quad bike…"

Fortunately, the officer was an understanding man and, as I have already mentioned, the sense of home is still very much alive in the Moroccans of the North. He realized that I was genuinely fond of my things, and after I had a chance to give him a detailed account of the merits and the history of some of them, and after expressing my concerns about water damage to stressed surfaces that had already endured the insults of time, interrupting me halfway through an impassioned peroration about my magnificent plan to reunite relatives separated by destiny and now by him too, he exclaimed "Bon! Bon!" and, shaking his head, he stamped the papers: shortly afterward—it was almost sundown—the truck was loaded once more.

Back home my treasures were hoisted onto many shoulders and laboriously carried along the narrow garden paths. Out of breath—the need to divide them over the three pavilions intensified one of my regrets: that of not being ubiquitous—I asked the carpenter Abderrahim to help us. Together with three children, he was framing a gigantic panel of Tunisian tiles, but he agreed willingly, assisted by the two gardeners, by Soufien our sculptor-cook, a couple of burly neighbors. and Moha, a boy from the Middle Atlas whom I had met on a construction site where I was doing the garden and he was working as a bricklayer. Won over by his rare aesthetic sense, I had hired him as a trusted collaborator: he had been living with us for a few months and I was blissfully happy about that, no one had ever put freer and bolder bouquets of flowers in our rooms, not even Abdelaziz from Jebila, famous since the days of the dry branches covered with *Clematis cirrhosa*. Although still sleepy (he usually got out of bed late in the afternoon, preferring to do the cleaning late at night upon returning home from his forays, only going to bed again when the day was done and everything was immaculate), the young Berber gave proof of the presence of mind that always delighted me, like the time we were stuck in the car after an avalanche had blocked the mountain track we were on and he had unexpectedly taken the necessary from his bag, filled half a glass with snow and squeezed a couple drops of lemon into it, before serving up one of the best gin and tonics I have ever tasted—just as a family of deer solemnly paraded past us. At around four in the morning, all the furniture was finally in its place, and we, a little tired but happy, inaugurated the living room by sharing one of the soups for which Soufien is famous. The *aménagement* was providentially aided by the large Venetian stone fireplace that the moving company had rejected because it was too heavy, while the truck driver-cum-smuggler who had taken on the job had dumped it in an open space near the customs office in Ceuta. The colossus eventually arrived in Tebarek Allah on the trailer of a tractor loaded with squawking chickens and local countrywomen singing as is customary here when going to a wedding. Afterward, with immense effort, the two lateral elements and the mantelpiece were built into the middle of the rear wall of the living room, where this new fireplace welcomed us with all the courtesy of an old host showing slightly intimidated guests where to sit. And so the new pavilion, like its older siblings in higher places, practically furnished itself. Hanging stuff up was much more difficult.

For days, weeks, months, hanging up panels of tiles and *azulejos*, hanging up the huge whale skull my friend Olaf had found on the beach at Sidi Mghait (the most exciting gift I have ever received, the eye sockets are so vast and deep that a man could curl up inside them), hanging up tapestries and long pieces of carpet with wavy borders, hanging up Moroccan shelves using lots of suspension rings at different heights, hanging up Islamic headstones in stone and marble with irregular profiles, hanging up sculpted beams, Koranic tablets, plates, corner shelves, mirrors, drawings, display cabinets, popular oleographs, and old photos in frames. Some objects weighed hundreds of kilos; first we had to lift them onto a table, then onto a second table precariously placed on the first one before swinging them, holding them and our breath until their tops met the wall, and then creating levers, improvising struts, tightening ropes and wires, pulling on chains, placing boards that tore apart under the stress and hastily replacing them with metal bars that bent like rubber, clenching our teeth amid the roar of drills and the thud of hammers, eyes, noses, and throats full of dust, hair covered in flakes of plaster, arms numb and backs contracted. But as soon as all this was over, and the group dispersed, Moha, Soufien, Abderrahim, and myself, each from a different angle, turned to survey the result…you would have said that the piece of ceiling, the whale ribs, and the front of the sarcophagus had always been there. We exchanged smiles. And for this, in my heart, I am grateful to Roberto, even though he doesn't appreciate this kind of exuberance in interior decor. On entering the loggia or the living room, to this day, every time a guest utters the fateful words: "How lucky you are to have found this old house here!" or "Who was the mad collector who built this pavilion?" I try not to laugh. And I no longer feel guilty of the crime of building a house here, where after all it would have been enough to plant a few trees and put up a hut and a chicken coop.

TEXTILES AND CARPETS

I like textiles. Between the warp and the weave, I feel the breath of time. It began when I was fifteen, in the store owned by a grave robber from Cairo with eyelashes like a doll's and an innocent smile contrasted by a massive body swathed in a threadbare djellaba and the air of an old fox. For some obscure reason, Mister Fathi—Fathi to his friends, "that likable delinquent Fathi" to museum curators and collectors—had decided to waste his time on me, and to see to the education of my "eye": "the eye is everything, remember that, my child." He gave me some practical lessons in the history of art. After two or three stays in the world's most beautiful city (every time I went into that dark little shop beneath the porticoes of Ezbekeya, cluttered with secondhand fridges and washing machines, I would find myself in the family album of the gods) expressions such as "Alexandrian sfumato" and "archaism from the twenty-sixth dynasty" would fire my enthusiasm much as the names of soccer players excited my school friends. From the table already jam-packed with the lids of alabaster canopic jars, votive terracottas, and small bronzes, Fathi would take a piece of Coptic or Fatimid funerary fabric and with the melodramatic gesture of an offering portrayed on the walls of a mastaba he would proffer it to me on the palms of his hands. With his peasant index finger, dark and stubby as a pestle (I can still see the eclipse of the nail with the small pale sun rising below; it's memories like this that make us realize how much we have loved someone) he would run slowly, paternally, over the outlines left on the fabric by the fluids of putrefaction. He would sigh: "*C'est la vie*, my child." I would nod, intimidated and already lost amid the flowering forest and the trimming hardened by blood, amid the scrolls of leaves baked by time and decay, amid fleeing hares and gazelles facing each other. In those scraps of tunics, soiled by dirt and bodies but still with colors, amid those stunted Cupids and those medallions of goddesses with bovine eyes, the pagan world still breathed, a world that monotheism had failed to smother. "Life is about this too, my child…It's sad that a piece like this costs nothing, but it's the mirror of our times, *le miroir de notre bêtise*…" And he would hand me ceramic potsherds from village kilns, a doll made of bone taken from a little girl's tomb, the pendant with which an artisan was buried... he knew better than I the depth of the cash-strapped pockets of a youngster like me who, in exchange for a fragment of an ex-voto, was prepared to skip his meals.

Thanks to those lessons, I began to understand that in the minor and provincial arts there endure—and sometimes result in surprising forms owing to the inventiveness of a single artisan—traces of beliefs that are obliterated by the contemptuous greater arts as they swagger along their marble-paved highway: it is precisely these paths in the sand that can lead us back to the womb, among mud houses next to the ruined temple still undecided whether to become a church or a mosque, among women who for three thousand years have worn a lily behind their ear and men who for another two will be using the same plow, and here we shall fall asleep in the embrace of a god with the body of Christ and the face of a dog from which a Santa Claus beard is already sprouting... If I really wanted to understand the mystery of late antiquity and the fabulous syncretism of its beliefs and superstitions, the poor remains of that popular world were more eloquent than any porphyry bust of a tetrarch.

Since then, I have developed a mistrust of all things courtly and a passion for the artifacts of everyday life. And I'm not just talking about Islamic, early Christian, or Alexandrian art. In the presence of a simple seventeenth-century table in dark walnut I immediately hear the clink of the small pewter plate from which the hand of a provincial notary grasps the biscuits to go with his afternoon cup of milk, I see the oriental design of his slightly frayed robe, I sense his worries about the increase in the salt tax (with the collapse in prices caused by the Fronde it is thanks to the salt pans that he was able to provide his lame daughter with a dowry) and his joy at the birth of a boy so late in life, while poor Marie Gismonde, thanks to Saint Anne and the zabaglione and the bloodletting, is already getting her strength back... A prince's sumptuous piece of furniture, on the other hand, protects itself from my gaze with the splendor of its bronzes and gilding and, hiding behind the shield of the technical skillfulness of its creator, plants a "No Entry" sign I am not inclined to contravene.

"You will become a collector," Fathi used to tell me. "A collector of small things, not one of those foolish men who are dazzled by masterpieces."

"Why?" He shrugged, a telluric movement raising and lowering his djellaba. "It is the destiny Allah has chosen for you, my child." And giving me a worried look, as if the prophecy was unlucky: "Seeing means listening. But the stories that objects tell, *les petits objects que nous aimons bien, toi e moi*, are often lies."

"Really, Mister Fathi? It seems to me that they teach..." He shook his head. "This is the problem, at first they seem like beautiful fables. But they are alive, they are desperate, dispersed, soon they will pester you to help them get back together... You will have to deprive yourself of bread to reunite them... Look at this." He took from his pocket the marble head of a child, the size of an apple. "Do you recognize it?" I nodded: it was the young Harpocrates, the god of healing, the same subject as the terracotta shard I had bought a few days before, sculpted with similar naturalism, but bigger, and made of a valuable material.

"Where is it from, do you think?"

I hesitated.

"Come on, don't be afraid. It's Parian marble, the jewel of antiquity..."

"Alexandria?" Fathi shook his head.

"From a villa on the delta?" He kept his eyes trained on mine. "Unless..." I narrowed my eyes to focus on it. "If the customer's work obliged him to stay close to the sea, he will have preferred to stay on dry land…Crocodilopolis?"

Finally, he smiled. "You were close. It was on the altar of a villa in Fayyum…It belonged to a merchant who had made a fortune in cotton, his triremes used to call in at the islands, and as soon as he could, he would return to his family in the oasis he hailed from…" I felt as if I had won a competition.

"*Très bien*, you are a quick study, *mon enfant*. It's from Fayyum, just like the fragment you bought the other day. Does it not say something special to you? Can't you hear it? Isn't this god child asking you to reunite him with his mortal brother? So that they can play together like all the children of Fayyum and the world entire, *un enfant de riches et un enfant de paysans*, before your very eyes?" His finger lingered on the little sculpture's slightly sulky upper lip. "Aren't you curious to compare them, study them, understand them, *mon enfant*? To watch the family prostrate themselves as they worship them? To see how they are dressed? The jewels? To guess the words of their prayers? And to help your good friend to pay the tuition fees for his son's school, which is ruining him, by Allah, ruining him?" And he put the little head in my hand, cold and boiling hot, heavy as lead. That rogue had an easy time of it with me, I who was only a few years older than that Harpocrates: the idea of placing them next to each other on the table in my hotel room made my heart beat faster, it was so irresistible that from that very evening I would no longer have either a table or a room, and I would move to the rooftop hut where a friend's mother, unaware of my presence, lodged her Nubian watchman. To console myself for the cold, and the diet of water and chickpeas I subsisted on when I was not invited to dinner and my friend didn't bring up the leftovers, I would spend the evenings contemplating the two heads placed side by side on the military blanket, just as I do today in Tebarek Allah when I miss Fathi and those years, and I put them close together. The very courteous Nubian watchman would call them my *poupées*, push his turban to one side to scratch his head before going to scatter handfuls of corn for his pigeons.

On my travels I have always collected fabrics: in Egypt and Syria, all over Europe, in Anatolia, in India, in Central America, and in various African countries I have filled my bag with ikat and embroidery, kilims, silk and raffia velvets, damasks and Polynesian tapa cloth, printed cottons, jacquards, and old chintzes. I have made many a boardinghouse room more welcoming with embroidery work from the Greek islands thrown over the bed or a towel from a hammam on the table (and I have also used them so I might feel less sad in the rooms of certain luxury hotels). It is my custom to make some changes in the decoration wherever I find myself: how many times Stephan has scolded me, in a hostel in Van or in the suite of a hotel in Damascus, because on returning to our room I would unroll a carpet I had taken from the landing or because I put next to the bedside table—on which I had already put the table lamp I had found in room 32 when someone had left the door half open—an armchair taken from the one next to the night porter's as he was snoring! How many tips have I handed to puzzled Bedouins so that they would bring to my room the little bookcase next to the piano in the living room—no, the peacock feathers in the howitzer shell were too dusty, while the Zoroastrian centerpiece should be immediately returned to the desk downstairs, thank you—because after all I had to maintain order in my little library of maps, guidebooks, texts on art history, anthropology, botany, zoology, and geology that no traveler can do without! How many vases have I borrowed from friends, acquaintances, and strangers to water the roses I asked a cemetery caretaker to give me, or for the buttercups picked from beneath the overpass, the crocuses and the fritillaries that a kind soldier handed me through the fence of an army compound with the inevitable "Off Limits" sign! I have always been able to make do with the bare necessities: after those nights in the hut on the roof in Cairo, all I needed was a patchwork blanket stretched between the walls by way of a partition to transform the corner of a Senegalese dormitory into a love nest, and with a piece of suzani fabric folded over to form a pillow I have slept like a baby on more than one railroad station bench.

EMBROIDERY

In Morocco, in those years, only a few of us collected these fabrics that express an aspiration to luxury on the part of those accustomed to living in otherwise bare houses. I began to accumulate them, from Fez, Salé, Azemmour, and Rabat, each city with its own technique and style, paying particular attention to those from the North, from Tétouan and Chaouen, and to fragments in which the technique differed from the standard one, or had an unusual color or combination of colors. They were made by a *mellemaa*, an expert embroideress, who worked with several apprentices, usually poor girls from the neighborhood. The base, of cotton, silk, and sometimes linen, was used to make the cloth bundles in which women packed the things needed for the hammam, as well as cushions, curtains that served as a screen for the bridal chamber, drapes to hang from the walls or lay on the chests, and veils, belts, and handkerchiefs for the henna ceremony.

Already in the late Middle Ages, handbooks on the art of embroidery were circulating in Europe (similar to those used by textile salespersons and decorators to this day), simple collections of motifs produced from woodcuts. To my amazement, I discovered that much Moroccan needlework features the same subjects—two-handled bowls with birds facing each other (previously dear to the Sassanids), dragons, storks in flight, stylized dancers holding hands, crosses, stars, moons, and flowers—and this is why, especially if the artifact is ancient, it is difficult to determine whether it comes from the North African Atlantic coast, from Toledo, or from Tuscany. But the fact that hundreds of years ago, in the home of a privateer from Salé or a shoemaker from Fez, they copied the same figures that Boccaccio's nuns and Don Quixote's Dulcinea worked on in candlelight, is further proof of the vitality of the popular arts: coarsely simplified, these archaic figures span the centuries.

In Tétouan they used to embroider *tenchifas*, long bands of cotton and later silk that were used on the wedding night to cover the mirrors so that evil spirits could not burst into the room clinging to the mane of a reflection. The embroidery work of Tétouan is an excellent example of how the minor arts can adopt and vary elements extraneous to the dominant figurative culture, perhaps of remote geographic origins but left to simmer in the cultural broth of the popular imagination.

Morocco was never directly dominated by the Ottomans and is the only North African country where their influence is absent. Yet the florilegium of long, plumed *saz* leaves, carnations, tulips, and dog roses that appears in embroidered eighteenth- and nineteenth-century fabrics from Tétouan made for the nuptial bed is part of the decorative repertoire of the Sublime Porte. It is certainly not the herbal of some erudite Grand Vizier, but the messy notebook of a provincial child. Moreover, in the mountains of Morocco those flowers bloomed almost three centuries after they flourished in the Anatolian steppes, and the bulbs and seeds likely arrived in the Napoleonic era following the French invasion of neighboring Algeria (which had been under Ottoman dominion), when many Algerians took refuge in Morocco. In

Tétouan, a town far from everything, a flora that has withered elsewhere suddenly revives, full of new sap and touching vitality: this is joyous embroidery, carefree as gypsy women singing as they toss their bags into the van, its excessive mannerism is the raised little finger of the weary young baker who hands you the bread; Sunday best and bare skin, stylization and naturalism, alternate and merge into each other in a dance music as fresh and indigestible as a glass of almond milk in the square on a torrid summer's day. Just like the striped silks woven in town, and the coeval Spanish-style embroidery of nearby Chaouen, this is African work, the fruit of the labor of naive, provincial pirates' wives who, when it comes to Turkish things, have probably seen a plate in their husband's plunder, at most.

For many years I have kept behind the headboard of my bed a piece of embroidery from Tétouan on a yellow damask background. In the first house where it was hung it must have occupied the same place: its carnations watch over my dreams as they did over those of a couple made up of… when I can't sleep and toss and turn in bed I try to imagine them, husband and wife, young and dark, her braids inevitably dyed with henna; the strange thing is that they almost always look different, he does a different job, and I catch them at a different moment of their story. This is the beauty of the tales that fabrics tell at night: they change all the time, and I still don't understand why on one occasion the sailor's adventures end in the arms of his young bride, while the next time I see only her, frightened as she hides her purse under the mattress before her newlywed second husband, the grandfather clock restorer, returns from the café. Many important things in life happen in the bedroom.

In Tebarek Allah, Moroccan embroidery is everywhere: monochrome cushions from Fez on the sofas, strips of Salé and Azemmour on the tables and chests, curtains from Rabat at the windows; brightly colored fragments, also from Rabat, are hung to form a backdrop to old framed photos, or thrown over chairs and armchairs, even tiny ones; as well as the aforementioned *mendil* of the Jbala and the appliqués of silk or fustian velvet called *hait*, which in traditional houses used to line the walls above the sofas. They play host to the Persian *kalamkari* and the striped silks of the Caucasus that until a few years ago you could find in junk shops in Istanbul, and to the beautiful French printed cottons and damasks from Lyon that were imported in quantity to Morocco in the nineteenth century. Enough stories to fill a thousand and one nights. Of course, they get worn and damaged. The sunlight, the dust, elbows, backs, and buttocks are merciless enemies. But this progressive decay, which mirrors that of those who live among them, has something consolatory about it. For now, the mutual drift has been kind, and destiny clement. Every now and then, to save a piece of fabric from the inevitable, I put it in the large seventeenth-century closet in the living room. But as I put to bed the amaranth border that has told me all sorts of things, my gaze unfailingly falls on one of its companions still lying in its rustling tissue paper nightgown. I lay bare a strip of it, and it already seems about to jump out: such freshness! What a rosy complexion! I didn't even remember it! I indulge it. And as soon as that piece of fabric embroidered in Fez or Rabat ends up on the back of a sofa next to its fellows, they immediately pick up the conversation from where they left off maybe years before. I hear perfectly well the tone in which they greet each other, the laughter ringing out, the pauses and the crescendos, but no matter how hard I try, I can't understand a word. Happy to meet up again, they speak their own tongue, light years away from the one they use when they speak to us at night, to tell us a story that is basically always the same, always and only our own.

CARPETS

Unlike oriental carpets, those knotted in Morocco are not very old—one hundred, two hundred years, rarely more. Even when they belong to a city tradition and come from small urban workshops such as those of Rabat and Mediouna, they were usually not intended for places of worship or the palaces of princes: they are bourgeois carpets. They have rarely managed to survive more than a couple of centuries in the inferno of domestic life, worn out by feet and elbows and knees, scorched by the kitchen fire, by embers from kif pipes and heaters in winter, soaked by blocked drains and by the buckets of water poured over the wool before it is brutalized with the broom—not to mention the custom of dividing every inheritance by cutting it all up with scissors: kilim, *hait*, blankets, even wide bridal sashes are reduced to ribbons. The Berber carpets that Morocco is famous for have had an even harder life: less dense, with less compact knotting, they served both as the mattresses and blankets of nomads who went from mud brick houses to tents, depending on where the grass for the livestock grew. And even in the settled tribes, the owners' ways and the climate of a region that is torrid in summer and mostly cold and rainy in the other seasons are not very conducive to the serene old age of household furnishings. Turkish kilims have a hard time of it too, yet some very old specimens remain. Why? Because in Anatolia everything old, *eski*, has always enjoyed prestige, has been respected and carefully preserved by the Yoruk nomads; Moroccan Berbers, on the other hand, are attracted to newness as magpies are to gold, and they have a gypsy indifference to objects. Heaven knows how many scraps of magnificent carpets have ended up in the fire for boiling the water for tea, or as a bed for a beloved cat and her kittens! Today, unless it has been able to find sanctuary in a mosque, a Berber carpet from the late nineteenth or the early twentieth century is considered every bit as old as a far older Anatolian prayer mat, which moreover is protected by layers of carpets gifted over the centuries to the place of worship where it can rest in peace.

The two most beautiful Moroccan carpets in Tebarek Allah come from the Marrakech area. It is possible to date them with certainty because at the beginning of the thirties they were given by Thami El Glaoui, the famous pasha who was a friend of Churchill, to James McBey, a Scottish painter who lived between Tangier and the rose city among the palms. They have an elongated shape and probably served as a bed for several family members. Like all artifacts from the same tribal area, they are very similar: on a dark orange background the geometric designs that, depending on the attention with which they are observed—or the amount of hashish smoked, or the book on the symbolism of Berber carpets you have just finished reading—evoke snakes, men, pregnant women, eyes, hands, and horses. I bought them thanks to a stroke of luck, or rather a gift from my memory. For years I had wanted to add a "classic" Berber carpet to my collection, but the few authentic ones in circulation were now too expensive for me. On the death of Marguerite, James's widow and a painter herself (an old dark-haired American lady who always wore a grin and who we were all fond of), my friend Christopher bought the McBey house on the Vieille Montagne from her granddaughters, along with some objects and furniture he liked. To get rid of the rest, the heirs, who lived in America, had organized a sale for the benefit of all of us foreign residents.

After having greeted each other politely and having lined up at the door, at the appointed time we flocked inside. Marguerite's old servants led us to her studio in the back; in the vast reception room with black-painted walls a great many things were piled up. Here, we were told, everything was for sale. It was like releasing wild beasts. Decrepit retired decorators used their walking sticks like machetes to cut a path to long-coveted baubles; sweet centenarian girls fell on your neck yelling that they were glad to see you while they snatched away the vase you had risked your life to get hold of; some pretended to bump into you to slow you down or knock you to the ground while an accomplice grabbed the frame or drawing you had spotted; some tripped you up, others shoved you against a table, others again slipped a stool between your feet—and in the meantime you had to keep responding to the declarations of "How nice to see you!" that rained down like darts dipped in curare, and bending down to kiss hands while taking kicks in the shins, trying to catch the attention of Marguerite's stunned granddaughter, or Christopher's who was giving her a hand, both standing against a wall so that they could consult the list and quote you a price before someone screamed: "Don't be ridiculous! I just bought it!" I struggled to recognize the room even though I had been there so many times, in the days of Marguerite's lunches where all the food was in different shades of the same color. In a corridor amid the stacks of furniture and objects, between human legs and those of tables and chairs, a few centimeters of red fabric protruded, a fringe... Suddenly I was pierced by a memory. "The two carpets!" Christopher shot me a questioning look. For a few moments he was engulfed by the throng of sweaty faces. "How much for the two carpets?" I had spoken so loudly that silence fell. The granddaughter looked at me in puzzlement: "Carpets?" My friend had turned pale.

Moving a table, I pointed to the edge of the hidden carpet. And Christopher, in a menacing crescendo of murmurs, told me the price. I hastened to sign the check. "I'll send for them later."

Here in Tangier I am fortunate to have many friends: I have made them over years spent in souks and beaches. That same afternoon a couple of strong boys came to move the furniture and load the carpets into the van to bring them to my home. As I often did when we were both in town, I had invited Christopher to dinner. At that time Christopher Gibbs, the greatest antiquarian of his generation, was already around seventy, and was very much tried by the chaotic sale, however he insisted on seeing my purchases, which I had spread out on the lawn in front of the "warehouse," as I call Mohammed and Ftoma's former house in which I store any new items until a place is assigned to them. He looked at them for a long time, in silence, first in amazement, then with an increasingly gloomy air. And as we went back to the sitting room in the middle pavilion: "I had never noticed them. Odd how in order to notice certain details you have to be a bit of a... 'carpet merchant,' in point of fact." He cleared his throat. "You got a great deal, dear boy. But I'm not letting you have this. It has sentimental value." And into his pocket he slipped a small pot that I had bought a few hours earlier because it contained the flight feathers of a crow. "I'll refund you tomorrow." I didn't say anything. We ate by candlelight, and we never mentioned those carpets again, even though they ended up in the lower living room, and he who had let them slip through his fingers had occasion to see them hundreds of times. Every friendship between collectors is dotted with minor incidents like this one. Christopher passed away two years ago, leaving a void in my life. I will never stop the car again on the old road to Asilah, and as I move away from him as he goes into the fields as big and confident as a moose, I will never take a furtive look to see how many times he bends down (before the *développement* there was a competition to see who could find more species of sage or Stars of Bethlehem in a quarter of an hour). I will never again swim with him in the Thames in winter—we needed to cool down after the painful scene in the living room—trusting that his invocations to some beloved seventeenth-century esoteric poets would save us from freezing to death; shivering, he recited the verses while beating his chest like the yeti and bellowing like a walrus. With the pretext of brushing it back off his forehead, I will no longer caress the thick white hair that would flop back over it again, making him look like an aged student. We will no longer vainly try to suppress our laughter like schoolkids, biting our lips, blowing our noses, coughing, but always looking each other in the eye, targeted in turn by the pieces of bread that the kippah-wearing master of the house started to throw at us as soon as we were seated, on the occasion of a dinner to celebrate—without our knowing, *en petit comité*—the Jewish Rosh Hashanah. I will no longer spread Nivea on his back and I will no longer hear him pronounce "Rothschild" in the British manner, seeing every time a whimpering child lying in the cradle of a diphthong stuffed with hard Maria Theresa thalers. But if when I am having supper I want to hear the warm and hesitant voice of my friend, who with his encyclopedic knowledge and anecdotes like those of a blithe memoirist would talk to me about the inventory of a large mansion or a forgotten wax-modeler, an Azerbaijani religious sect or a stuffed leopard, a party for rogues in Piraeus or a manuscript that had reappeared in Dublin, I have only to look at the piece of marble he left me. Standing regally erect on a wooden plinth in front of the place where I usually sit, "the *kouros*'s bottom" was my favorite among his treasures. I can see the previous owners and their fellows, the young lords of the Grand Tour, Diaghilev and Bakst, Bertie Landsberg, a callow Bruce Chatwin visiting with two friends at La Malcontenta. Depending on how I position the *kouros* in the morning to wish it good day I see them floating in the V of the groin or filling like ectoplasms the two bulging sacs of the buttocks, which are all that remains of the young archaic hero who can no longer smile, yet with his smile he reduces me to ashes as he did to them ... "Dear boy, it's like the salt in your food, the lining of your glove, or flowers in a room. What matters in an object, what makes the difference, is not only its adventure in history, its provenance, not even its beauty ... it is ... How would you define it, that way of being ... bruised? ... That certain je ne sais quoi ... that seduces good-hearted hawks like us?"

FRAGMENTS

The reason why I collect fragments of classic carpets—Turkish, Caucasian, or Persian, knotted between the sixteenth and the eighteenth centuries—is not only that I don't have enough money to buy complete ones. The fragment is a culture—indeed, we collectors are a secret society. The sentiment that moves us is less romantic than the one aroused by my piece of ancient *kouros* or a fragment of a predynastic Egyptian bas-relief, that is, the pleasure of completing and healing them only with the imagination, of making them coincide with our ideal—intact, the same sculptures would perhaps leave us colder. It is not just a matter of suggestion. Every fine carpet is already a fragment, and every fine carpet is infinite. And since every part of infinity is infinite, when we observe every piece of carpet it obliges us to extend its pattern as far as the eye can see. It does not prompt us to do this, it makes it inevitable. Its unlimitedness is contained in its very limits. In the visible world this only happens with fields in bloom and with Iznik tiles. In both cases, every ear of grass, every tulip the color of sealing-wax, coincides with the blissful expanse in which we all yearn to lose ourselves. It is a rather mysterious matter of rhythm. The meander of an arabesque at first welcomes you with a gentle invitation, before immediately capturing you and making you hurtle headlong down its twists and turns as if on a roller coaster; you don't have time to catch a breath before the next chasm is already yawning before you, you plunge downward at breakneck speed and then emerge from it, and so on, in a dizzying series of descents and ascents, curves and counter-curves, to which you abandon yourself heart in mouth but trusting. You are no longer there, you coincide with the energy that is carrying you along, you are a river, you are the wind, you are the meadow you are running through, the madness of the dash. This never happens with Western art, not even with marvelous millefleur tapestries, which exclude you and leave you standing there like a spectator, and to penetrate their leaves, to fly among their corollas, you have to disguise yourself as a bee or a fly. It is curious that this experience of fusion can be had both with something living—nothing is more alive than a field in spring—and with the abstract designs on a piece of old carpet. Maybe it has to do with the women who knotted it. They were nomads, they came from the steppes, they loved the outdoors: their faith did not bristle with spires that pierce the sky. It expressed itself in domes that seemed made of sky. Their luxury was not gold, but to lie down and chat on those carpets woven with flowers.

I bought one of my favorite fragments at a garage sale on Long Island, in front of a house with an ugly wooden porch. I wandered about on the dry grass among the pots, the flayed dolls, and the three-legged chairs that constitute the allure of this type of sale along with the deranged memoirs of television actresses and chess manuals. I was in hunter mode—and when I get this mouthwatering sensation, I have learned to look around carefully. I was drawn to a pile of doormats, probably because they were the shabbiest thing amid all that junk. I picked one up. The back was lined with a piece of something caked with mud and dirt, but that didn't prevent me from recognizing a couple inches of a certain pattern. Wool? It looked like linoleum, but on scratching it with a fingernail the pile stood up and softened. The seller, the usual middle-aged lady with a silver bob and fake tortoiseshell glasses, approached me suspiciously. "So you're planning to settle in our little community!" she exclaimed, weighing me up. "Great choice! Like all useful things, they've become hard to find. These coconut-fiber ones are the best. Did you notice there are five others? They're all one lot." I muttered something, paid the asking price of a few dollars and, arms loaded with worn-out doormats, I walked away and headed for the car. Tossing them in the trunk, I left. I didn't dare stop until I was a few kilometers away. I couldn't wait to get to my friends' house where I was staying. When I pulled over at the side of a small street, no one in sight, I got out. I found the first mat and I began scratching it again for a few minutes. I couldn't believe my eyes. I took a look at the others, but the shamelessness of fortune has its limits: none were lined. I put an end to their existence by throwing them in a garbage can. An hour later, locked in the bathroom, I unpicked my fabric with some nail scissors. I lovingly washed it in the tub with warm water and shampoo. Once, twice, three times, and then a long rinse. I tamped it down with a towel. And finally, I went back to the room and laid it on the bed. It really was a sixteenth-century fragment of a medallion Ushak carpet, and now it shone with its blues, its greens, and its sumptuous reds, on which the slim arabesque of yellow palmettes formed a grid that might be called golden. As if by magic, the half medallion was transformed into the whole medallion, or rather into the complete carpet, and my American bedroom already overlooked the Golden Horn, the call of the muezzin and the scent of the countrywomen's bunches of daffodils wafted in through the window... I didn't wonder how it got there. The destiny of things is no less unpredictable than that of men: a mere nothing can divert their path, and they must submit to the eccentricities and whims of their ephemeral masters. Unless they come across someone who recognizes them, rescues them, reunites them with other members of their dispersed family—but it takes very little, an accident, a theft, a death, for the infernal gymkhana to begin again, and once more the poor fragment of a courtly Ottoman carpet tossed hither and thither ends up pierced by another needle to line another doormat. We collectors are only the caregivers of the glorious oldsters who will survive us, and therefore we do everything possible to indulge them and keep their spirits up.

    Among the classic types, the so-called vase carpets of the seventeenth century are my favorites. These creatures—who would dare to call them "objects"?—seem to have just emerged from an ocean floor populated by sea anemones, swishing algae, and corals, pulsating ocean fossils beneath which lie the mountains and deserts that might have witnessed their birth. In their fields, in their blue and turquoise abysses, are woven motifs of a color that leaves me ecstatic. We shall call it "orange": it is a salmon pink, icy yet boiling hot (all the great colors are united by this vast range of temperatures, only the mediocre ones are "hot" or "cold"), which as it floats amid all that indigo and tourmaline produces a sound that transports you to a grotto. It is a song. In the underwater cave sirens sing; crouching on their tails, they weave their patterns of peonies and octopuses. The apricots that some of them are eating are of the same orange color, and how sad the sirens would be without those ripe apricots, they who are gluttons for them! With a gesture, they invite you to sit on the white pebbles, where you lie down and contemplate the sunset that filters through the wall of water. You feel good with them, happy in a way you didn't know.

    The first time I heard the song of the curly-haired and most beautiful Persian sirens was in an antique dealer's in Paris. I was holding a piece of carpet on which a couple of motifs were woven with their apricots and their underwater sunset. I did what I do when I have to conceal my emotions: I yawned. But I couldn't take my eyes off it: Baltic amber, persimmons, Cordoba leather, a bunch of canna lilies at dusk—and the sirens bent over the loom, knotting and chatting... A dozen years later I was in London at an antiques fair, where at a dealer's stand, among stacks of small carpets, I was attracted by a hem. A mere touch was enough to reveal the stiffness of the "vase" technique. I uncovered it and I was back in the grotto. When I got back home, I realized that the two fragments were connected. It was one of the most exciting moments of my life: side by side, that piece of trim and field was maybe a little over a meter and a half by two, but the fabric extended beyond measure, it was the seabed that, little by little, would have covered the world with its net teeming with scorpion fish, jellyfish, and hermit crabs, the same ones carved in a Byzantine bowl in the Treasure of Saint Mark's that was transformed into a lamp (my favorite artifact), where they dart motionless in the rock crystal.

    Years later, leafing through an old issue of *Hali*, a magazine dedicated to fabrics and carpets, I came across an advertisement placed by a Californian dealer: the photo was in black and white but there was no doubt that the rectangle of "vase" consisted of my two pieces plus a third. Someone, the dealer or some wretched colleague of his, must have cut them up, certainly thinking that by selling the pieces to people like me, disciples of the brotherhood of the fragment, they would have made more money. Overcoming my repugnance, I called Los Angeles. The number was no longer working. From antiquarian friends I learned that the Californian had retired years ago, and later that he had died, while his stock had been liquidated. I am still looking for that third piece, and I am confident I will find it one day. Of course, for the boundless seabed the survival of my few handsbreadths of carpet will suffice. And the sirens? They have other things to do rather than encourage me: they carry on weaving and singing, and when I'm sad I even suspect they are the Fates. The wonderful underwater grotto in which they welcome me couldn't give a hoot for my work of recomposition: when you have curtains of emerald-green algae, pillows of purple sponge, and beds of sea anemone and mother-of-pearl, an extra fragment of seabed is certainly not going to change your mood. In fact, the grotto drowses blissfully, yawning like an oyster on the sea bottom. So what is the real reason for my search? Is it only because I'm a glutton for apricots?

  I keep most of my pieces of carpet in Tebarek Allah. Legend has it that carpets began to be knotted in Moroccan coastal cities after one fell from the beak of a stork in flight. If it was Anatolian it would explain why, in a country that was never a part of the Ottoman Empire, city carpets are so mysteriously affected by its influence. In the living room of the middle pavilion there is a rare carpet from Rabat that many clues lead me to date to the eighteenth century. With Giacomo, the friend and expert on weaving who sold it to me, we spent hours finding affinities between it and prayer mats from Ladik, which are contemporary but already decadent carpets, with those opium poppies standing upright like skittles and awkward as soldiers who cannot scratch their lice during inspection, the zigzag bands of the borders, rigid and formal, the saw teeth that connect at random in the corners, the leaves that were once sinuous phoenix wings and are now only the feathers of a chilly sparrow. Before they started making carpets like this on the Atlantic coast, house floors were probably covered with mats (what Elizabethan and Jacobean inventories call Tangerine mats) while in the richer houses there were certainly Anatolian, Caucasian, or Persian carpets, as was also the case in Italy, France, Portugal, Spain, and England. For centuries now, classic rugs have been familiar to us: this is why they are so at ease in the rooms, this is why they make us feel good. When I put an *Iris pseudacorus* from the water basin in the garden into an ancient turquoise ceramic and observe how the brazen yellow flower on the mantelpiece converses with the sumptuous Ushak fragment hanging on the wall that serves as a background, I feel I have done something right, the same act that many people have repeated for centuries before me, a simple everyday miracle: the flower that inspired the lily of France, with the old sultan watching over it. Without sirens weaving in the scent of apricots, without bejeweled viziers, without boundless backdrops enclosed in the space of a handkerchief, without the Jbala women who wove the *mendils* laid over our sofas, our life would be sadder. And these worn-out fragments, freed after centuries from the task they carried out when they were part of an entire carpet (and were used to rest one's forehead on during prayer, or to caress the calloused feet of so many people) can finally relax, let themselves go. Stephan calls them "your loafers."

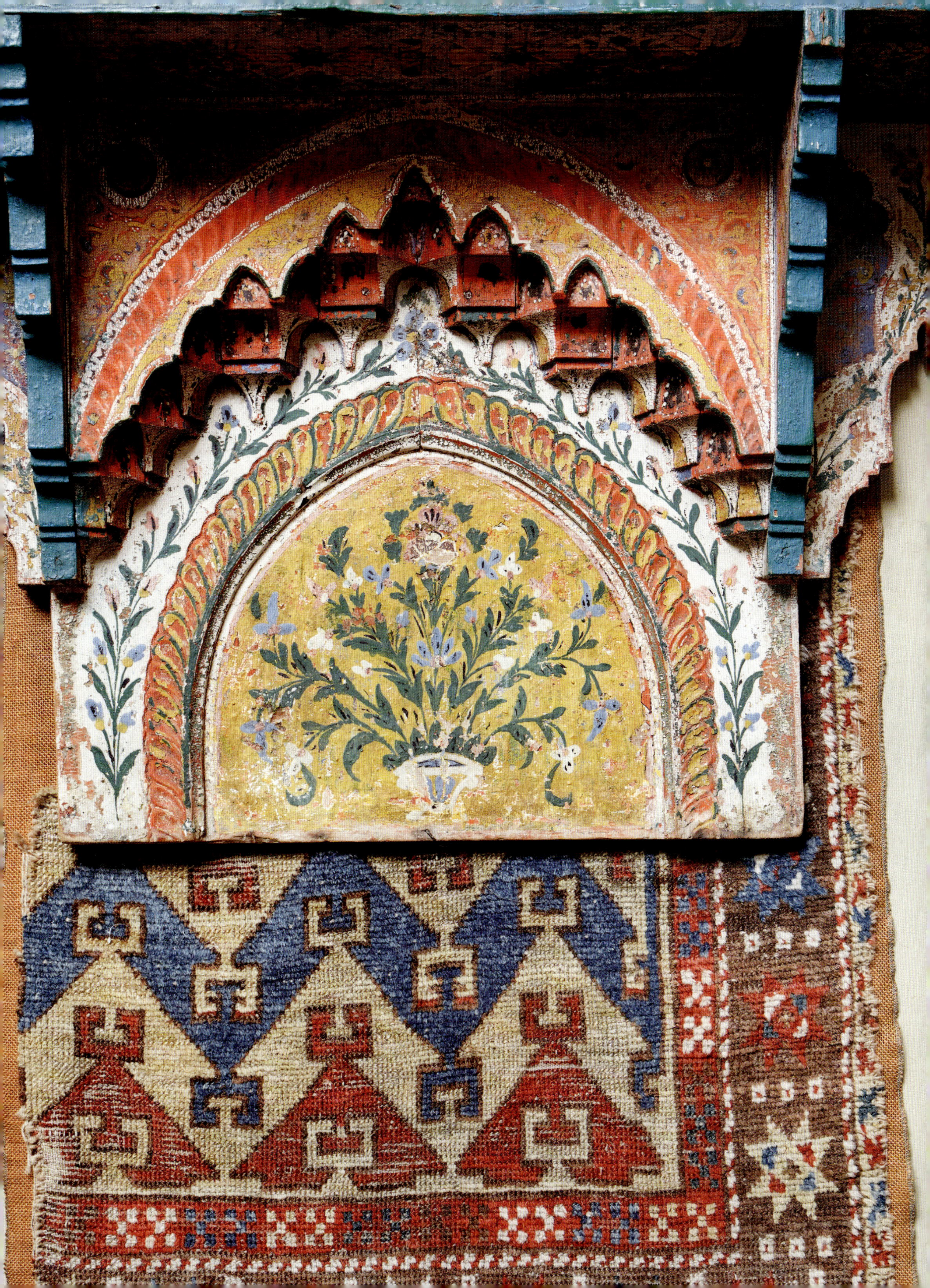

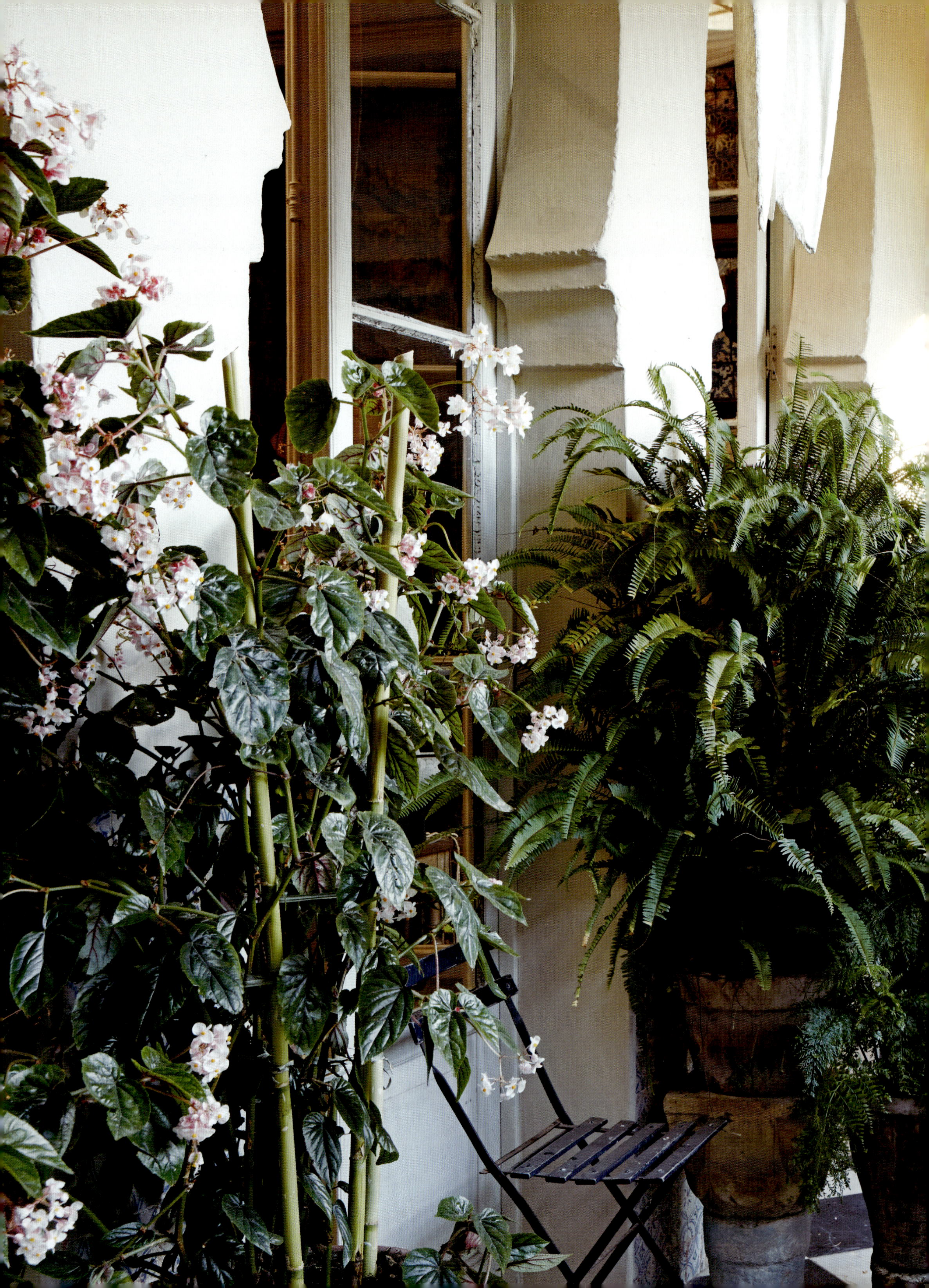

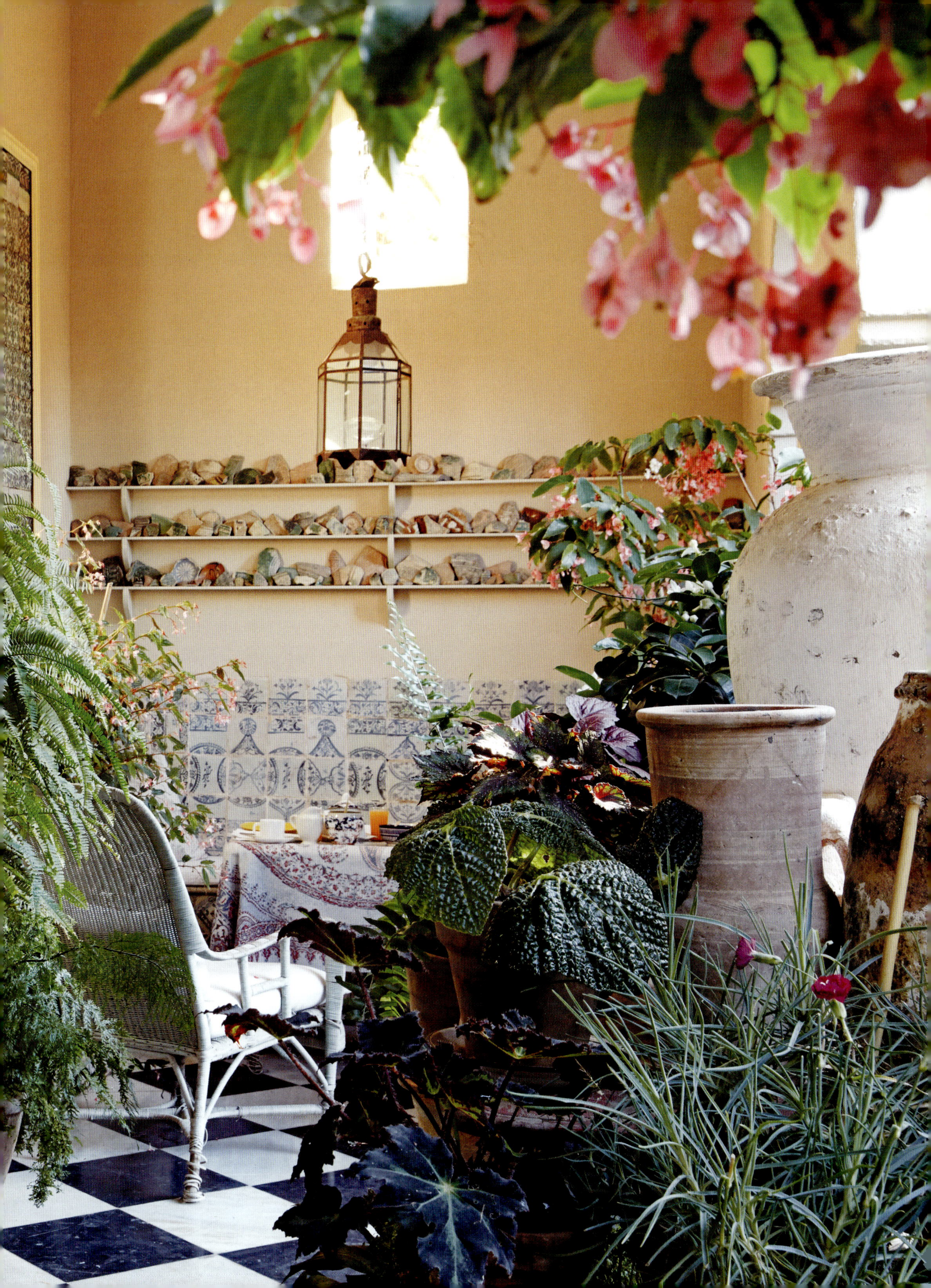

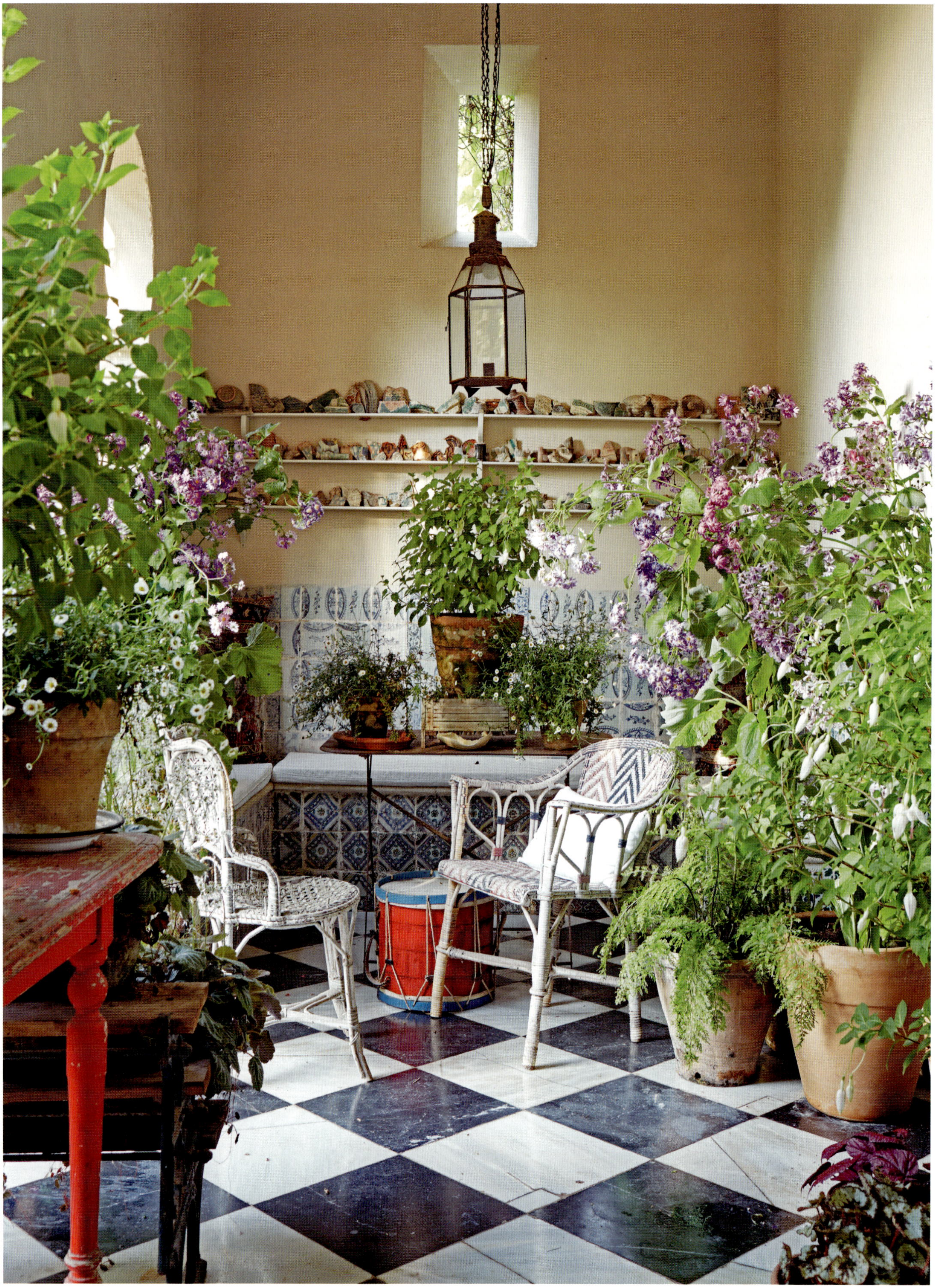

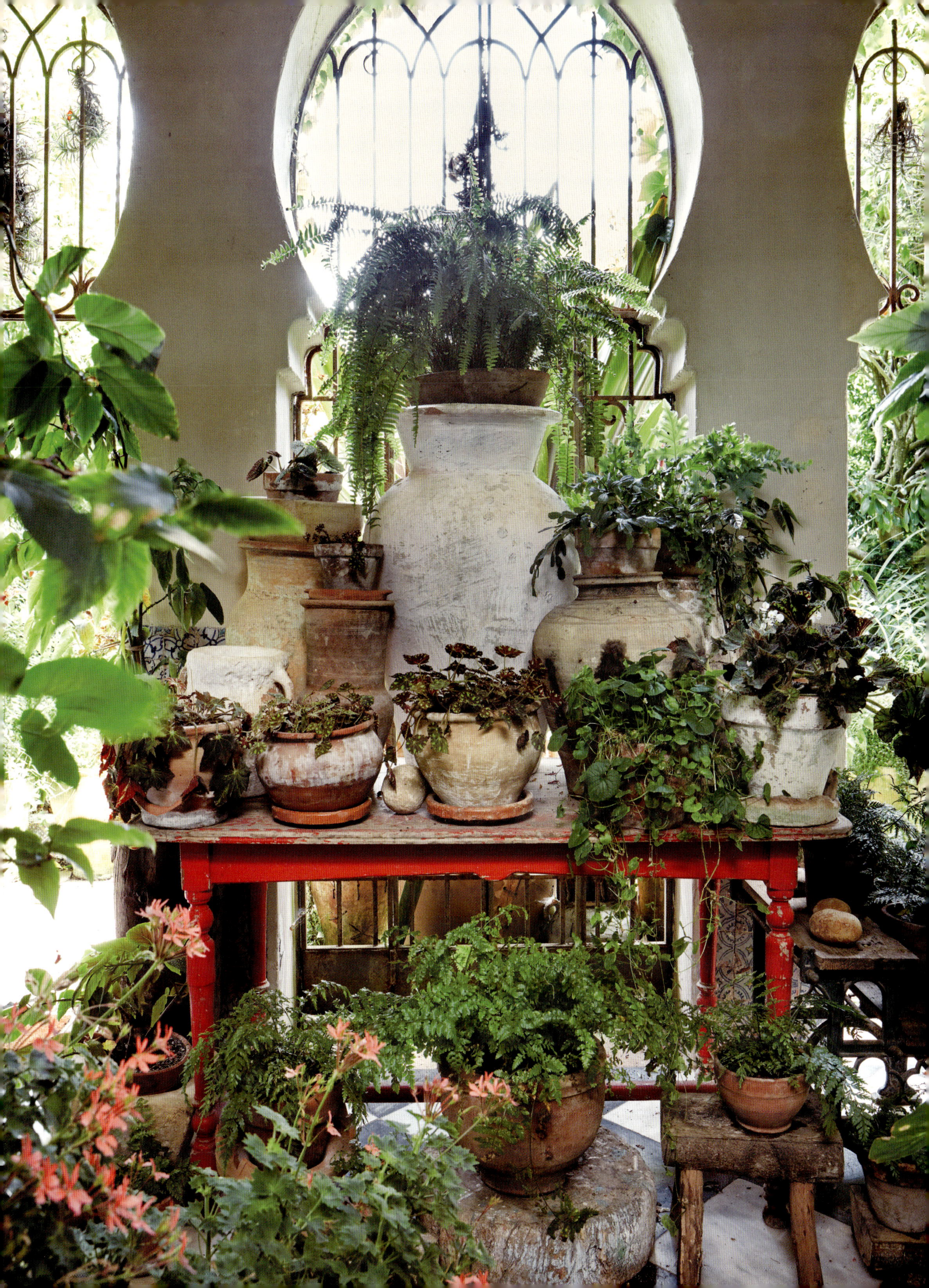

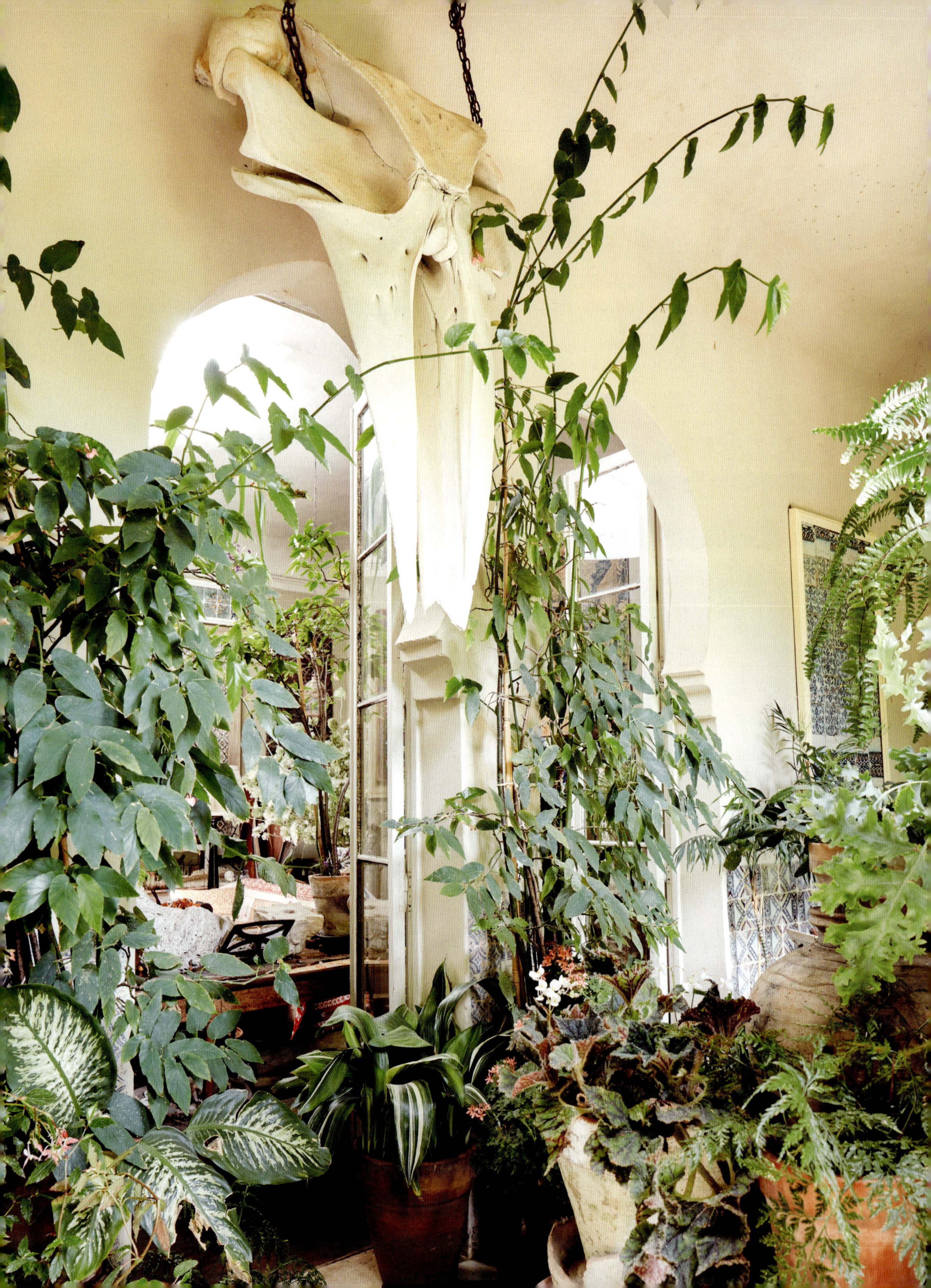

PAGES 146-47: *The eighteenth-century tiles on the walls are from Fez. The motifs and the glazes, similar to those of the bowls, jugs, and vases collected in abundance for almost two hundred years, make it possible to date them with a degree of certainty; yet neither these blue-and-white tiles nor the contemporary geometric tiles in multiple colors, all taken from the buildings of the old medina, have yet been studied. Was it perhaps because they were intended only to "play the wallflower"? At both ends of the loggia, on iron shelves, a collection of medieval shards that I inherited from an old gentleman in Tétouan who shared my passion for Almoravid, Almohad, and early Alaouite pottery. Ferns and begonias are all over the place.*
PREVIOUS SPREAD: *The red table from a rooming house in the medina playfully winks at the Moroccan drum.*
OPPOSITE: *The begonia tickles the skull of the whale that my friend Olaf found on the beach and gave to me—one of the most beautiful presents I ever received. Unfathomable, looking a bit like E.T., the skull meditates on the transience of life.*
FOLLOWING SPREAD, LEFT: *Surrounded by wildflowers, members of old tile and fabric families enjoy a long, lovely picnic.*
FOLLOWING SPREAD, RIGHT: *The skeleton of a dolphin and a little pharmacy display case full of treasures on a kitchen table. Kitchen tables are among my favorite pieces of furniture; they evoke the past much more than "official" furniture. In this room alone there are three of them.*

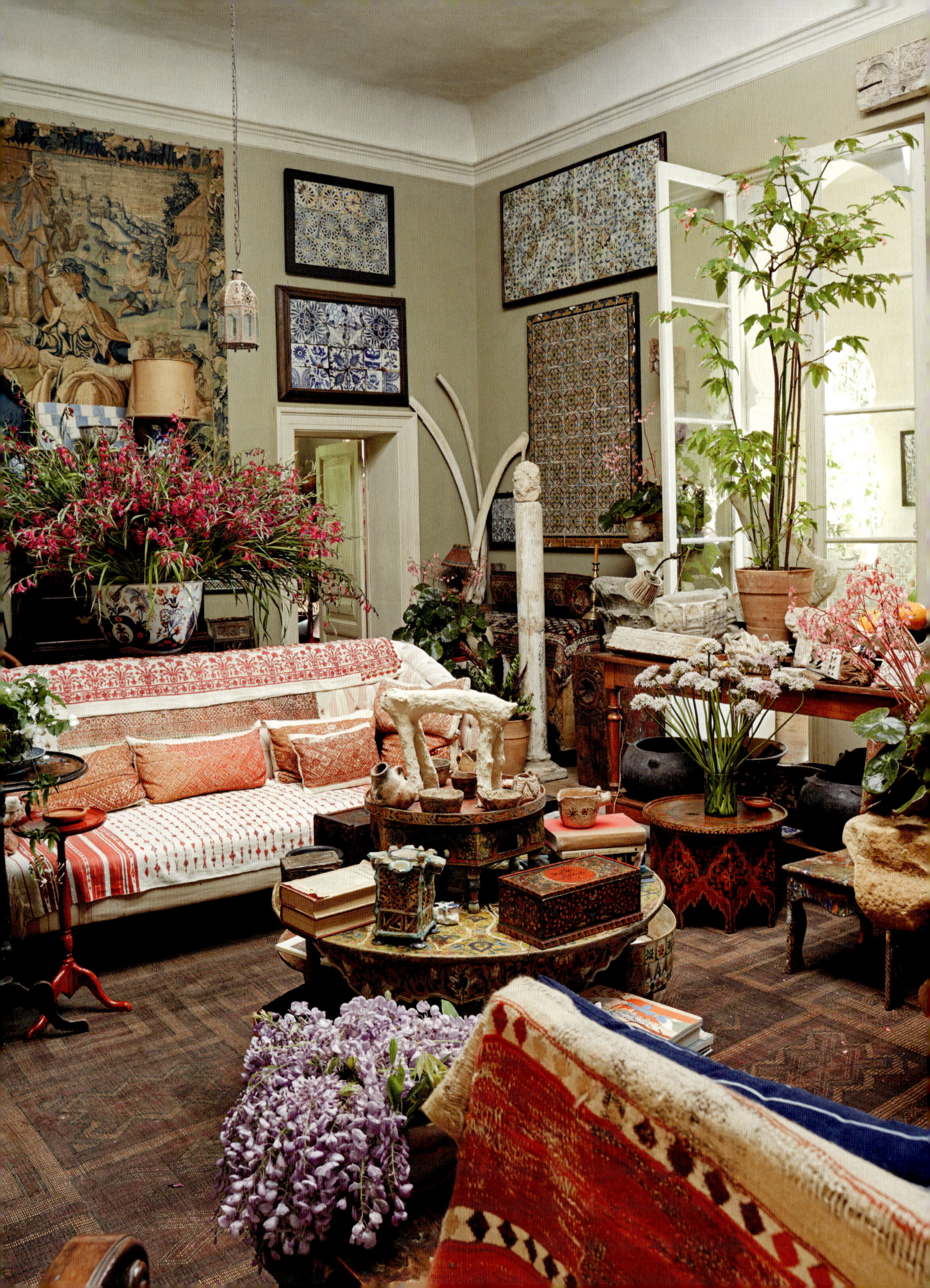

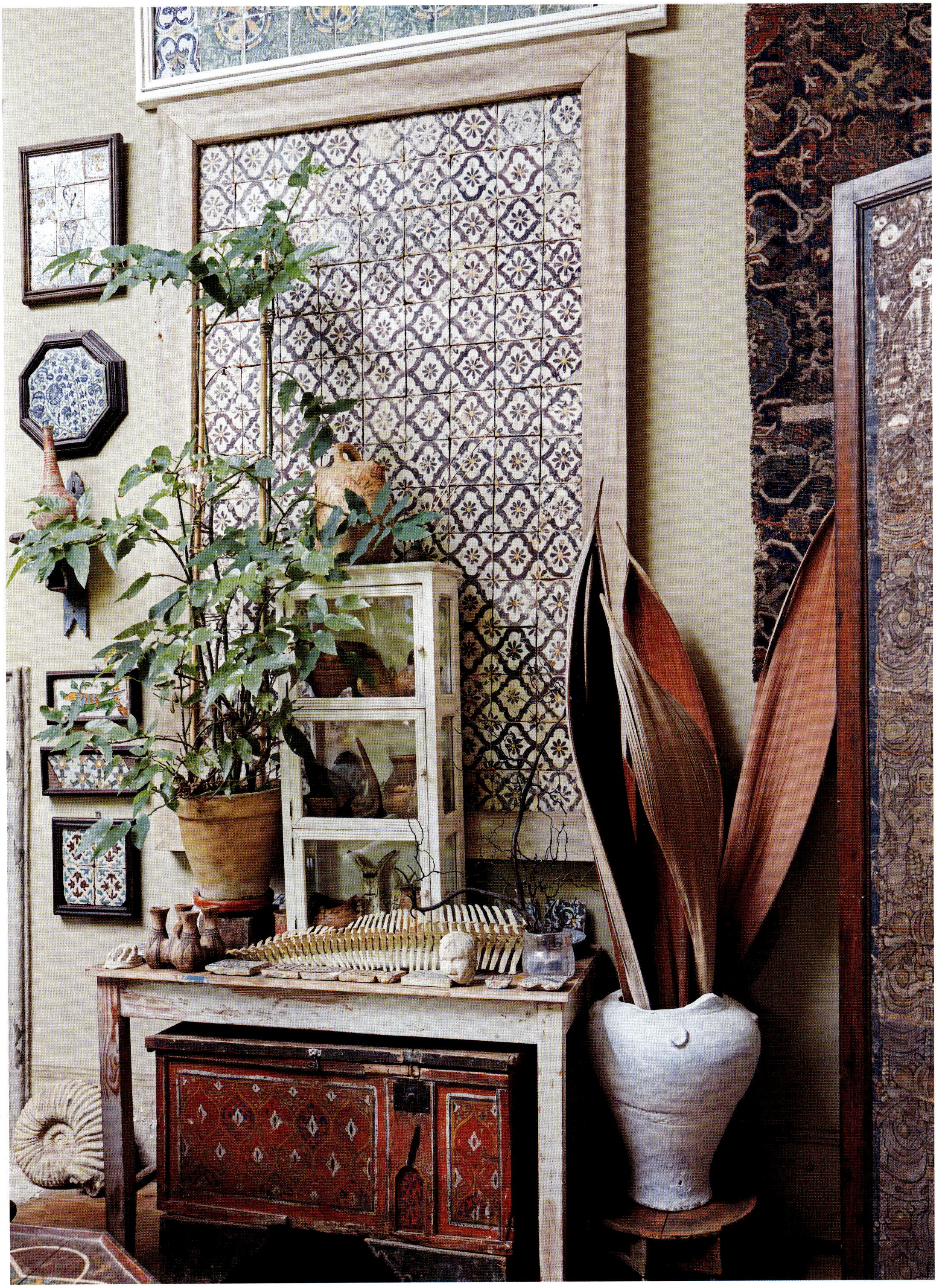

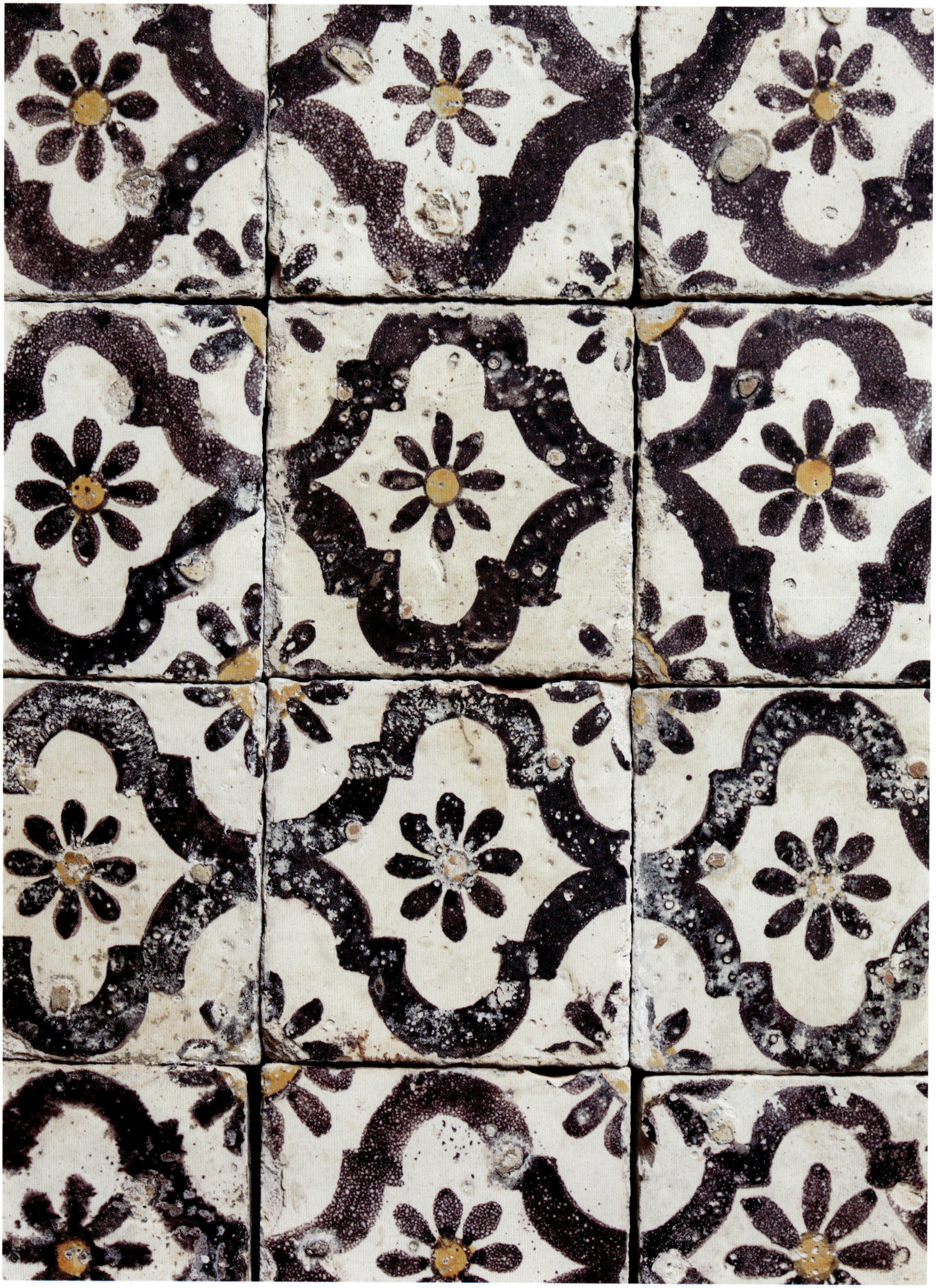

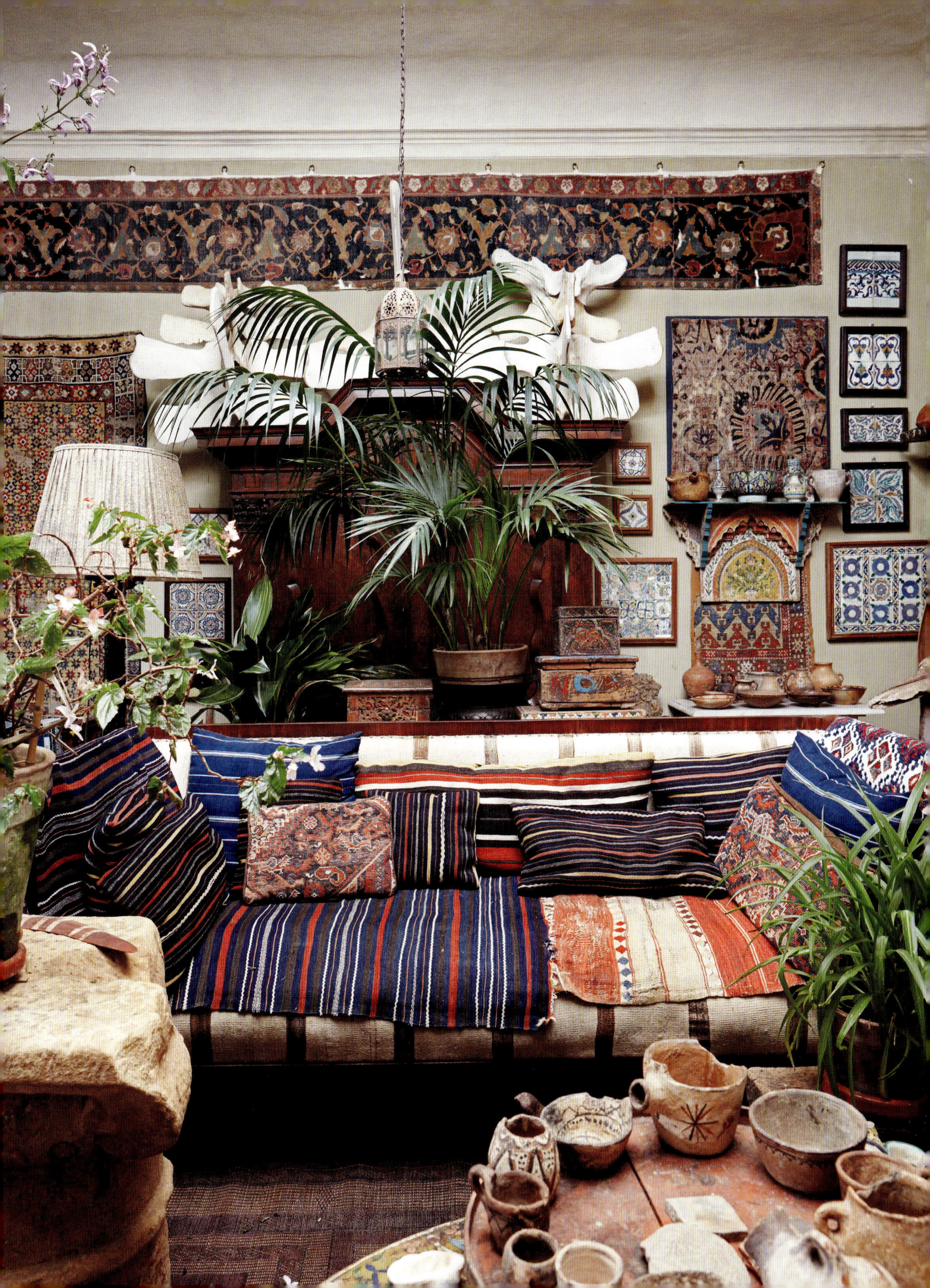

PREVIOUS SPREAD, LEFT: *nineteenth-century Qallaline tiles.*
PREVIOUS SPREAD, RIGHT: *A few whale vertebrae sit on the German wardrobe; they were stools used by the fellows selling pottery on the Larache road. The long carpet fragment is a seventeenth-century Safavid bordure from Ispahan. The cushions on the Biedermeier sofa are upholstered with old Berber shawls from the Ait Haddi and Ait Haddidu tribes of the Middle Atlas.*
OPPOSITE: *eighteenth-century blue-and-white Fez tiles are among the most beautiful works of art ever made in Morocco.*
FOLLOWING SPREAD: *An eighteenth-century Qallaline tile panel that I found in a flea market in Paris. It came from an old collection where it was misdated as seventeenth century.*

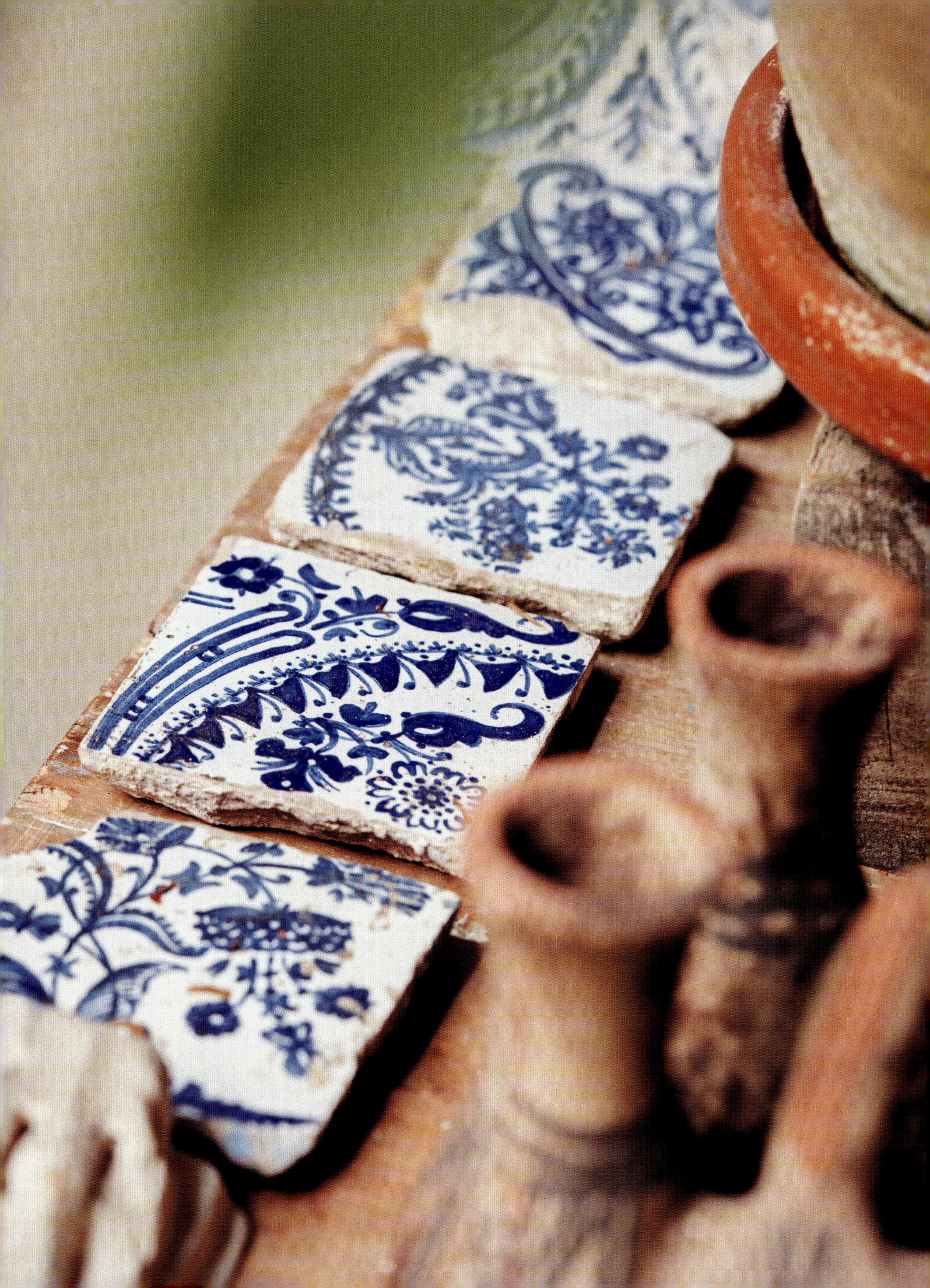

ALGER (FAIENCE ARABE du XVIIIe SIÈCLE DU PALAIS DE LA CASBAH)

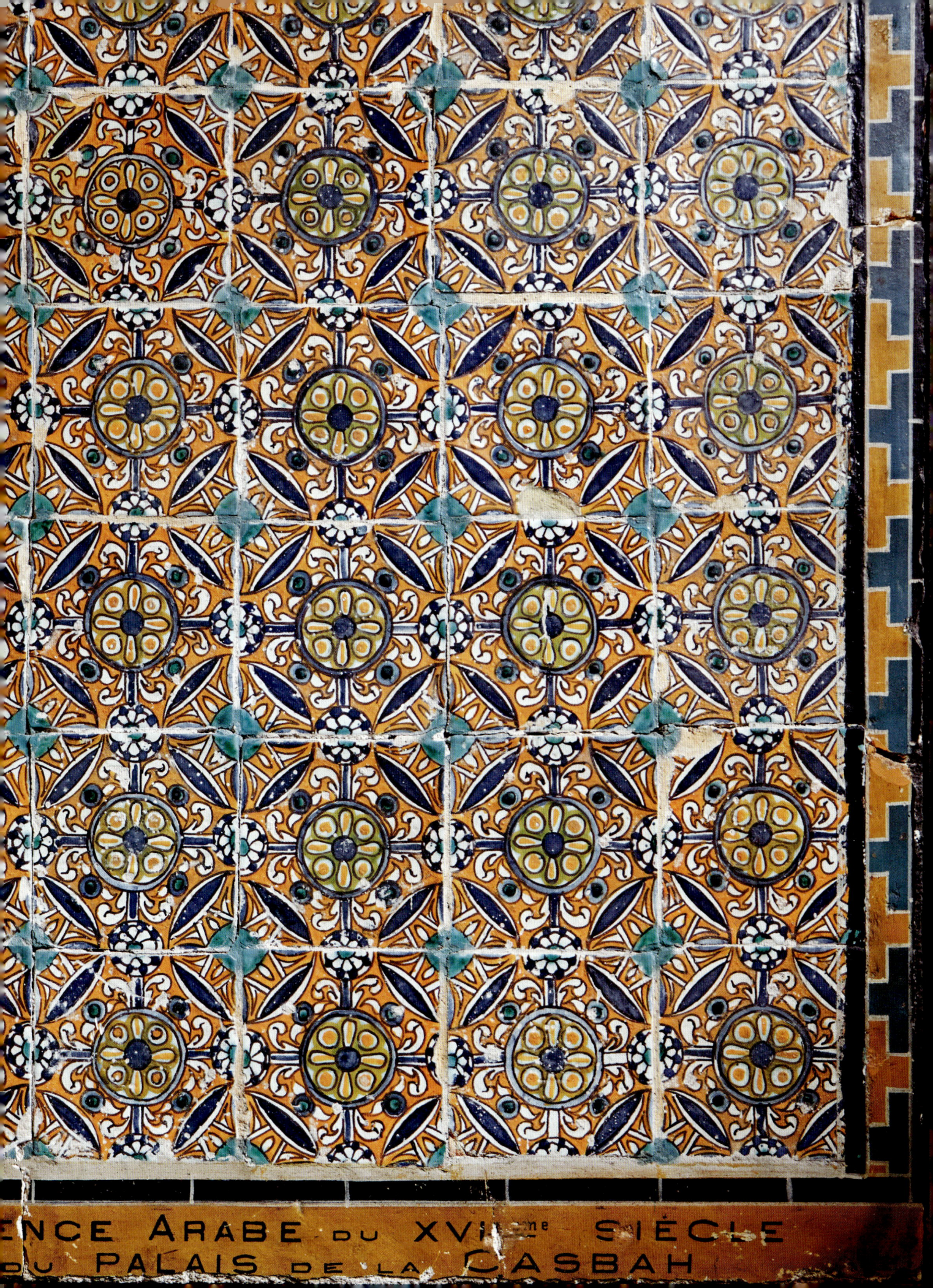

ENCE ARABE du XVIème SIÈCLE
DU PALAIS DE LA CASBAH

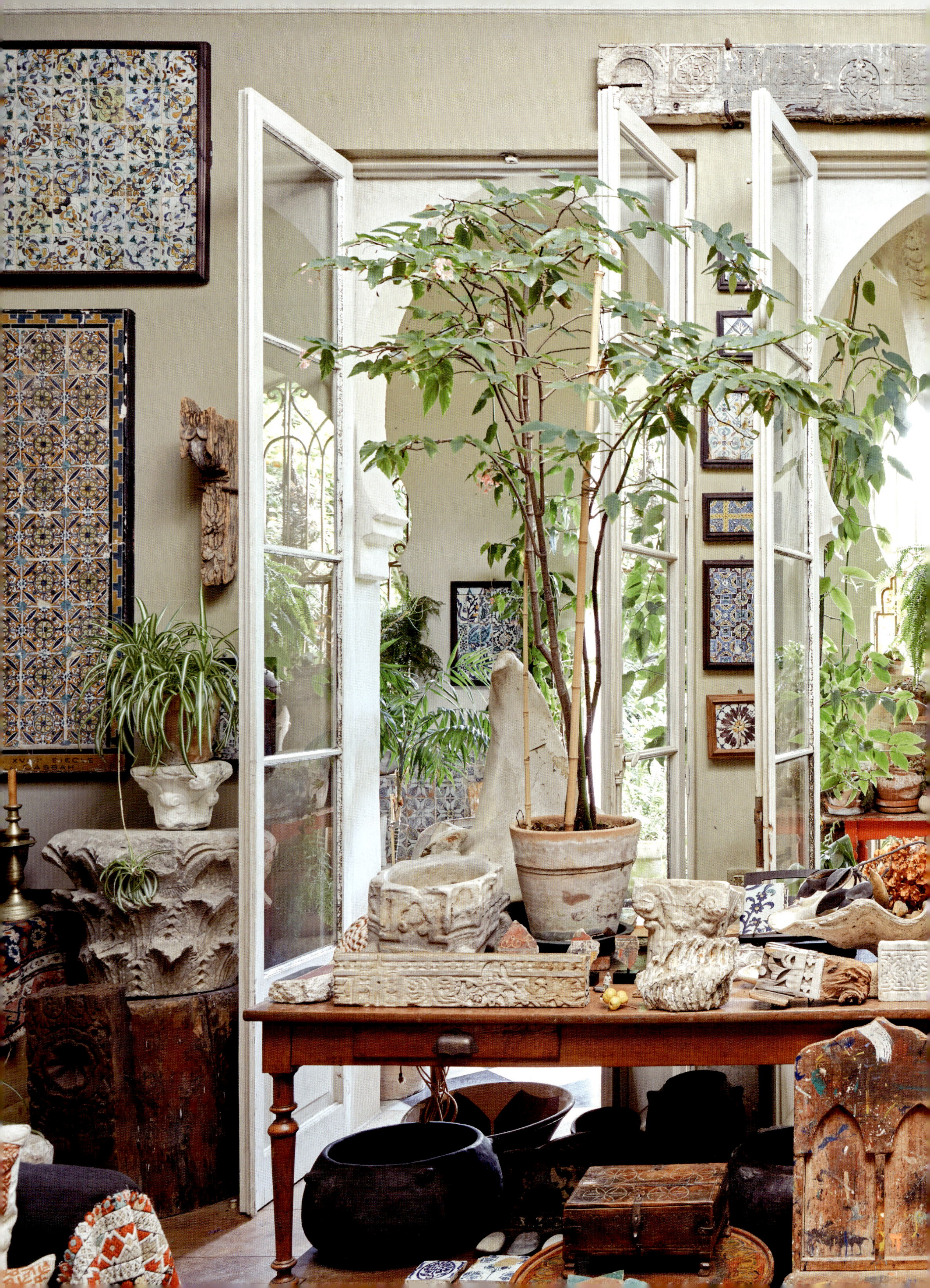
SIECLE
CASBAH

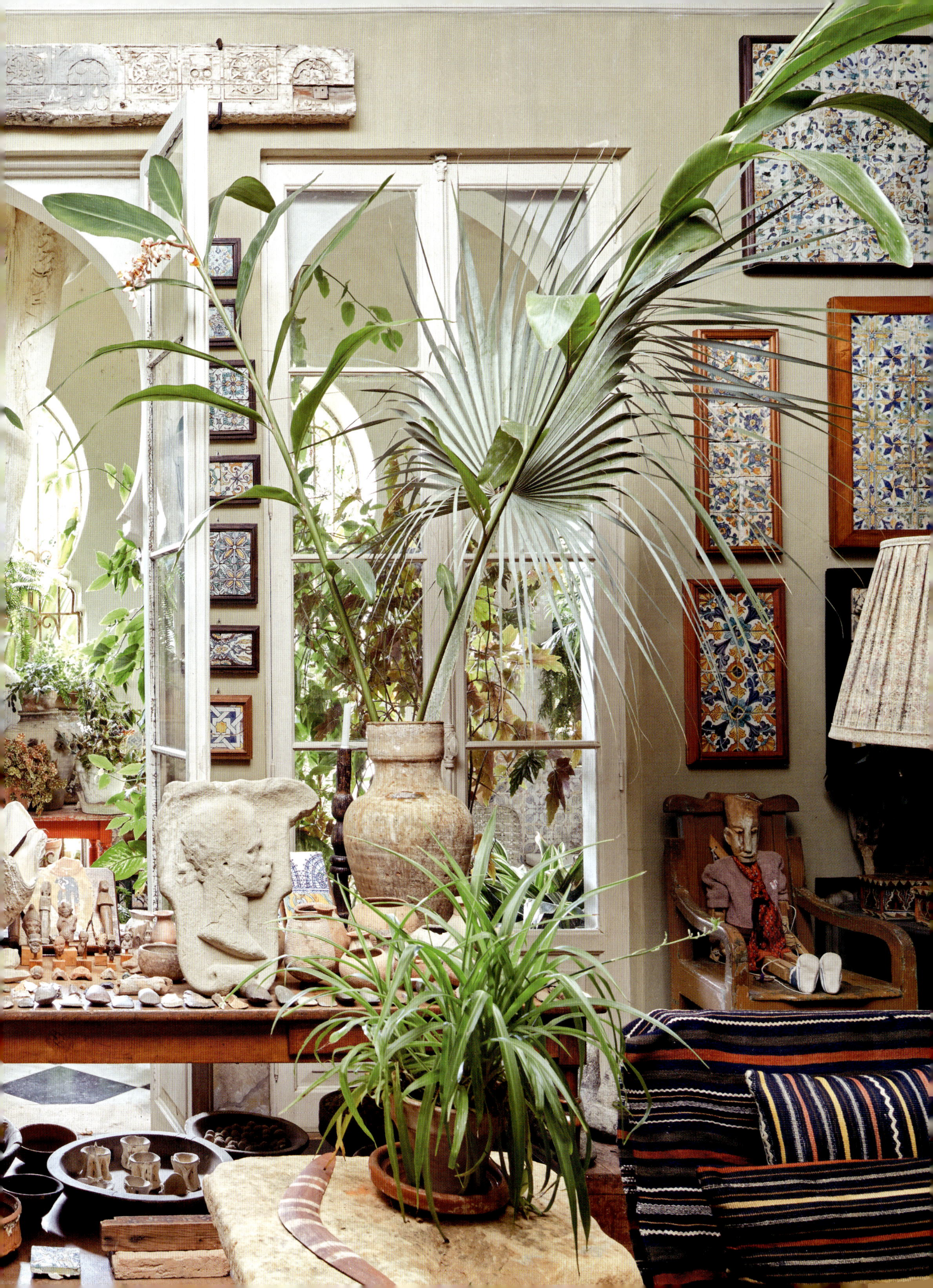

ALGER { FAIENCE ARABE du XVIIIe SIÈCLE
DU PALAIS DE LA CASBAH

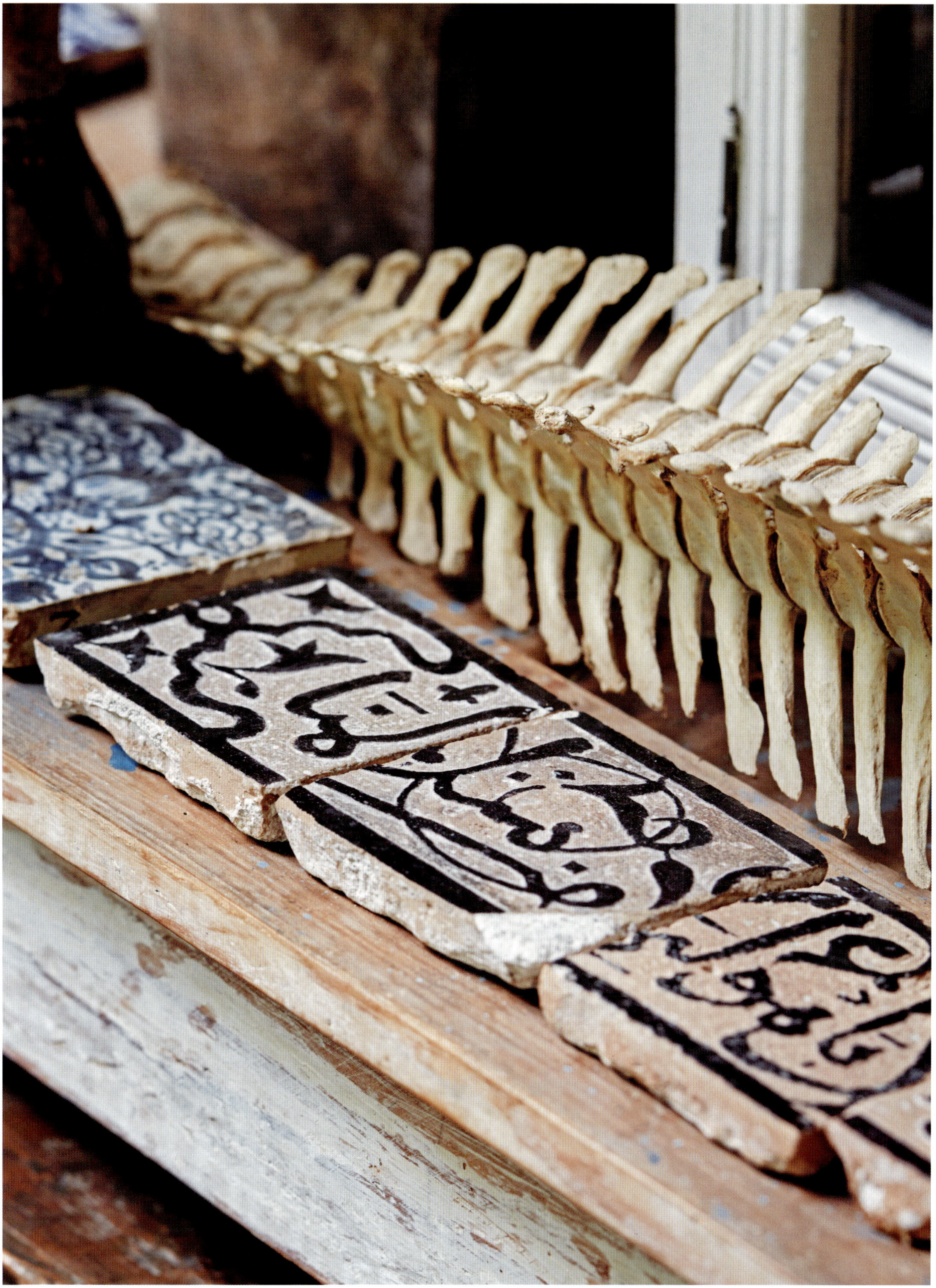

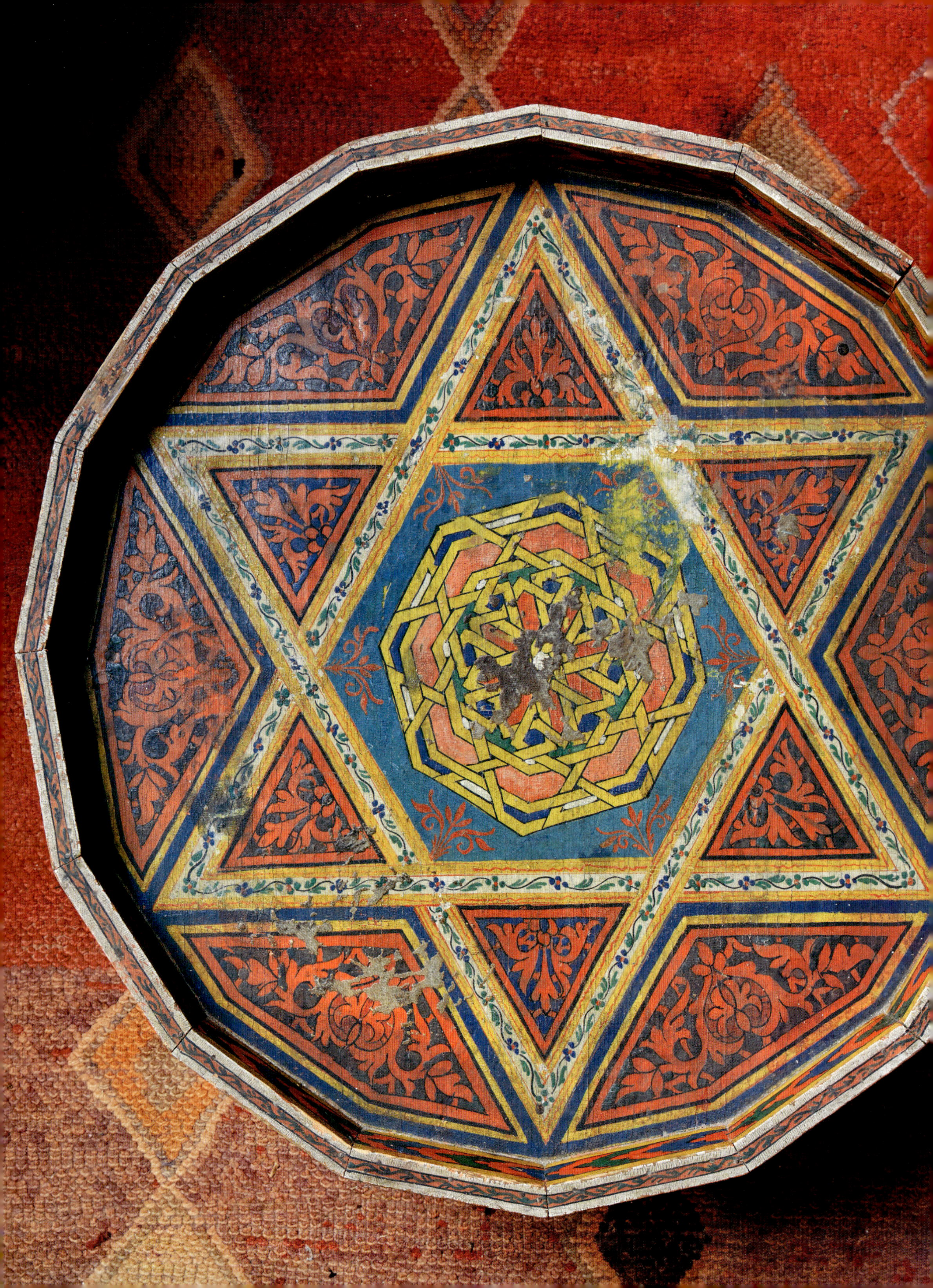

PREVIOUS SPREAD, LEFT: *A nineteenth-century painted cradle from Tétouan.*
PREVIOUS SPREAD, RIGHT: *seventeenth-century* sgraffito *tiles.*
OPPOSITE: *The top of a beautiful* taifur *from Tétouan.*
FOLLOWING SPREAD, LEFT: *The fields of wild irises (*Iris tingitana*) are the reason why we moved to Tangier. They have now disappeared. The embroidery is the border of an eighteenth-century Cretan skirt found in a bazaar.*
FOLLOWING SPREAD, RIGHT: *In front of the seventeenth-century Venetian fireplace, a few Roman capitals that I found thirty years ago while I was redoing this garden. Upside down in the dirt, mixed up with other stones, they had been buried in order to support the terraces. I never found out how they ended up here. The carpet is a fragment from a sixteenth-century Star Ushak.*

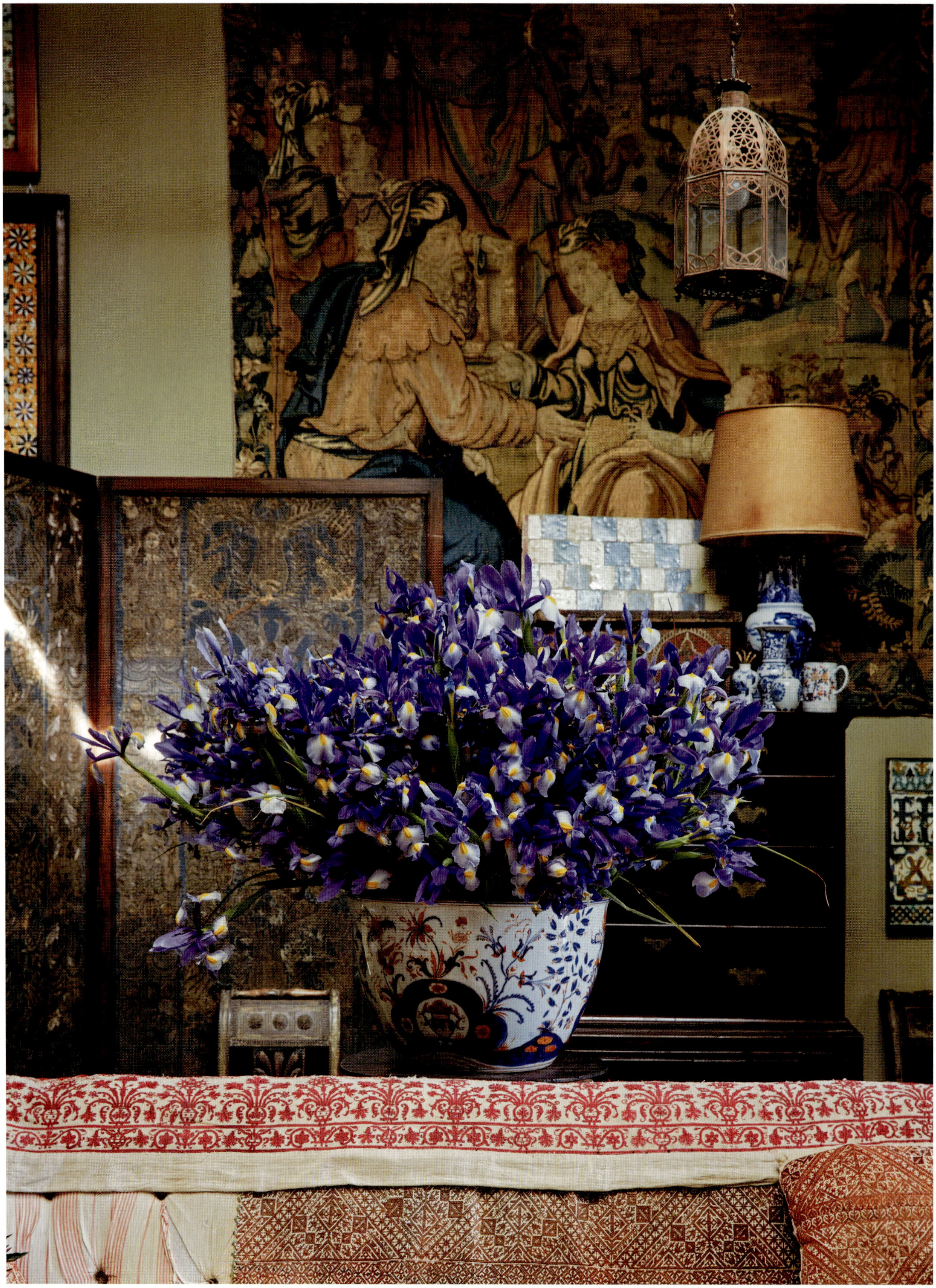

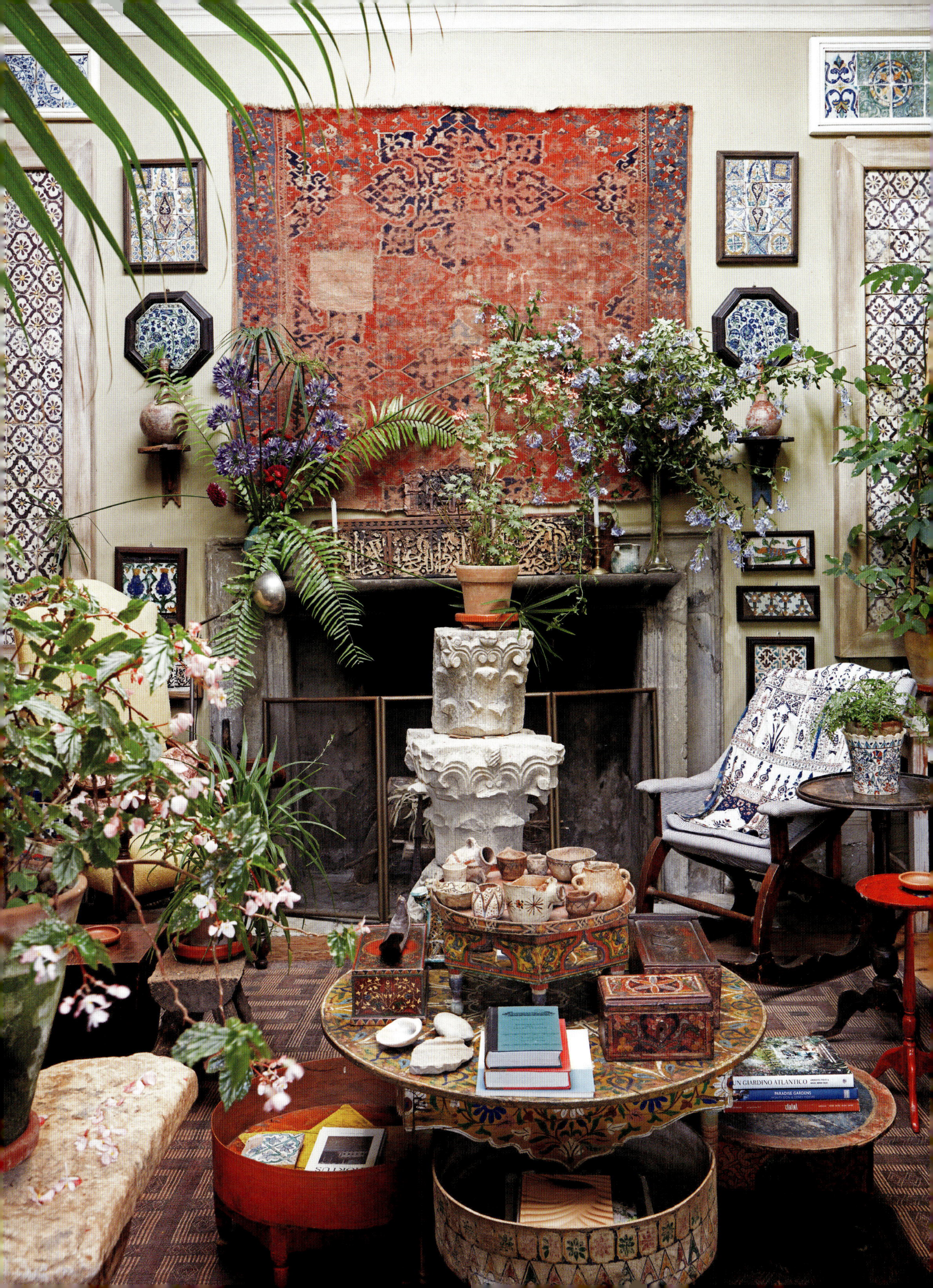
UN GIARDINO ATLANTICO
PARADISE GARDENS

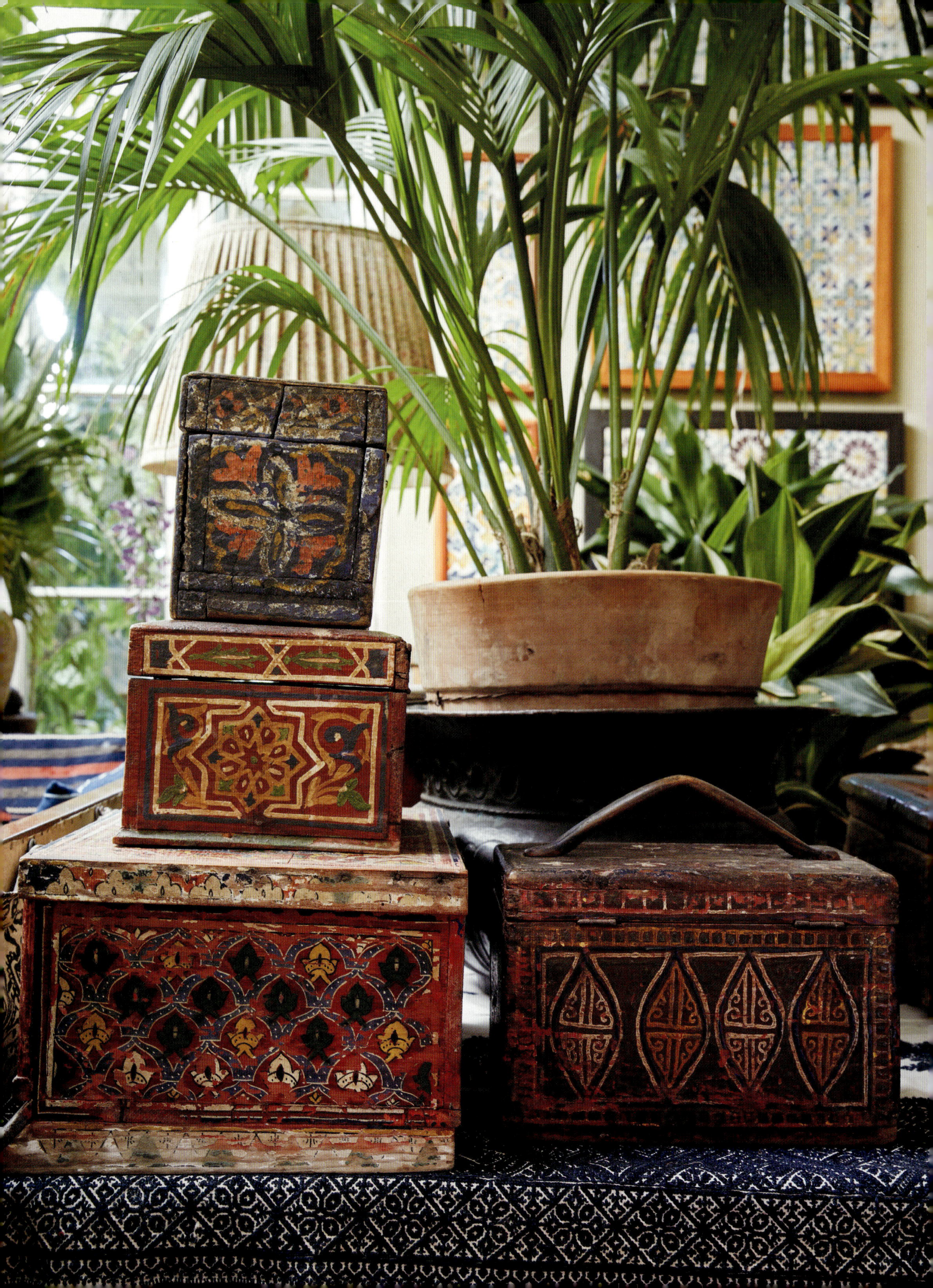

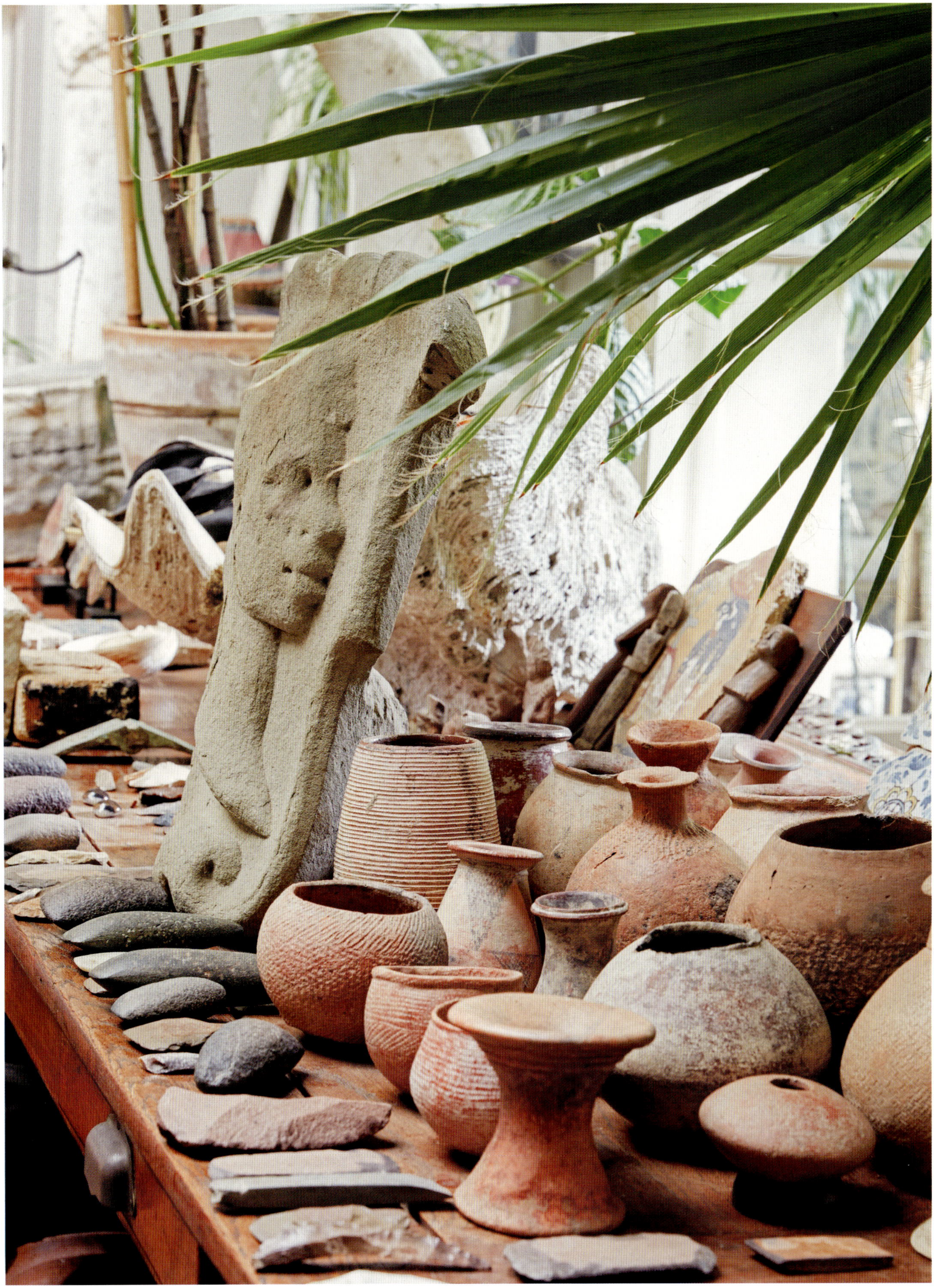

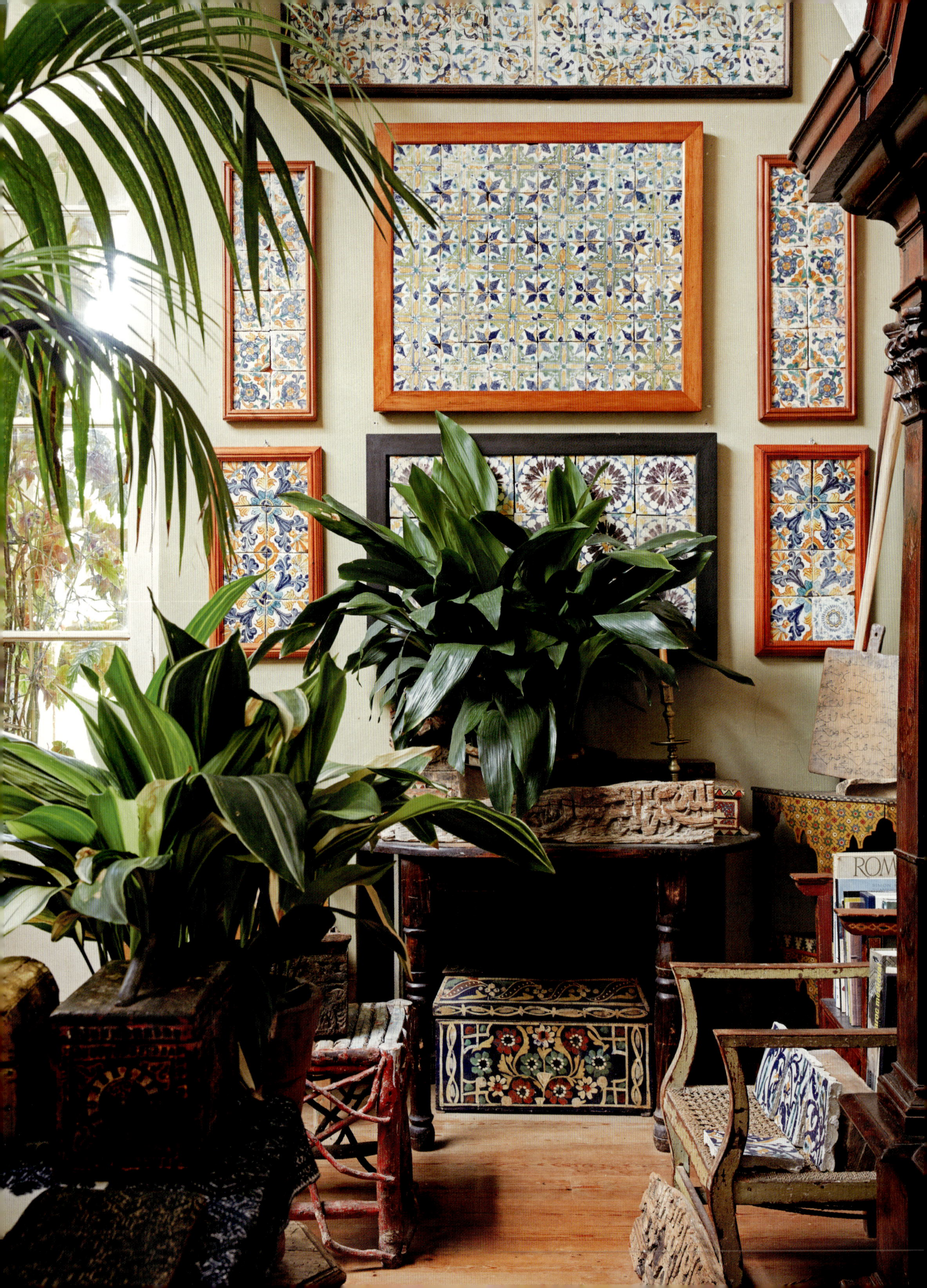

PREVIOUS SPREAD: *I will never have enough Jbala painted boxes... nor Niger Delta potteries and Neolithic axes.*
OPPOSITE: *A few more Qallaline tiles.*
FOLLOWING SPREAD, LEFT: *Another whale skull, this one from a* Balaenoptera acutorostrata.
FOLLOWING SPREAD, RIGHT: *The two fragmentary wooden Merinid beams date back to the fifteenth century. I consider them the most seductive objects in this room, certainly the sexiest, for the dance of naked letters that, panting, slip out of the embrace of the wooden base that grabs them again every time.*

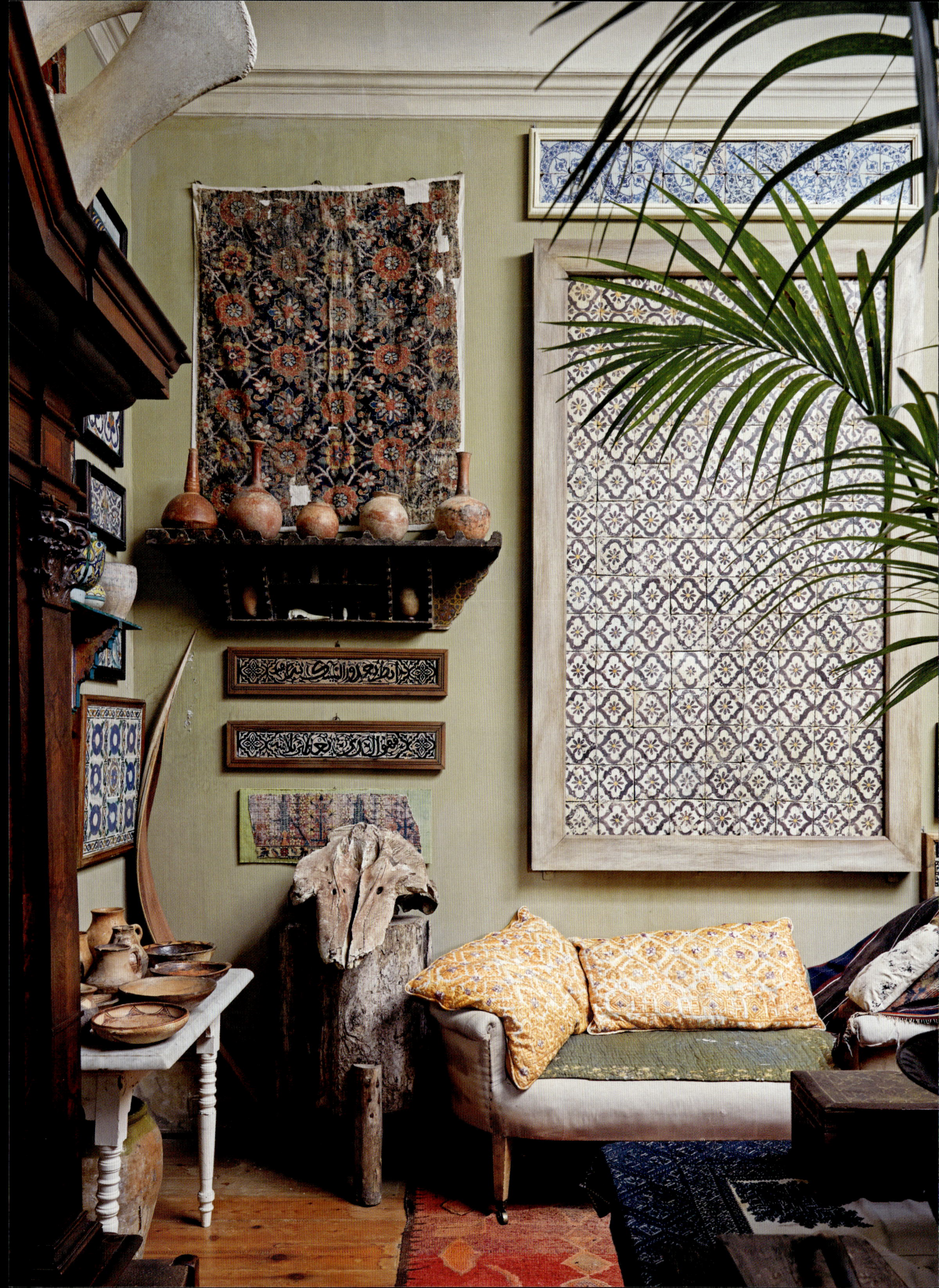

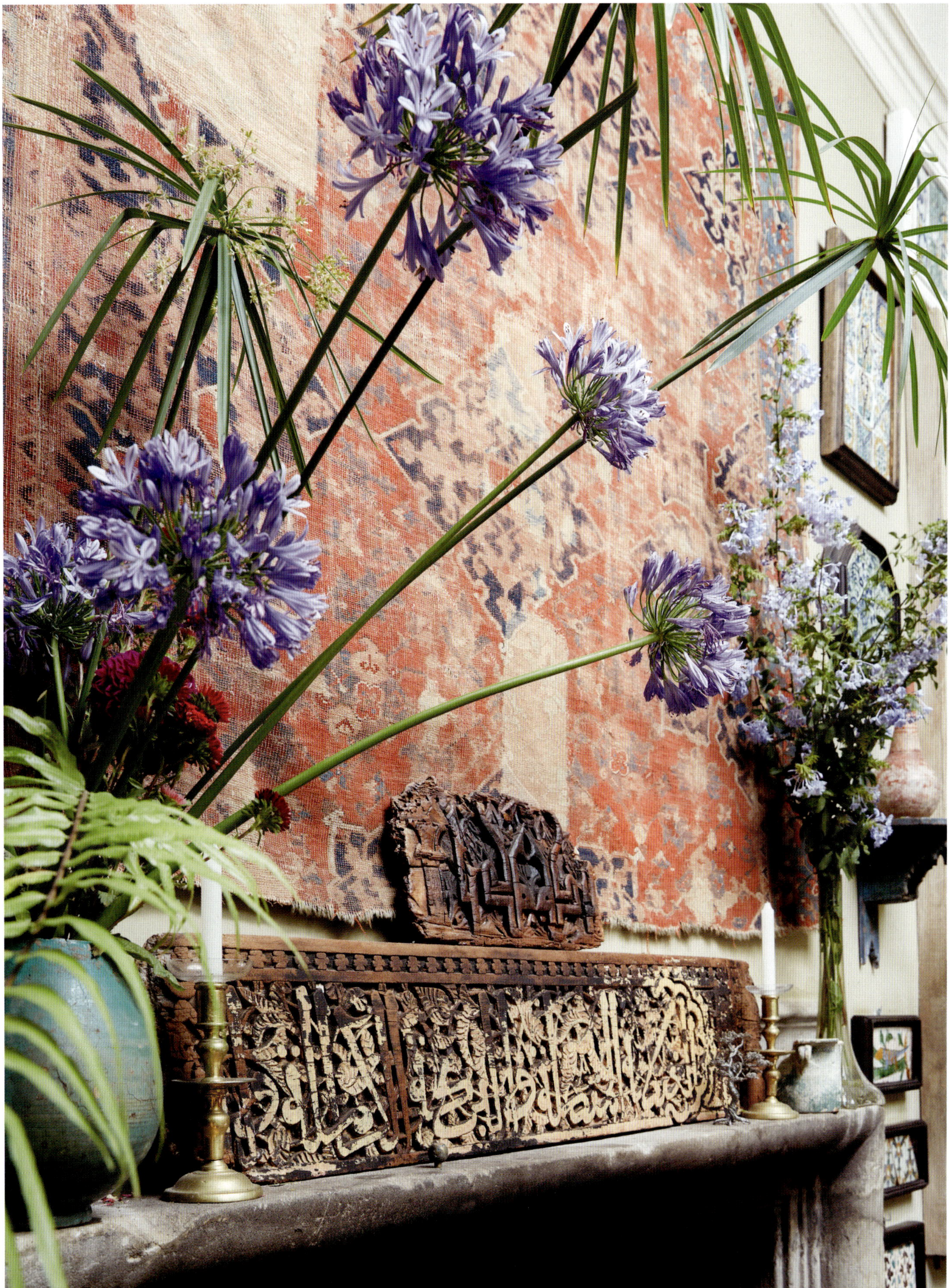

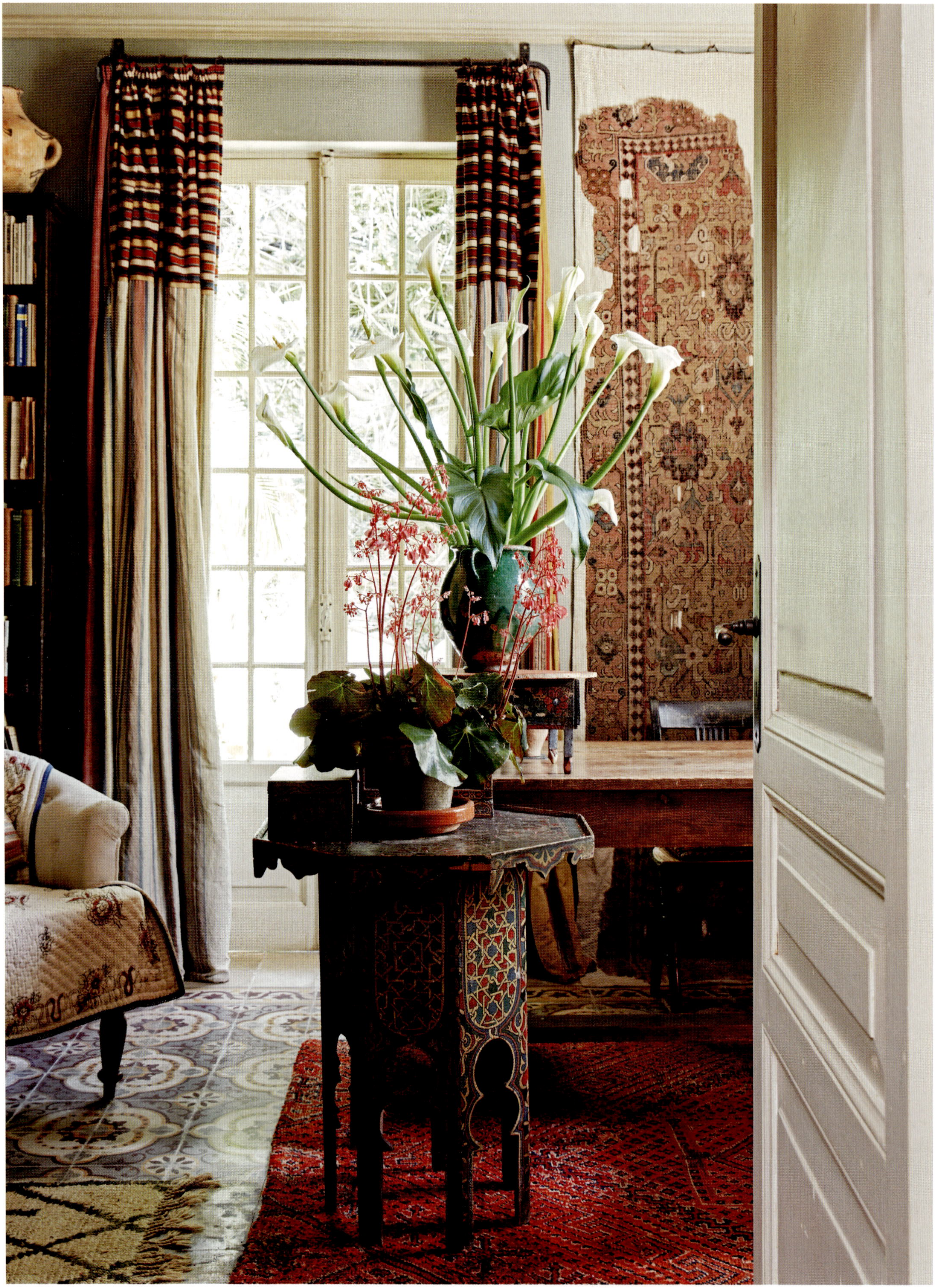

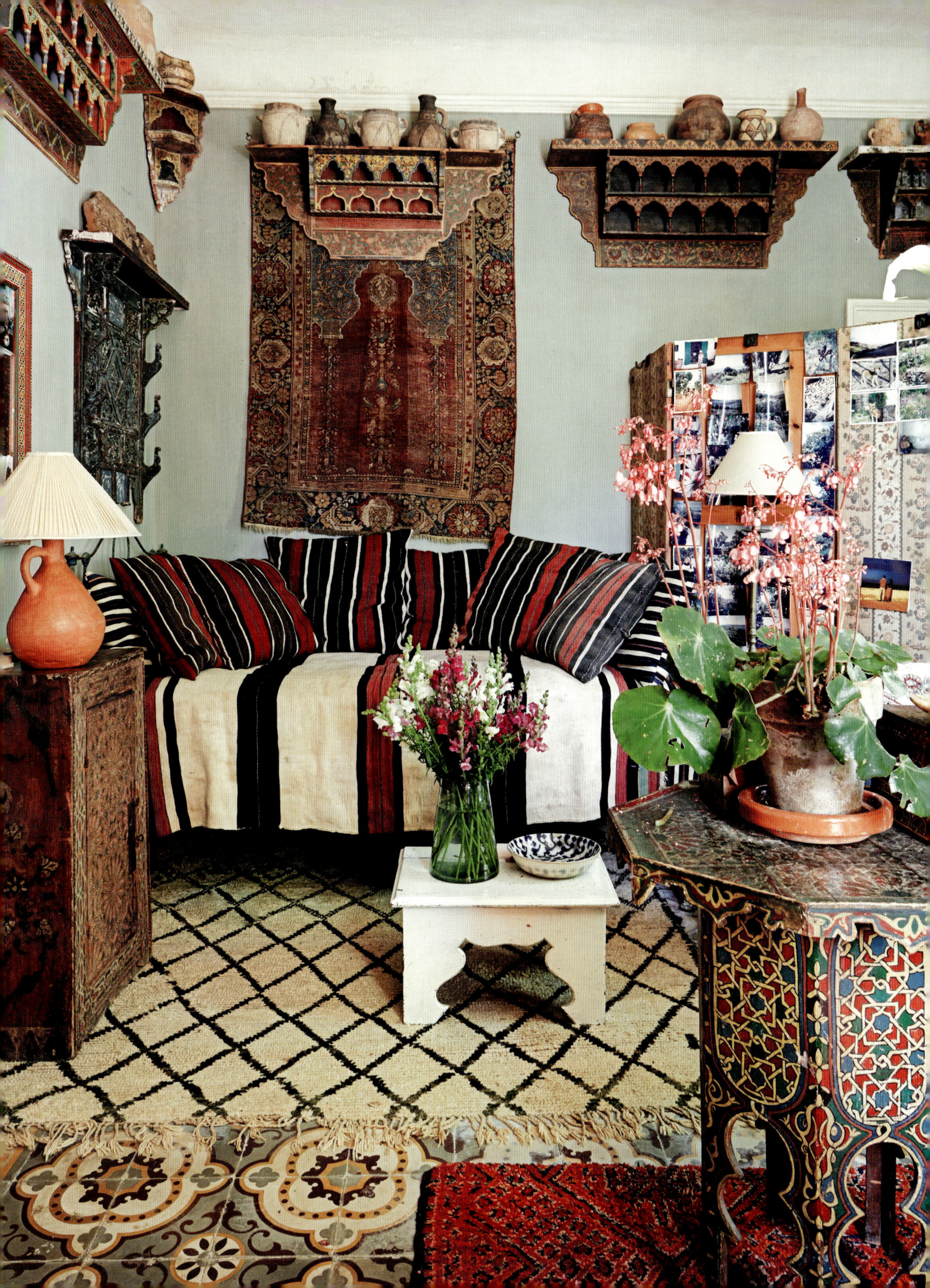

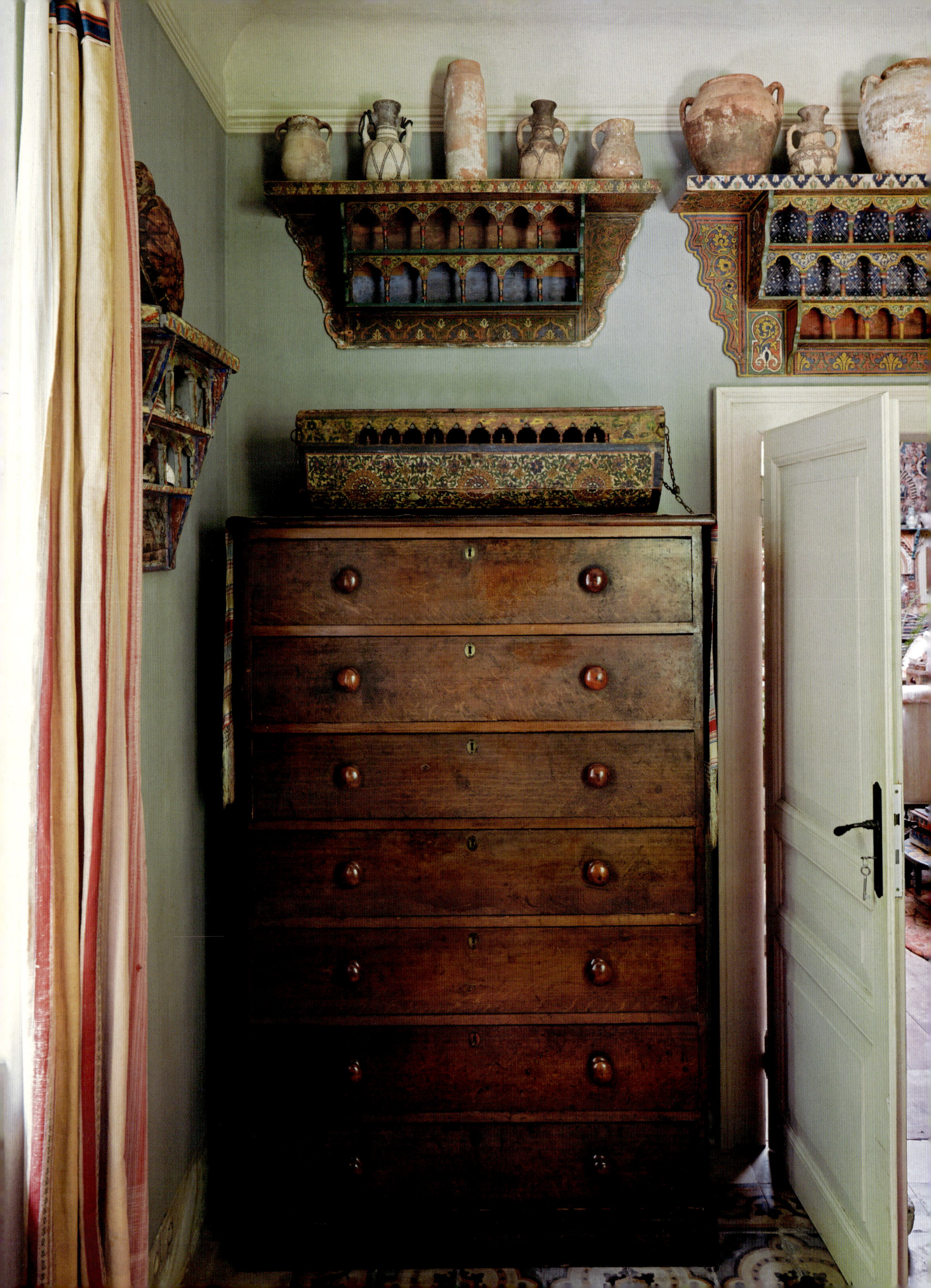

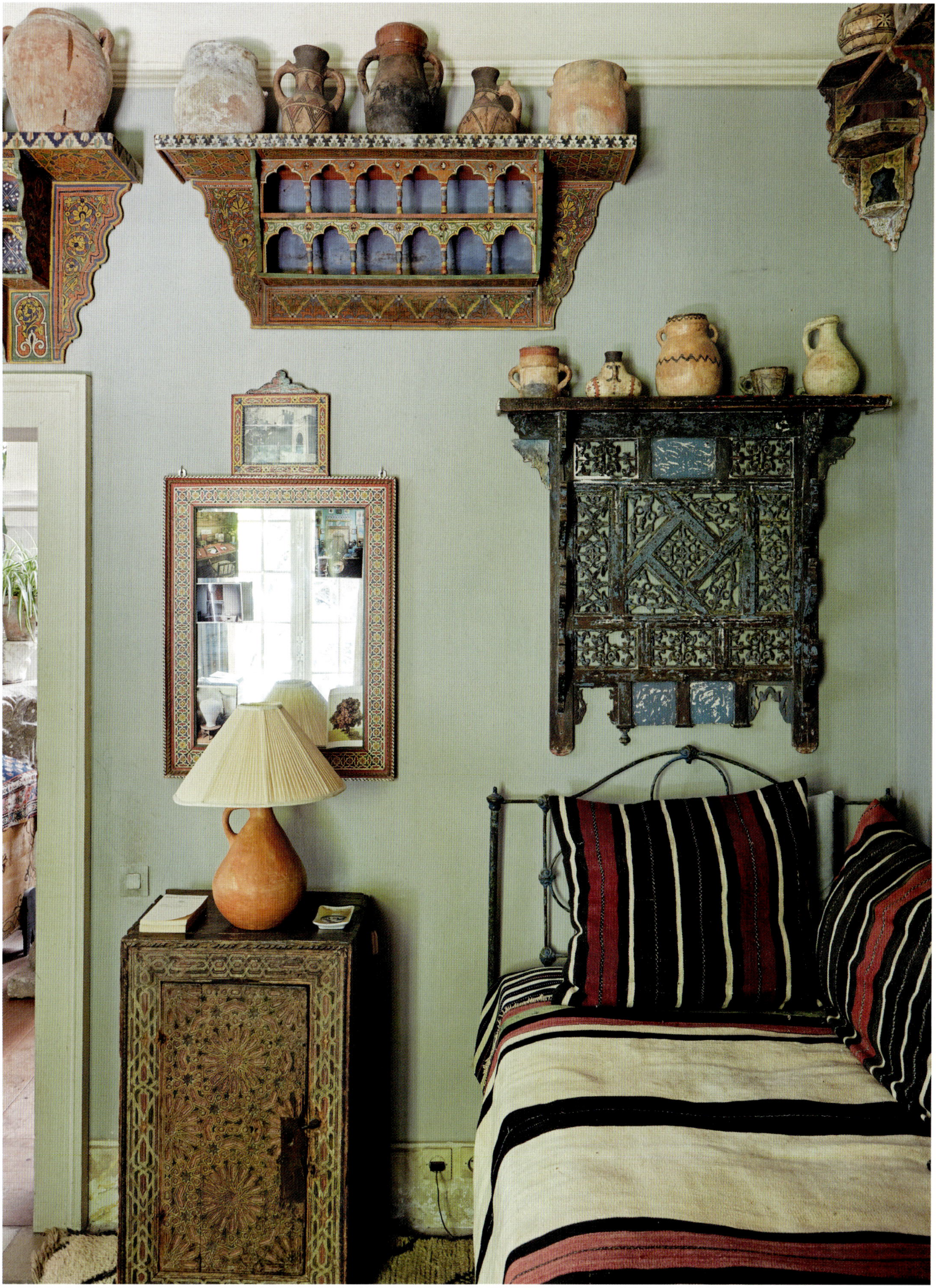

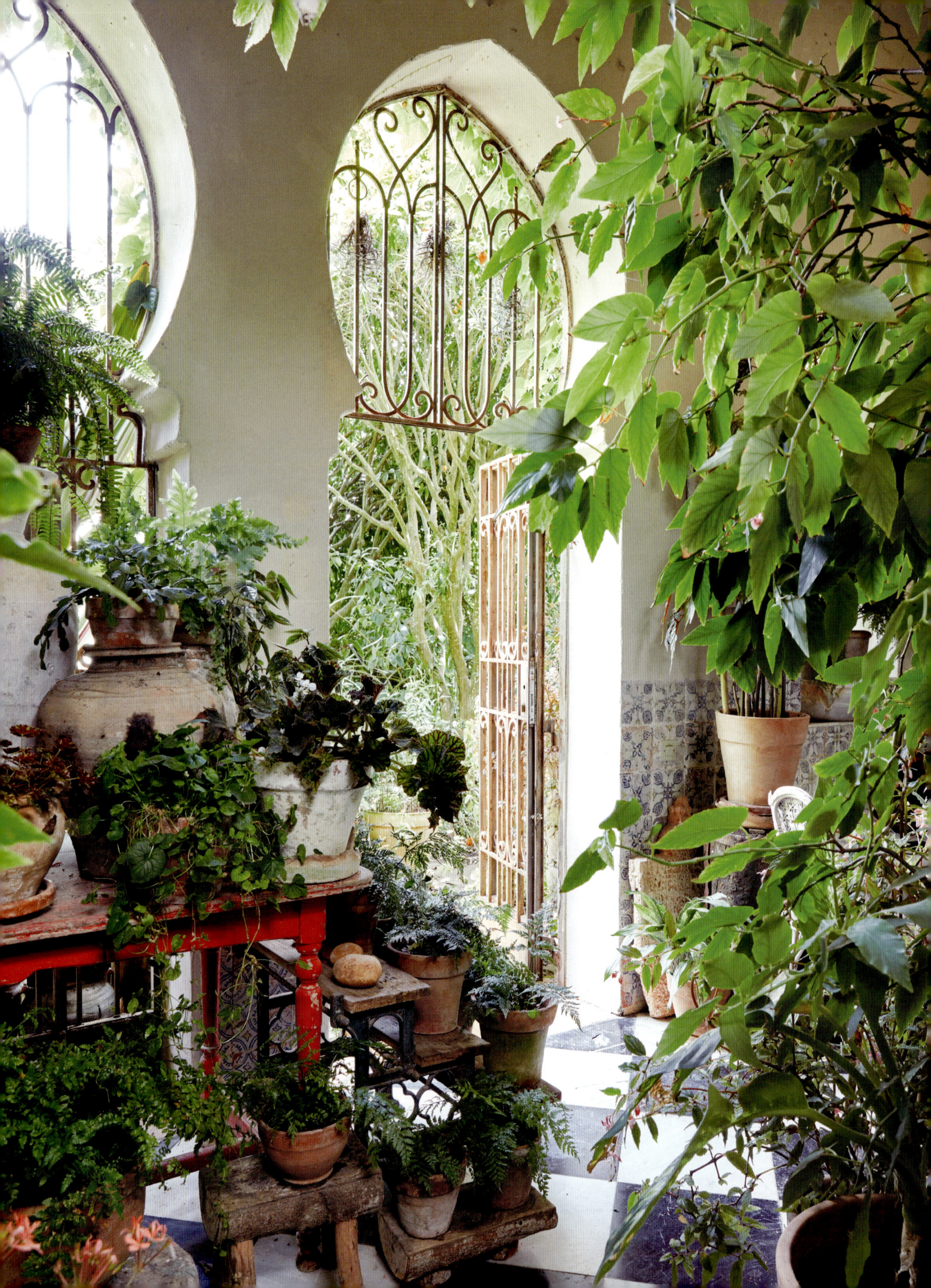

PAGE 174: *In the small bedroom that was Stephan's studio and that I have invaded, a painted* taifur *from Tétouan. I'm very keen on this kind of furniture—we host more than fifty of them in this house. The curtains are a patchwork of nineteenth-century Tétouan and Daghestan striped silks.*

PAGE 175: *On the bed, fabrics from the Middle Atlas. The seventeenth-century prayer rug is Anatolian. But who forgot the shoes?*

PREVIOUS SPREAD: *Above the Victorian chest of drawers, another cradle from Tétouan. On the walls, a collection of nineteenth- and twentieth-century* marfas *from Chaouen with some pots from the Rif. Unlike what generally happens in Muslim countries, the ceramics of these mountains are made only by women, modeled by hand and not on a wheel. Unglazed, they are decorated in black, using a sort of ink from the bark of the terebinth tree. The motifs resemble those of Neolithic and Minoan pottery. Until a few years ago, before the invasion of plastic, they were used in all the houses in the region to cook in and to store water and milk. Accept an invitation to lunch and you would step a few thousand years back in time.*

OPPOSITE: *The arches and the iron railings designed by our friend Roberto Peregalli twenty years ago look as if they have been here for two centuries.*

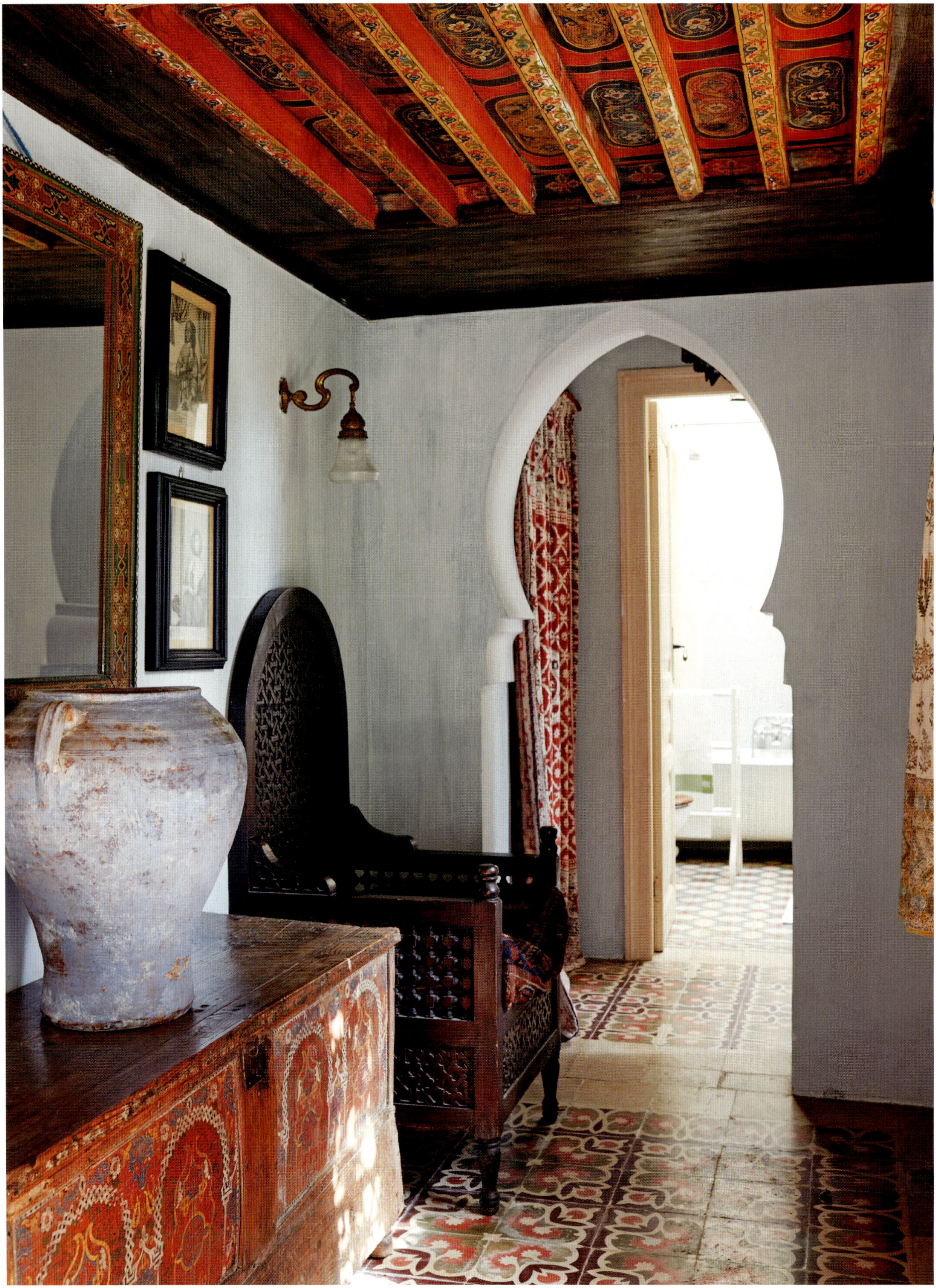

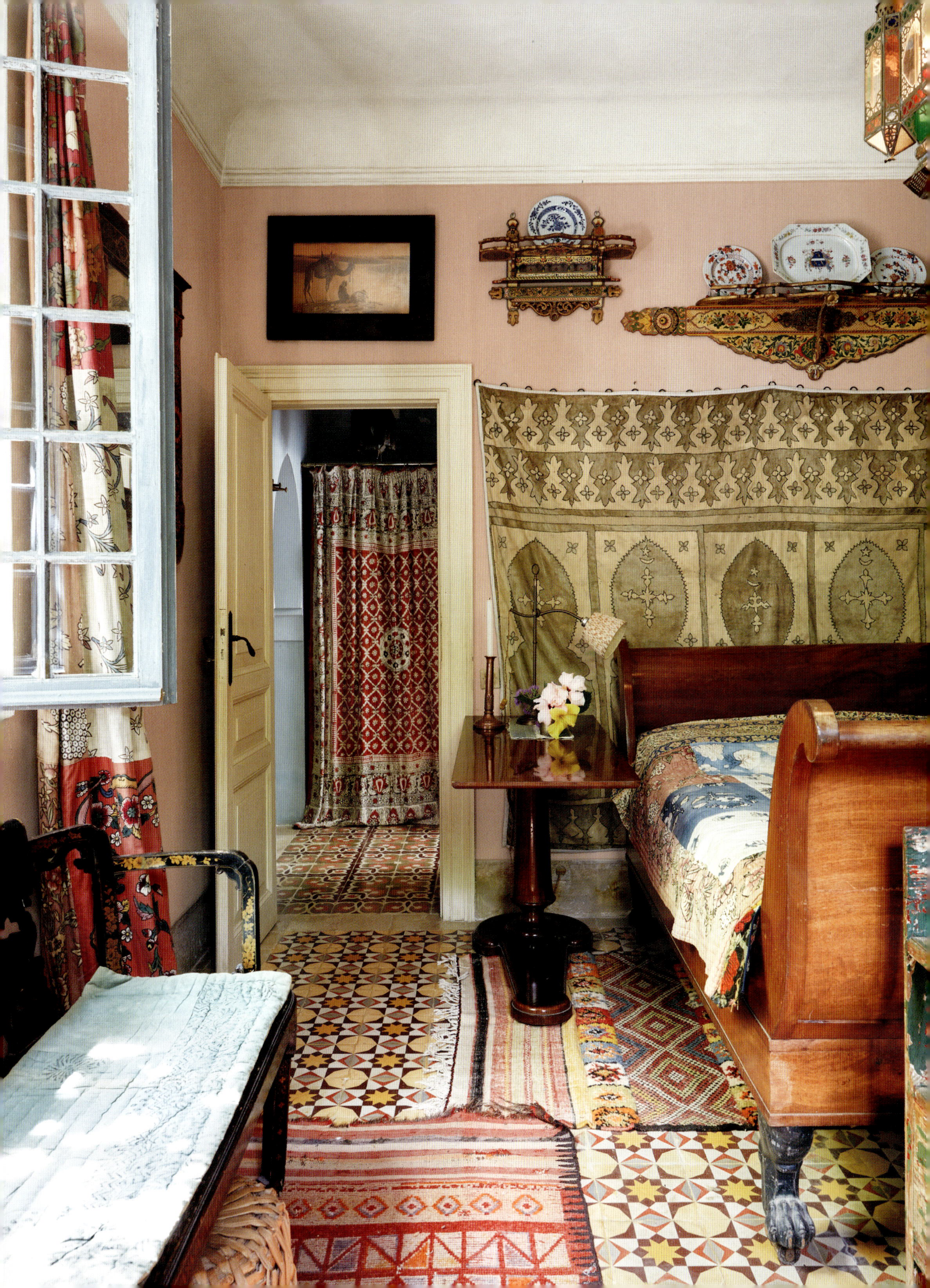

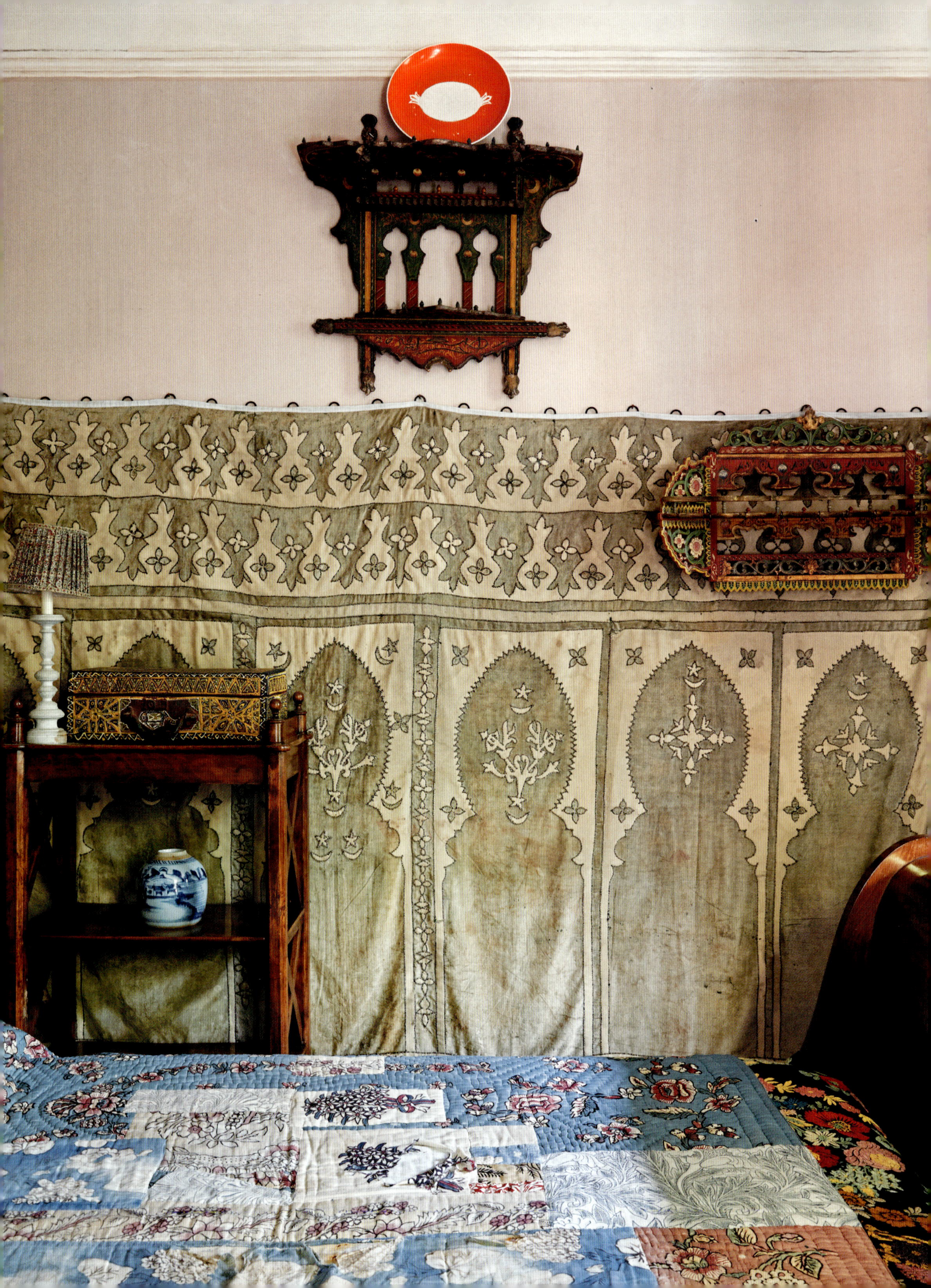

PREVIOUS SPREAD, LEFT: *All the tiles in the guest suite floor were rescued from an old house in Tangier.*
PREVIOUS SPREAD, RIGHT AND OPPOSITE: *We call it "The Algerian Room" because all the painted* marfas *come from Algeria. The floral motifs, a bit Turkish and a bit French, are a peripheral expression—but no less moving for all that—of that courtly style known as "Ottoman Rococo," which for a few decades of the nineteenth century transformed Istanbul into a bonbonnière of marzipan and filled the salons of Damascus and Cairo with those curly gilded armchairs known as "Louis-Hamid." On the wall behind the Austrian bed, a velvet* haiti, *the tapestries hung in old Moroccan homes.*
NEXT SPREAD, LEFT: *A magnificent 19th-century painted ceiling from Chaouen.*

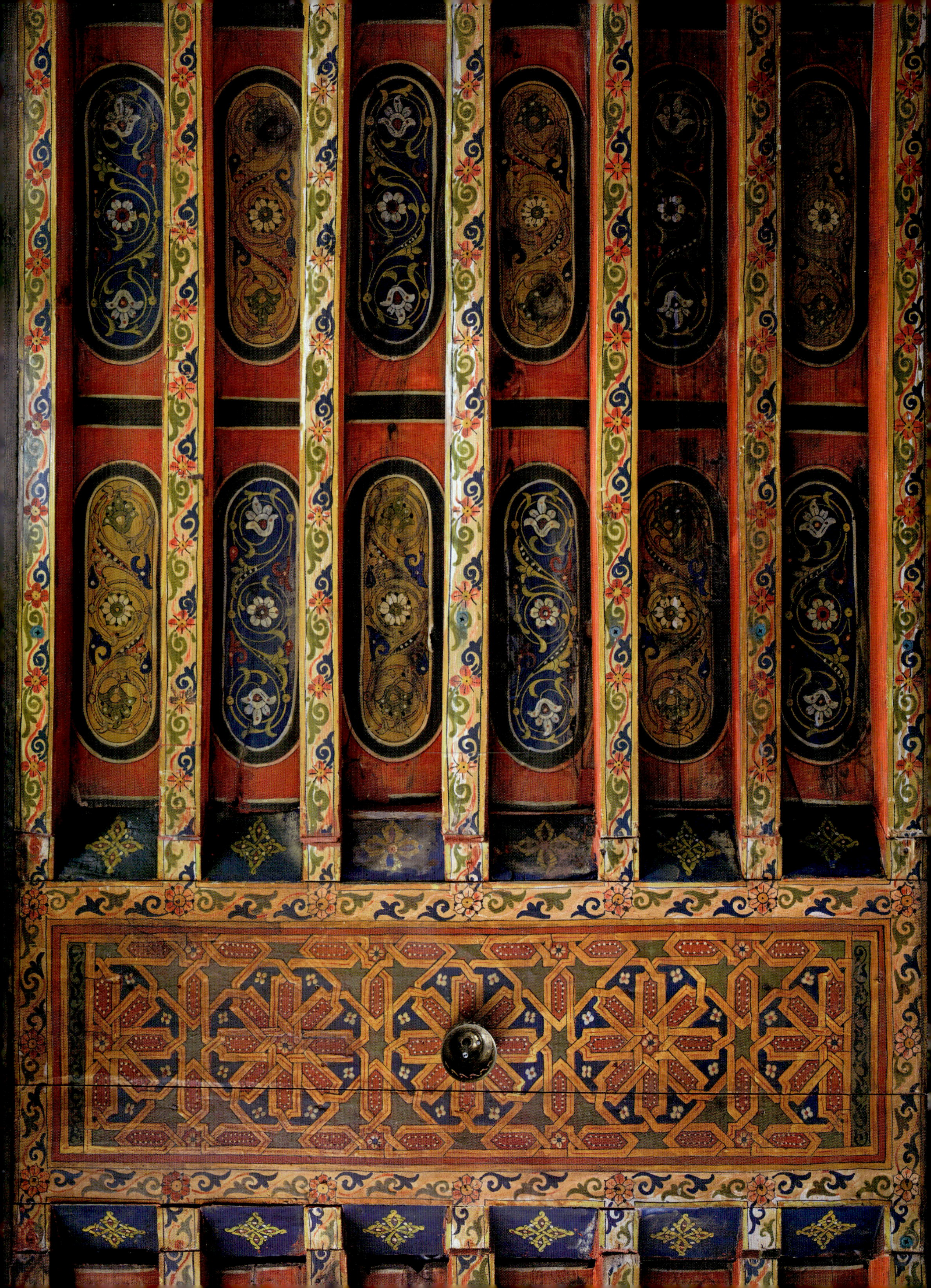

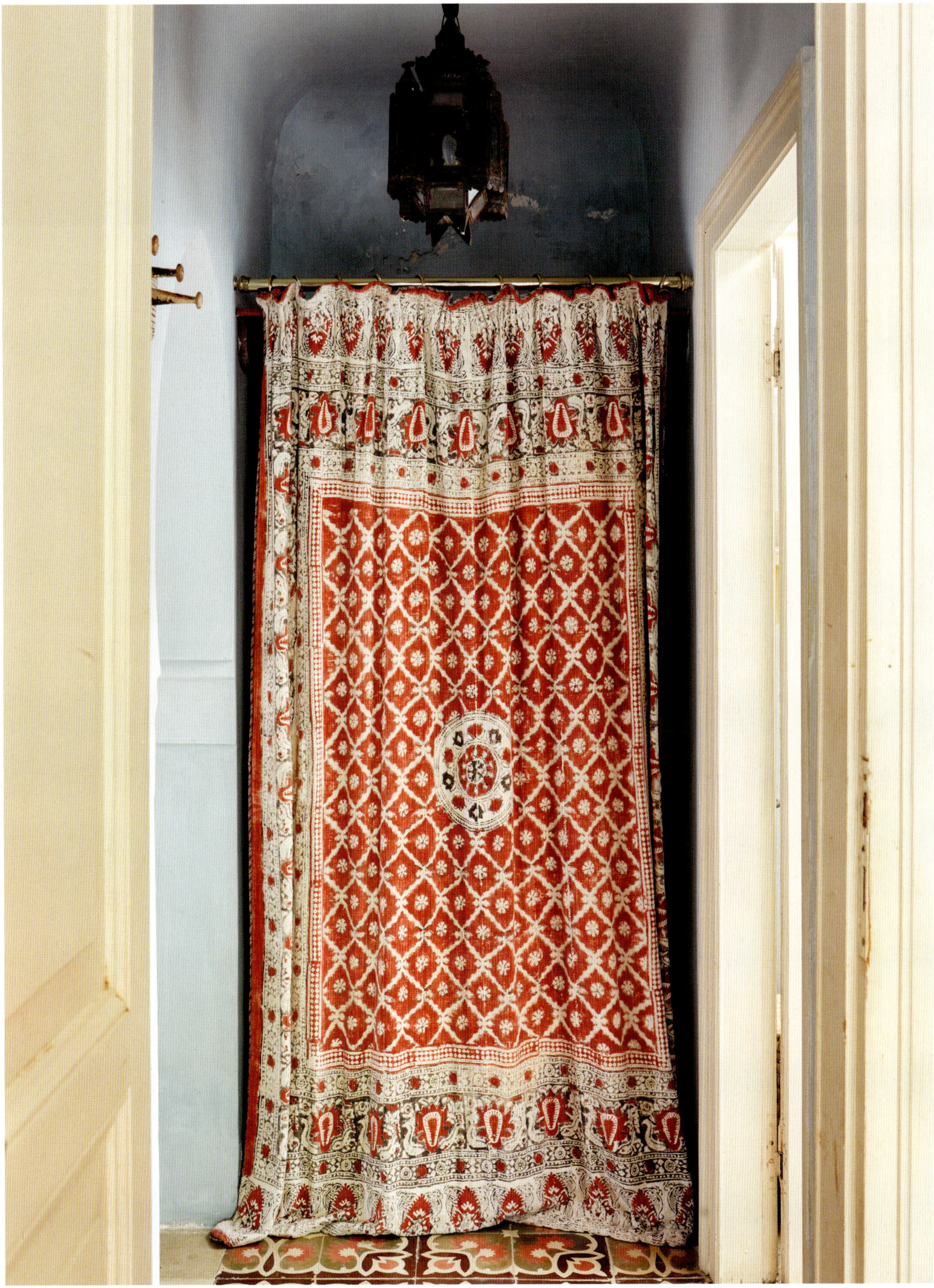

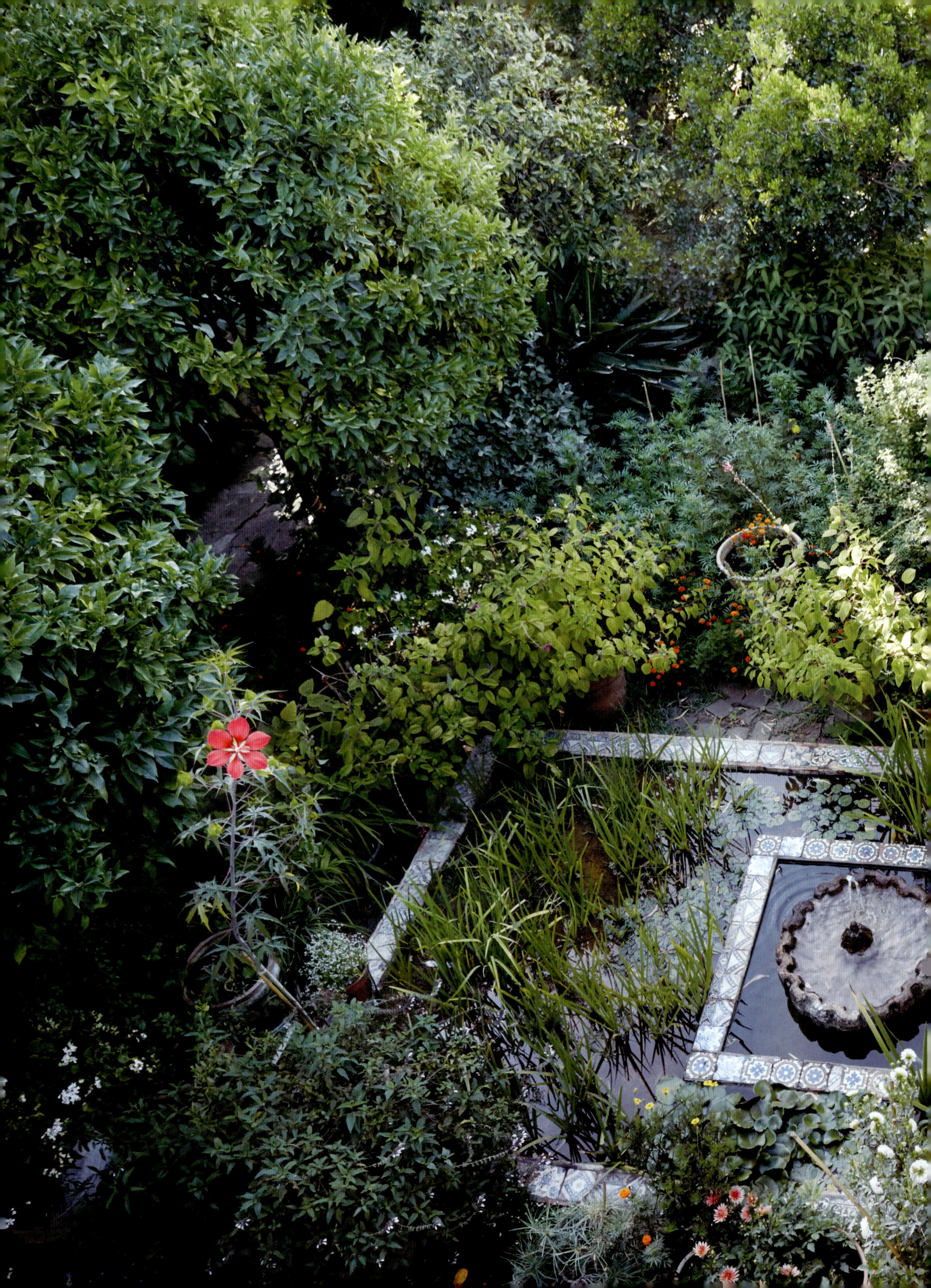

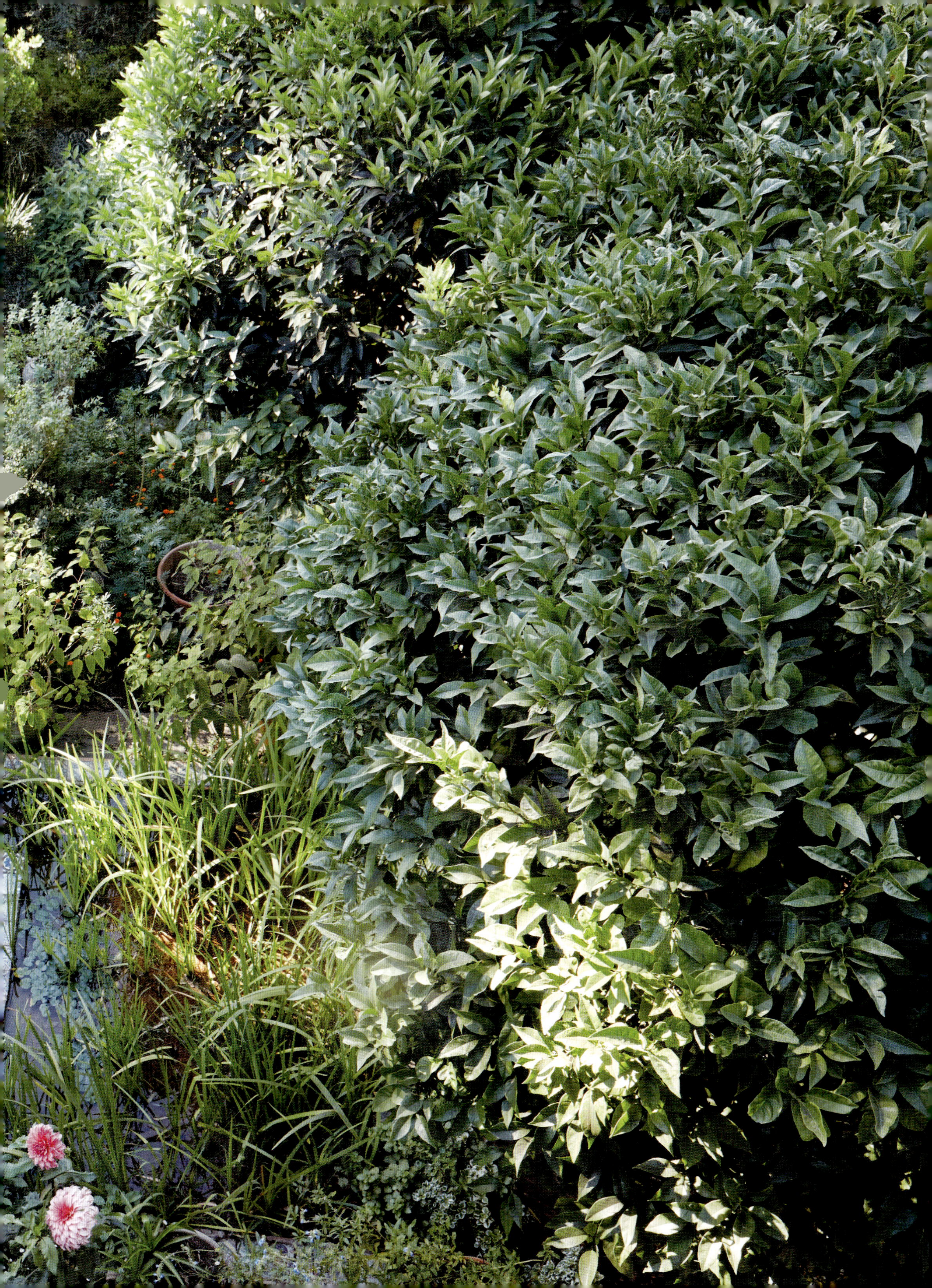

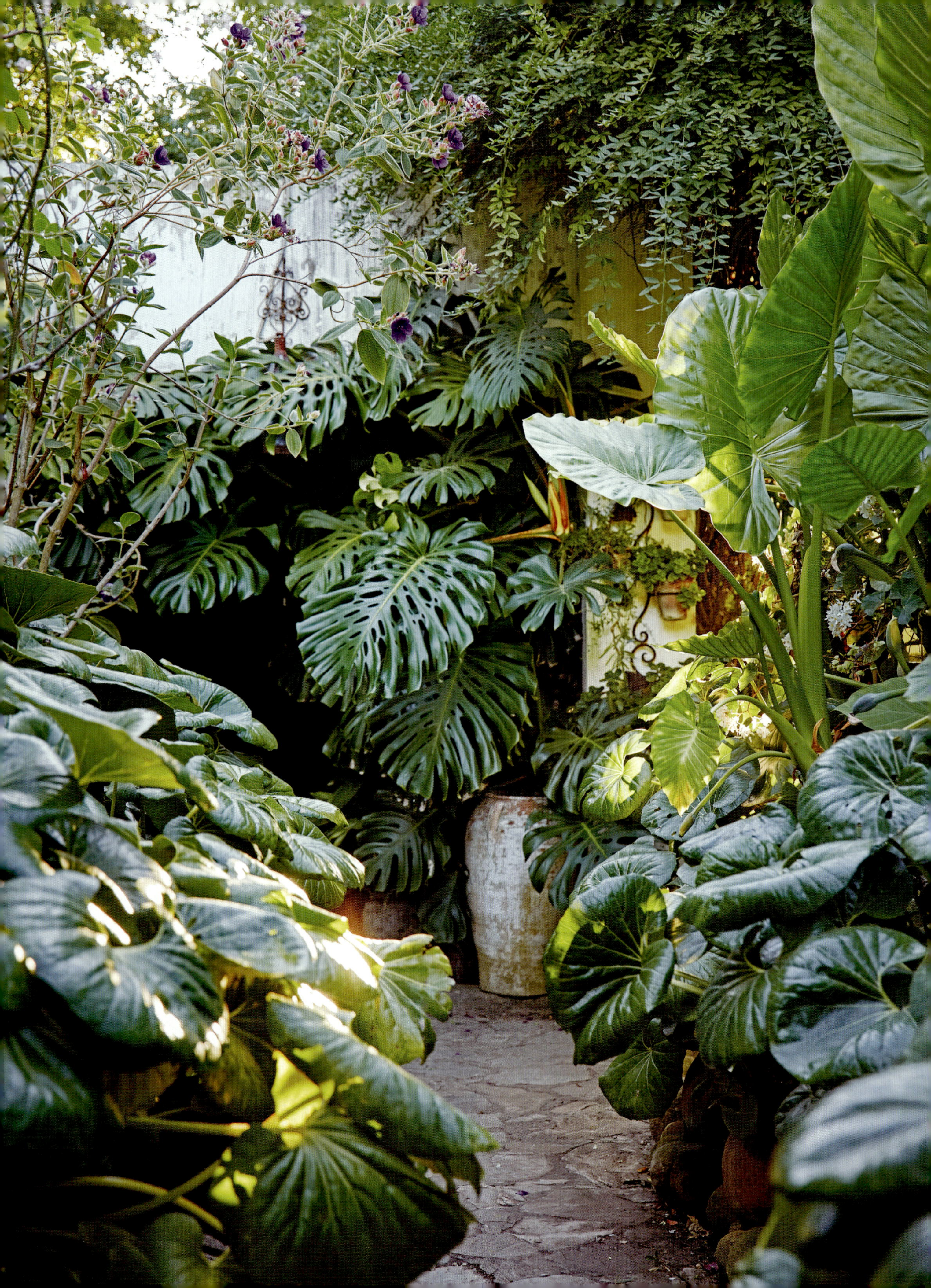

THE GARDEN

Thirty years ago Mohammed was just over fifty, but to us kids he seemed old. Stocky, high forehead, laughing hazel eyes, well-groomed gray beard. At dawn, rain or no rain, he went every day to pray at the mosque. On Friday, dressed in his immaculate gandoura, he stayed there for several hours, and on his return he smelled of incense. On Sundays he would fish with his pole on the rocks at Agla and return at sunset with some little fish in his basket. The rest of the time he worked in the garden.

When he was a boy, in his parents' hut in the forest above Al-Hoceima, he woke up one night from a long fever. The noise was deafening. He caught a glimpse of a black horse rearing up and pounding its hooves on the floor, dodged the terracotta heater as it shot through the air, the frying pan was violently banging on the ceiling, his grandfather's stick exploded into a thousand splinters, the stool rolled from side to side as if in a ship during a storm. Then, finally, the *jennouns* flew out of the window. They had cut off his tongue and poured molten lead into his ears. A few years later the family had had to leave the Rif for the city, where the father had found a job as a night watchman. By then their deaf-mute son had become a burden, he had to start earning his bread. Luckily, he had two weapons: physical strength and, even more effective, a cheerful nature. Together with his faith, they made him the most serene man in the world. In a laborious stammer, for all his life Mohammed called everyone *ha-bi-bi*, beloved—when you are the beloved of Allah (no sound here, only the index finger pointing Leonardesque at the sky) you can rest assured, enjoy the water if you are thirsty and if you want beauty just gaze upon creation. In exchange for bread and a blanket he had worked for a farmer who sold vegetables in the souk and had labored as a longshoreman before working as a servant to a Spanish woman who slapped him, spat on him, and skimped on the potato skins. He had arrived in Tebarek Allah around the age of twenty, hired by the Gramonts, for whom he had built both the middle pavilion and the two shacks where he was living with his family when we arrived. After uprooting the prickly pears and the reeds, he dug up and broke the stones, built the drystone walls that to this day surround the four main terraces of the grounds, paved the paths, delimited the flower beds, and planted the trees that had come to keep the original palm trees company. The cypresses, the great Judas tree, the olive trees, the quince trees, the two medlar trees, the apricot tree, and the cherry tree had grown thanks to his care, along with many creepers (the wisteria being the most glorious) and many bushes.

Ftoma, his wife, was a widow with five children from the Anjra, the steep lunar mountains that plunge into the strait east of Tangier, where they knead dried tubers and roots to make bread and lick the condensation from the roofs of caves where they worshipped a goddess with goat's feet. The four eldest sons had gone their own way and the youngest had stayed with the couple, who had had two girls. The blood of Shousha and Karima was a concentrate of the beauty of an ancient, bastard race. They were little girls with doe eyes, brown hair, and a golden complexion that tiredness or ill humor could turn white as plaster: when they quarreled, their graceful movements became those of panthers and their fits of pique worthy of a duchess, and when they finally calmed down, their beautiful childlike faces resembled those of the two boxers from Santorini. Family life had all the coziness of the nest, with continuous play and joking—but when the daughters greeted their father, they kissed his hand. For his part, Mohammed attributed the decline of our world to specific causes, one of which being that women (whom he designated by running his index finger over his chin, because that is where the women of his tribe were tattooed) had begun to paint their eyelids and lips. Yet he never dreamed of preventing his teenage daughters from wearing makeup (they both did so with a certain exuberance), and when they were finally ready to go out he would admire the result of hours of work on their faces with the same emotion as in front of a flower. And once, when Shousha went to visit an aunt and had made herself up like a fifties diva at the Oscars ceremony and I, astonished, complimented him on the beauty of his eldest daughter, he nodded vigorously several times and got out a whole word several times: "*Mzuina, mzuina!*"—beautiful, beautiful! He was too good to forbid his girls a practice that clearly made them happy, and too free and sure of his faith to bother with the comments of bigots.

 Mohammed loved this garden as you can only love something you made from nothing with your own hands. I realized this from the first day I set foot in Tebarek Allah when, on leaving George and Stephan on the terrace to exchange pleasantries as they gingerly tackled the matter of the sale, I followed him along the paths among the plants. I had never met him before, I still didn't speak a word of Arabic, and he was deaf and dumb, but in a quarter of an hour, with the urgency of a prisoner who has a chance to pass a message to someone who can rescue him, he managed to explain to me that the situation was desperate. Among flower beds parched and cracked from lack of water and suffering saplings, he showed me the half-collapsed well that George was too stingy to have repaired: water was scarce, the soil hadn't received a handful of manure for years, he pruned with his bare hands because he had no shears anymore… he took advantage of the rare rain showers to plant the cuttings that his friends, gardeners for other Nasranis, had given him (he pointed to roses, marmalade bushes, datura) and carried on a little at a time with his sedum and drought-tolerant sage borders. He proudly showed me, on the last terrace, where the owner never came, the little patch of annuals, zinnias, cosmos, and some dahlias that he cultivated by secretly connecting the barrel to a tap in the house for a few minutes: his treasure, like all treasures, was stolen. From his isolation, this gardener condemned not to work made a silent plea for help to the stranger whom fate had put in his path. As I walked up to the terrace where George was waiting for us, I was shaking with indignation and impatience. Thirsty and starved by the avarice of a despicable master, the garden did not deserve this treatment: I would do all I could to make its true owner happy.

 I had liked wildflowers since I was a child, when I discovered them on walks in the countryside or in the mountains; later, on observing still-life pictures in books and my mother arranging cultivated flowers in the vases, I had learned to appreciate others of a less insolent beauty. But I had never looked after a plant. I was twenty-eight, late for a first love: I threw myself into it with all the ardor of a neophyte who needs to make up for lost time. I frequented nurseries, consulted experts, visited gardens, questioned collectors. And I read, I read all day and a good part of the night—in those years before Google there were only books, and you could only order them by mail or by calling a bookseller… but the most valuable school of all lay right before my eyes: I began to look around, and I realized that I was learning more by observing what sprouted after a rain shower in the safety island on the state highway to Rabat than by filling a notebook with jottings on the parterre of a historic English garden. Together with Mohammed we set out to find the plant sellers of the region. Everyone knew the *zenzen*, the deaf-mute. The nurserymen were countryfolk who had arrived in the wake of a relative who was a gardener in the villa of some European; mountain men who had managed to buy a small patch of land where they grew flowers, vegetables, and fruit to sell in the souk, eccentric enthusiasts, industrious good-for-nothings who would consider anything to make ends meet, misfits intolerant of the rules of the city, old shepherds who would never give up their goats, lonely gatherers of blackberries and arbutus fruit, kif smokers, silkworm breeders, itinerant junk dealers, people who loved the outdoor life.

Behind crumbling walls, beyond the canebrakes, at the end of unknown paths among the eucalyptus trees, beneath the villas of the Europeans and Saudis where the nouveau riche Moroccan drug barons would soon arrive, stood shacks made of poles and corrugated iron surrounded by flowers and vegetables. Old women in shawls and boots reigned there, who, in addition to milking the cow, drying almonds and figs on sheets, ripening bunches of bananas on the tree by wrapping them in jute bags, and cooking giant pots of apricot and plum jam, also sold cuttings of subtropical plants. My supplier of agapanthus and old roses was a shaggy giant who took care of wounded birds in a reed hut deep in the thicket, splinting the wings of crows and hoopoes and caressing the vultures without fear of their shearlike beaks or the sudden lunges of their swanlike necks. To feed them, he picked up dead dogs. Every now and then he tried to palm me off with some "Phoenician" statuettes he said he had found in a cave, but they came from a tourist bazaar.

Zorah, Mohammed, Anwar, and Redwan were my heroes: every evening we would return home in the car loaded with plants grown in those gardens, the most beautiful in the world, our pockets full of the bags of fried sardines and little doughnuts we had received as gifts; every morning we resumed our rounds, returning the empties, cans of preserves, cans of oil, egg cartons, polystyrene boxes, ready to be filled with earth for resowing and replanting. On the roof of a ghostly apartment building where the widow of one of Mohammed's friends had opened her nursery, we bought ruby-colored tradescantias and farfugium and philadelphus three spans tall but already in bloom; I found a rare epidendrum in a hut buried beneath a banksia rose that looked like a flock of canaries in love; Mjiddo, who lived in his sheepfold behind the spring, cultivated thirty varieties of sansevieria and almost as many of aspidistra, and washed himself shirtless in a stream filled with calla lilies that came up to his shoulders, whiter than his skin; Fatna was a master at reproducing peach and apricot trees; Jemila cultivated mysterious species of begonia and fuchsia in the courtyard where she sewed on her machine watched by dozens of cats; and Tarek was the god of sages, purple, blue like his eyes, orange, scarlet; and all this a few miles from the city center, with the sea glittering in the background. Now that the well, newly repaired and cleaned, gave us a plentiful supply we could water the dozens, the hundreds of shrubs we brought back from our expeditions. I was so excited that I began to tremble. Then Mohammed placed his warm hand on mine: an enormous task awaited us. Little by little, a truck had unloaded tons of goat manure in front of our door, and even at dusk there was no way to convince my gardener reborn to stop going back and forth with the wheelbarrow that lulled me with its creaking, making me fall asleep over my Brian Mathew book on bulbous plants, or over the volume of the *Flore de l'Afrique du Nord* on amaryllidaceae. We built pergolas and huts that would be covered with vines, we ran wires between the branches so that the roses and the new jasmine would climb from tree to tree to create a fragrant shade, we filled pots and lined them up on the terraces and along the paths, we used poles and reeds to support the new trees, removed the dead wood of the old ones, added fertile soil, planted bulbs and rhizomes, sowed, planted, and mulched.

One day, to satisfy Mohammed who wanted an audience for his miracle, we invited about ten guests to lunch, the youngest of whom was in his seventies—in Tangier such old glories were nicknamed "Cro-Magnons." On the eve of the event, Mohammed triumphantly announced that he had bought a new brand of poison for rats, which have abounded in the city since the time of the Crusades, and therefore nothing was liable to disturb the harmony of the banquet.

The aperitif on the lawn, served by Mohammed who prided himself on being an impeccable butler—and as he was never servile, he really was—went off without incident. The fact that Jane, pretending to stumble on her high heels, clung to a giant colocasia leaf and sheared it clean off seemed to me a good sign: her garden was one of the most beautiful in the city, and everyone knew that when she was envious of something she destroyed it.

"Forgive me, dear, I didn't do it on purpose. But don't you think you've gone too far with the greenery?"

Luckily, she was immediately approached by Margot, and the two resumed their squabble over the garage affair: according to Margot, who had rented the garage from her friend to use it as a storehouse, rainwater seepage had caused irreparable damage to her late husband's furniture. "Stuff and nonsense, my garage has always been drier than a martini," Jane shot back. "Believe me, darling, those poor chests of drawers were already soaking wet when they arrived…didn't your mother-in-law grow mushrooms on them?"

Meanwhile, Yves complimented me on the quality of the little orchestra (Ftoma's son must have left a transistor radio on somewhere), the French consul was singing the praises of the magician who would brighten up his next fundraising evening for the restoration of the grottino dedicated to the Madonna in the park of the Résidence in Place de France, while Alfonso, having taken his golden sandals off, showed us his tapering feet and, for the umpteenth time, told the story about the famous Peruvian sculptor who had made a cast of them for his Apollo of Machu Picchu.

When we went up to the terrace and sat down at the table, the new pergola of plumbago, morning glories, and roses brought a murmur of admiration from everyone. Stephan and I were at the head of the table with the older ladies to our right. "These plates are lovely!" chirped Claudine. "They remind me of our picnics in Pakistan!"

"I didn't feel a thing, Madame Leyla is a genius!" Rose said, winding up the epic story of her callus. "You shouldn't trust that slattern from Tétouan!" Jane scolded her. "Tessa's daughters are all on antibiotics and their feet are in bandages because of the fungus they got from her filthy instruments!"

Shousha had appeared at one of the French windows leading onto the terrace. She looked anxiously at the table and then into the garden, as if she were looking for someone. I was beginning to get nervous: why hadn't Mohammed come to help?

"Are they shooting a costume movie?" Geneviève asked: Shousha was made up for the grand occasion. Everyone turned to look at her. "Divine," David murmured with a nostalgic sigh, and swung his head from side to side as if listening to a tune from his youth: "Divine." Some nodded, others smiled, rolling their eyes. It was evident that the old gentleman, an intimate of the Queen Mother and nicknamed the "Queen of Tangier" in many books, was returning in memory to one of the ancient pantomimes in which, to play the role of the odalisque with the heart of gold, he had run through the entire stock of mascara and eyeshadow held by the only French perfumery on the boulevard.

"Is everything all right?" I asked Shousha, who instead of answering disappeared indoors. I imagined her mother was struggling with some kind of drama in the kitchen. I filled the nearest glasses for the second time, and Stephan did likewise.

"That furniture was already soaking wet. Practically fished out of the *Titanic*. Otherwise you wouldn't have left it on the roof all summer, before resigning yourself to selling it in bulk to that ethnic restaurant," Jane went on. The first Neapolitan pizzeria in Tangier had opened only a few months earlier, it had been one of the most celebrated events of the season. "If I left them on the roof it was in the hope that they might recover from the shock of your garage, but not even the sun of the Sahara would have been hot enough. The proprietor, who by the way is a beautiful boy from Bolzano, complained to me because it wouldn't burn at any price!"

"OK, OK, it's all the fault of my poor garage! However, goodness knows why Michael's and Cherry's books are perfectly preserved after twenty years in crates…" Suddenly there was a rustling in the grass, then a scuffling, and from the path that led to the middle pavilion our gardener came running.

"*Kibir! Kibir!*"—big, big—he repeated with enthusiastic guttural sobs, holding up his arms to let us see… some of our guests jumped to their feet in unison, as if on an agreed signal; glasses wobbled, a chair fell, Jane screamed, Claudine pulled her shawl over her eyes and looked like a mummy, even Yves, a great big man famous for his military aplomb, was clinging like a child to the consul, curiously petrified in the same pose as the bust of De Gaulle that dominated his office. Alfonso was no longer visible, perhaps he had taken refuge in the house, or under the table. With hands held high, Mohammed, breathless and exultant, was dangling two enormous rats by the tail.

"*Ashouma* Mohammed! Shame on you!" I exclaimed with a frown. I realized that the news of the poison's effectiveness was too happy to wait for a better moment, but I had to show my indignation. He shrugged and ran off. When all the diners had recovered, Margot rearranged her silver bob and commented: "Let's hope he wasn't the one who washed the salad, it would be ridiculous to catch the plague for a *tajine*." And staring into space, as if seized by an inspiration, she pontificated: "But this garden is beautiful. Yes, very nice. And you know what, Jane dear? The primacy of yours is at risk." Some protested, her words sounded sacrilegious even on the lips of a contrarian like her. Like some aging Nefertiti, Jane had already raised her fine turbaned head. "Yes, I know, I know that your garden is the most beautiful in the city," Margot resumed immediately, preventing her from replying, "but on seeing this one I realized that yours has always had something…" She paused for an unusually long time, the group's attention was focused on her. "…*straitlaced* about it?" she asked in the innocent tone of a child trying out a new word.

"Gardens are important," Yves broke in smoothly. "Because if there are too many people, you can sit and enjoy the cool and play the tom-tom while looking at the bicycles." An exchange of bewildered glances and forced smiles ensued. The rumored stroke suddenly seemed confirmed, gliding over each of them like a threat. "Amen to that!" Jane hastened to approve, "Gardens are important." And grabbing her glass, she held it up and exclaimed in a voice that was a little too loud: "Here's to our boys!" But no one was paying any attention: Shousha had finally appeared with the serving dish, and forgetting good manners, hungry after the wait, and suddenly sadder and even older, everyone threw themselves on the overcooked quiche lorraine with which I had hoped to surprise them instead of the usual *tajine*. Stephan winked at me: somehow or other, we had pulled it off.

Some time afterward an acquaintance asked me to do his garden. "Me? But I'm still learning to look after mine!"

"Stop being modest and look around you," he replied.

On observing the cascade of white begonias with ruby stems that poured down the wall, and the fragrant wisteria hanging from the branches of the false pepper tree that responded from the other side of the path, a thought occurred to me: everything was dying of love for its neighbor. Since then, every time I arrive on a construction site, I remember that April morning, I feel what it means to die of love, and I miss Mohammed once more.

The more I learned about plants, the more our garden grew richer and more complex, and the more I loved him. Mohammed and I were two happy obsessives. Both continually tormented by the need for new combinations, we tried one plant after another with the urgency of a thirsty man at a stream: a few moments of contemplation and then we were back at work, rain, wind, or shine, forgetting to eat, always battling against the clock; branches of the strawberry tree had to be thinned out so the bells of the climbing fuchsia got enough sun, the "mermaid" needed to be pulled up onto the cypress to see if it came out as nicely as it did in that Persian miniature, dozens of Boston ferns had to be planted beneath the viburnums whose ugly legs showed more and more as they got older, and it was necessary to prepare a nest for the Kaffir lilies, to replace the ferns with plectranthus while paying attention to the dialogue between the leaves, and to insert the commas of the iresines, the semicolons of the amaryllis, the exclamation points of the strelitzia—closing the quotation marks with a bowl full of crassulas or a round stone heavy enough to break our backs ... And could we neglect the dialogue between scents? The Four O'Clocks making fun of the jasmine, the backyard chatter of the night blooming jasmine with the white ipomoeas, the roses squabbling with the daffodils, obliging us to make continuous additions, continuous transplants, in search of an ideal balance that existed only in our heads and maybe not even there, everything dying of love for its neighbor, everything, love, together ...

Stephan and I decided to give Mohammed a present. It had to be a great one. He liked to fish, but no fishing pole would fit the bill in this case. We racked our brains. Then Stephan had an idea, and I immediately knew it was the right one. The head of the travel agency said he was moved by such attention from two Nasranis. "The gates of heaven are opening for you." He even offered a rate that in addition to the trip included transfers, the hotel with full board, and a guide who spoke Moroccan Arabic. We bought the two packages, and having gathered all the members of the family we announced that we had thought ... I handed the envelope to Shousha, she opened it, turned pale, welled up, hugged me: "*Merci merci merci.*" For the benefit of Mohammed, Ftoma mimicked the flight of the plane and prostrations. He gave a little laugh, winked at me, and went off to water the plants.

The *hajj*, the pilgrimage to Mecca, is one of the pillars of Islam: every believer must do it before dying. For this trip, many save up for their entire lives and often do so in difficult conditions. But despite the assurances of the agency employee—they would always be together with other pilgrims from northern Morocco, health care and insurance were included in the rate, the organizers would think of everything—as the days went by the daughters were more and more concerned, and I too was uneasy: of a reserved nature, Mohammed and Ftoma weren't used to the company of strangers and had never taken a plane in all their life. In fact, they had never even left the Tangier region. In our enthusiasm we had forgotten that they were no longer young, in Saudi Arabia the heat is hellish, the mere thought of them doing the ritual rounds in the courtyard of the sanctuary crowded with thousands of people made me feel ill. I remembered the wasted, gaunt look of an acquaintance of mine who had just returned from Mecca. My anxiety was compounded by the fact that Mohammed seemed troubled, and in any case less cheerful than usual. "Are you afraid of the plane?" I asked him. He shrugged. "Of the heat?" No, he liked the heat. And the crowd would have been all *habibi*, beloved ones, and so they would have been fine. Except... "*Henaia*," and he pointed to our flower beds. Who was going to take care of the garden in those three weeks? Moved, I immediately found a solution in another Mohammed, Ftoma's son, who worked on the nearby property of a Saudi prince. We persuaded him to quit. But before long this too stopped sounding like a good idea to me: his stepfather was making his life hell. Was that any way to water plants? Did he want to give the plant time to drink or was he in too much of a hurry to have fun in the city? And had he noticed the little stream that had formed behind the hibiscus? Did he think he was still hosing the Saudi's lawn? Did he understand what a tree was? Did he understand that taking care of a garden means keeping the plants clean and not waiting for them to collapse under the weight of the withered parts? Flowerpots are important, did he understand that? That when the leaves droop, it means that they're not draining properly and you need to do something about that? Or did he prefer to see them rot? If I tried to intercede for his stepson, Mohammed pretended not to understand. There's none so deaf... also applies to the deaf. Fortunately, as the departure approached, excitement took over from ill humor. In the final days he devoted himself to putting his things in order, his fishing pole, hooks, and lines, the clothes and the tools he kept in the woodshed, and the Sunday best he had been carrying around for a lifetime. After taking our pilgrims to the airport we handed them enough victuals to keep them alive in the desert for a couple of months.

  Finally left alone, little Mohammed, as we had now nicknamed him, seemed to breathe a sigh of relief, and with him the garden. When I saw that he had learned to control the anxiety that causes inexperienced gardeners to water the epiphytic ferns too much, and was leaving ours thirsty as happens in nature, I knew I could trust him, and I was not wrong, since almost twenty years later he is still with us.

  On the appointed day, we all left together before dawn to pick them up. The *hajj* falls on set dates, during the last month of the Muslim calendar, and in those years, in the short period when the pilgrims returned, the Boukhalef hills near the airport (the same hills where Stephan and I got lost in a sea of irises on our first visit) were covered with a strange tent city. Leaving the car more than a kilometer from the parking lot, we made our way through the crowd. There were thousands of families gathered from all over the North of Morocco to welcome their loved ones, grandmothers lying chrysalis-like on plastic mats, mothers boiling water for tea on camping stoves, fathers hunkered down without being able to smoke or kneeling prostrate in prayer, children with tired faces wearing their good clothes, and uncles, cousins, distant relatives, even simple neighbors—and those without a tent slept under a canopy of branches or cardboard, or wrapped in a blanket. As soon as an announcement was broadcast over the airport loudspeaker (that the distance, the fatigue, the waiting, and the crackle of the faulty microphone transformed into an encrypted interplanetary message), all those in that multitude who were able to move, some autonomously, others leaning on a stick, some supported by a couple of young people, others on the shoulders of a strong man, began to approach the barriers that had been crowded since the previous evening by those who had not wanted to give up their place. Every one of them wanted to be the first to throw himself into the arms of their loved one, kiss him in the hollow between his neck and shoulder, three times, six times, on his hand, on his head, caress him, touch his gandoura, hoping to extract from him a few drops of *baraka*, the divine blessing that the pilgrim has absorbed in the holy places. Every time the automatic door opened and a group of pilgrims dressed in white emerged dragging bags and cartons, a roar went up from the multitude. Sometimes a barrier gave way and the military lashed out with their nightsticks. Finally, Mohammed and Ftoma also appeared on the threshold, thin, black, and bewildered as shepherds who have fallen from the crèche: almost without realizing it I jumped over the bars, swerved to dodge a nightstick, wriggled free, and with another leap I was in the arms of my beloved, my flower brother—my Mohammed whose beard always smelled of incense. At home other relatives and many neighbors were waiting for us. Ftoma took gifts for everyone from a bag, plastic bottles for holy water, fridge magnets, seed rosaries, handkerchiefs, and sandalwood fans, all of which the recipients received with grateful groans and sighs. The couscous was delicious, but I withdrew almost immediately and left them to celebrate in peace.

    I woke up at first light and went down to the garden. Still all in white, Mohammed was contemplating the flower bed with the oleanders and laurel. "*Qulshi mzian,*" all right. The birds began to flap around in the branches. He slowly looked around, repeating: "*Qulshi mzian.*" Then, pointing to the horizon from which the sun was about to rise, he stammered: "Mec-ca, Mec-ca." He raised both hands in prayer, added *daiman*, always, and smiled at me. I understood that he had prayed to Allah for the health of our garden. He loved it so much that he had remembered it on one of the most important days of his life. And at the same time he took advantage of the moment not to give any credit to poor little Mohammed. The garden was all about him and me, no one else.

    But arthritis forced him to part with it. At that time we still had enough money to finance the construction of a house for him on a piece of land he had bought years before in Rehreh, not too far away, when prices were low. There, he would spend his old age with Ftoma, coming to see us when he felt like it. Mohammed threw himself into the work on the house with the same enthusiasm he had dedicated to the garden. That was the beauty of him, his enthusiasm. And I carried on with little Mohammed, who, relieved by his stepfather's absence, continued to improve. But when Shousha and Karima married two boys who emigrated to Belgium, I realized that life in Tebarek Allah would never be the same again. In their place there came in succession: a devious couple of Jbala who hid bags of kif in the woodshed and received customers at night while I slept; a beautiful young man from Meknes who spent most of the day in front of the mirror because he was obsessed with getting a nose job; a boy from Larache who had married an aging beautician from Chaouen with golden blond hair and insisted on getting me to try her massages; a very kind, decrepit carpenter from Asilah convinced that he was a great chef who brought me a broth every night with gestures so ceremonious as to make me feel obliged to simulate delighted surprise every time; and an Italian ice cream maker—together with a black Molossus mastiff named Luna—who had been living in Morocco for years working here and there without ever holding down a permanent job. When he tried to stab me, shouting that he was going to cleanse me with my own blood and forcing me to push the dining table against him, and with the help of little Mohammed and the postman who happened to be passing by we tied him up with a rope, I understood why he had been fired so many times. He smoked too much hashish; it wasn't good for him. And finally Soufien, the melancholy sculptor-cook with his fur hat and motorbike, came into our life.

Although drawn like a magnet to Rohuna, even here in Tangier I continued to design and supervise the new terraces, paths, stairs, fountains, and outdoor rooms for reading and chatting, and when Mohammed, leaning on his new walking stick, came to visit us, the first thing I did was show him our progress. When he saw the wall of the new pool, he made a face and gave me some instructions. The mixture of water, goat manure, and expired yogurt that I tossed over it in bucketloads has been one of my secrets ever since: it only takes a few weeks before foreign, hostile surfaces begin to fill with lichens, mushrooms, and small ferns, turning into old friends. Since then, taken up by the adventurous story of Rohuna I tell in my novel *Lost in Paradise*, every year here in Tangier I just planted a dozen bare-rooted roses, a few shrubs, and a couple of saplings, adding a few pots, a headstone, a mortar, and a capital. Probably sooner or later I would have ended up admitting that our garden had gone from madcap lover to comfortable husband with no more surprises, if our landscape architect friend Madison hadn't one day insisted on bringing home a new discovery of his, a Belgian who knew plants in a way that… "You'll see," he said, "you'll see."

Bernard Dogimont seemed a bit wooden to me, that surname I had mistakenly transformed into d'Ogimont made me think of a provincial aristocrat who used to pass the time by visiting stately homes and holding conferences in the country. After a tour of the garden, over lunch there was talk of a variety of white-flowered dombeya that according to Madison was impossible to find in Morocco. I objected that my friend Aysha was growing some seedlings and suggested Bernard accompany me to visit her. After saying goodbye to Madison, who was in a hurry, I found myself in the car with Bernard, on the road to Cap Spartel. He wasn't talkative and he didn't like Tangier very much. He had visited a few gardens and found them disappointing. He didn't say a word about ours. But when we reached the spot where the old countrywoman was selling plants by the roadside, I saw him smile for the first time. His eyes are very beautiful, ice blue. With Aysha leading, we hopped and skipped our way down beneath the pines to the clearing near her house, where she grows the mother plants and repots those for sale. On the hill overlooking the valley stands a hollowed boulder with a muddy pool in which frogs swim: the water flowed down onto the terraces below, in full sun, a trail of calla lilies and yellow flags meandered through strawberry trees and the trunks of fallen mimosas. In a few minutes we had leaped back thousands of years. "Tangier has its secrets," I said, excited as I am every time I look out over that radiant Neolithic that redeems the present and expands the future. Everywhere, on the hillside and around the bushes, stood rows of black plastic bags containing Aysha's plants. At that sight, Bernard became a happy sprite: he ran from one to the other, bent down, named the plants as if finding old friends, pointing out their characteristics, their rarity, and suggesting which ones to buy and for what reason, and… "I would put that pelargonium between the crinum on the sides of the last flight of steps to fill the gap left by their summer rest, this aspidistra with virosis should be added to the collection that you keep below the upper pergola, and the jasminum sambac—are you aware that this is your lucky day? Because it isn't the usual 'Grand Duke of Tuscany!'—should go in the pot of euphorbia you keep next to the entrance… And put the euphorbia somewhere else because it's not got enough room, that eupatorium would look good below the tetrapanax in front of the studio, there are too many ferns around that beautiful yellow justitia, variation would be welcome, and this very rare oreopanax… Look at that stem! Resplendent quetzals go mad for its fruit, so grab it like a shot!"

I was speechless. He had been in our garden for no more than half an hour, and he already knew it as well as I who had planted it. We went back up the hill loaded with plants. When we were sitting in the car once more, he said: "Thank you." Then he went back to being as taciturn as before.

We saw each other again a couple of times for supper. At first I tried to make conversation to get to know him better, but I soon realized that with him the only topic was plants. Not that it's a sacrifice for me. One evening, I asked him point-blank if he liked my garden. It was beautiful, he replied, but when I pressed him a bit he added that there was a lot of work to do. On the third bottle (another thing we had in common was the pleasure of red wine) he confided to me that in the place in town that Madison had found for him he had to share the bathroom and kitchen with other people. He said "people" as I would have said "cockroaches" or "vampires." I took the plunge: "Why don't you move in with us?" He hesitated. I insisted: the middle pavilion was empty, he would have a bedroom, a living room, a bathroom, and a kitchen all to himself. "I won't have to eat with you?" I reassured him. "Nor meet your guests?" No, I would warn him in time and he could disappear until they left. "If I recommend a plant, will you trust me and not ask for explanations?" This was more difficult, but I accepted. He moved in the next day. Then he came to Rohuna and love blossomed.

Officially in return for our hospitality, actually for the same law of nature whereby a fish thrown into water will swim, Bernard has begun to look after our gardens. He does this with the same enthusiasm that Mohammed and I used to have, but where we groped, he goes straight to the point, thanks to his knowledge. He knows the habitats, and the climatic and water needs of thousands of species, but above all he identifies with plants. He is one of them. He is able to tell you without fail which ones will get along and which will not, he is a cross between a telepath and a go-between with the plant world. A consultant to various European gardens, every time he returns from a business trip—to avoid humans he sleeps in the car and washes at the fountains—his car is overflowing with plants, bulbs, and cuttings, the pockets of his old jacket are chock-full of seeds. He throws a handful of them on the table and recognizes them without hesitation: these come from the yellow umbellifer that grew next to the highway, these were given to him by a worker in a botanical garden, those are of a rare double-flowering montanoa just in from Guatemala, while those tiny ones are of an unusually pale variety of poppy... and he knows how to germinate them, he knows which ones should be immersed in water overnight, which should be scorched with flame, which de-hulled, and which tossed into the wind.

Little Mohammed is happy to have found such an expert guide (he calls him "professor") and even the kids at Rohuna, initially wary, were won over by the skills of *beljiki* (the Belgian) and began to bombard him with questions. Bernard tries his best to satisfy them, but his dream is to be left alone. In fact, with him life is no bed of roses: he is moody, touchy, and sensitive, he can sulk for days just because a guest dared not to notice the new leaf opening on the kentia, or because I refuse to scold the gardener who watered the aloe for a few seconds before remembering his order to leave it dry for a month. But all it takes is a new shrub to plant and he is immediately happy again: at six in the morning I find him among the flower beds, ready to suggest thirty or so possible improvements, illustrating the strengths and weaknesses of each one, and urging me to visualize the result of the combination at a date probably much later than that of our death. Unlike me, he has the virtue of ruthlessness: when a plant dies, I despair; he just spreads his arms and moves on. He has learned from nature to be indifferent. It is one of the characteristics of the great gardeners, their motto is "Next, please!" They know very well that there are countless species to try out. To become attached to a plant that is struggling, to get all worked up out of anxiety and cowardice, is absolutely detrimental.

The son of a Belgian worker, born in a village where no trees grew and the soil was ruined by monocultures, he had an unhappy childhood: he didn't like his peers, he detested adults, and he did badly at school. In desperation, his mother had sent him to be a florist's assistant, and when after a while the florist had called asking her to come see him she had gone with a heavy heart, expecting new troubles. But the only trouble was that the boy was so enthusiastic and knew the plants so well that he was wasted among the red roses and chrysanthemums of a provincial store. At this point a botanist comes on the scene—how? I don't know, on the rare occasions Bernard talks about his past it is always in vague terms, and then just when it gets interesting he cuts things short and goes off to bed. However, this botanist worked in one of the largest gardens in Belgium. Thanks to him, Bernard ended up under the wing of an eccentric collector (every time he mentions her he smiles like a David Copperfield who has found his aunt): a smart woman at last, good enough to plant thousands of trees and cultivate them properly, a woman who called the queen by her first name, and refused to take care of her state parks; above all, in a row of plants a hand's span high with almost invisible leaves, she could tell you which of the hundreds of species of fuchsia each of them belonged to. Thus began Bernie's career: apprentice, undergardener, gardener, and finally globetrotting consultant, until the moment of weariness that led him to accept Madison's proposal to come and spend some time in Morocco.

He has all the patience and passion you need for the effort gardening requires: partly out of perfectionism and partly to spare himself the hassle of providing explanations, he is often the one, armed with the saw and shears he never parts with, who prunes the large shrub that needs to be thinned out, the one who climbs the tree that gives shade to one of his beloved desert plants. He cuts rapidly, without having to stop and think about it, as if the tangle of branches were inside him, the buds an extension of his fingers. He does it with an ardor, a furious passion that sometimes leads me to avert my gaze—we seldom talk about personal things, he strikes me as an animal that mates with its shadow, and that involuntary display is an insult to his decency. There is something brisk and sensual in the way he plants out and repots, a few precise gestures where mine would be hesitant: he has a talent, a kind of orgiastic madness, for putting thirty plants where there seems to be barely room for three, but he already knows that the shade provided by the taller ones will favor the development of the shorter ones, and that in the search for light the stems of some will grow thinner, while those of others will curve. Angelic, criminal, at the foot of each one he plants a creeper, he ties an epiphyte with raffia to each branch, and puts one ground-covering plant for every span of earth: they will live together for years, they will help each other and in the long run, perhaps, they will end up overwhelming and smothering one another, but that's what a garden is, a theater of nature, the beauty and truth of struggle, dying for love, certainly not the oleograph of a little family smiling on a well-cut lawn. Today, the garden of Tebarek Allah, where a few hundred species grew before his arrival, is an increasingly intricate jungle that is home to over two thousand of them: dozens of ferns, our favorite begonias, plectranthus, tillandsias, rhipsalis, sansevierias, aspidistras, alocasias, clivias, small shade palms, and hundreds of aralias and araliaceae, all creatures that fear direct sunlight and raise merry hell in the humid half-light of our forest. But this confusion requires constant dedication and maintenance: Little Mohammed and young Nassar work there every day; Bernard and I help out when we can.

After four years of living together, following a quarrel for which I take all responsibility, he moved out, but we remained very good friends, and Bernard the *beljiki*, with his encyclopedic knowledge and his hunger for new plants, continues to help me with this garden and with that of Rohuna. I learned many things from him, and perhaps the most important one is that the garden is a drama. Being aware of this, feeling the responsibility of growing even a single basil or tomato plant, is essential to our enjoyment as gardeners. We labor under the delusion that we are all-powerful while we are weaker than the humblest aphid. We have the hands, head, and heart to try to encourage life, and if we manage to lose ourselves in work and contemplation, we find ourselves swimming along singing like whales and frogs. The garden is a slice of that beautiful world that many call paradise: even the smallest and scantiest garden, even a windowsill, is larger and deeper than the ocean in which my beloved mermaids knot their carpets. But there is another reason why I am grateful to Bernard: he introduced me to a fellowship of dauntless globetrotters, far more exclusive than that of the provincial aristocracy with which, on the day of our meeting, I had naively associated him. They are... how to define them? Gardeners of the world. Boys who live in a shack next to the plastic tunnel where they are the only ones in Europe, to grow hundreds of species of ferns; explorers in rubber flip-flops scouring the jungles of Borneo for new begonias; hermits who have learned by themselves to reproduce very rare South African bulbs from seeds; men even of no fixed abode, who care nothing for money and success; happy outcasts who live to exchange information on other forms of life. Often the plants that Bernard brings back from his travels were given to him by one such as them, who trusts in his ability to grow them in the best way, if not in the best of worlds. Today our neighbors, the countryfolk who sowed and reproduced, have all disappeared, their heavenly gardens have been replaced by reinforced concrete villas, the overexposed shots of the Tangier of myth have curled up and burned to ashes, but a little of that light still comes from the urban gardens of Bernard's friends, their camper vans, their suburban rooms full of cuttings—the torn anoraks, the bowl of boiled vegetables gulped down amid the condensation of the humidifier bought in installments, that sleeping bag dream of a world covered with plants and full of free and happy animals. My hope springs from this.

  When I walk the terraces of Tebarek Allah, which is one of the most species-rich gardens in Morocco, I am amazed by the density of the vegetation, by the constant changes of atmosphere, and by how my moods change thanks to the combinations of the species: every day, several times a day, my walks are journeys that teach me something. I know every step, every tile plinth of a vase, every one of the thousands of containers of every shape and age, every shrub, every plant, every component of the mulch up to the most remote corners of this garden. And yet, if I have to find a place for a new sage or the right spot for the headstone or the big bronze pot I insist on saving from oblivion, what still moves me are the traces of the country priest's parched garden that won my heart almost thirty years ago. In this mature garden I see the child that it once was, that I was. I am a child too. The plants converse, the roots laugh, the leaves sing, the branches mutter, the objects sometimes whisper and sometimes speak aloud, stories and characters crisscross in a net ready to welcome me like a cradle, more comfortable even than the old cobweb that right now is dangling between the two branches of the viburnum beneath which I have lain down to take a nap... Reverting to being ourselves can be as easy as licking an ice cream, but also a hard slog. Flints and axes from the Paleolithic to the Neolithic, pottery of all ages and origins, colored marbles, potsherds, Islamic tiles, pieces of carpet, painted furniture, rags, baskets, photographs, postcards, old toys and reference books, ferns, begonias, irises, daffodils, seeds, roots—and stories. I have always been a collector, and like that of any collector my destiny is two-pronged: at one and the same time a couch potato who loves to study in his ivory tower, and a restless traveler in search of new things. A rescue dog who has to extract orphans from beneath the rubble, sniff out the lost, identify the forgotten … in short, to bring together families so as to be happy contemplating their happiness. A home is not just a mother's embrace, there is no return to Ithaca without a long and risky journey. Some encounters helped me stay afloat: for the garden a deaf-mute Moroccan and a young Belgian in love with plants—woe betide you if you call him a botanist! For my home, a grave robber from Cairo and the last English aesthete worthy of the name. My house and my garden, as much as I love them, will never be a Noah's ark, but merely the foam and reflections of a rubber dinghy that passes without stopping. Ithaca cannot be far, but I already know that as soon as I land those blessed sirens will oblige me to leave again. "Go for it, my warrior for beauty!" Stephan will say. Deep down, he has always encouraged me.

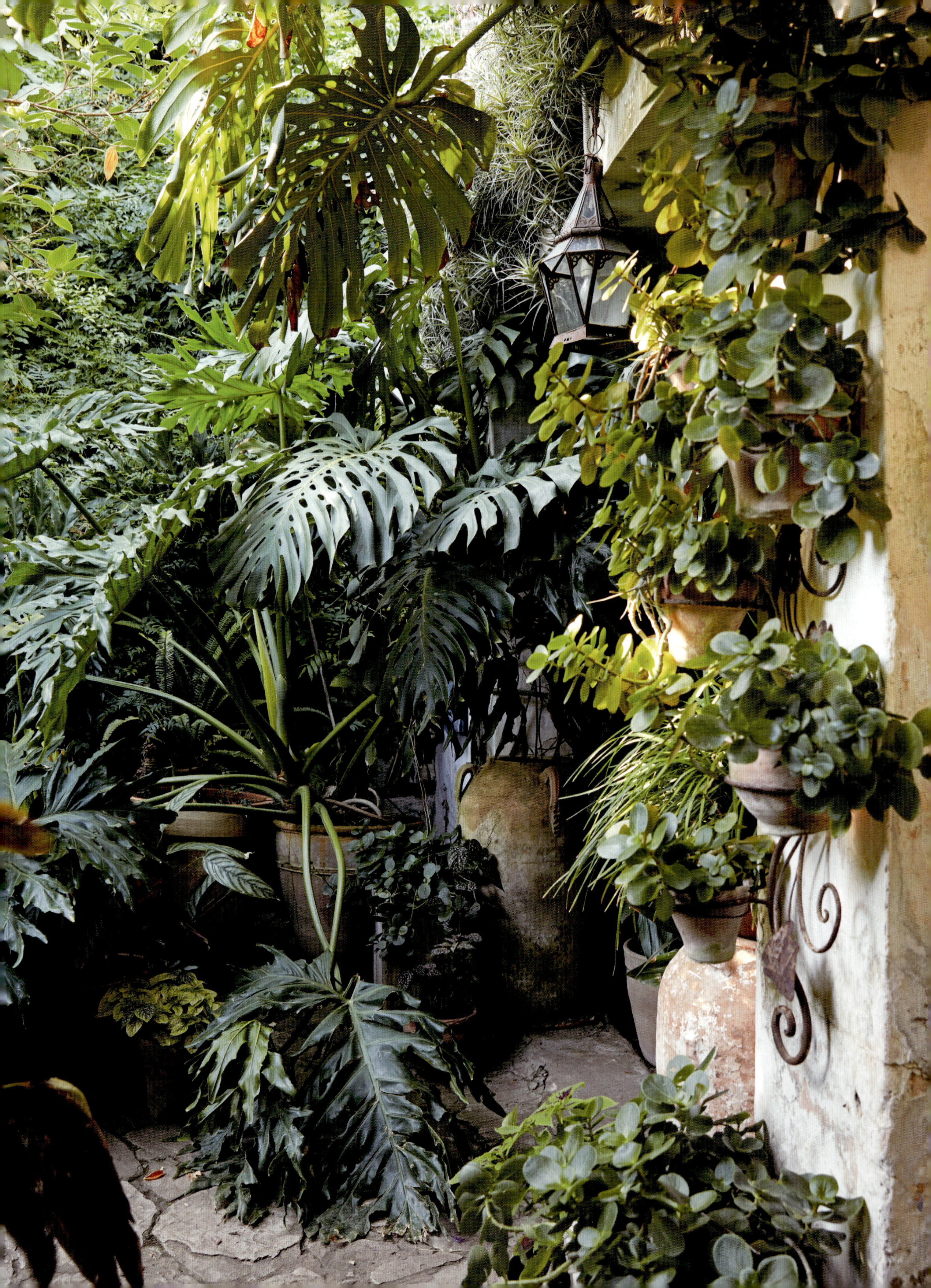

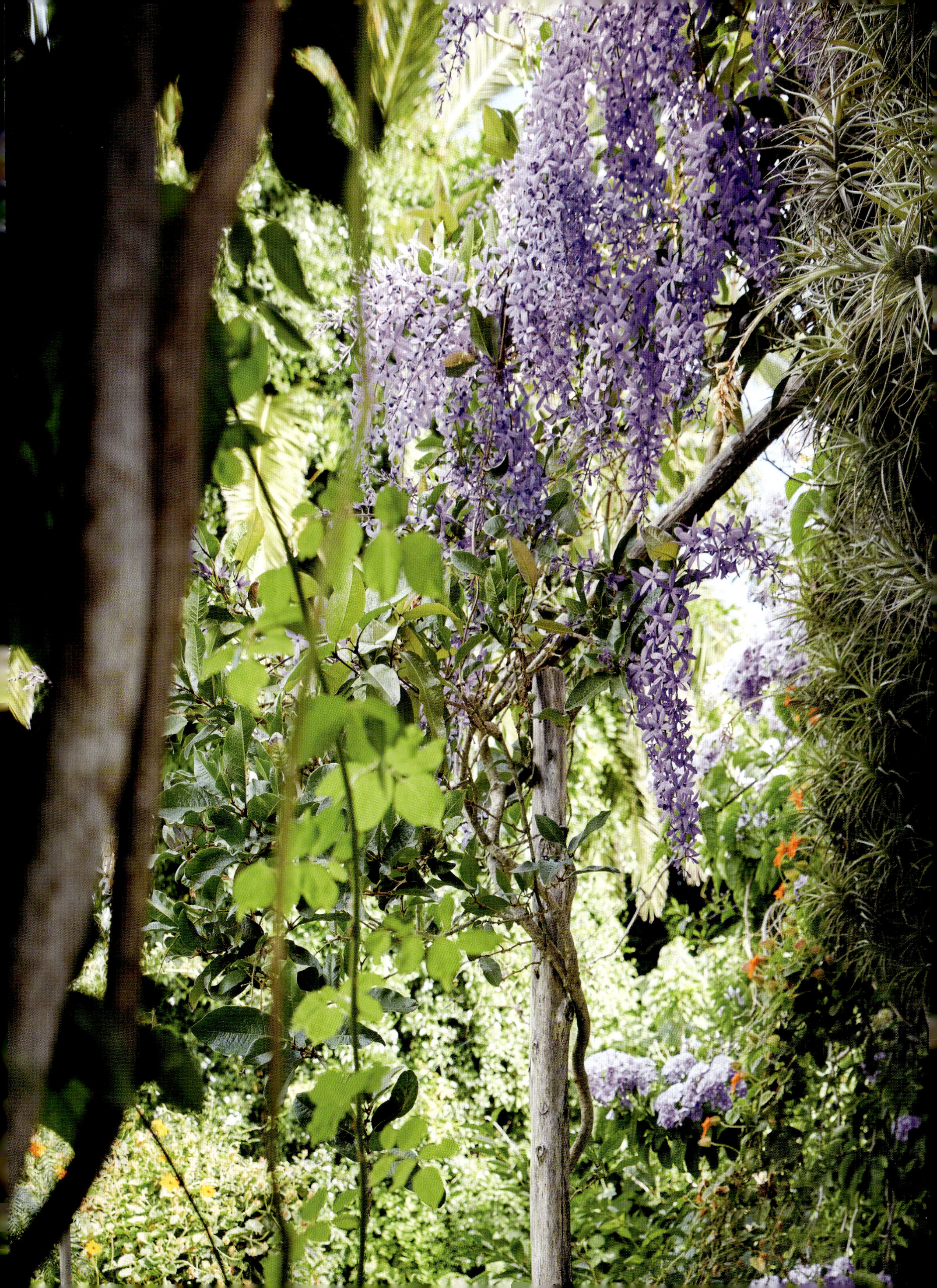

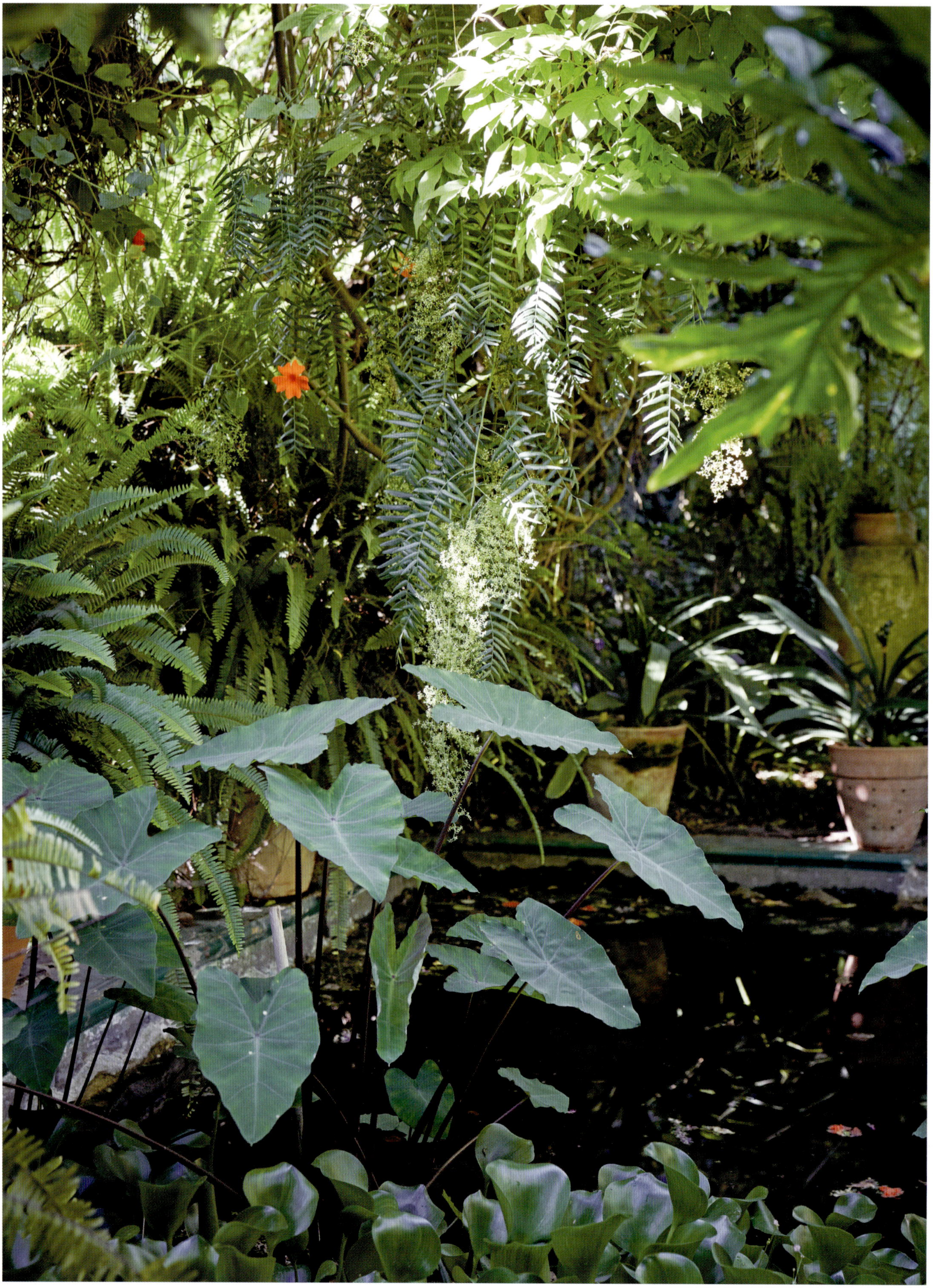

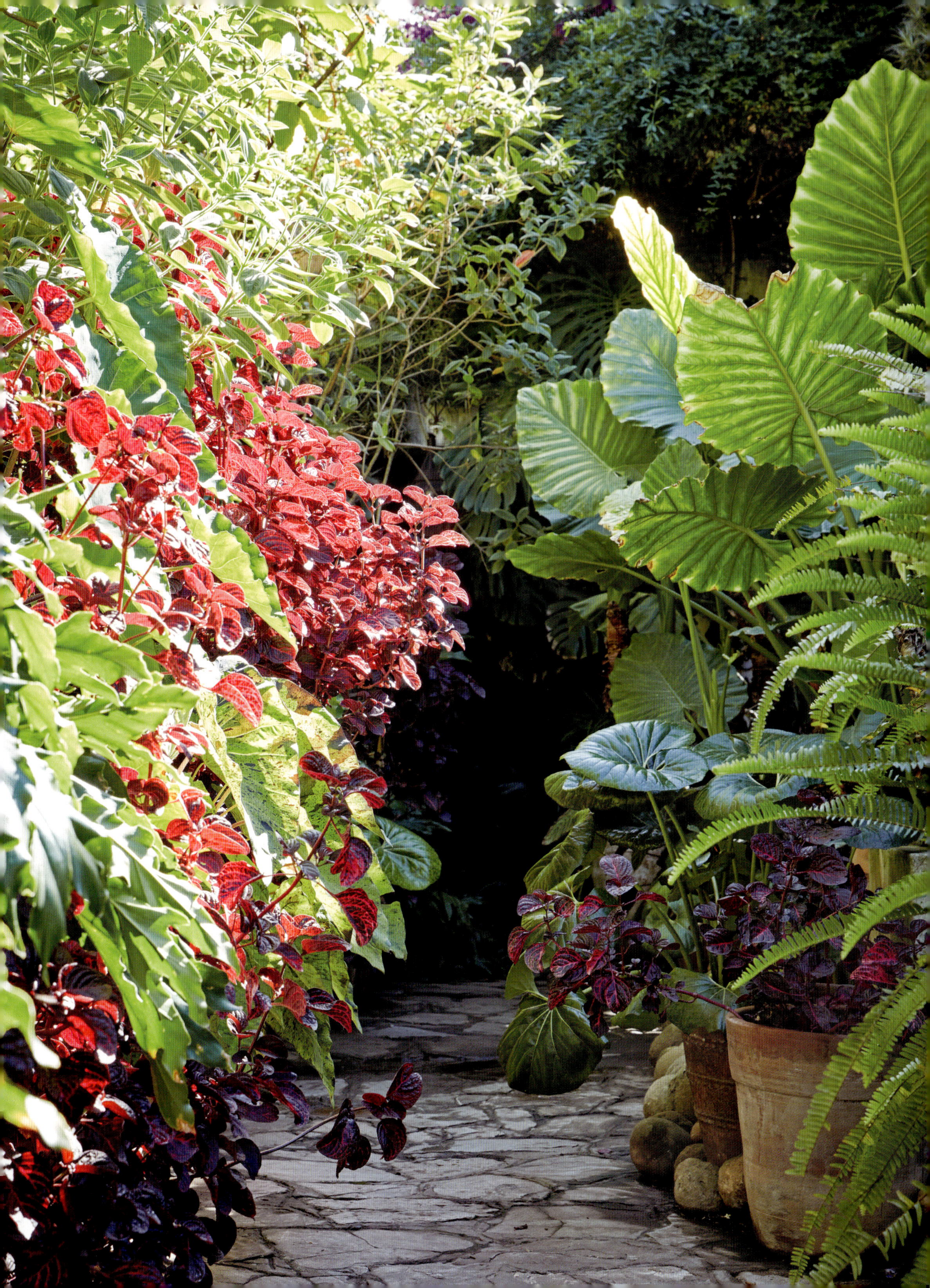

PAGE 202: *By the main entrance, pots of* Monstera deliciosa. *No name could be more appropriate.*
PAGE 203: *It looks like wisteria but it is* Petrea volubilis. Tillandsia bergeri, *the Brazilian epiphytic plant often seen for mysterious reasons on old Jbala houses, is cascading from the wall.*
PREVIOUS SPREAD, LEFT: *In this small pond I grow* Colocasia esculenta, *more commonly known as taro, and* Eichhornia crassipes, *the water hyacinth, to allow my pet frogs to hide from blackbirds.*
PREVIOUS SPREAD, RIGHT: *The lovely show of steakplant (*Iresine herbstii*) in the backlight.*
OPPOSITE: *The white "rustic" table is made by NOW on the Ocean, the furniture workshop I started ten years ago in Rohuna with my young friend Najim. The oleander chairs are made in the Charf, the area of Tangier where they made all the traditional furniture for coffee shops. To make space for ghastly new buildings and roads, the shops have been recently moved by the powers that be to another district, which is a pity because their beauty and the skill of the artisans would have been one of the biggest attractions of our poor Tangier, which is on its way to become a faded copy of the hideous Abu Dhabi. In the pot,* Thunbergia battiscombei *with its blue flowers.*
FOLLOWING SPREAD, LEFT: *To repot the big fern in the corner I had to go on the street and ask help from two strong gentlemen passing by. Even if we were six, it was hell.*
FOLLOWING SPREAD, RIGHT: *Begonialand I.*

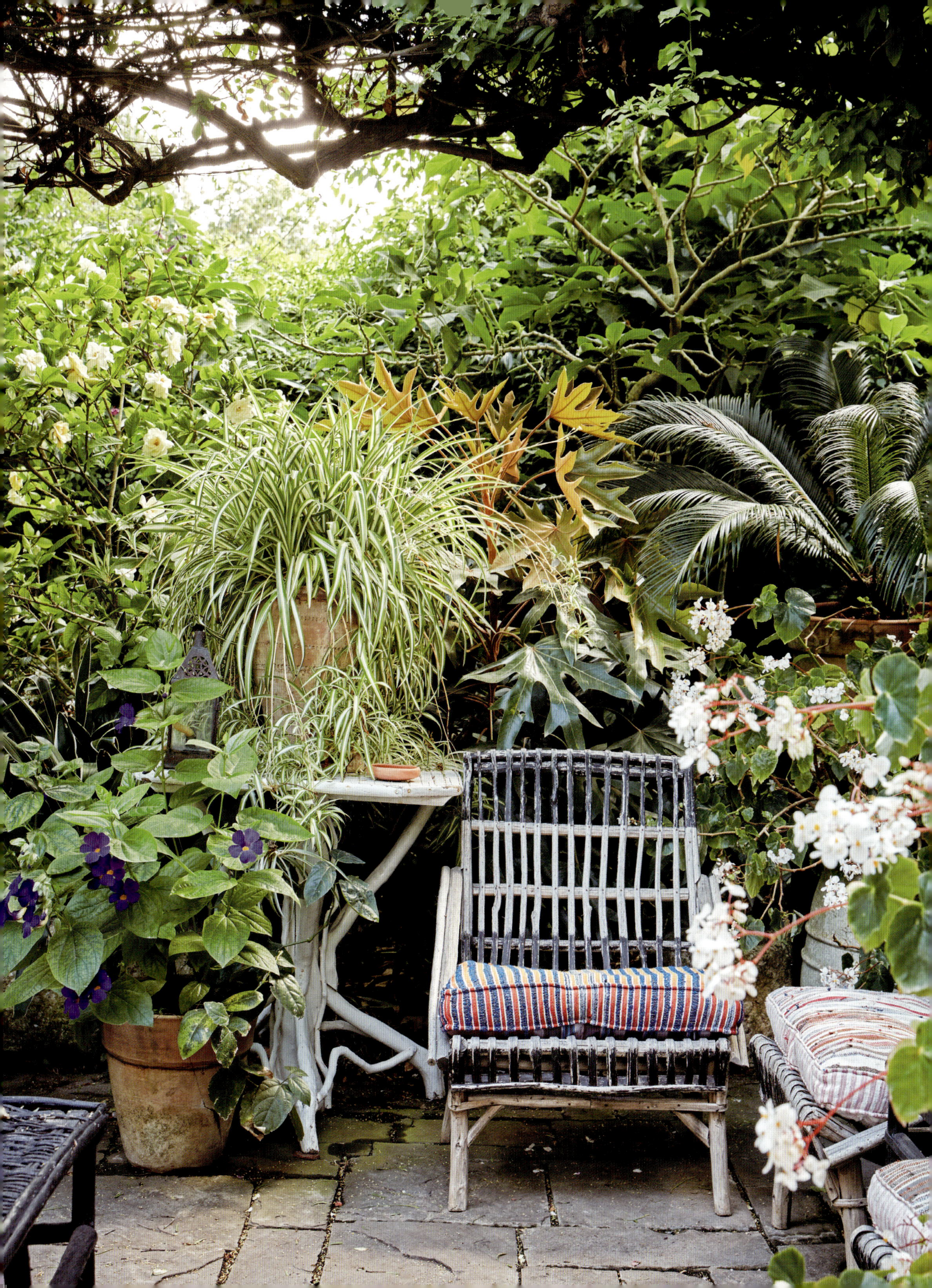

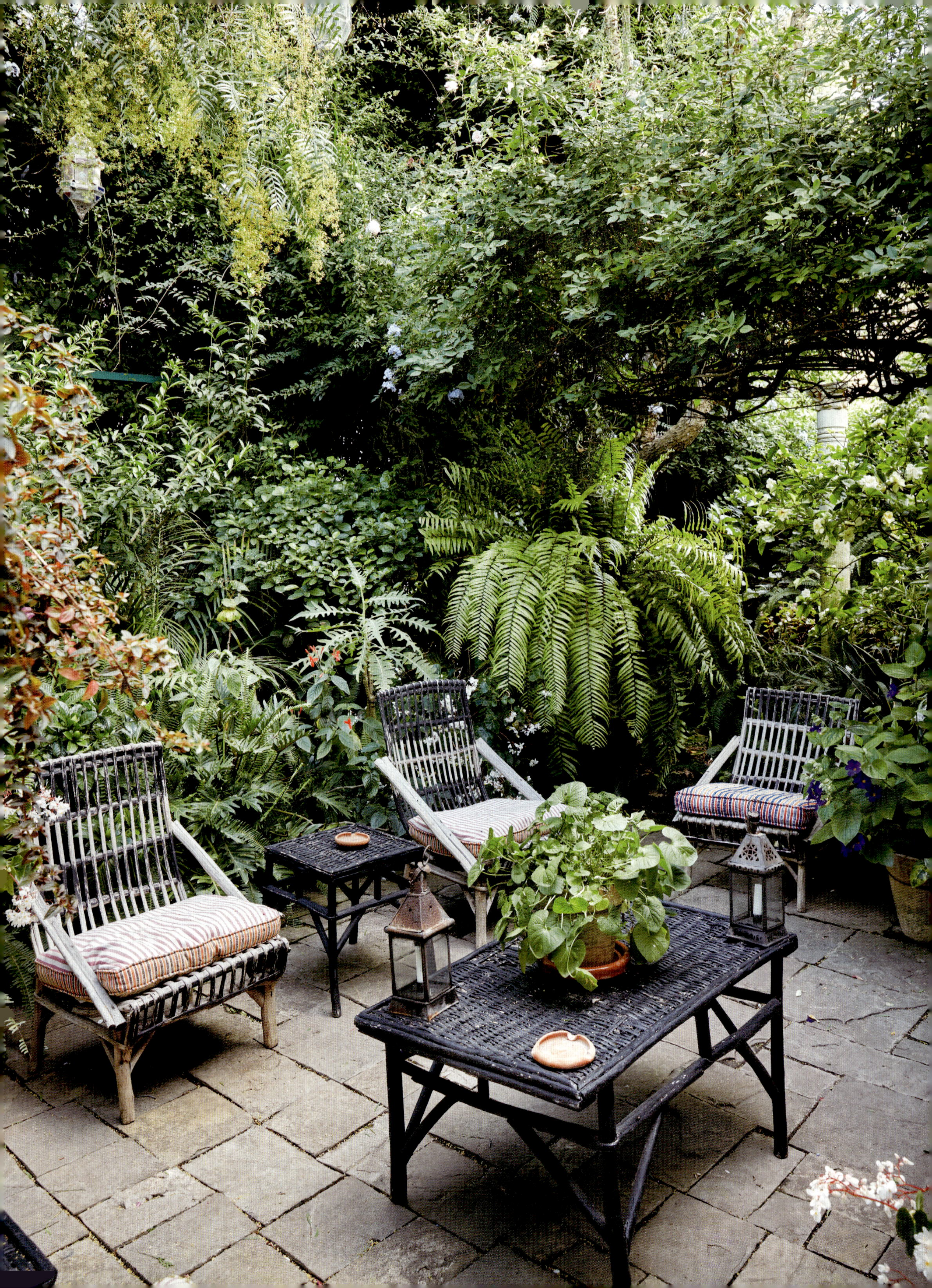

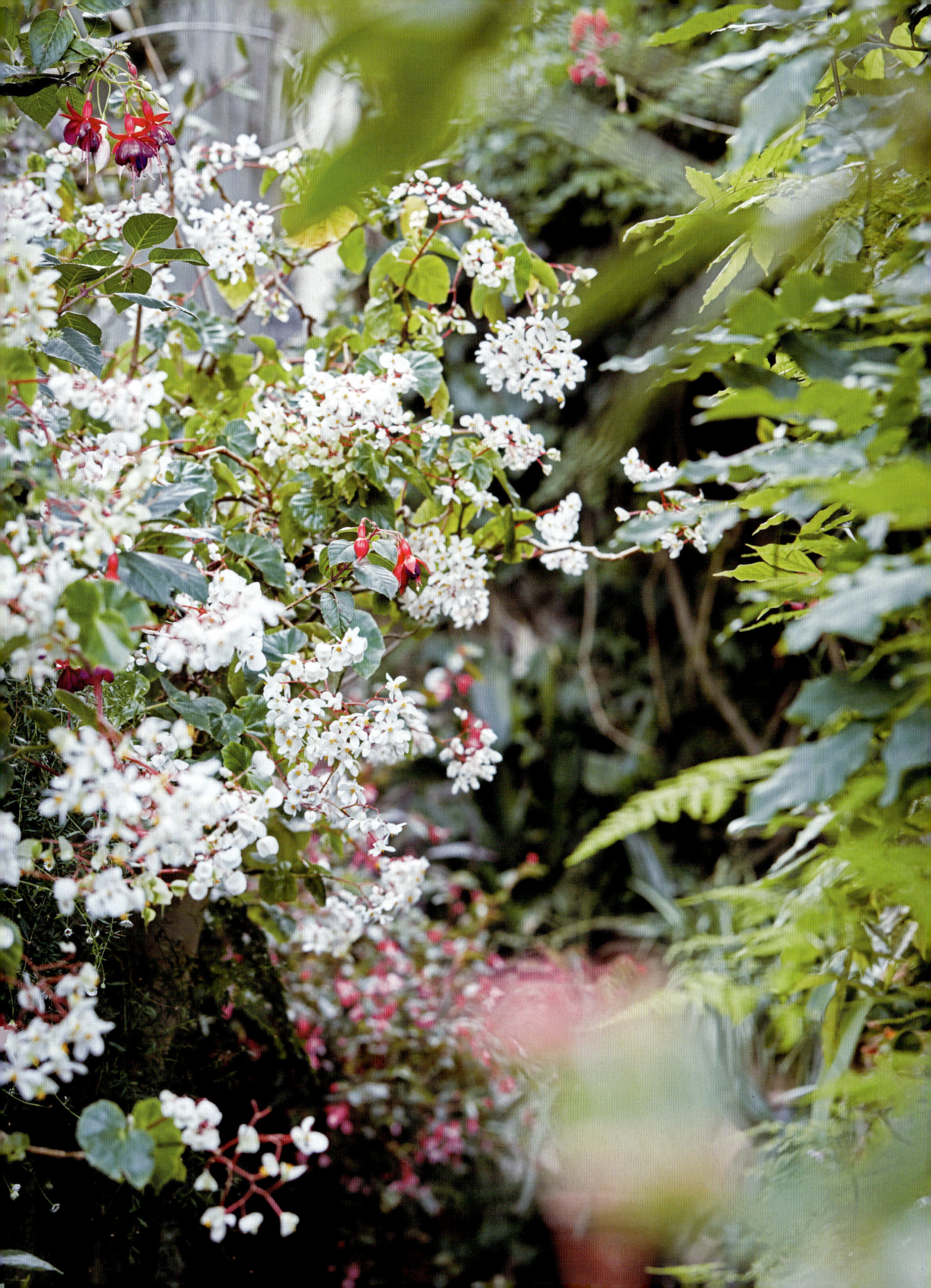

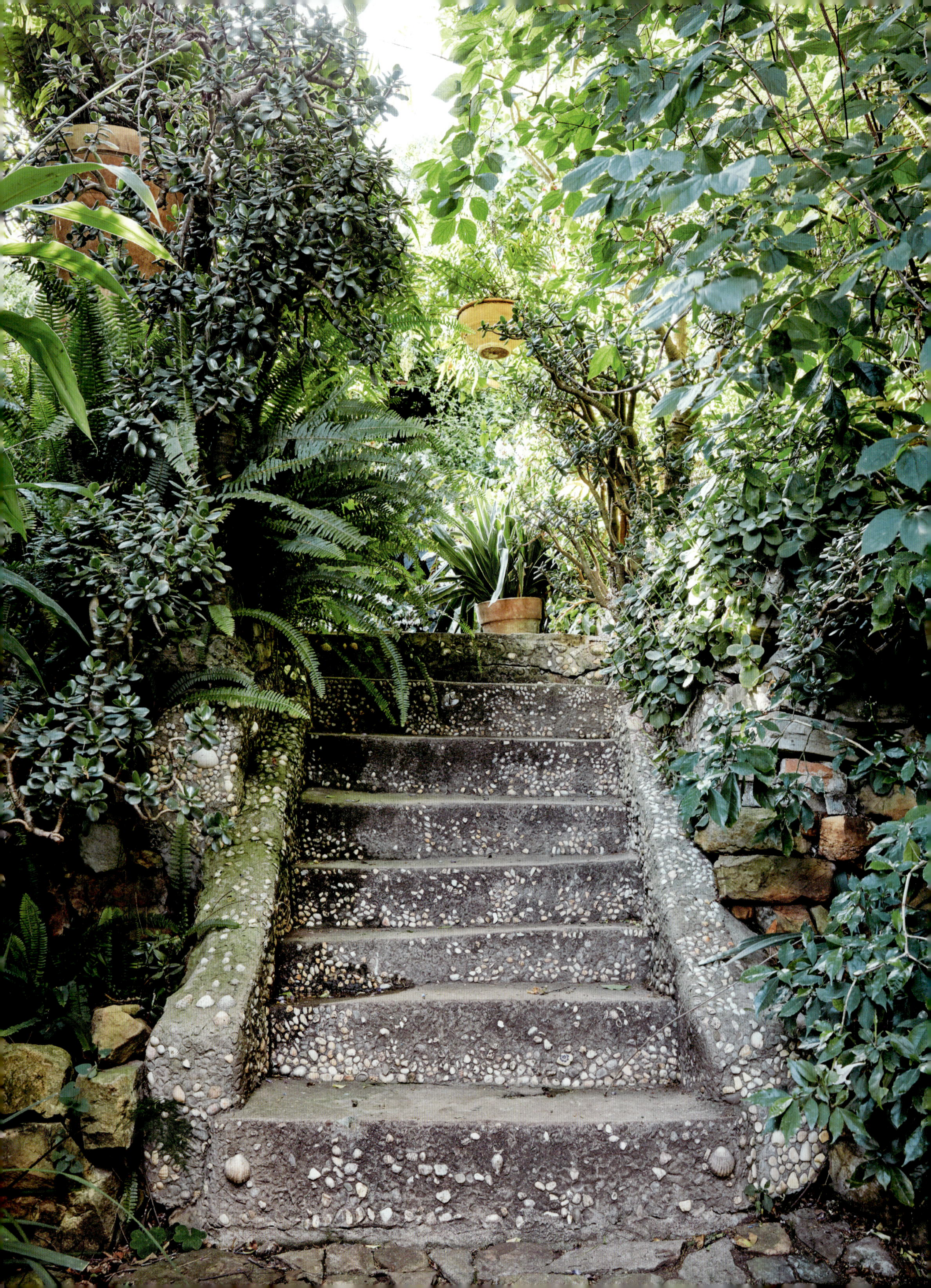

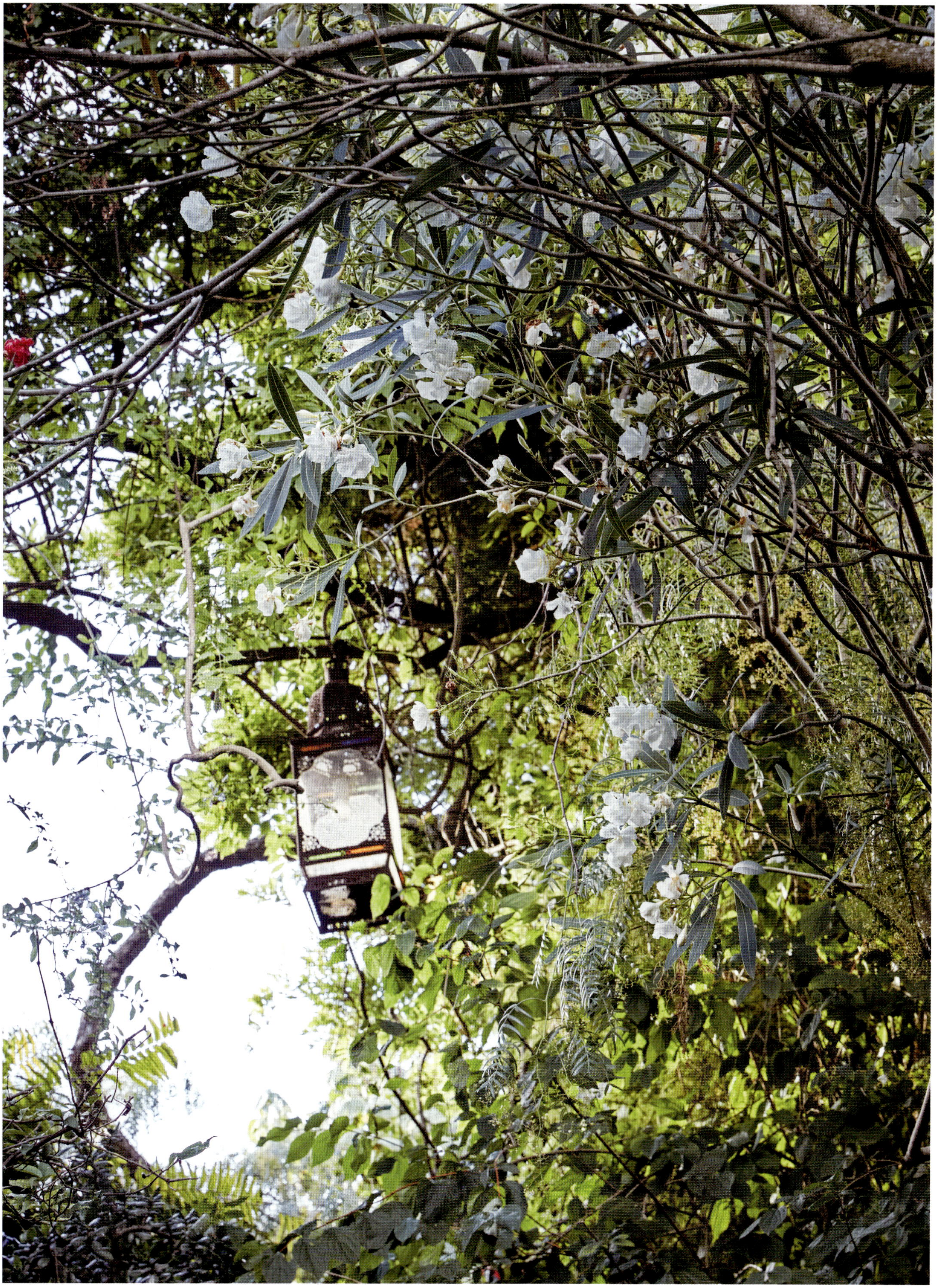

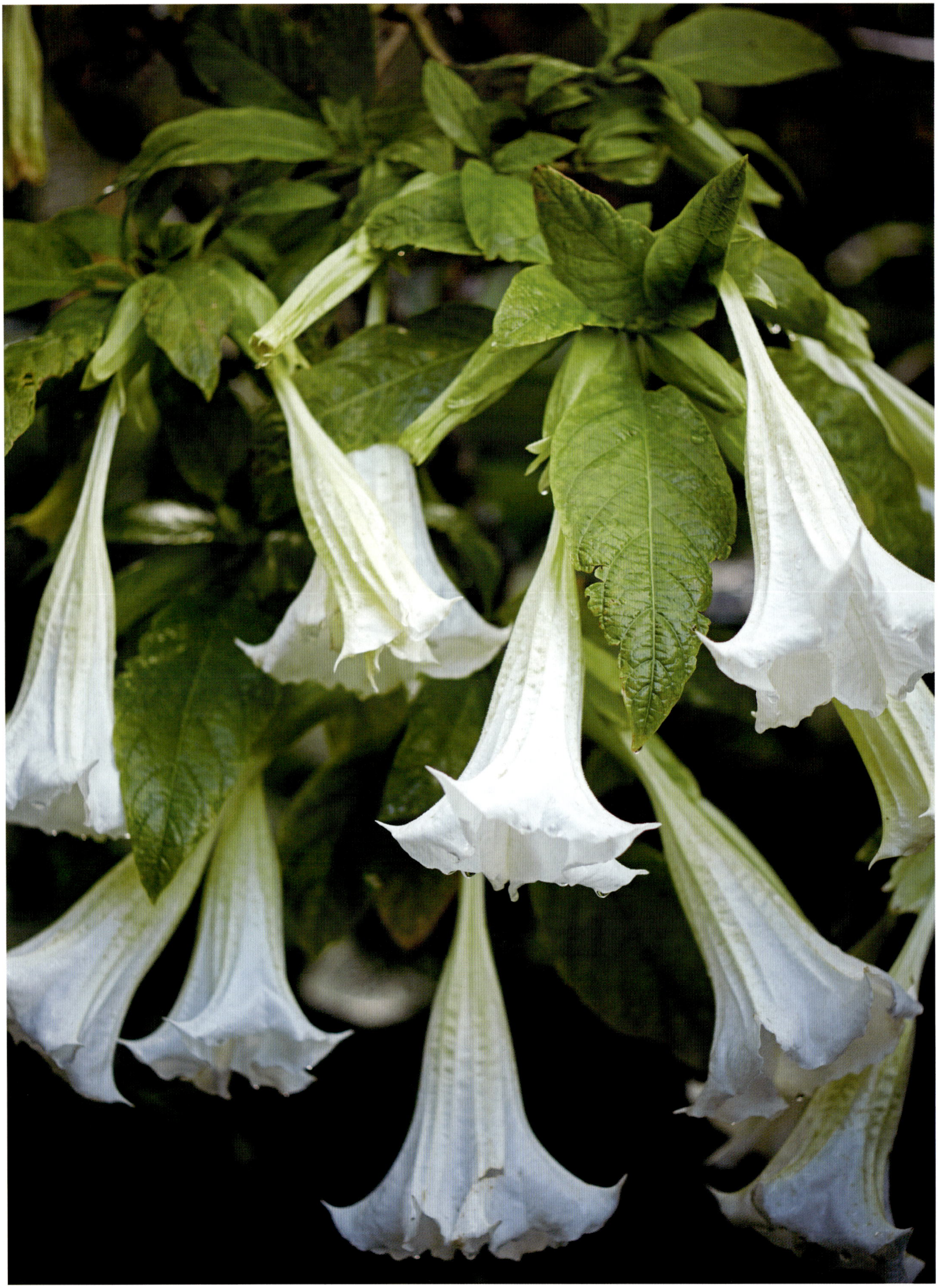

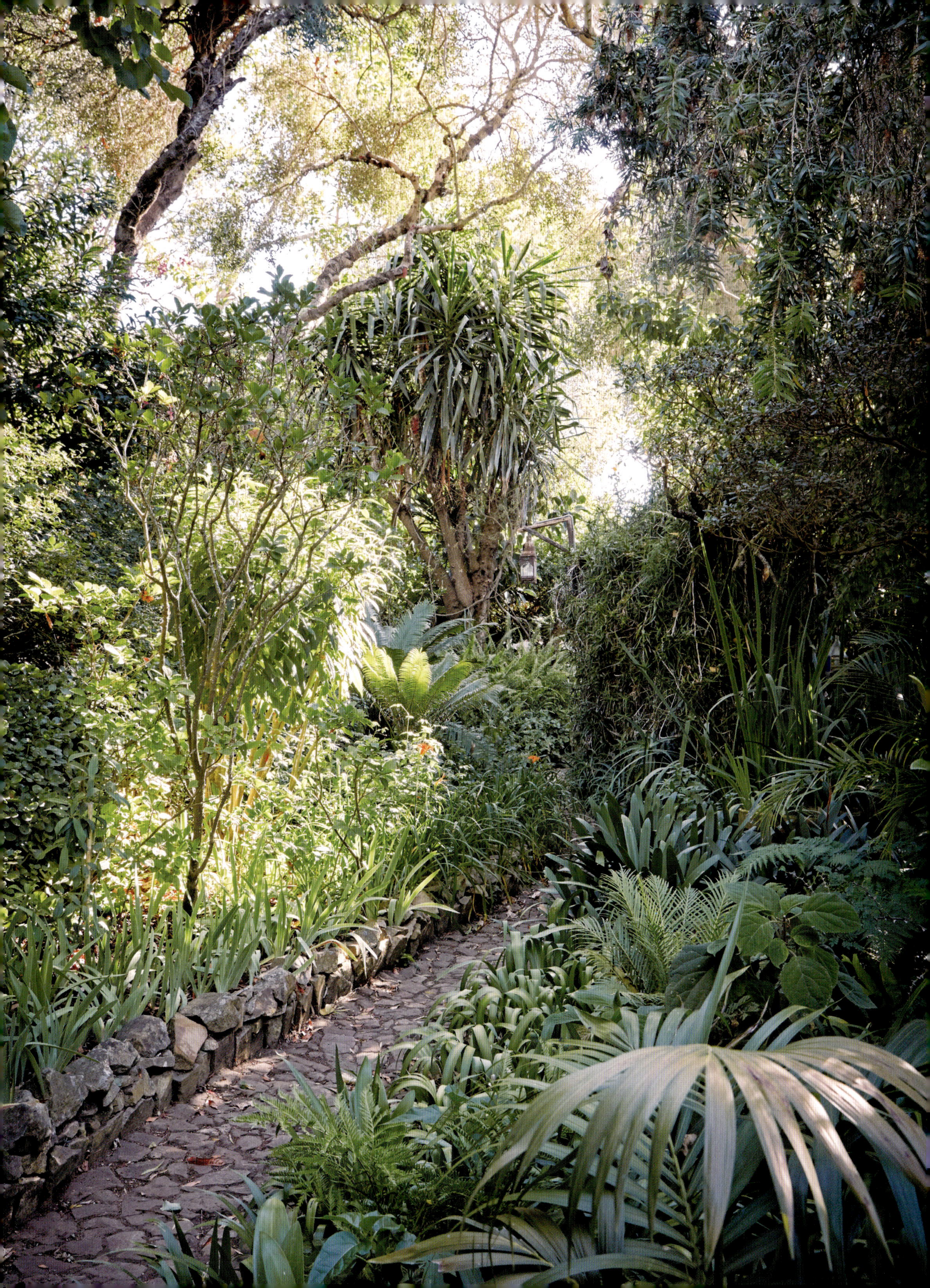

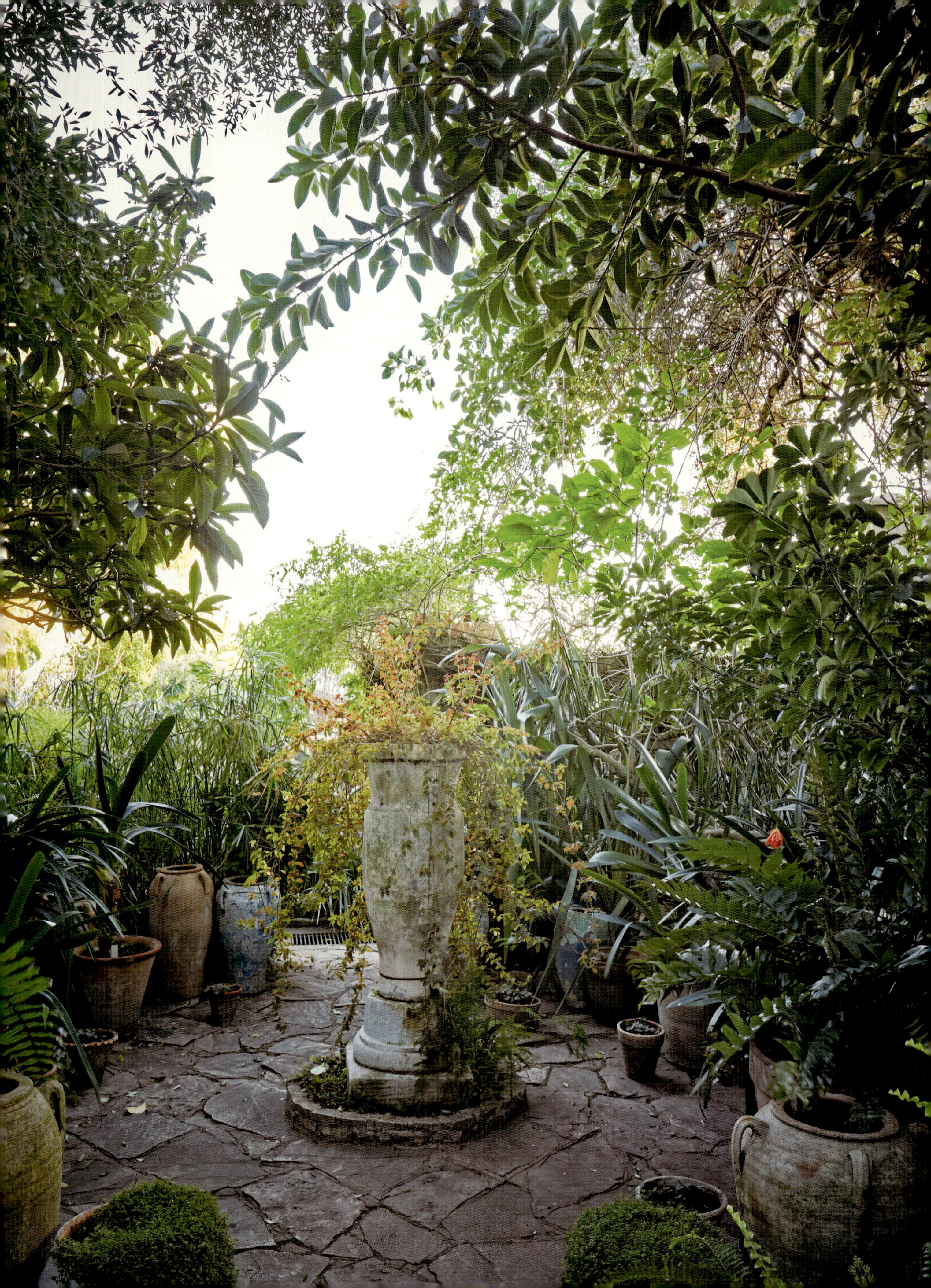

PAGE 210: *Mohammed made the stair with shells we found on the beach.*
PAGE 211: *At night the Moroccan lanterns hanging from the trees create little fairy worlds.*
PREVIOUS SPREAD, LEFT: *I will always call the* brugmansias *"daturas."*
PREVIOUS SPREAD, RIGHT: *A little path made by Mohammed. Few things are as difficult as to trace a curved path that doesn't look suburban.*
OPPOSITE: *The family of the Clivia species, quietly resting in their pots in the semi-shade.*
FOLLOWING SPREAD, LEFT: *The lower pavilion is covered in* Muehlenbeckia complexa: *I like the contrast between its tiny leaves and the feathery leaves of the palm tree nearby.*
FOLLOWING SPREAD, RIGHT: *The leaves of* Tetrapanax papyrifer *look like pharaoh fans. Unfortunately, no leopards in the garden, and very few ambassadors from the Kingdoms of Kush.*

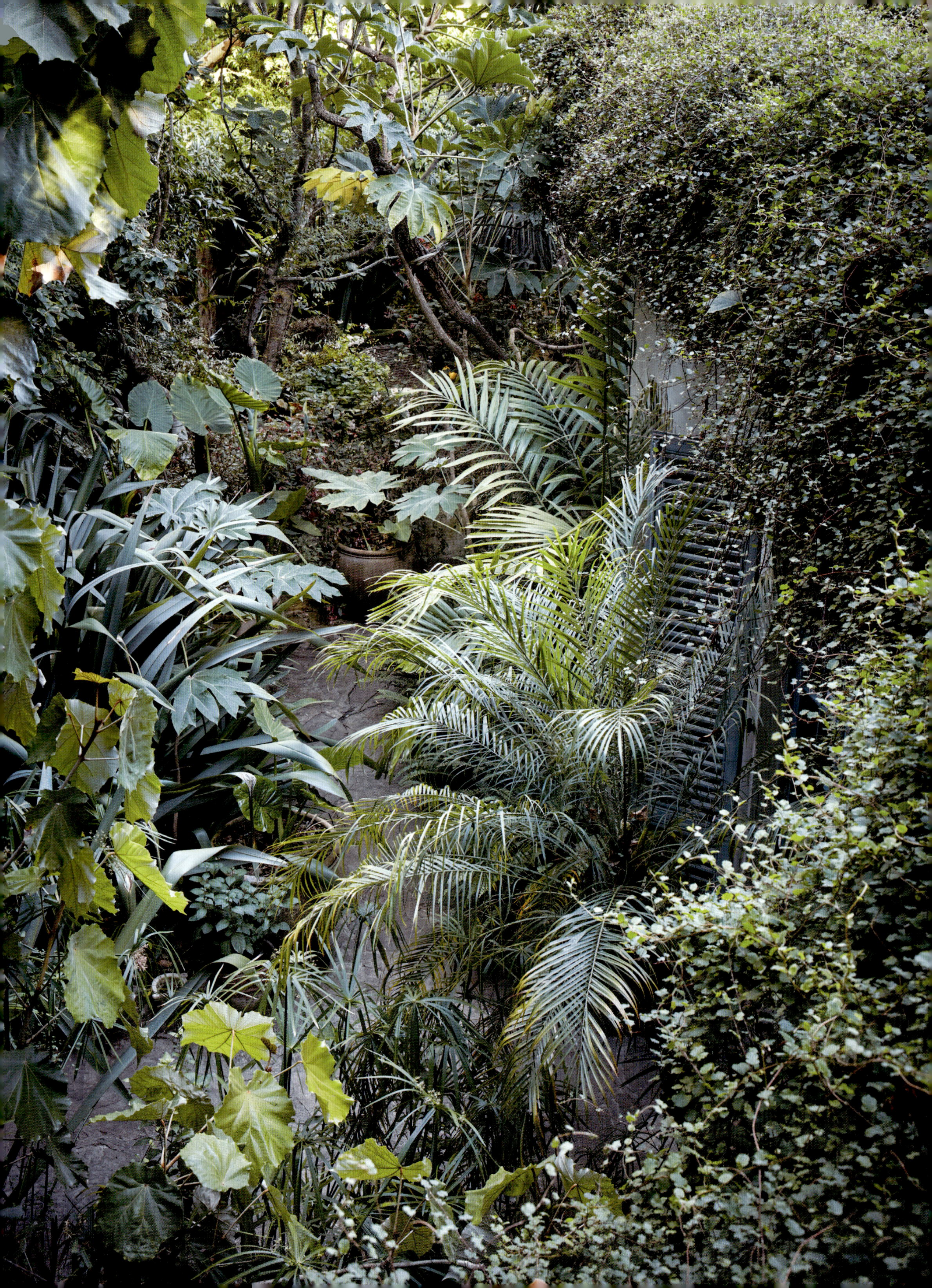

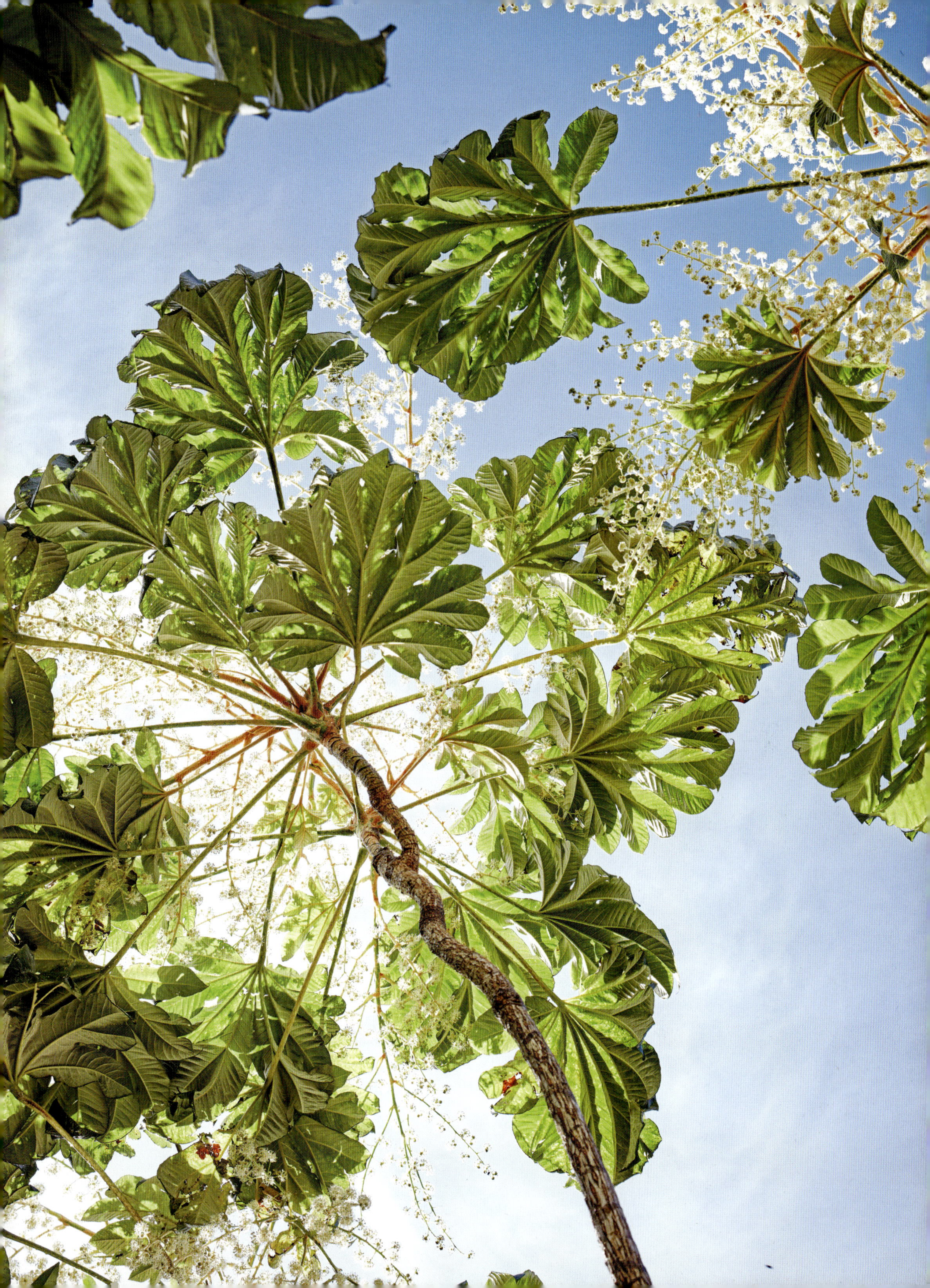

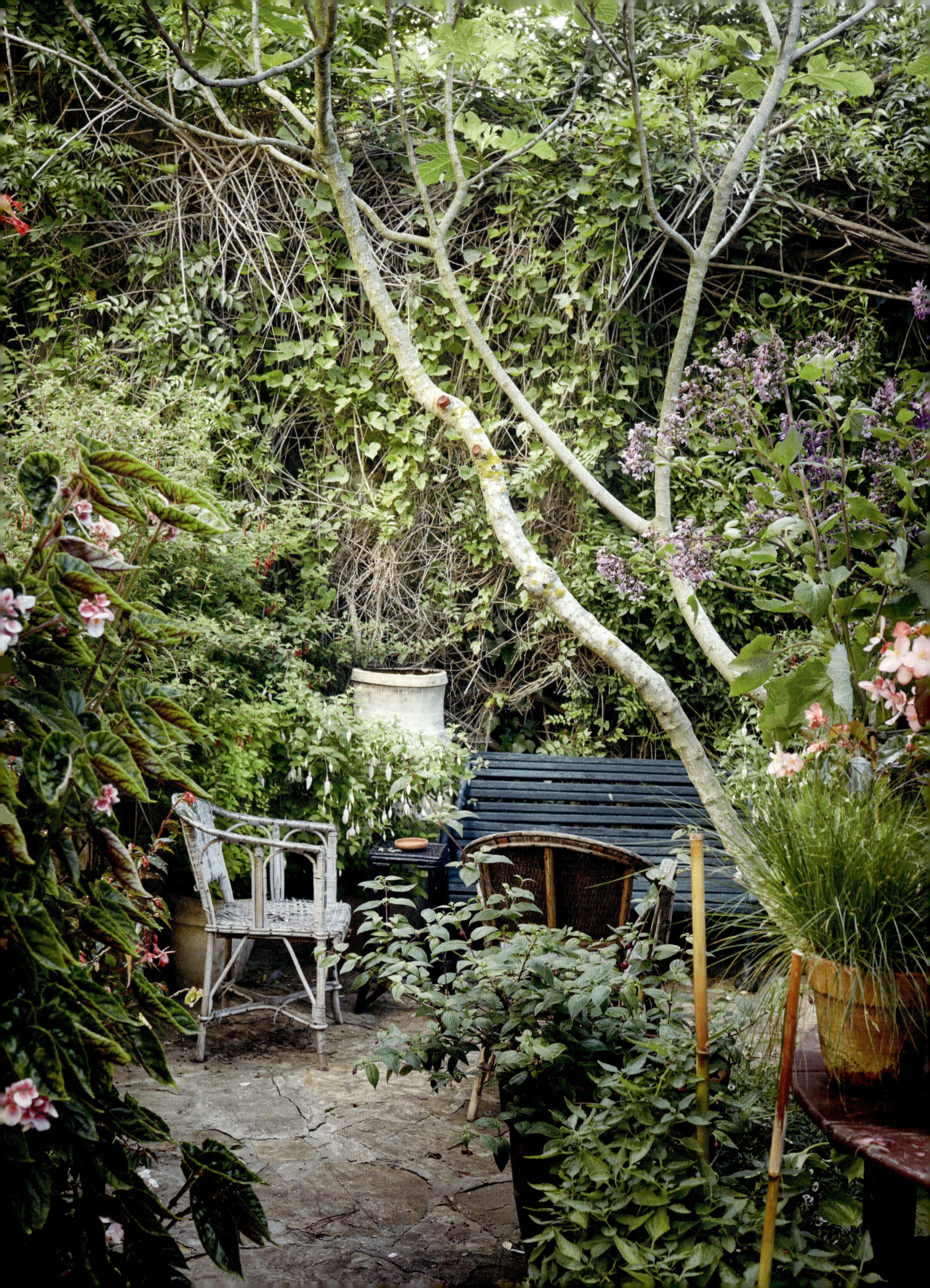

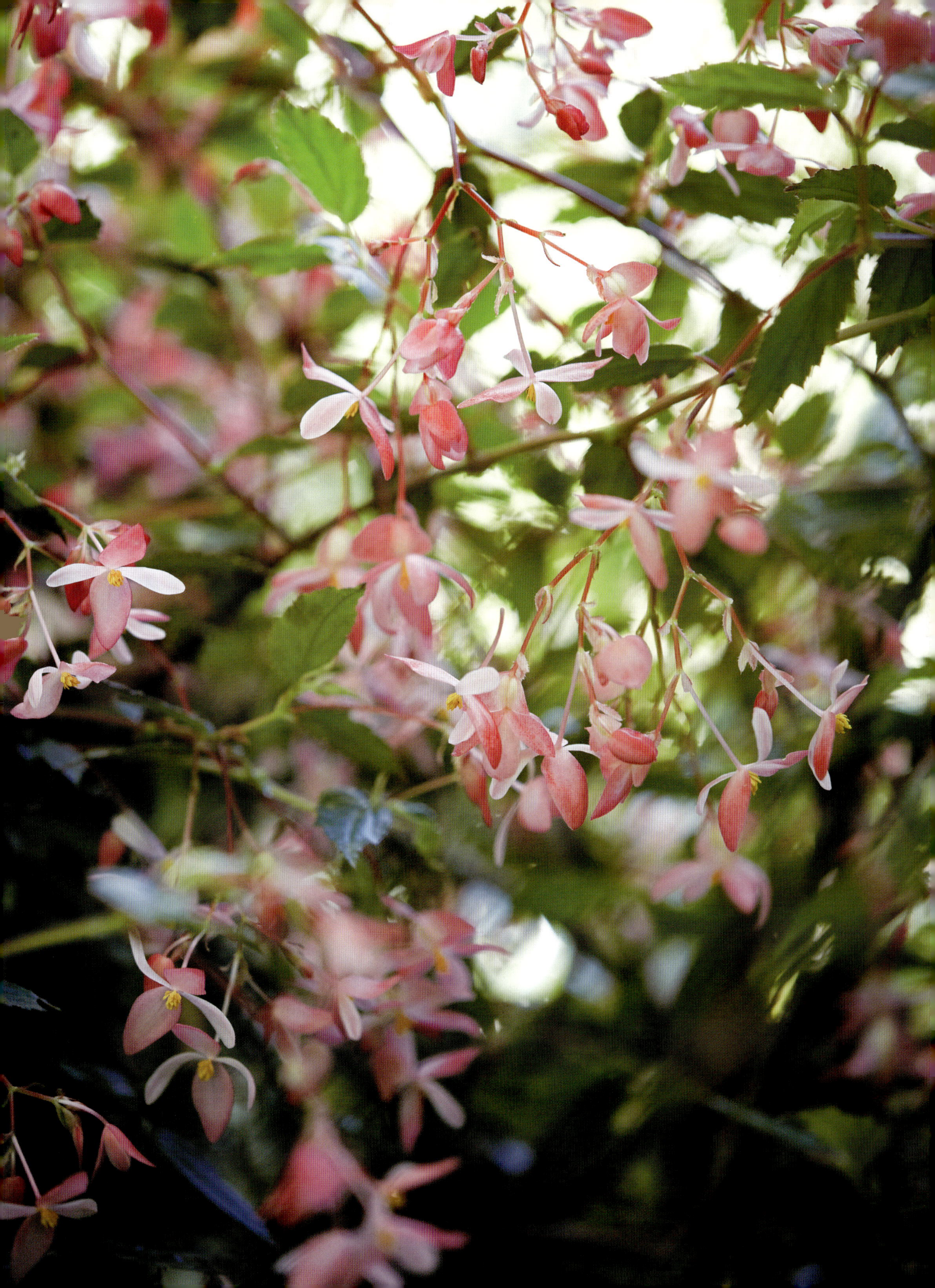

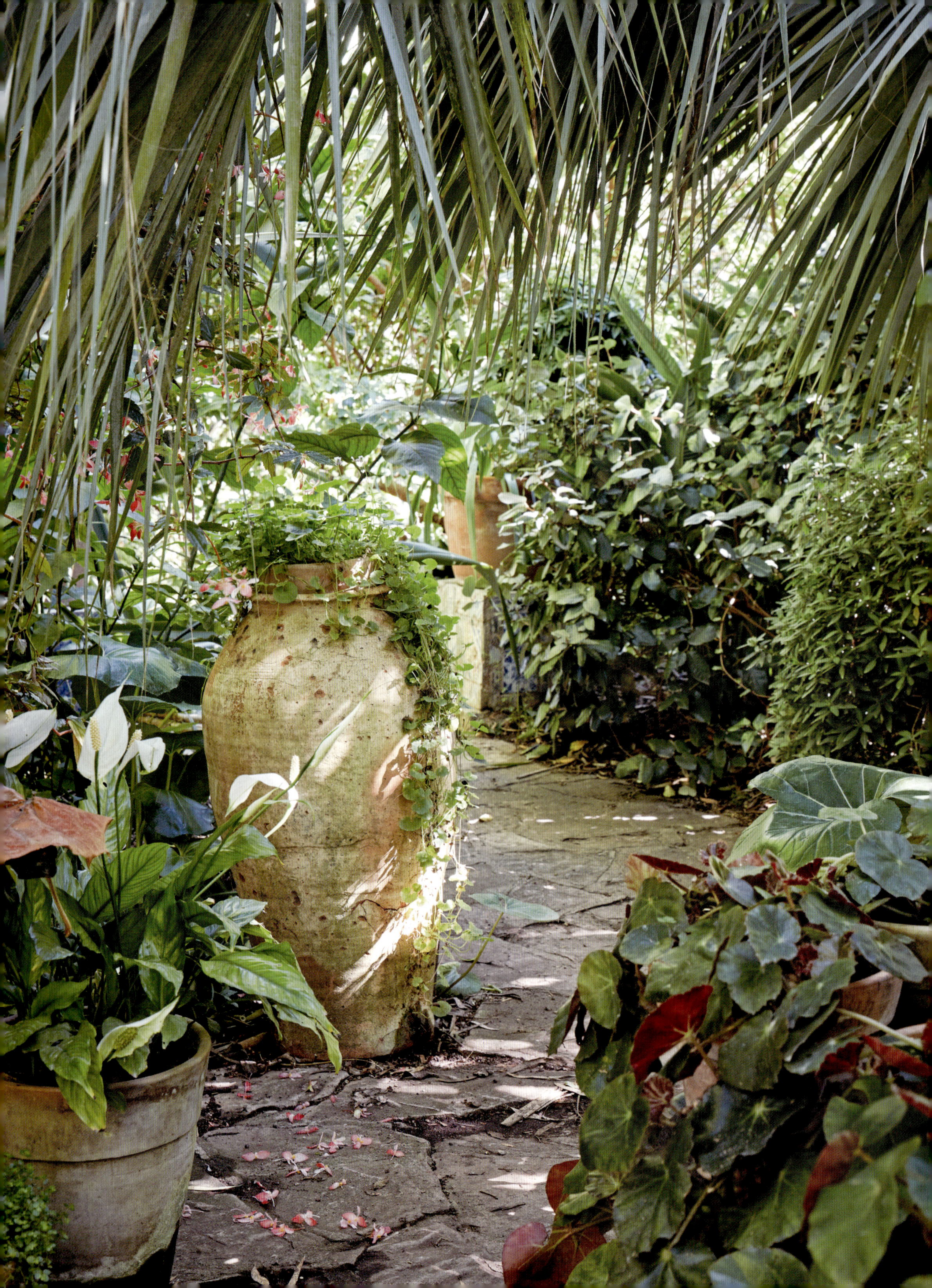

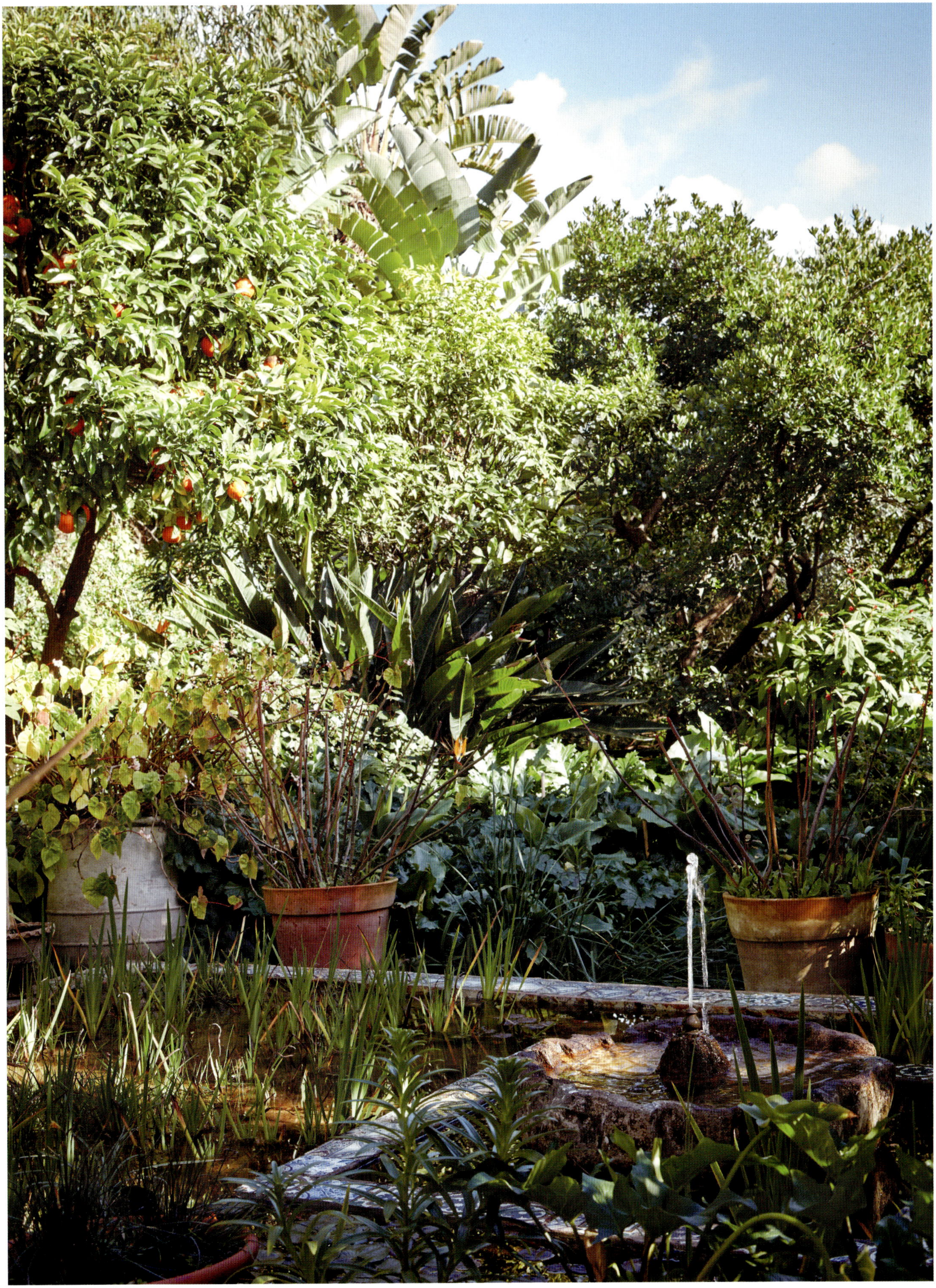

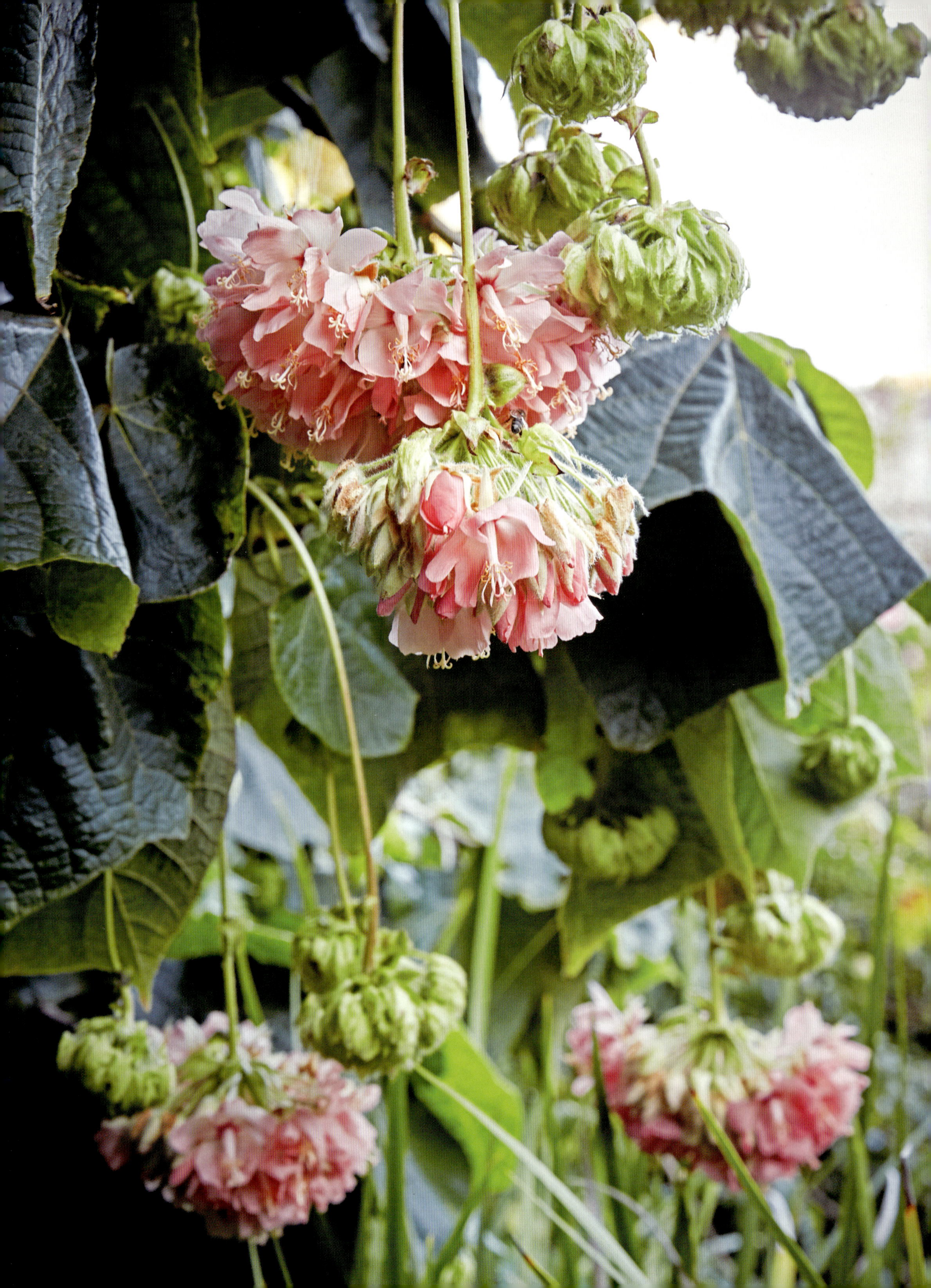

PAGE 218: *A Tcheckhovian sitting room under a fig tree.*
PAGE 219: *Begonialand 2.*
PREVIOUS SPREAD, LEFT: *I love* tonnas, *the Moroccan jars that keep the water fresh.*
PREVIOUS SPREAD, RIGHT: *The stone fountain is surrounded by two basins covered in old tiles. The yellow flags have just been cut back.*
OPPOSITE: *Dombeya smells like honey.*
FOLLOWING SPREAD, LEFT: *Begonialand 3.*
FOLLOWING SPREAD, RIGHT: *We make jam out of our bitter oranges.*

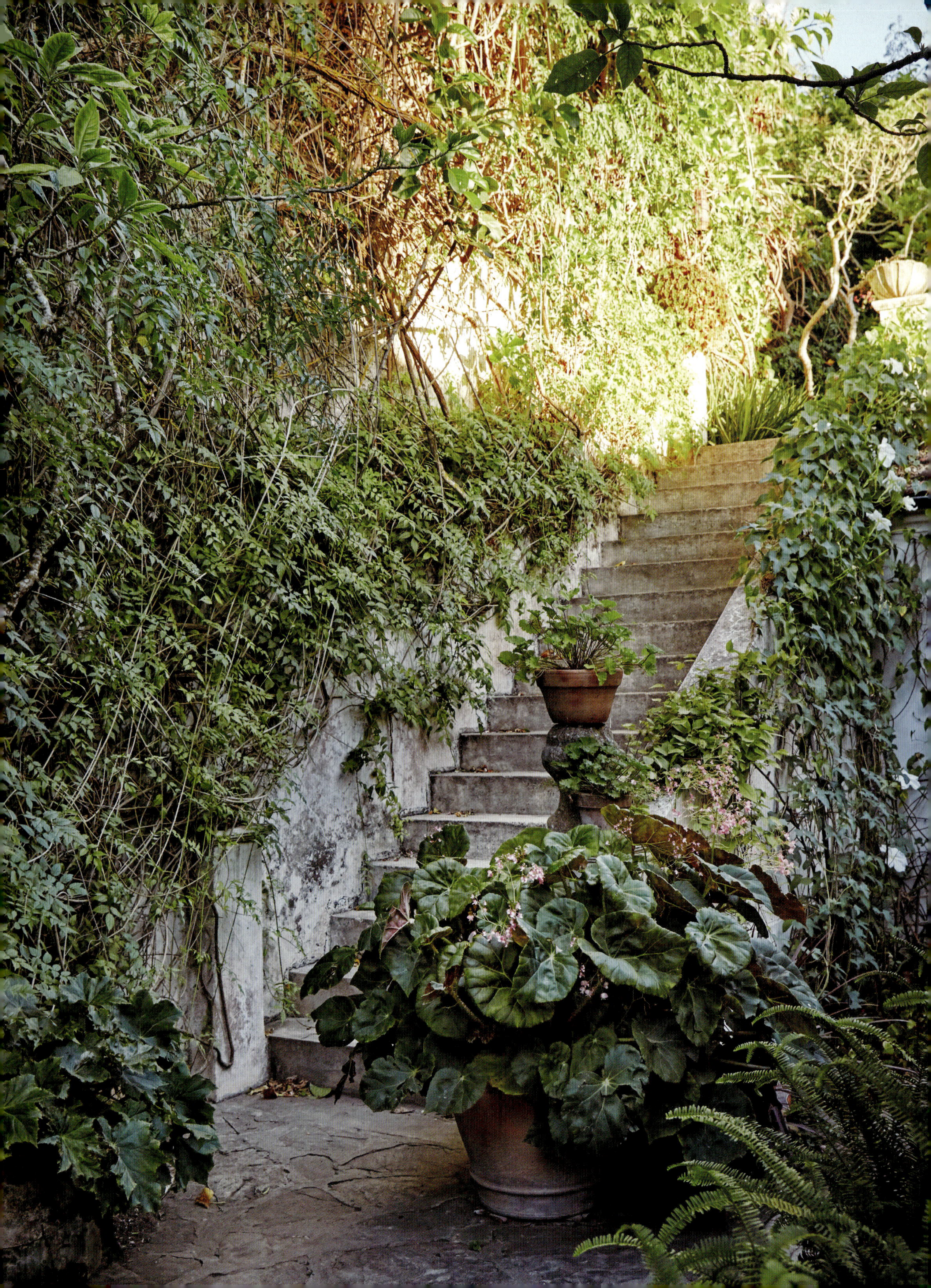

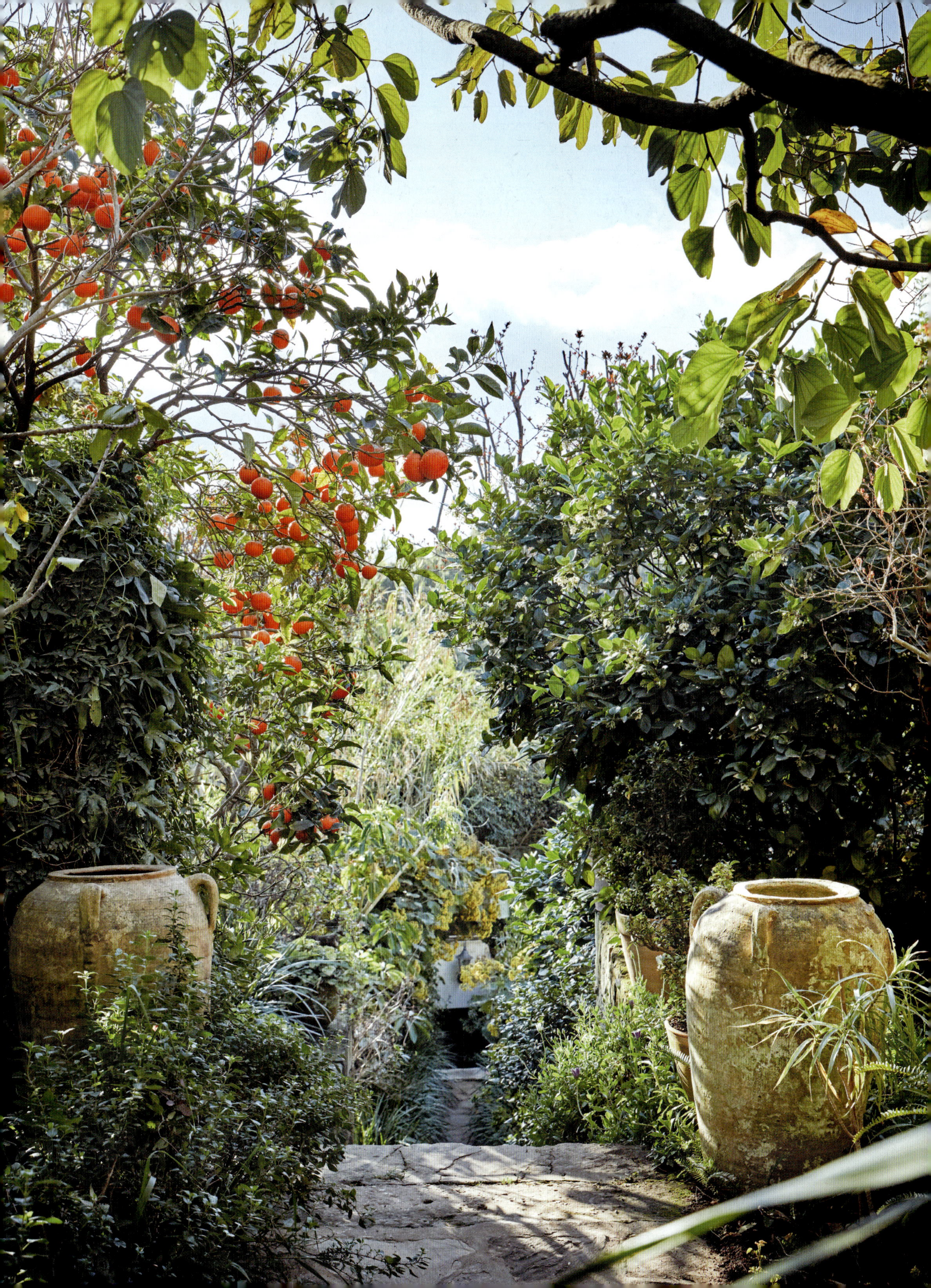

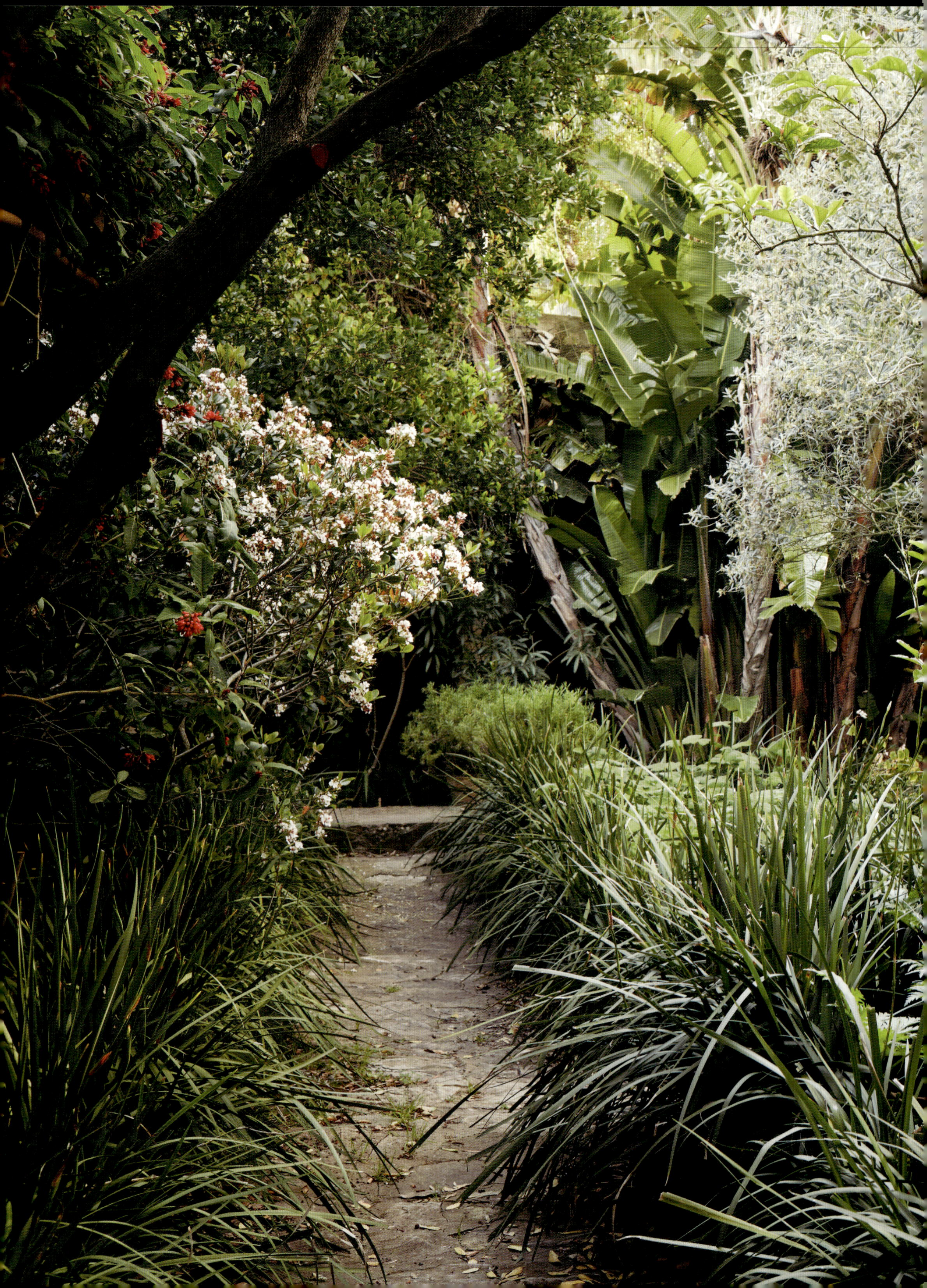

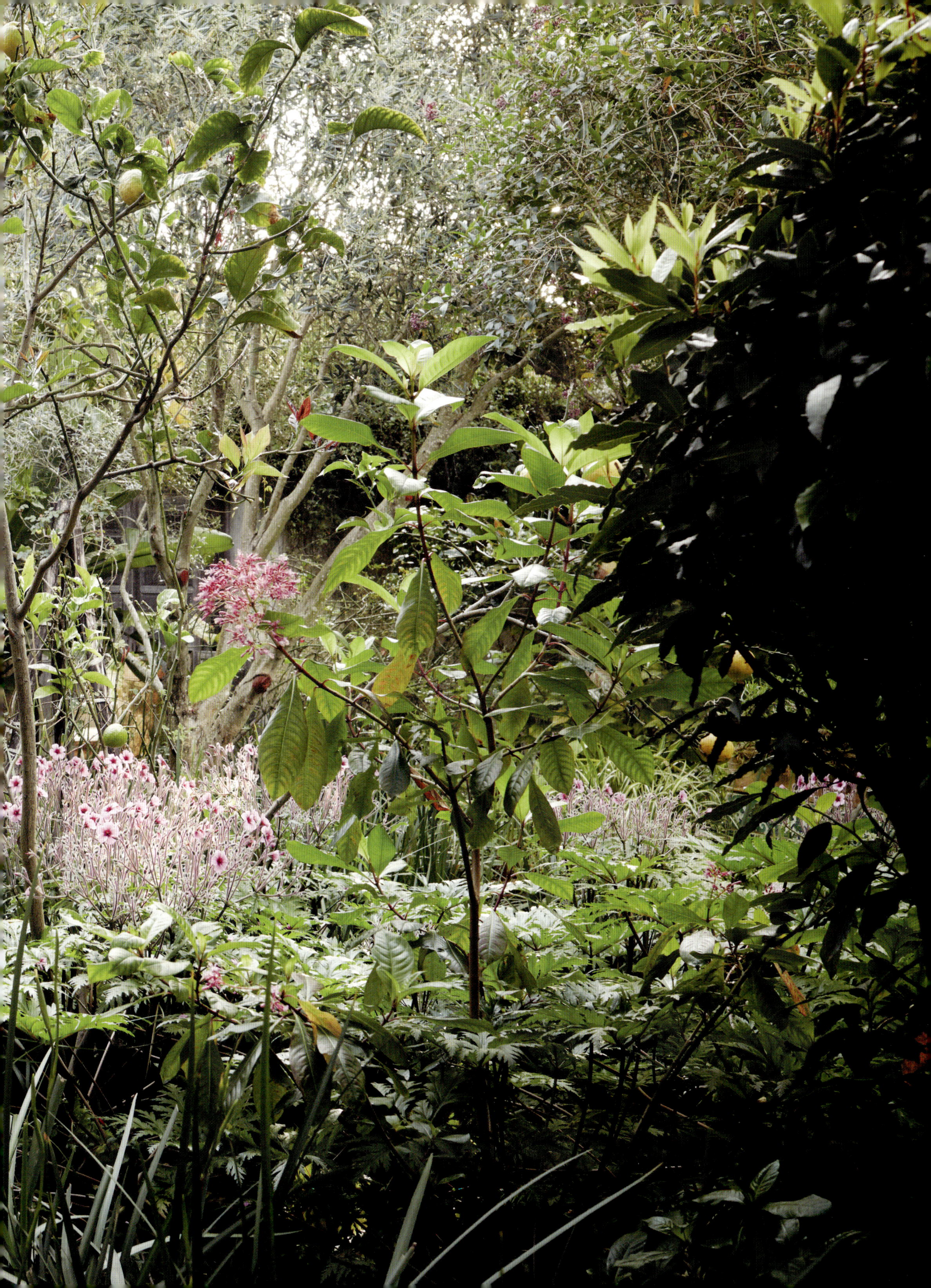

PREVIOUS SPREAD: *On a terrace, Madeira cranesbill (*Geranium maderense*) in bloom is like a pale fire—I'm sure Nabokov would agree.*
OPPOSITE: *A plum is a plum is a plum.*
FOLLOWING SPREAD, LEFT: *Aspidistras can become an addiction.*
FOLLOWING SPREAD, RIGHT: *My secret corner where I like to read. The bench was made by NOW on the Ocean. I'm quite proud of having achieved this tropical look in Mediterranean Tangier. Bernard Dogimont, the greatest plant expert I have ever known, helped a lot.*

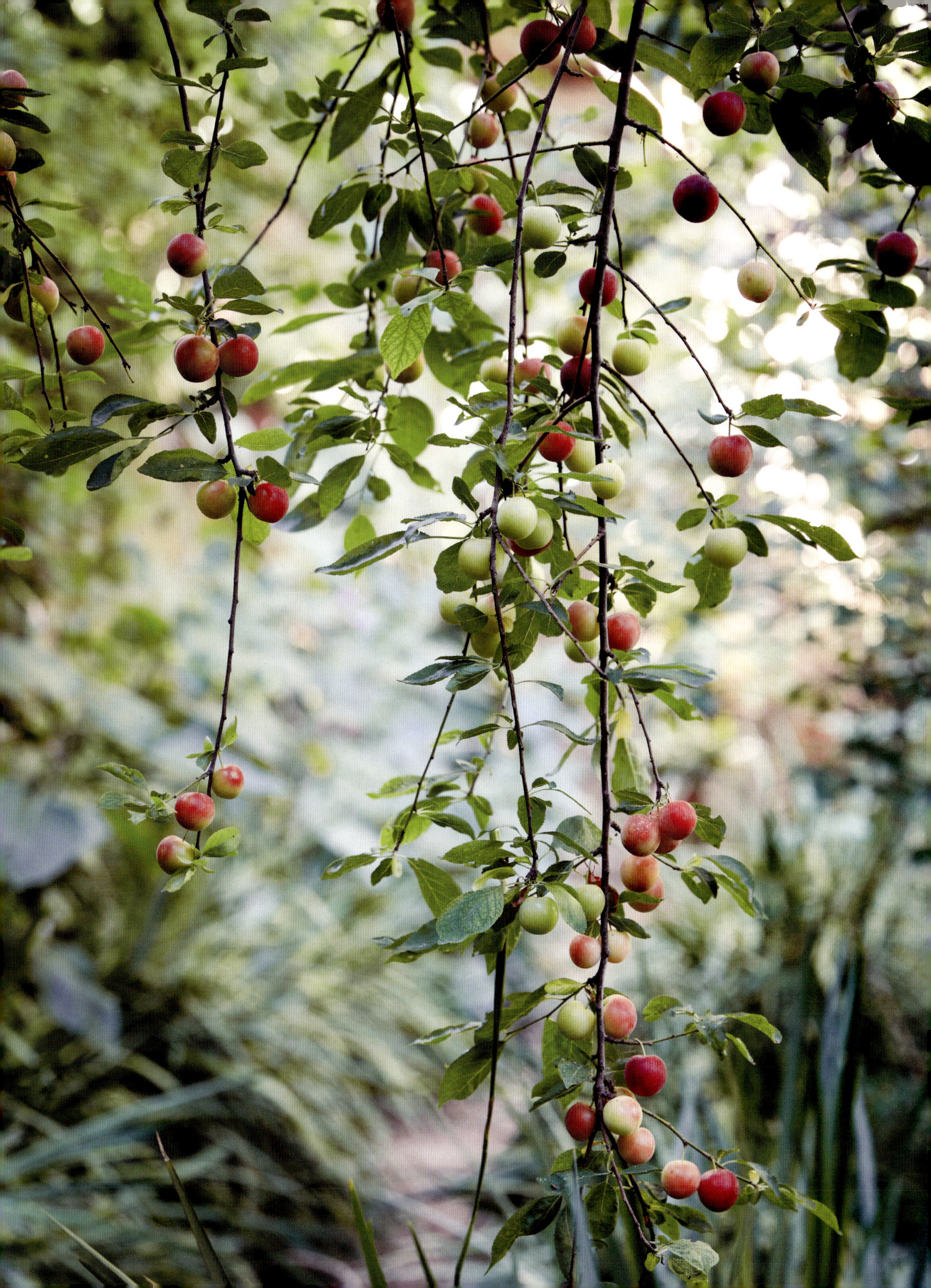

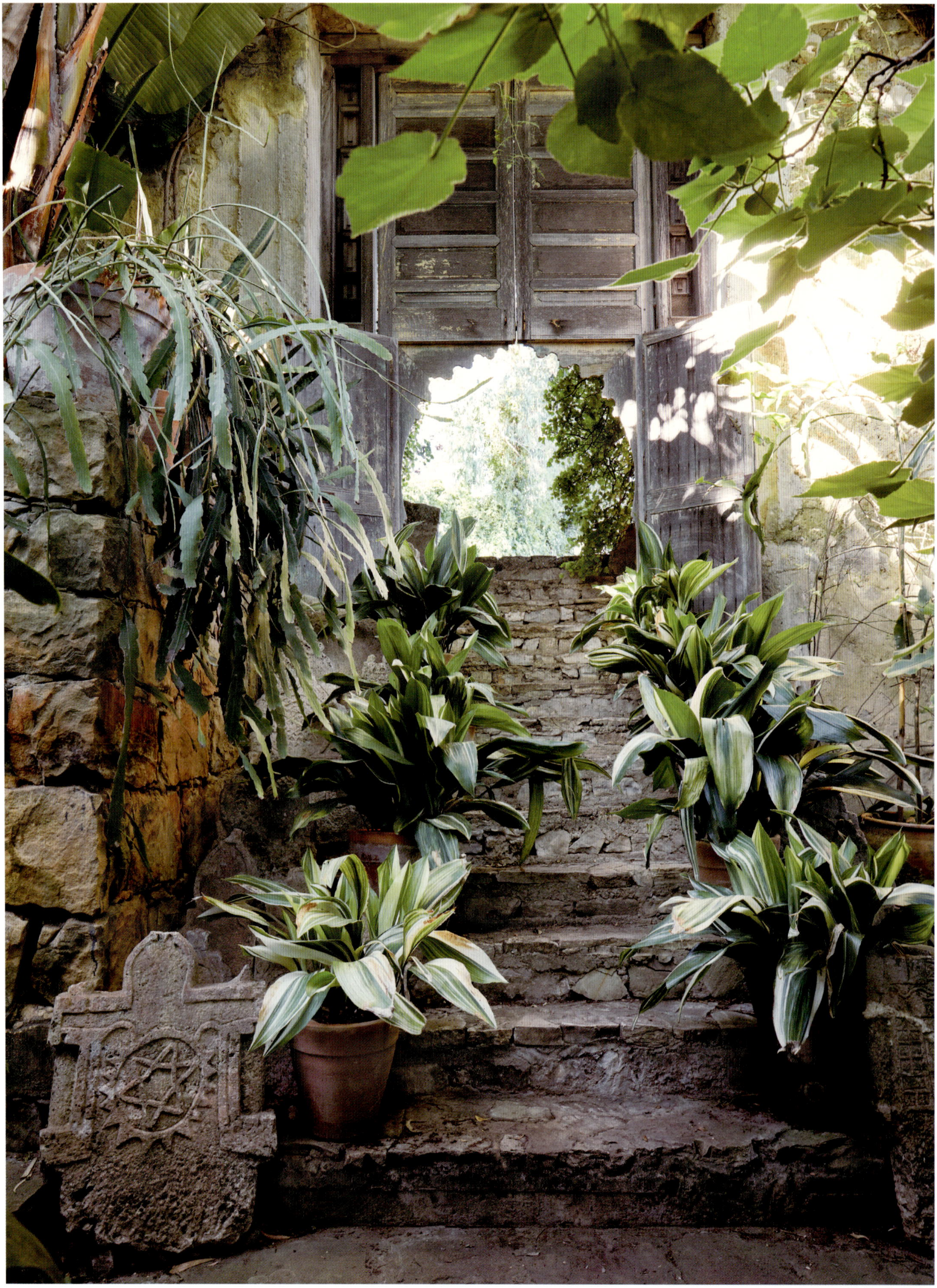

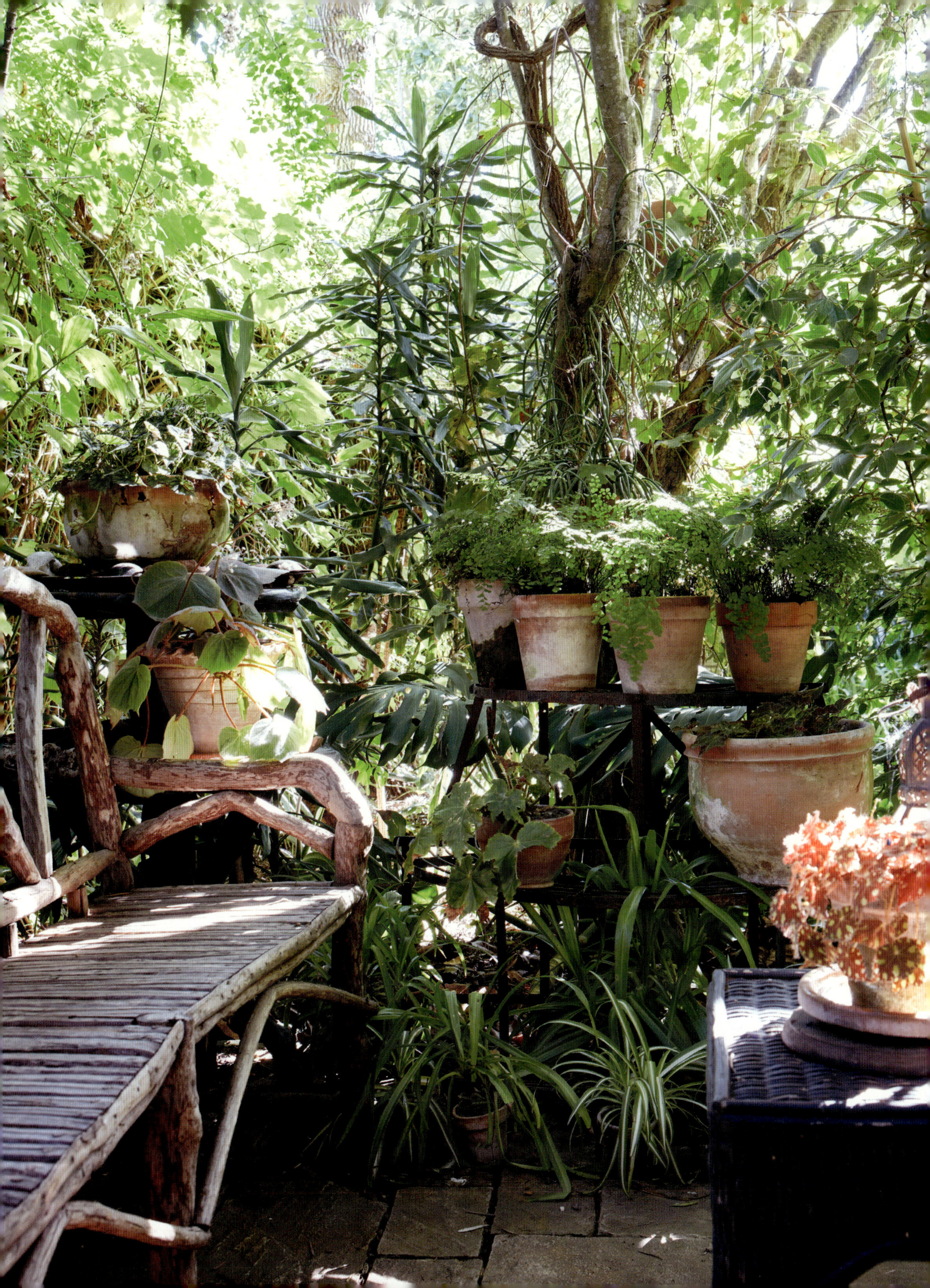

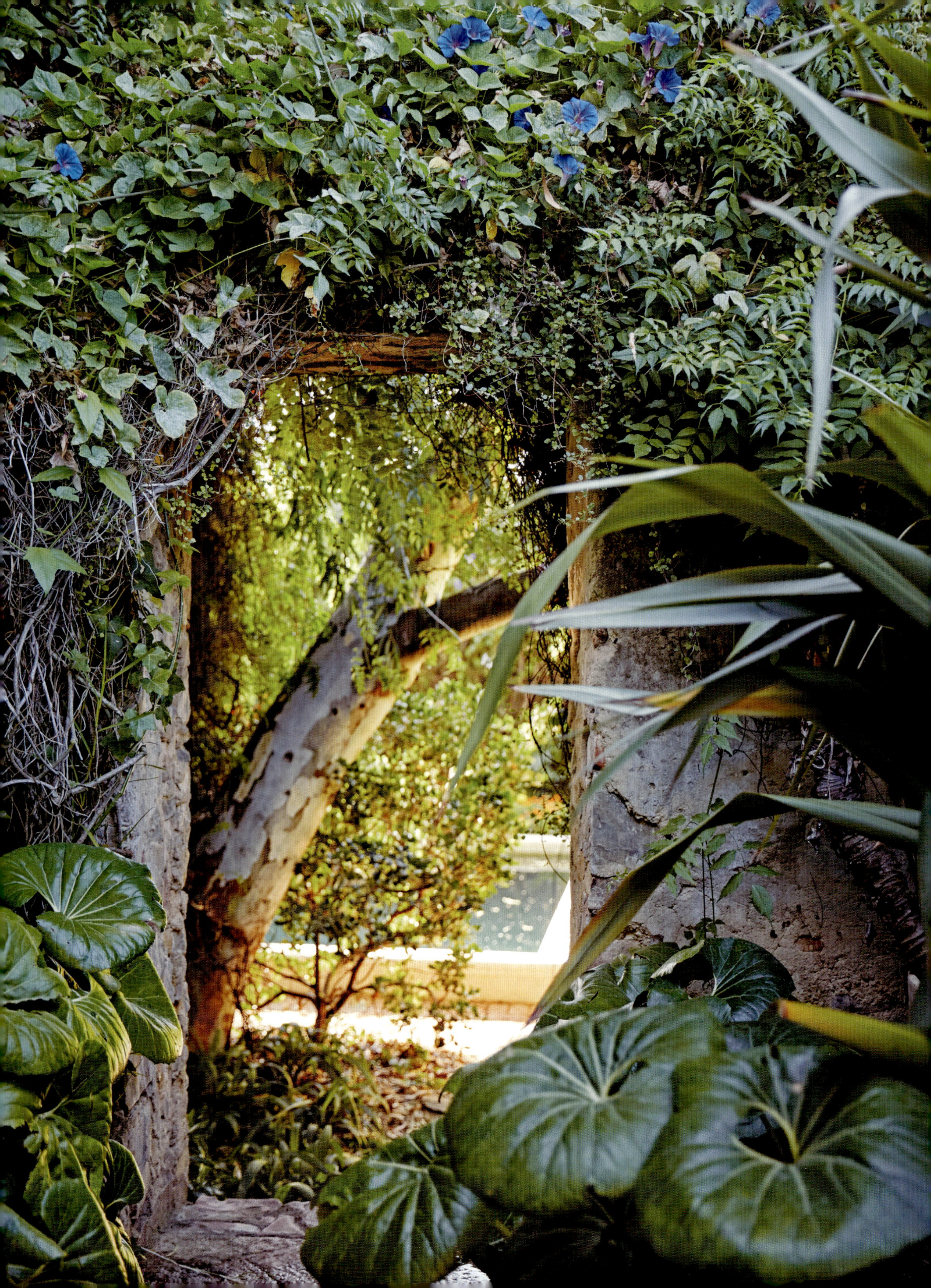

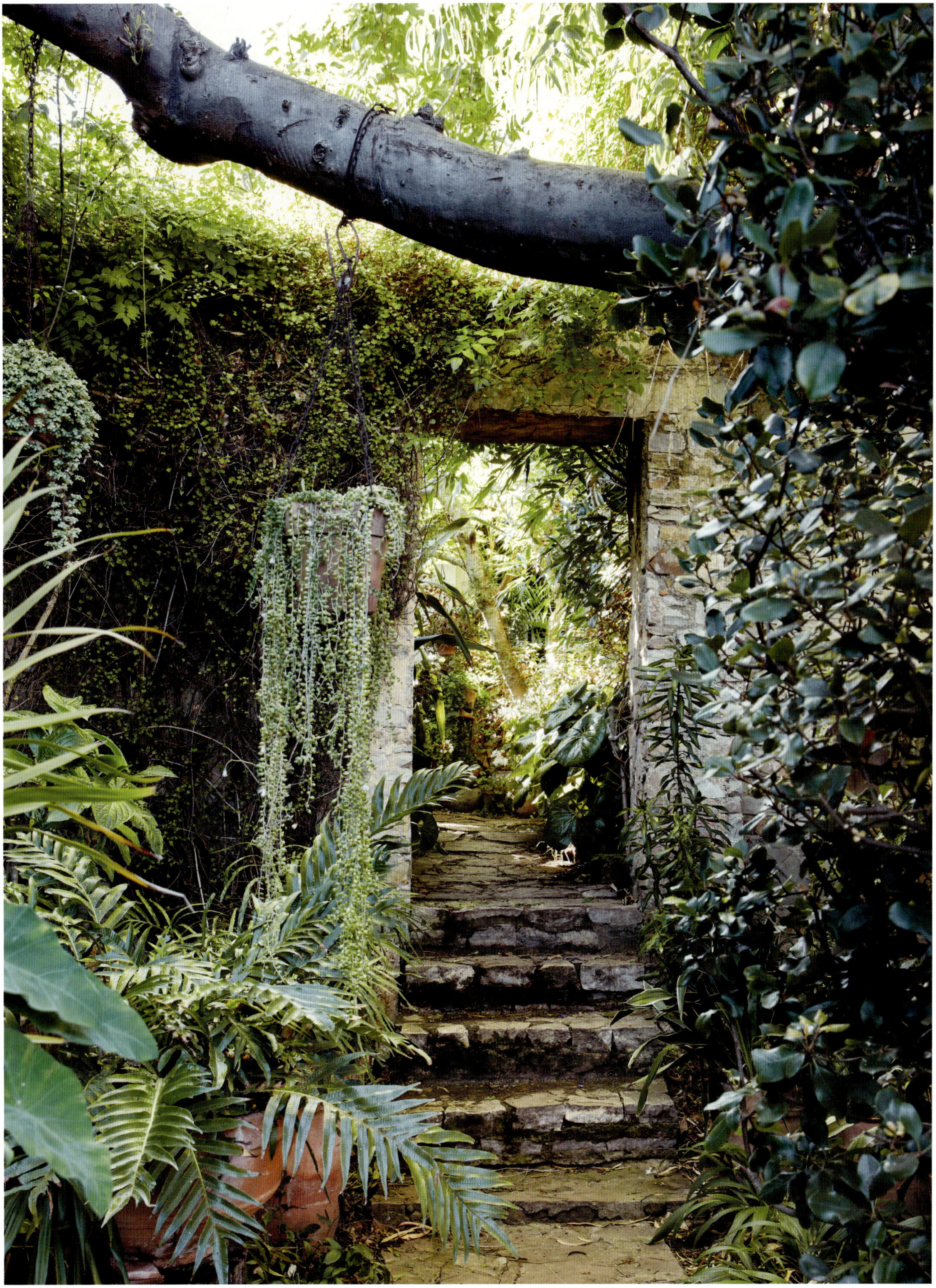

PREVIOUS SPREAD: *Both sides of the small door leading to the pool room.*
OPPOSITE: *The wooden door comes from a palace in Tétouan.*
FOLLOWING SPREAD: *The swimming pool room—never enough old pots and old stones in a garden.*
PAGE 239: *The pool, beautifully designed by Roberto, is painted in a very dark green. It looks like an agricultural and slightly otherworldly basin.*

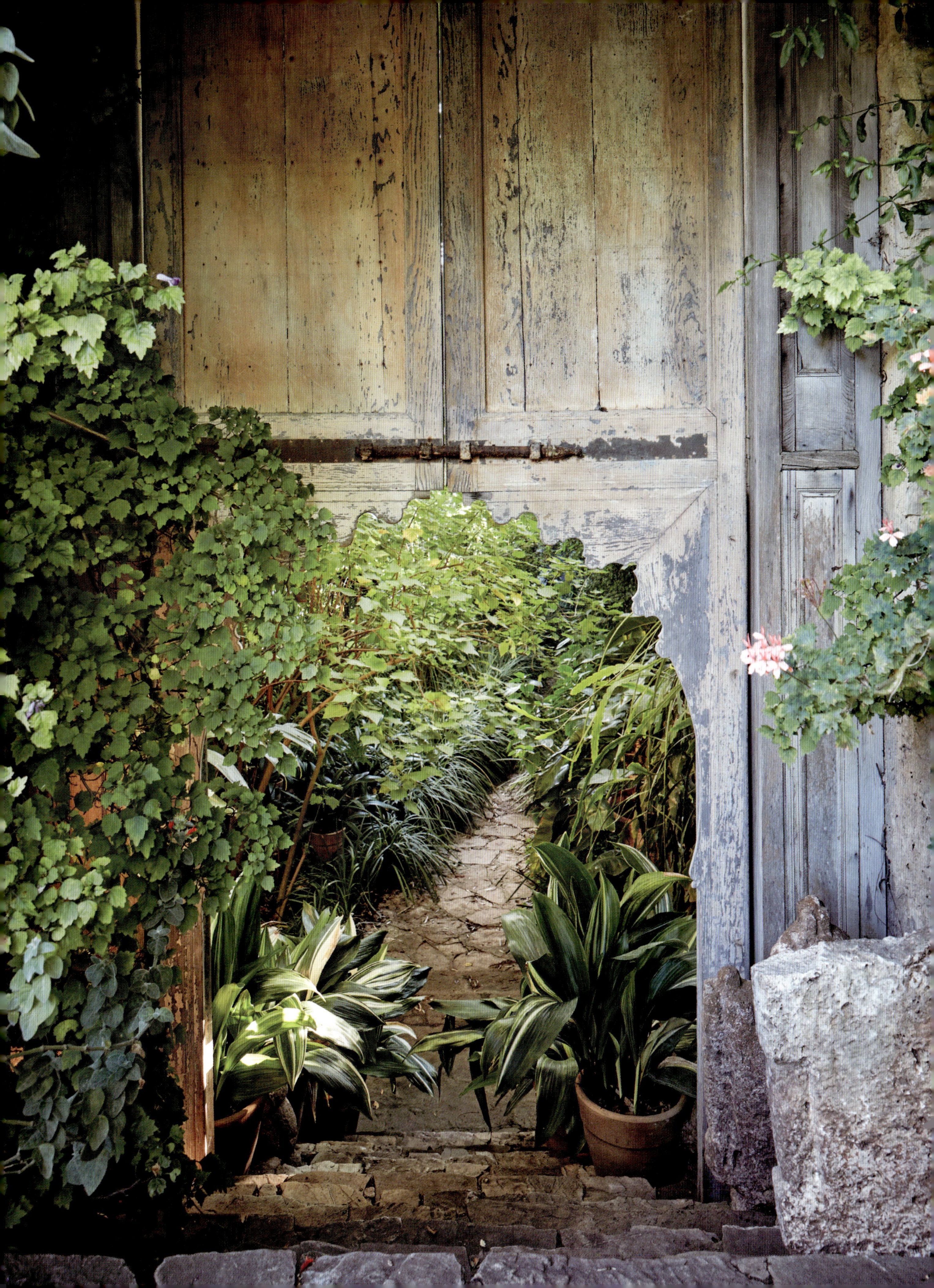

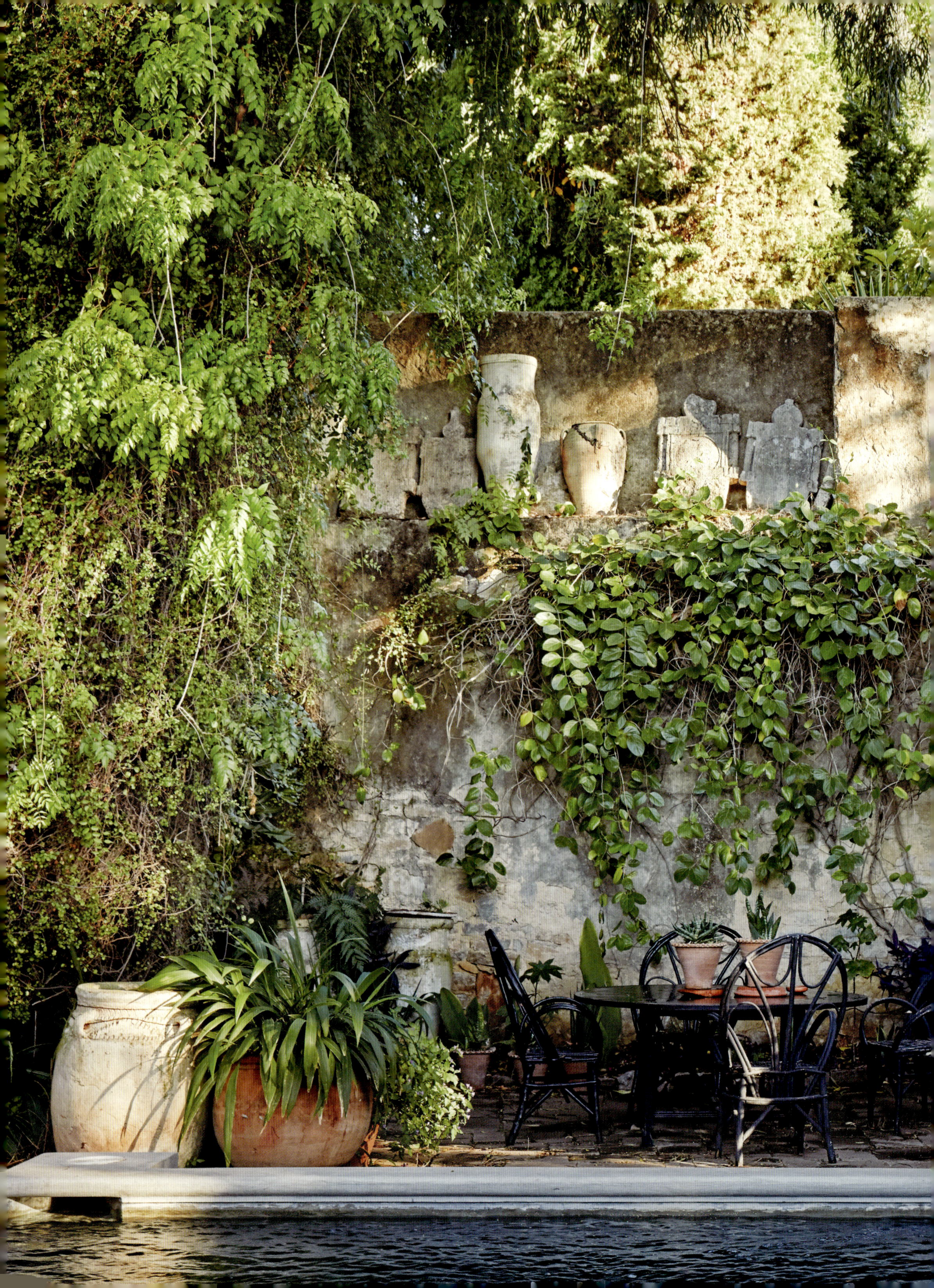

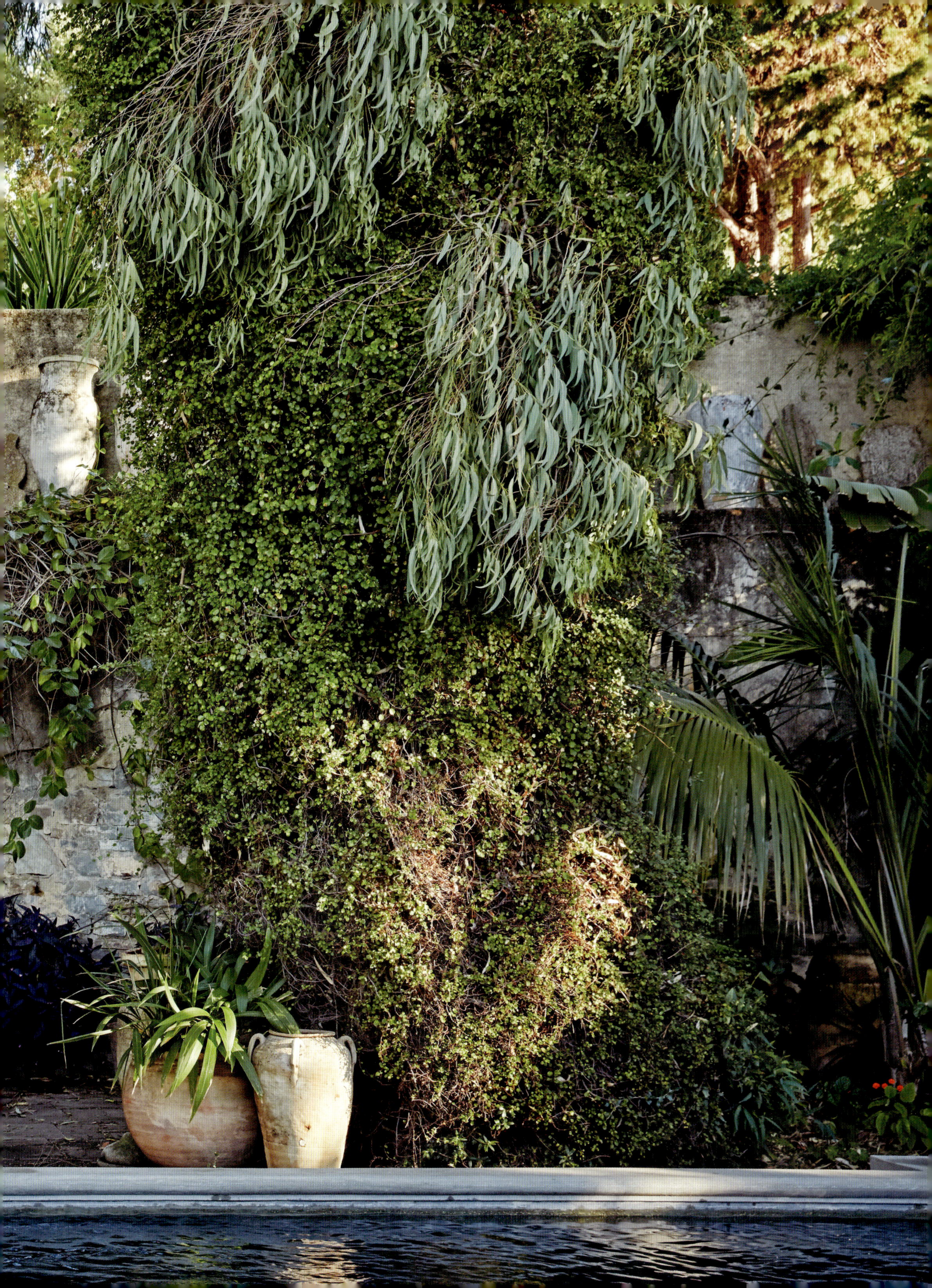

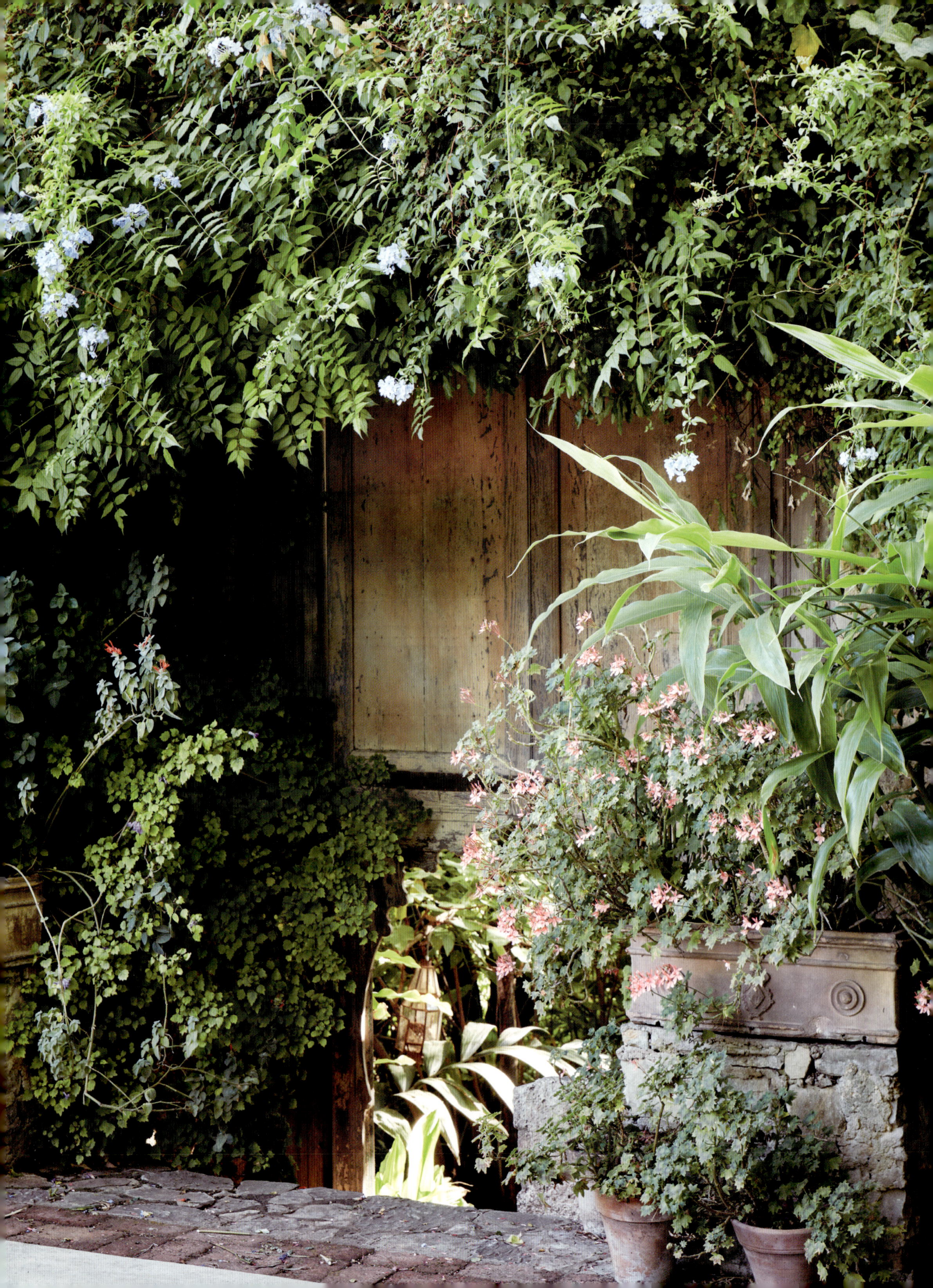

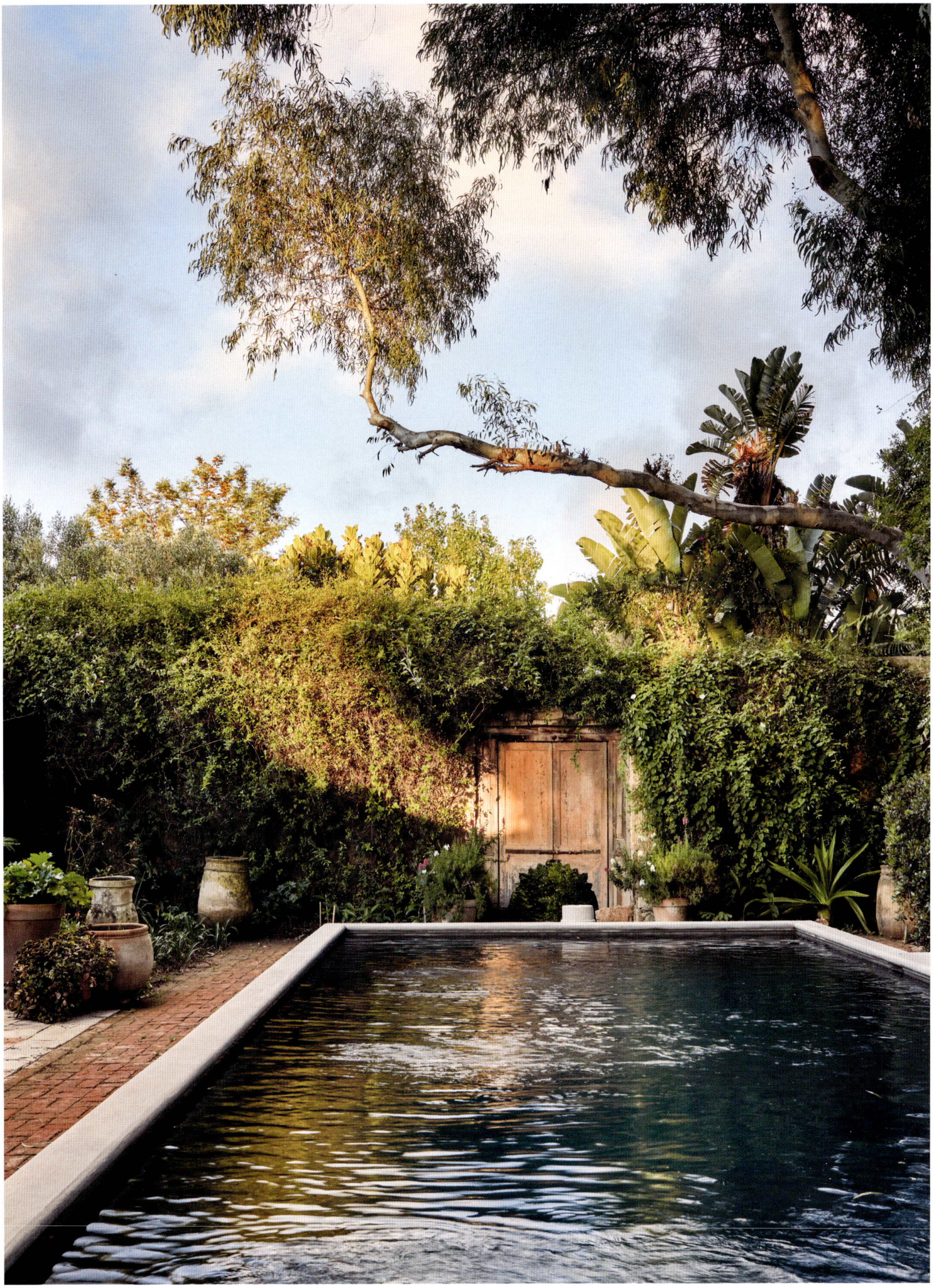

First published in the United States of America in 2023 by

Rizzoli International Publications, Inc.
300 Park Avenue South
New York, NY 10010
www.rizzoliusa.com

Texts Copyright © 2023 Umberto Pasti
Foreword Copyright © 2023 Madison Cox
Photographs © 2023 Ngoc Minh Ngo

Publisher: Charles Miers
Design: NGO Studio
Editors: Dung Ngo & Klaus Kirschbaum
Translator (Italian to English): Alastair McEwen
Production Director: Maria Pia Gramaglia
Managing Editor: Lynn Scrabis

All rights reserved. No part of this publication may be reproduced, stored in a retrieval system, or transmitted in any form or by any means, electronic, mechanical, photocopying, recording, or otherwise, without prior consent of the publishers.

ISBN-13: 978-0-8478-9913-5
Library of Congress Control Number: 2022944714

2023 2024 2025 / 10 9 8 7 6 5 4 3 2

Printed in China

Visit us online:
Facebook.com/RizzoliNewYork
Twitter: @Rizzoli_Books
Instagram.com/RizzoliBooks
Pinterest.com/RizzoliBooks
Youtube.com/user/RizzoliNY
Issuu.com/Rizzoli